Faith, Food,

and Family

in a

Yupik Whaling

Community

Faith, Food,
and Family
in a
Yupik Whaling
Community

CAROL ZANE JOLLES

With the assistance of
ELINOR MIKAGHAQ OOZEVA
Elder Advisor

A McLellan Book

University of Washington Press
Seattle & London

This book is published with the assistance of a grant from the
McLellan Endowed Series Fund, established through the generosity
of Martha McCleary McLellan and Mary McLellan Williams.

Copyright © 2002 by the University of Washington Press
Designed by Veronica Seyd
Printed in the United States of America

Library of Congress Cataloging-in-Publication Data
Jolles, Carol Zane.
Faith, food, and family in a Yupik whaling community / Carol Zane Jolles;
with the generous assistance of Elinor Mikaghaq Oozeva.
p. cm.
Includes bibliographical references (p.) and index.
ISBN 0-295-98189-X (cloth : alk. paper)
1. Yupik Eskimos—Alaska—Gambell.
2. Yupik Eskimos—Food—Alaska—Gambell.
3. Yupik Eskimos—Alaska—Gambell—Religion.
4. Whaling—Alaska—Gambell.   I. Title.
E99.E7 J59 2002   305.897'1407986—dc21   2001048086

The paper used in this publication is acid-free and recycled from 10 percent
post-consumer and at least 50 percent pre-consumer waste. It meets the
minimum requirements of American National Standard for Information
Sciences—Permanence of Paper for Printed Library Materials,
ANSI Z39.48-1984. ♾ ♺

In loving memory of

LINDA AGHNAGHAGHPIK WOMKON BADTEN,

Yupik educator and scholar, 1926–1997.

Her life was an example to many.

She left this life carried on songs of praise.

This book is for my husband,

ARNOLD HENDRIK JOLLES

His faith in me has been my support.

And it is for my mother,

JANET AISENBERG SMITH

Her stubborn strength has been my example.

Contents

Acknowledgments

It has been twelve years since my first trip to Gambell. I would like to thank each person and each organization that has helped me over the years, but with so many, it is hard to know where to begin. The people of Gambell have treated me with tremendous kindness and generosity and I am truly grateful for their support. In 1987, the Session Elders of the Gambell Presbyterian Church endorsed my work on community religious history. In 1990 and 1991, Sivuqaq, Incorporated (the Gambell Native Corporation) approved my work on community traditions and values with elder Elinor Oozeva as project manager. In 1994 and 1996, the Native Village of Gambell (the Gambell Indian Reorganization Act Council or IRA) endorsed new research on women's contributions to community life and history. I appreciate the support I have received from each organization, and I am especially thankful to Mrs. Oozeva for her loving and thoughtful guidance.

Of course, it is the individuals, the many people at each stage of my journey, who have made all this a reality. Regrettably, some of those I would like to thank are no longer living, and I can only commemorate them here. They are Thelma Apatiki, who welcomed me into her home as her guest and companion; Leonard Nowpakahok, whose words of wisdom and devotion to his Yupik heritage were inspirational; Bessie Kaningok, who offered to be my Gambell mother; Wallace Ungwiluk, who gave me my first "woman's share" of *mangtak* on the beach one spring; Ronald Kingeekuk, Herbert Kiyukluk, John Kulowiyi, Nathan Noongwook, and Walter Wongitillan of Savoonga, who shared their memories with me; and Linda Womkon Badten, who taught me so much and whose friendship and advice I so much appreciated.

In the community today I especially want to thank the Apatiki family. So many members of the Apatiki family have helped me and watched over me through the years that I shall never be able to repay them. Michael and Debbie Apatiki and their children have always made a place for me in their home, fed me hundreds of good meals, and cared for me when I was sick. It has been an honor and privilege to be their guest. Three Apatiki women are especially important and dear to me: Deborah Kaningok Apatiki, Edna Apatiki Anungazuk, and Lucy Walunga Apatiki. They have been my friends in every sense of the word, as well as my teachers and my counselors. I never had any sisters. If I could have chosen them, I would ask that these women be my sisters.

Among the elders, I would like to thank Elinor Oozeva, Estelle Oozevaseuk, and Beda Slwooko. These three women have spent hours with me and my tape recorder. Some of the other women who contributed much to the research are Gail Angi, Lydia Apatiki, Luceen Apassingok, the Rev. Agnes Brady, Alayne Booshu, Susan Campbell, Helen Christiansen, the Rev. Alice Green, Beulah Nowpakahok, Ora Gologergen, Mitzi Shinen, June Walunga, and Nancy Walunga. Many men have also befriended, helped, and advised me: Holden Apatiki, Jerome Apatiki, Ralph Apatiki, Clarence Irrigoo, Gerard Koonooka, Job Koonooka, Conrad Oozeva, Dave Shinen, the Rev. Sigurd Christiansen, Vernon Slwooko, Jimmie Toolie, Clement Ungott, and Willis Walunga. I have tried to thank those who have worked with me as research assistants, translators, and interns within the pages of the book itself. While I am grateful to many, the work is my own, along with any weaknesses or misinterpretations or misunderstandings of what I have learned. To the people of Gambell, I can only say "thank you." I have tried to present what I have learned in a way that will have value for the community, especially the young people. Forgive me for the errors. They are truly my own and not yours. You have been wonderful teachers.

Among my colleagues I would like to thank Noel Broadbent, David Hales, Stevan Harrell, Charles Keyes, Fae Korsmo, Tsianina Lomawaima, James Nason, and Eric Smith. The late Charles Hughes served as my mentor and resource, and his wife Leslie became my friend, although, regretfully, only after Charles' death. Herbert Anungazuk, Lydia Black, Jean Briggs, Julie Cruikshank, Roger Harritt, Chase Hensel, Allen McCartney, and Phyllis Morrow have offered helpful criticism and support. Thanks also to Susan Smith-Hughes for preparing the book's index. Finally, of course, there is my family. My husband Arnold has been my most enthusiastic supporter. Without him, I might have lost heart.

From the very first, I received financial support that made the research possible. In 1987, I received a financial gift from the late Mrs. Illsley Ball Nordstrom of Seattle, Washington, which paid my fare to Gambell that spring. I also received an award from the Phillips Fund of the American Philosophical Society for research in the Presbyterian Historical Society archives in Philadelphia. The Anthropology Department and the Graduate School of the University of Washington (Graduate Faculty Award, Royalty Research Fund) provided funding from 1987 to 1993. The National Science Foundation's Social and Behavioral Sciences Division funded my dissertation research (Grant No. NSF-8721726) on religious history and identity in 1987 and 1988. In 1991 and 1996, two grants (Grant Nos. DPP-9122083, OPP-9796084) from the Arctic Social Sciences Program, Office of Polar Programs, National Science Foundation, supported work on the transmission of traditions and values among Yupik families and on Yupik women's life histories. At the completion of this book, there is still more work to be done.

Faith, Food,
and Family
in a
Yupik Whaling
Community

1.1 St. Lawrence Island, Easter Sunday 1987.

CHAPTER 1

Introduction

I often think that for those who were born and raised on St. Lawrence Island, Alaska, the landscape itself must be part of their being. Even people's names tie them to this land: some come from the island's geological, topographical, and marine features. Others come from the plants and animals found on the island or from the weather that molds the character of each day and from the daily activities and relationships that bind people together in the community. Mary Catherine Bateson notes that "objects summarize histories. Passed from hand to hand, they represent new relationships and meanings on each passing" (1994:24–25). I believe that landscape itself, expressed through the repetition of names taken from the land and through the daily experience of traversing the land, with its multitude of names, in order to hunt or to visit family or to seek comfort and assurance through prayer, also summarizes and affirms histories. Surely, this deep familiarity affects how people feel about their homeland and how they think. Still, I do not pretend to describe the feelings that the sight of the island and its many landmarks generate among islanders. My own experience of the land has come slowly, marked by my outsider status and my gradual understanding of the traditions and experience of local people.

When I first saw St. Lawrence Island, on Easter Sunday, April 1987, I was struck by its stunning beauty and its isolation from all that I knew. Its stony, snow-hardened surfaces on that brilliant, sunny spring morning endowed it with an almost mystical presence. I still have this feeling each time I see the island, which often rises straight from the ice-calmed sea into clouds of crystalline mists. The clouds hang across cliff tops or perpetually encircle the outer shores. Snow covers the land in blotchy patches until the end of June. Ice is always present—sometimes solid and piled in great chunks to the farthest horizon, at other times blanketing the sea in smooth blue-green patches. Sometimes it is broken and in shards, moving in the wild currents that swirl around Northwest Cape. The full hundred-mile length of the island is seldom visible except from the air. The curves and inlets of the indented shore hide its drawn-out shape, while the fogs, storms, and winds that assault its shoreline 300 out of 365 days a year effectively complete its cloak of obscurity.

The island has two villages, Gambell and Savoonga. This book is intended as a narrative of community life and history in Gambell, the older of the two, and it is dedicated especially to the St. Lawrence Island *Yupiget*[1] who live here. In one sense, it is a retrospective of community life. Some would call it a community study and others an ethnography of local life. It is also a personal documentation of continuities and changes over the last decade, with special attention given to the voices of elders and others whose experience is the stuff of community history. The narratives give expression to three important motifs that underlie all village life: faith, devotion to a subsistence life way, and family. Many of my teachers in the community have been women elders, and most of my close friendships have also been with women. As a result, more women's voices fill these pages than men's voices. Overall, the narratives give local expression to these motifs and suggest some of the pleasure and the pain of rural arctic life.

The village of Gambell sits lightly on a graveled spit a few feet above sea level at Northwest Cape and is bounded by black, lava sand beaches. The cape is a slanted, knife-edged corner at the extreme outskirts of town. The spit is surrounded on three sides by the Bering Sea. Along the southern edge of town is Naayvaq, a lake that once supplied drinking water, but is now polluted. Throughout the winter and spring months, Naayvaq is a wide, smooth ice road. People used to use it to travel to the airport runway, which is caught between the southern edge of Naayvaq and the beach, close to the village's southern brink. The west and north beaches front the sea without unusual interruption, unless one counts the village

1. *Yupiget* is the plural of *Yupik*, meaning "a St. Lawrence Island person." Yupik is also the name of the language people speak. It is sometimes called Siberian or Chaplinski Yupik and at other times St. Lawrence Island Yupik.

dump and the newly constructed waste water field at the northwest turn of the beach. Along the entire eastern perimeter of Gambell, the blunt, imposing promontory of Sivuqaq Mountain rises into the air, defining the community and limiting its spread. The Yupik name for both Gambell and the island is Sivuqaq.

When I arrived on that memorable Easter Sunday in 1987, it was whaling season. The community hummed with the activities of men and women going about the business of bowhead whaling. Citizen band (CB) radios filled in the quiet times with men's voices as they talked excitedly to their families at home and to men in other boats. The weather and whales were on everybody's mind. Above all else, Gambell is a modern whaling village.

In the ten years since that first visit, babies have grown into independent ten-year-olds, who compete in school spelling bees and play with their cousins all night in the sunlit summer months; one-time first graders hunt walruses, whales, seals, and birds for their families; those I met as fourth and fifth graders are raising families of their own; and parents have become grandparents. Many whose voices I loved and whose stories I was privileged to hear are gone now. I miss them. From the very first, St. Lawrence Islanders opened their homes to me and offered their friendship, their assistance, their generosity, and their good humor, while they patiently overlooked my mistakes and my ignorance of Yupik good manners. Ten years later, I am still the grateful recipient of St. Lawrence Island hospitality and Yupik patience. Occasionally, still, someone says to me with a smile, "Now you are sounding like a *laluramka* [a white person]!" Friendships have deepened and widened, and I find, not surprisingly, that my own life has been changed and enriched by the people I have come to know here. While I am sure that it happens, anthropologists do not often admit that the people who have allowed them to enter into their homes and lives have become like "second family" to them. For me, that is what happened. Throughout the fall and winter of 1998 as I listened to the voices of many people on tape, I found myself thinking again and again how important this woman or that man had become to me. It was a humbling and thought-provoking experience.

In the pages that follow I describe some of what I learned from a decade of life lived intermittently among St. Lawrence Island people and from searching among archives and libraries for other evidence of the

1.2 *Gambell, May 1987, as viewed from Sivuqaq Mountain. Naayvaq is out-lined on the south side of the village.*

community's long history. Our conversations, our shared experiences, our different observations, along with the observations and experiences of those who have preceded us, comprise a narrative of contemporary Yupik tradition, belief, and life within the St. Lawrence Island or Sivuqaghhmiit (people of Sivuqaq) community. I hope our voices together will speak to islanders and strangers alike. The narratives and commentary reflect the desire of elders and others to tell their stories. If some stories have a de-cidedly religious flavor, it is a natural consequence of the philosophies of the storytellers and the abiding faith and spirit that underlies the thought world[2] of St. Lawrence Island people.

2. Robin Ridington (1988:ix–xv) uses "thought world" to indicate a local knowl-edge basis of understanding.

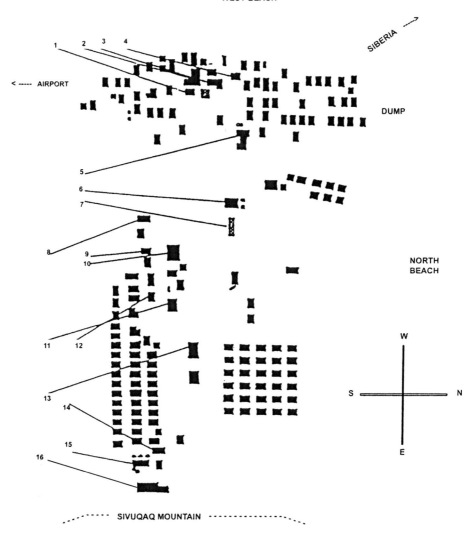

WEST BEACH

SIBERIA ----->

<----- AIRPORT

DUMP

NORTH
BEACH

W

S ====== N

E

····· SIVUQAQ MOUNTAIN ····················

1. Clinic
2. Gambell Elementary School
3. Teachers' quarters
4. Principal's quarters
5. Presbyterian Church and manse
6. Village fuel supply tanks
7. Gambell Native Store
8. Community freezer

9. Seventh-day Adventist Church
10. National Guard Armory
11. Store (G&E Enterprise)
12. Library
13. Post Office
14. The City (municipal building)
15. Laundry & public showers
16. John Apangalook Memorial High School

1.3 Gambell in 1987–88.

Gambell is the most recent settlement of many in this ancient outpost. As both archaeological research[3] and island oral and historical traditions suggest, Gambell sits where generations of Yupik, proto-Yup'ik,[4] and Inupiaq peoples have lived for some two thousand years. While this book is mainly a narrative of recent family life and tradition, it depends on that centuries-old history and prehistory. The story line of island history and tradition is constructed from Native voices drawn from the past and from the dynamic context of contemporary community life. The framework is social and religious, with the intention to present island culture as a source of implicit meaning, enduring values, and familial continuity. Each chapter incorporates the rules for living mentioned by elders[5] whom I and my island co-workers[6] have consulted over the years. These rules, which extend backward in time, embrace the non-literate past—a time when the humans, the land, the sea, and the animals and plants that sustain human life and livelihood were the dominant elements, a time when obstreperous technology and the presence of foreigners interrupted

3. See, for example, discussions of the island's archaeological history by Geist and Rainey 1936; Collins 1937; Rainey 1941; Bandi 1969; Ackerman 1962, 1984; Dumond 1998.

4. There are two spellings of this word, "Yupik" and "Yup'ik." They reflect differences in the Yupik variants spoken by, on the one hand, St. Lawrence Islanders and their Russian Yupik relatives and, on the other, by Central Yup'ik speakers from mainland Alaska. There are cultural distinctions, also. Inupiaq peoples live further north on the Bering Sea coast, on Little Diomede Island, and across Canada and Greenland. The differences between Yupik and Inupiaq are similar to the differences between English and German.

5. The elders include Gail Angi, Steven Aningayou, Lily Apangalook, Luceen and Anders Apassingok, Ralph Apatiki, Linda Badten, Alayne Booshu, Susan Campbell, Ora Gologergen, Clarence Irrigoo, Ronald Kingeekuk, John and Alice Kulowiyi, Nathan Noongwook, Elinor and Conrad Oozeva, Estelle Oozevaseuk, Beda and Vernon Slwooko, Jimmie Toolie, Clement Ungott, Nancy and Willis Walunga, Walter Wongitillan, and many, many others.

6. Many Gambell people shared the work of this book with me: Dawn Apangalook, Delma Apassingok, Deborah Apatiki, Jennifer Apatiki, Lucy Apatiki, Tanya Apatiki, Trudy Apatiki, Reena Booshu, Susan Campbell, Beulah Nowpakahok, Elinor Oozeva, and Tamara Slwooko. They conducted interviews, translated and transcribed texts, typed transcriptions onto the computer, served as interpreters, or, in the case of high school students in Gambell, did a bit of everything in their roles as interns. Rebecca Klenk (University of Washington) and Cheryl Stonestreet and Michelle DeFields-Gambrel (both of Indiana University) also assisted me.

1.4 *Paul Silook, Native historian, and his wife, Margaret, look out from the interior room of their mangteghapik (traditional walrus-hide house) in 1940. Photo courtesy of the University of Alaska Fairbanks Arctic and Polar Regions Archives.*

the flow of everyday life only intermittently. These same rules for living are integral to the community's present dialogue about the future direction of the island, the goals that parents envision for their children, and the confusion found in this and many northern Native communities about the best way to survive in an ever-changing and constantly encroaching outside world.

When I began, I thought I could create a chronological and cultural outline of Sivuqaghhmiit life. Using ethnohistorical records, contemporary documents and elders' recollections, I sought to provide a fairly continuous reconstruction of island history with an emphasis on socioreligious activity and belief. While I still hope that a historical pattern is evident, islanders themselves have changed my perceptions about island history. Critical to these perceptions are the women in the Gambell community who have worked most closely with me as researchers, translators and advisors and the elders, both men and women, who have recounted their memories. Most especially though, my eyes have been opened and I owe my thanks to my teacher and elder advisor, Elinor Mikaghaq Kulowiyi Oozeva. Many times her quietly raised eyebrow or subtle query turned and reshaped the path of research, perhaps more than she even realizes. From Elinor I learned that not every story can or should be told. In fact, many times as I sat with a woman recording her story, she would ask me to turn off my tape recorder so that she could discuss something of particular importance that she did not wish to appear on any record. I have honored those requests. As Elinor reminded me in her gentle way, sometimes the social costs of a bit of information may be more than the community is able to bear. While some might argue that history must be as "complete" as one can make it, I would answer that all written history is selected and arranged by the many contributors to its pages. Thus, the history presented here is colored by an implicit Sivuqaghhmiit bias in recognition of and out of respect for the community members who have contributed to its telling.[7] Many elders did not wish to interpret their parents' and grandparents' actions.[8] They perceived such behavior as distinctly un-Yupik. In some cases, they felt that it would not be appropriate to describe certain events from the past, and thus some recollections have gone unreported. Other events have been presented without interpretation.

After the turn of the century, the Sivuqaghhmiit gradually changed. What had been a self-sufficient community, relying mainly on locally hunted and gathered resources—that is, an autonomous subsistence-

7. The notion of bias as a part of the representation of thought worlds is essential to multi-vocality, which was widely discussed by anthropologists in the 1990s. It is a critical component in presenting the "other," whatever that may turn out to be. See, for example, Pratt 1986.

8. In Yupik discourse, one person seldom interprets or analyzes the actions of another, particularly of an elder. For a description of the circumspection of mainland Yup'ik discourse, see Morrow 1990.

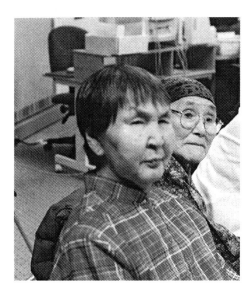

1.5 *Elinor Mikaghaq Oozeva with Beda Avaluk Slwooko.*

based economy—became a dependent community with a mixed market-subsistence economy. Such economies combine subsistence hunting with extensive trade and importation of goods. Until the late 1800s, the community also had its own distinctive religious and political traditions. Today, the community is recognizably Christian, with two well-established churches, the Presbyterian and the Seventh-day Adventist. The Native Village of Gambell is a recognized tribe, and three formal socio-political organizations administer the affairs of the village: the Gambell Indian Reorganization Act Council (known as the IRA); Sivuqaq, Incorporated (the Corporation); and the mayor's office and city council (the City). The community supports two general stores, a laundry, and many other small businesses both non-profit and for-profit.

The oldest members of the Sivuqaq community sometimes feel uncomfortable if they are asked to speak of the old ways, especially of the traditional religious system in which they and their parents participated. Younger men and women, those in their forties, fifties, and sixties, have struggled to maintain local hunting and bowhead whaling traditions, in

1.6 *Traditional mangteghapik. These were commonly in use during the early 1900s. Photo courtesy of the University of Alaska Fairbanks Arctic and Polar Regions Archives.*

spite of pressures from the outside world. They frankly admire their ancestors and are generally more comfortable with the idea of the "old ways" than those in their late seventies and eighties. On the other hand, the younger group's experience of the old ways is substantially diminished. They observed their parents and grandparents when they themselves were small children. Most have commented that one of the strict rules for children was the admonition *not* to listen to their elders when they were speaking of adult matters. In the confined one-room spaces of *manteghapiget* (traditional homes) of the previous generation, not to listen was a disciplined and deliberate act of consciousness and will.

HANNAH[9]: There were serious things that grown-ups talk about they didn't want children to hear. So there was a general ruling

9. Pseudonym.

that you weren't supposed to listen to them, you weren't supposed to grow up listening to all these tales. [At] Night time . . .
you were permitted, though, when they were talking about general history, history really. When they were relating history . . . in
the past.

CAROL: Well, since you were all in the same relatively small
house space, you must have had to train yourself not to [I was
about to say "listen" when Hannah continued her sentence].

HANNAH: Not to be boisterous, not to be meddling with other
families. Yes, those were taught from the beginning. ("Hannah"
1995, in Jolles 1987ff)

Elders today follow their parents' and grandparents' admonition. They
speak openly only of that which is considered generally acceptable to all,
that which "ought" to have been heard. To some extent, then, in order to
honor the wishes of elders themselves, this discussion of St. Lawrence Island history and culture reflects their concerns.

While I have respected the desire of elders not to probe too deeply for
uncomfortable memories, I have also reflected upon the comment,
which I heard over and over again, that children were not supposed to listen to the serious discussions of their elders. And, while I am willing to
accept local interpretation of this comment that children were not strong
enough to deal with the heavy and serious thoughts of their elders, it is
also possible that this admonition is not, as I originally assumed, an indication of very old practice. Perhaps, instead, it was a response to the considerable pressure to give up the older system placed on the parents and
grandparents of the present generation of elders. Like Native Americans
in the "lower 48" who refused to teach their children their Native languages, this decision not to have children listen to discussions about the
older religious traditions, particularly the spirit forces that assailed and
supported elders, may just possibly have been a reaction to the presence
of missionary teachers and outsider officials in the community from 1894
onward.

The interwoven narratives that follow come from many sources: elders'
recollections, focused conversations with local community administra-

1.7 *An honoring of elders in the gymnasium of John Apangalook Memorial High School, May 1987.*

tors, elders and others whose stories represent distinct and different ancestral backgrounds because of *ramka*[10] (clan or, as some islanders call it, tribal) affiliations, and ethnohistorical documents and scholarly texts. These accounts are often highly personal recollections, interpreted through the multifaceted lens of the community storytellers and a vast assortment of scholars, adventurers, and community recorders.

As in other northern Native communities, Yupik people seldom describe history in linear terms. Thus, moving "back" into history and non-literate oral history is conceptually difficult. Community life occurs as a

10. I have struggled with the terms *ramka* and *ramket*. Islanders translate *ramka(et)* as both clan and tribe. *Ramka* is both singular and plural when used alone. *Ramket* used alone means "those people" (in contrast to "these people"). When used as an ending, *-ramka* is singular, while *ramka* is plural. Throughout the book, I use *ramka* except in a few cases. It is difficult to reconcile Yupik and English, although Elinor tried hard to guide me through the linguistic landscape.

series of interwoven cycles. That life is caught in seasonality, in the ever-present forces of winter and summer weather, and in the return of animals. The cycles are heralded by bird migrations, by walruses along the ice edge, by the appearance and retreat of winter ice, and, most spectacularly, by the northern and southern migrations of the bowhead whale. In similar fashion, but with greater poignancy and distress, humans, the Sivuqaghhmiit themselves, cycle through the landscape, a community of valued names and persons. The emphasis is on family and kin. While Sivuqaghhmiit children attend public school, they do so preeminently to learn how to make more informed decisions about local community life in their seafaring community, not to become adventurers in distant lands where skills are useful only in foreign, urban environments. Sivuqaghhmiit parents try to imbue their children with a special sense of place and belonging that derives from their unique island home and their language.

Sivuqaq history is a record of family life, of peoples known and almost known until that retreating edge is reached where history transforms into legend. When community co-workers and I collected the stories and recollections of historical events presented here, it was inevitable that they would reflect this immediacy, this sense of place epitomized by a circular and sometimes wavering rather than a linear perspective. History moves across the landscape of memory like the tree line, sometimes deep, sometimes quite close to the shore.

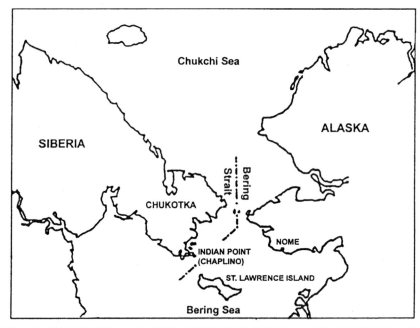

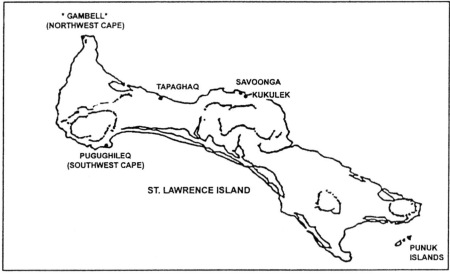

2.1 *St. Lawrence Island: Two views.*

CHAPTER 2

Where It All Takes Place:
The Village of Gambell

Gambell is one of two second-class cities[1] on St. Lawrence Island, the largest island in the Bering Sea. Including the three small Punuk Islands near its northeastern edge, the island covers an area about the size of New Jersey. It is located at 63° 10' north latitude, 172° 12' west longitude, approximately 150 miles south of the Arctic Circle. On clear days, one can see the high mountains of Chukotka (the Chukchi Peninsula) on the north Russian mainland, only 38 miles away. The nearness of Chukotka reminds one that both the International Date Line and the Russian coast are closer to St. Lawrence Island than Nome, Alaska, which is more than 200 air miles to the east. Travel to Gambell or to Savoonga, the island's other village, usually begins in Nome, from the small airport lounges of several northern commuter airlines: Bering Air, Olsen Air, Cape Smythe, and Baker Air.[2]

St. Lawrence Island is a mountainous, treeless, volcanic, rock and tundra expanse that stretches 104 miles from Northeast Cape, at its eastern tip, to Northwest Cape, on its western edge. On average, it is 20 to 30 miles across. Mt. Ateq, at 2,070 feet, is the highest point. Cliffs mark much of the shoreline and rise hundreds of feet in places on the north-

---

1. Alaskan cities are classified by population size. Because Gambell is small, I refer to it as a village.

2. This is not strictly true. In July 1997, Gambell native and boat captain Wade Okhtokiyuk and his boat crew made the 200-mile trip from Gambell to Northeast Cape to Nome using a traditional skin boat (*angyapik*) with an outboard motor set into the motor well designed for that purpose. They hoped to return using only a sail, but tricky wind conditions and rough water, plus strict instructions not to sail from clan elders living in Nome, prevented them from completing the return trip.

west and southwest coasts. Elsewhere, rock, gravel, and sand beaches give way to rolling tundra, laced with lakes and lagoons. While the island is, strictly speaking, subarctic, the treeless landscape, the small catalog of animals and plants, and the cool summers and fierce winters point to a land that is more arctic than subarctic.

Because the island is surrounded by the Bering Sea, temperatures seldom drop below minus 30° Fahrenheit. Winds batter the island almost every day, however, and create extremely low wind chill factors for most of the winter. With winds that blow steadily at 12 to 25 miles per hour (mph), heavy parkas with deep fur ruffs to protect the face are most welcome from late October to mid-May. Occasionally, winds have been recorded as high as 100 mph.[3] In the spring of 1997, for instance, a blizzard peeled roofs from houses and caused general havoc. Further north in the Bering Strait, the same storm destroyed a sea wall and beach causeway that had served the community of Ingaliq on Little Diomede Island for years. Generally, the wind blows from the north or northwest in winter and from the south or southwest during the brief summer. Ripple patterns in gravel and snow reveal the wind's signature.

Winter weather is usually generated in the northern Arctic or in Siberia, to the northwest. The island sits in a weather corridor and from November to April, blizzards sweep the village, often making it impossible for small children to walk the short distance to school for fear of suffering frost bite or even being blown away. I remember once walking from one house to another, a distance of perhaps 200 yards, with two little girls, on a brilliant sunny day in late April just after a storm. Although I had been through a Gambell winter, I still did not respect the wind as much as I should. My young friends Amamsi and Uvegtu and I held hands as we charged across the snowy, gravel-covered space between two houses. In my free hand, I clutched Amamsi's snow pants. I didn't think she needed to wear them for such a brief walk. Suddenly, the wind gusted sharply, ripped Amamsi's snowpants from my hand, and, in a matter of seconds, flung them into the air like a new kite and then blew them directly more than a half mile out to sea. With a red face, I tried to explain to Amamsi's

3. See Williams 1977:9 for a discussion of wind and weather factors on St. Lawrence Island.

2.2 *Traditional walrus-hide boats line the west beach.*

mother that somehow I had lost her daughter's snow pants on that short trip. Such is the wind in Gambell.

In 1988, Gambell had a population of 522.[4] By winter 1997, it had reached 640. The oldest part of this modern village is on the west beach, where small houses have clustered in some fashion since the 1890s. Until the 1960s, village sled dogs were staked near these houses. Now every house has a collection of snowmobiles and all-terrain vehicles. Many of the driftwood and imported lumber homes in the west end of town that are still in use were built in the late 1920s or early 1930s, when local trappers could receive high prices for their harvest of arctic fox furs. Newer houses are spread in two "branches," one between the north beach and a broad corridor filled with village service buildings, and the other between the corridor and Naayvaq, the southern boundary of the village. Sivuqaq Mountain, a bluff 614 feet above sea level, sits at the back of the village and defines the village's eastern edge.

4. Figures are from unpublished statistics of the City Council clerk (February 1989) and the Gambell IRA (1997), and from the Alaska census (1990).

In 1987, when I first lived in Gambell, the community had no running water except at the John Apangalook Memorial High School, the elementary school, and two of the schoolteachers' living quarters. The pump station for the village water supply was on the mountain's slope. In good weather, water could be obtained from a pipe outlet inside an open shed near the village laundry. By midwinter, however, the outlet, the shed floor, and the shed steps were usually completely draped in heavy ice and impossible to use. Once a day someone in each family had to go to the mountain side for water, either to one of the small springs along its flanks or to water sources farther along the slope just below the road that leads out of town along the foot of the bluff. These trips were always exciting. Sometimes the water container blew away. Sometimes the slope was so slippery that just standing near a spring presented a challenge.

In 1994, under the guidance of the incumbent mayor, Deborah Apatiki, and the city council, the village obtained funds to install a running water system. By 1997, most homes had inside plumbing, except for houses in the "old village" along the west beach and a few others, which still relied on the pump station and the mountain for their water. When the pump fails or the water lines to the pump freeze, those without running water hook-ups still must travel up to the small springs dotting the mountain's frozen slope or to the outlets by the road.

Sivuqaq Mountain itself is a monument to the past. Along its western crest and down its sides, wherever it is flat, the village lays its dead to rest among the rocks in coffins of imported lumber. The mountain top and its western side have served as funeral grounds for more than a century. At its base, on a slight rise, the community built the high school in 1977.[5] In 1996, a new elementary school building was added to the high school, replacing the older elementary school near the west beach. East of the school, the mountain divides "the town" from the vast open space of the island: the camp settlements, family cabins, hunting blinds, fishing spots, egging cliffs, greens-collecting spots, favorite picnic areas, and the lagoons, streams, and open tundra.

---

5. Gambell built a local high school following the 1976 decision in the Mollie Hootch court case that determined that it was insufficient to educate rural students in remote regional or national boarding schools.

The buildings and other facilities that mark Gambell as a modern, rural community are just beyond the school, in front of the mountain. To the southwest is the "washeteria," which contains commercial clothes washers and dryers as well as public showers. Huge water tanks for the laundry and other water utilities are near. Next door, in "the City Building," the mayor and city clerk, the St. Lawrence Island Ivory Co-op, and the federally supported Elders Lunch Program operate. The building was always busy, especially in winter, when the lunch program was in full swing and Beulah Nowpakahok and her sister cooked meals for the elders. In spring and summer, men wander into the offices of the Ivory Co-op to buy walrus tusks to carve and to sell their finished carvings. The tour ships that stop off at the island each summer always bring their clients to the Co-op to shop for carvings and other island souvenirs.

In 1987, the broad corridor that separates the north and south sides of the community was relatively empty. Between 1990 and 1996, several new buildings were built there. The Bessie Kaningok Clinic was completed in 1995 and expanded in 1996. Qerngughvik, a public meeting space, built in 1994, is used for community gatherings and nightly bingo games. The postmistress and her family dragged a vacant house from its former site near the airport to its present location next to the post office. I'm not sure that's where they wanted it to go, but that's as far as the village tractors managed to pull it, seated on its precarious roller supports, one spring afternoon. The post office has occupied the middle of the corridor for at least ten years, but it used to sit conspicuously alone. Older men passed time in the post office when the postmaster was elder Herbert Apassingok. After Herbert died, the men began to use the outer entryway (*saayguraaq*) of the Gambell Native Store.

Until 1995, the Corporation had offices in the City Building. These have moved to a building in the middle of the corridor donated to the community by the firm that erected the new elementary school. Workers had lived there while they constructed the school. In 1997 the Corporation's new home included offices, a meeting room, quarters for out-of-town visitors and tourists, and a delicatessen ("the Deli"). Rhoda Boolowon, who had cooked for the Elder Lunch Program for many years, became a Deli cook, making desserts and other fare for the Deli. The Corporation's main tasks are land and natural resource management.

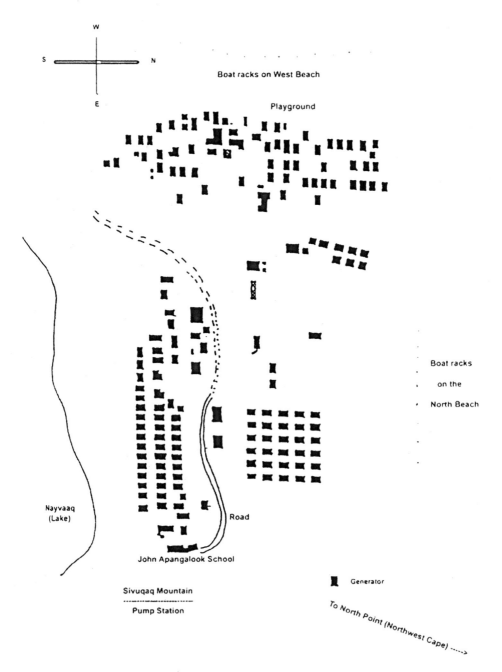

W

S   N

E

Boat racks on West Beach

Playground

Boat racks

on the

North Beach

Nayvaaq
(Lake)

Road

John Apangalook School

■ Generator

Sivuqaq Mountain

Pump Station

To North Point (Northwest Cape) ---->

2.3 *Gambell in 1987–88, showing the road and the lake.*

The tribal offices of the Gambell Indian Reorganization Act Council are not far away from the new Corporation offices. The IRA uses two mobile home trailers and a permanent building that used to house nightly bingo games and is still the place to go to take a chance on "pull tabs"[6] during the day. The community library is also in the corridor but is no longer staffed by a library worker. Instead, it houses other IRA offices. The library facility was still staffed with a library clerk when I first came to Gambell in 1987, and small children came in after school to look at books and play board games on the carpeted floor. Night classes through Northwest Community College have been held here for many years; they are in session after the tribal offices close for the day. The problem of what to do with the books still on the shelves in the library building had not yet been solved at the end of 1998. Other buildings in the corridor include the Army National Guard Armory, the Teen Center,[7] a privately owned store, three private rental homes, and the Seventh-day Adventist Church, where Sabbath-day (Saturday) services and other religious meetings are held.

The community jail space was located on the outskirts of town, away from this central corridor, close to Naayvaq and the road to the airport. The jail, really an old house equipped with an office for the village police safety officer (VPSO) and a secure holding area for offenders, was destroyed in summer 1997 by a local person. The police quarters were back in operation by summer 1998 in a new location.

Gambell is essentially a seafaring village. Beyond the houses, pairs of split walrus-hide *angyapiget* (traditional walrus-hide hunting boats used in whaling) and aluminum "runabouts" or Lund[8] boats (*angyat* or general-purpose hunting boats) line the north and west beaches. The boats perch on racks constructed of driftwood and whalebone. They generally belong to a single boat captain or, more often, to several members of a particular family.

6. Pull tabs is a game of chance, somewhat like "lotto," found throughout rural Alaska.

7. Between 1995 and early 1998, the Teen Center was closed and its windows and doorways boarded up. It opened again, in 1998, after the IRA obtained funds to remodel the building.

8. Lund is a brand name, but it is used locally to refer to aluminum runabouts, regardless of their manufacturer.

On the southern edge, the airport runway is sandwiched between the sea to the south and Naayvaq to the north. Two boarded-up service buildings sit near the edge of the runway. Winter storms and the ever-encroaching sea eroded the runway, and so in 1997 the community requested bids to repair the existing runway or to build a new one. Air transport keeps the village alive. In July 1997, however, some elders worried that workers hired to fix the runway might ignore the warnings of a previous generation of elders not to move boulders from the mountain. According to these elders, any tampering with the mountain might anger the forces that reside within it, causing imminent danger to everyone. One proposal was to build the runway closer to the mountain, using rock from its base for the foundation. Another was to take rock from the mountain to bolster the eroding runway. By summer 1998, the decision to reinforce and revise the position of the original runway had been made, bids were accepted, and construction was in full swing. Backloaders, steam shovels, and dump trucks were parked along the southern edge of Naayvaq when they were not in use.

School buildings bracket the community to the east and west. The old elementary school and its playground, the school district storage buildings, fuel storage tanks, assorted teachers' living quarters, the old community health clinic, and the Presbyterian Church defined the village's western boundary. In fact, the original Presbyterian church-school complex, built in 1891, was one of the oldest modern landmarks. Under the direction of the Bureau of Indian Affairs, which ran the school, it was torn down to make way for a more modern elementary school in 1965.

After the new combined elementary–high school was finished in 1996, the 1965 school building became teachers' quarters. The "old" clinic nearby was used briefly as a mobile classroom, but, in 1997 it was closed and the community attempted to dispose of the asbestos from it. Seven houses, built by the Civil Aeronautics Administration in 1943, sit out along the northwestern extension of the community. A few are empty, but most had families living in them in 1997. Between the Gambell Native Store and the first houses on the western side of town is a long stretch of enormous oil and gasoline storage tanks. At the far northeast end of the village, away from all else, is the electrical generating plant. It is a grim reminder that the old generating plant, located close to the cluster of store buildings, houses, and fuel tanks, burned in 1985. It caught fire, exploding the fuel tanks one chilly night, eventually destroying ten homes. The fireball that accompanied the explosion was almost as high as the mountain, and the entire village evacuated to the road running along its foot to escape the flames.

The village garbage dump occupies a corner of the northwest beach and is protected by a wire fence. What is left of the storage tanks from the fire can be found here. Inside the fence, the community deposits and burns whatever trash can be gathered up, including "honey bucket" contents and refuse produced in the village. The dump attracts polar bears, so throwing the trash away is sometimes risky.

The village has two stores, the Gambell Native Store and Angaaya's, or G&E Enterprise, owned and operated by Gerard and Esther Koonooka. A few women sell knickknacks from their homes, and some give haircuts and home permanents for a fee. Many people make local crafts for sale, using traditional techniques to create products for the modern commercial market. Several commuter airline agents work from their homes, too. The agents carry mail back and forth between the post office and the airport runway. They also arrange village air travel. The village has usually had at least two combination bakery–coffee-shop–restaurants operating. One used to be open in the evening and was popular with "night folks," those who stay up most of the night playing cards and listening to music. For several years now, the Deli, mentioned above, has sold sweet rolls, coffee, hamburgers, hot dogs, chicken, spaghetti, pizza, and home-baked desserts. It is successful and seems likely to become a permanent fixture. The local IRA Council, like many church organizations in the lower 48, sponsors community bingo games (four to six nights per week) and sometimes advertises stakes as high as $1,000. Proceeds of community-sponsored games support programs like Head Start, college scholarships, and bereavement airfares for travel to attend funerals of relatives. Bingo is one of the few amusements available every week. There's not much to do in a small arctic village.

Most residents travel the village, which is spread out over approximately a square mile of gravel, on snowmobiles and all-terrain vehicles. Locally, these are called "Hondas" or three- or four-wheelers. There is only one road in town, a raised dirt and gravel strip that stretches from the high school to just west of the post office, where it dies into the village land-scape. It roughly follows a path used until the 1960s by dog sleds and the like. In 1987, people complained to me that teachers were responsible for the road. The road is often muddy or dusty in summer. In winter the north wind blows snow across it, forming high drifts. Teachers believed that the community wanted the road to transport supplies and children between the old elementary school on the west beach and the high school. By 1997, with the entire K-12 education program housed in one building, such travel was no longer critical. Besides, the road had become so familiar that most people just took it for granted. The minor tensions gathered around the road are characteristic of relations between Natives and non-Natives in the village. There is often low-keyed grumbling, but few major eruptions.[9]

Having only one legitimate roadway means, essentially, that any open space is a potential thoroughfare. Actually, "roads" come and go in re-sponse to the appearance and shifting of drifts and hard-packed, wind-driven snow paths. The foot traveler often ends up in the drifts, since walking is safer there than along a four-wheeler superhighway. Old peo-ple, children, and families without a working vehicle are most often the ones trudging through the village on foot. Few walk who can afford to ride. With no "rules of the road," even pre-schoolers sometimes zoom through the village on Hondas.

Life in Gambell is similar to that in other poor, northern rural villages. By Alaska standards, Gambell is relatively large. It is one of the oldest vil-lages in rural Alaska and compares in age with Point Hope and certain sites in the Aleutians. Studies conducted in the 1980s indicated that house-hold incomes were not large, and the community is, in general, low-income (Williams 1977; Little and Robbins 1986). The 1990 census figures confirmed this pattern. Low income, however, did not mean that anyone went hungry, unclothed, or without shelter. As I helped some residents to prepare their income tax forms in 1988, I realized that the community-wide tradition of caring for family meant that many financial burdens were shared among several different related families. Thus, a household might

9. There are exceptions. Several teachers left one year, after a disagreement over teachers' attitudes toward their students' Yupik heritage. In the 1997–98 school year, the community felt that the new principal did not share their vision for their children. He left the community at the end of the year.

have several families under one roof. Food was generally shared. Those with cash income provided cash items to those without. In some cases, housing itself is fully subsidized, that is, rent-free. In others, housing receives a partial subsidy with rents relatively low by Alaska standards. The new water system is costly, however. Families paid a flat rate of $76.00 per month for running water in 1994. While fuel costs are high and heating at consistently low or sub-zero temperatures creates a constant expense, most families qualified for energy assistance in the late 1980s and early 1990s. Proposed changes in state and federal assistance programs in the late 1990s, including federal energy assistance subsidies, will undoubtedly affect this community. Some families use their carving and needlecraft to provide additional cash. Both hunting and wage work—for community agencies, the state school district, and federal granting agencies—support more than nuclear family units. Medical treatment at the village clinic is free. And, the Indian Health Service and Medicaid subsidize necessary travel for hospital care. Various researchers have shown that hunting costs can run more than $4,000 to $6,000 per year (Jorgensen 1990; Little and Robbins 1986). In Gambell, these costs, too, are shared among families, with the largest cost burden falling traditionally on the boat captain, as well as the greatest prestige and the greatest benefits to his immediate family members. Several studies (Burgess 1974; Williams 1977; Little and Robbins 1986; Ellana 1988; Jorgensen 1990) show that the Sivuqaq community depends on the sea for 65 to 80 percent of its meat and also depends on the land for a substantial supply of eggs, greens, and fruits (berries). Perhaps the most significant "store" purchases (other than fuel, ammunition, and other goods required for hunting and vehicle maintenance) include tea, sugar, salt, flour, disposable baby diapers, infant formula, pilot bread (a kind of dry, salt-free unleavened cracker)—and, in large, but undetermined amounts, candy, chewing gum, soda pop, and sweet drink mixtures (such as Tang or Kool-aid). Tea, lump sugar, flour, pilot bread, and diapers are consistently included in family sharing networks. Some are offered in the gift giving that accompanies marriage ceremonies.

The community has three main sections. Until 1997, the north side or section was home to many Aymaramka families, members of a *ramka* or clan group with close ties to Chukotka. Some families, like the Walungas, are descended from Siberian Yupiget who immigrated to Sivuqaq in the 1920s. Others, such as the Kulukhons, trace their families back to those who immigrated in the late 1800s. In 1988, Aymaramka families occupied about 21.7 percent of the houses in the community (26 of 120 occupied residences).[10] Many of those living on the south side of the village were Pugughileghmiit families, members of a *ramka* or clan group with ties to Southwest Cape and the island's south side. In addition, several smaller groups, such as the Iyakitans and the Aningayous, live here and are thought to be the descendants of the oldest original Gambell people. In 1988, Pugughileghmiit occupied approximately 30.8 percent of the houses (37 of 120 residences). Thus, ten years ago, 52.5 percent of the households were associated with two large clan groups (sometimes called "tribes" locally). Of course, families from several *ramka* were intermixed on each side. Along the west beach, there seemed to be even more intermixing among the thirteen or more *ramka* (clans) currently in the village. Thus, these divisions were by no means absolute.

Starting in the 1970s, government agencies (Bering Strait Regional Housing Authority and Kawerak, Inc., the local arm of the Bering Strait Regional Native district) began to build new houses in the village. Families that demonstrated need eagerly signed a waiting list. Once a family qualified, the household head selected a house. More often than not, husbands or other male heads of households selected the new house for their family. They chose based on a number of criteria, only one of which was the nearness of clan relatives. In one case, for example, a large home, located near the southeast edge of homes, went to a widowed clan elder with a very small immediate family, to honor her advanced years and her status in the family. A two and one-half bedroom house half the floor size of the former went to a family of nine. The husband liked the view that the house commanded of Sivuqaq Mountain. New home residency did rearrange older *ramka*-based living patterns somewhat, although it did not erase social boundaries between *ramket*. Much of the visiting that goes on in the community is still among close relatives.

In 1997, the community added twenty new homes to the north side, at the northeastern end of town (see fig. 2.4). The homes were built in Ana-

10. Residence and clan information comes from a 1988 residence survey, local census data, data recorded by Dr. Lynn Robbins of Western Washington University from elders Nancy and Willis Walunga in 1982, community records developed by Anders Apassingok and Willis Walunga, and my own field data.

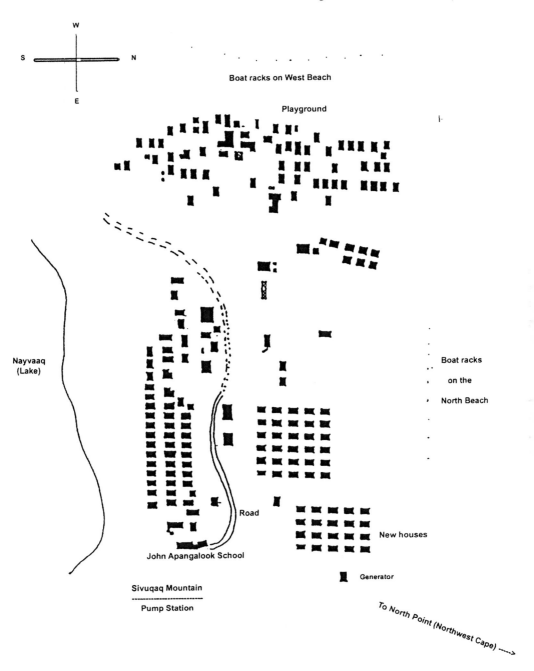

W

S —————— N

E

Boat racks on West Beach

Playground

Nayvaaq
(Lake)

Boat racks

on the

North Beach

Road

John Apangalook School

New houses

Generator

Sivuqaq Mountain

Pump Station

To North Point (Northwest Cape) ----->

2.4 *Gambell in 1997, with twenty new houses.*

cortes, Washington, by workers drawn from several northwest Alaska villages, and men from both Gambell and Savoonga traveled to Anacortes
to help build them. The following spring, the houses arrived on huge
barges.[11] In a remarkable engineering feat, the houses were swung from
the barges onto the gravel beach shore on huge cranes and loaded onto
giant flat-bed tractor-crane vehicles. They were taken to foundation pads,
which community members had constructed, lifted off by crane, and set
down, already built. With the addition of the latest houses, there has been
even more mixing of *ramka*. In addition, the practice of settling nuclear
families in the new homes based on income qualifications and immediate need has created a mix often based on age (the majority of the new
homes were filled with young families) rather than on *ramka* membership—a continuation of a process begun two decades ago. That the face
of Gambell is changing has been especially apparent since 1994.

A PERSONAL VIEW OF GAMBELL

I came to Gambell in 1987 to learn about the community's religious history. I had "studied" the community for several years, but, like many others who set out to "do" research, I had never even been to Alaska, much
less a rural Alaskan Native community only 38 miles from the Russian
mainland. I had only a scholar's knowledge of the community, based on
extensive reading and on contacts with other scholars who had visited the
community over the years. I had little acquaintance with the community
and its distinctive *ramka* system. One of my research advisors, anthropologist Charles Hughes, had discussed *ramket* at length in his publications
(Hughes 1958a, 1960), but he told me almost nothing of his life in the
small house that he and his first wife had rented from Vernon and Beda
Slwooko in 1955. Several researchers warned me that Gambell was not a
friendly place and that as a woman I should certainly avoid it. Thus, I
worried as I prepared to visit Gambell for the first time in April 1987.

Today, although I have lived and worked in Gambell intermittently for

11. Approximately 180 homes were built and distributed along the northwestern
Alaska coast in the summer of 1997. Savoonga, too, received twenty homes. Some
mainland coastal villages also received homes.

more than a decade, my understanding of the community is still incomplete. In many ways, I will always be an outsider looking in, not an insider looking out. My personal experiences within this community have radically changed my life and my views on the importance of family in both the theoretical and pragmatic sense. Yet, I suspect that while I have made many close friends in Gambell, I cannot be considered a major influence on the community.

My first experiences among Gambell people were more imaginary than real. In summer 1986, I worked in the Presbyterian Historical Society Archives in Philadelphia. There I discovered the writings of two schoolteacher-missionaries, the Rev. Edgar Campbell and his wife, Louise Kellogg Campbell. They had lived in Gambell from 1901 to 1911 and had made daily entries into a series of journals. They described their emotions upon entering the community and gave detailed accounts of their interactions with many families. Of course, in 1901 only about 150 people lived in Gambell itself. The rest lived in settlements scattered around the island. Altogether, there were perhaps 230[12] people on the island at the turn of the century. Reading the Campbells' journals and letters opened a slender window for me into the world of early twentieth-century community life and the people who lived there, but their writings hardly prepared me for the same community in 1987. In the archives, I also discovered addresses of more recent former missionaries and ministers, to whom I eventually wrote, hoping to learn more about the island. One, the Rev. Sigurd (Sig) Christiansen, had moved to Nome with his family and was using part of the large apartment he rented from the Nome Lutheran Church as a small chapel for island people living in Nome. Another, the Rev. Alice Green, had retired from active preaching and lived in a trailer home on the outskirts of Anchorage. Later, I met them both and became a guest in their respective homes. In fact, until they left in the mid-1990s, I stayed with Sig and his wife, Helen, whenever I was in Nome.

After my visit to the Presbyterian archives, I wrote to the woman who was Corporation president in 1987 and asked permission to spend a year in Gambell to conduct research on the community's religious history and

---

12. Statistics come from Edgar Campbell's diaries (1904–1911).

life. Response came about a month later. The Corporation's Board of Trustees had not yet acted on my request. I was disappointed and feared outright rejection. Perhaps my colleagues' unflattering remarks about the community were about to be confirmed. My imaginary encounter with the Campbells and the ancestors of today's islanders had absolutely convinced me that Gambell was the place I should be, and so, hoping that the Corporation did not intend to refuse my request, I continued to seek permission to work in the community. Eventually my wish was granted when Marina,[13] the Corporation president, invited me to come to Gambell during spring whaling season. With a hospitality and graciousness that I later learned was quite as characteristic of Gambell as the less friendly receptions described by my colleagues, Marina offered me a place to stay in the home she shared with her mother, Rhea.[14]

On that first visit, it was made clear that I had been invited as a guest and not yet as a formally endorsed researcher. Although the Corporation never told me of its decision, I learned from a board member that the board was not ready to endorse any researchers and that they had considered suggesting that I seek permission from their relatives in the neighboring community of Savoonga. Since the Corporation never actually told me of its decision, I was not sure how to proceed. I knew that I must have permission to enter the community, since no researcher in a northern Native community can expect to work without it. I believed in the value of the work on religious history that I proposed to do. My task was to convince community members of its worth and to gain formal endorsement from one of the large community organizations. In May, several Corporation board members suggested that I go directly to one of the two community churches for permission. At the end of eight weeks, I wrote to the Session Elders of the Presbyterian Church in Gambell for endorsement and waited for yet another two months for them to consider my request. The Session, led by the Rev. Eng of Savoonga, formally endorsed my request early in the summer of 1987, and, at the end of the summer, Marina called to ask me to care for Rhea, in her absence.

My initial trip to Gambell in the spring of 1987 occurred in three

13. Pseudonym.
14. Pseudonym.

stages: first I traveled to Anchorage, where I was met by the Rev. Alice Green, who had been a Presbyterian missionary to Savoonga for eighteen years. Alice looked for all the world like my fifth grade teacher, with the same knobby gray hair and formidable appearance. But appearances are often deceptive. She offered me lodging in her tiny house trailer, submitted willingly to being interviewed, and introduced me to others who might help me to research the religious history of Gambell. She even gave me her bed while she stayed up half the night sitting in an ancient recliner in her living room, until sleep forced her to lie down on an equally ancient sofa. She did so, she explained, in order to be able to watch TV at any time or meander through the stacks and stacks of books and papers that filled her home without disturbing her guest. Later I learned that Elinor, my advisor, and other women from the island also slept in Alice's bed whenever they came to Anchorage to visit.

The second phase took me from urban Alaska[15] to the edge of the bush. From Anchorage to Nome one flies over approximately 500 miles of open, relatively uninhabited areas of mountain, forest, river, and marsh—the vast reaches of the Yukon-Kuskokwim Delta, the lands over which the Iditarod dog sled race is run each year. Villages are only occasionally visible, and the overwhelming impression is of emptiness.

Nome, my next stop, was a town of 3,000 in 1987, large by rural Alaska standards. It hangs along the breakfront wall of the Bering Sea on the underside of the Seward Peninsula and has a mixed Inupiaq, Yupik, and non-Native population. The city serves as a resource center for the peninsula, for northern coastal villages, and for St. Lawrence Island. Along with a real airport, grocery stores, hardware stores, churches, bars, a community center with swimming pool and bowling alley, museum, library, hospital, and schools, it sports running water, hotels, tourist shops, and a small network of roadways that allow for automobile traffic. All of this is to say that for residents in bush Alaska, Nome is perceived as a flourishing rural metropolis.

In Nome I stayed with Sig and Helen Christiansen. Helen gave me a

---

15. Roughly half of Alaska's population lives in or near Anchorage. The only other large cities are Juneau, Fairbanks, and Sitka. Rural hub cities like Nome, Kotzebue, and Barrow have fewer than 5,000 people.

parka to wear in Gambell, and both offered a great deal of advice. Here, as in most homes I entered in Nome, and later on the island, I found myself wrapped in a blanket of spiritual concern. Prayer was conducted at meals. Conversation sometimes turned to the state of one's soul. Visitors to the house were often there to request prayer. I found myself gradually immersed in a religious world view.

The day of my departure for the island, I hoped to meet Marina in the lobby area for Ryan Air. I did not yet know her except from our telephone conversations. She had suggested that we fly together on that Easter Sunday afternoon, and I planned to stay with her and her mother for six weeks. I hardly knew what to expect but was certainly surprised to be met by a young woman in her late thirties. I had expected someone older. We boarded a small eight-seat aircraft that took off for the island shortly thereafter. Soon I was almost breathless with the beauty of the icy mosaic of the Bering Sea stretching out below me. I wanted to see great masses of walruses sprawled out on the ice-strewn sea, but it would be another twelve years before I saw live walruses swimming through Bering Strait, and I have yet to see a live polar bear. (In the meantime, I have become accustomed to eating sea mammal meat day after day and have learned to feel hungry and deprived when none is available.) Because the weather was extremely beautiful, the pilot took us on an unscheduled tour over the island,[16] flying over the site of the most recent whale harvest by the men of Savoonga on the island's south side, pointing out whaling camps along the southern shore, and circling the high cliffs above Southwest Cape. As we flew above the cliffs, my own excitement increased when Marina exclaimed that we were flying over the cliffs that had inspired her Yupik name. Later I learned that many members of her *ramka* were named for landmarks associated with her family's history on the island. Family and ancient residence were woven together in a person's name.

Gambell, like most bush communities over which I have flown, appears as a series of grouped black cubes against the white, relatively undifferentiated arctic landscape. Most buildings are one-story rectangular

---

16. I felt privileged to have that tour, and, to this day, I don't regret it. However, these same "unscheduled" habits of Ryan Air eventually led to some disastrous accidents and to the demise of the airline.

structures built of imported lumber and prefabricated building components. Many structures long ago lost any paint they might have sported. To the newcomer the landscape appears to be featureless with the exception of shorelines, sharp rises or bluffs, and the beach itself, a reminder of the isolation and vulnerability of these seafaring people who reside along the shore. We landed on the long tarmac that passes for an airport in Gambell. It is distinguished from the "road" by its smooth surface and its electric directional lights. In the spring of 1988, a polar bear made off with a section of the directional lighting, effectively destroying the system, and planes landed without benefit of lights for the next two months. It seems somehow typical of the short-term problems that face bush communities like Gambell: amusing, annoying, and a liability for the inhabitants if ignored.

My anticipation grew as we walked across the icy landscape toward the jumble of unpretentious houses clustered along the snow-covered gravel spit that contains Sivuqaq. We carried some of our luggage, leaving the rest on the runway. Normally relatives and friends careen across the snow on snowmobiles and Hondas to bring air passengers from the airstrip. But on this Easter Sunday, no one anticipated our arrival. We arrived, finally, at a typical home, although, as I later learned, a little more tidy than some.

Newer houses, constructed by the Bering Strait Regional Housing Authority or other agencies with federal funds, tend to have the same kinds of spaces within and the same distribution of amenities. Each has two entrances, facing either north-south or east-west. Doorways open into an outer entry way (*saayguraaq*), which serves as a cold barrier. Outer gear, garbage bags, and food needing refrigeration are kept in these spaces, which can vary in size from a mere 4' x 5' to a large, room-sized entry way. Entrances lead to kitchens or living rooms. I learned that it was proper to remove my boots and stack them along one wall with the other boots and shoes of the household upon entering someone's home. The newest houses in 1987 had wood-paneled walls and tile floors. Inside this home, as in many others, there was not a lot of furniture. In the living room I saw a sofa, a TV set, a small desk, and a file cabinet. On the floor near the cabinet was a huge rock that Marina's nephew, who also lived there, used for weight lifting. In the kitchen I saw a Formica-covered table, four chairs, a small chest freezer, an under-the-counter refrigerator, and a

2.5 *House A, where I lived with Rhea and her grandson, Isaac, in 1987-88.*

stove. The kitchen had a sink, and the bathroom, just down the hall, had a sink and a tub. There was no running water, of course. Both sinks held basins of water. In the bathroom there was a honey bucket[17] near the tub. The tub itself held a remarkable array of items, including old magazines, clothes, boxes of bullets, and a pleasant display of seashells along the rim. There were four bedrooms, each filled with mattresses, an occasional bed, and clothing and toys of all kinds.

On one side of the kitchen was a propane-fueled cooking range. Such stoves, found in almost every home, often served simply as additional storage units. In 1987, it was not uncommon for a family to forgo purchase of propane for cooking and to use two-burner Coleman camp stoves with small amounts of "Blazo" (white gas) for cooking. The sink was stacked with unwashed dishes. A small dog named Rosie[18] was tied with a short

17. Honey bucket toilets are plastic containers with disposable garbage bag liners, topped with detachable seats. Pine Sol disinfectant is dumped into the empty plastic bags to reduce the odor.
18. Pseudonym.

rope to the door handle. She barked excitedly. Except for Rosie, the house looked empty. Shortly after we entered, however, a small boy arrived— Marina's grandnephew. At that time, Marina, her mother Rhea, Marina's older brother's son (her nephew), and her niece—the daughter of another of Marina's brothers—all lived in the house. Marina's grandnephew lived sometimes with her and sometimes with his parents. At times, the youngest children of Marina's older brothers or their sons (two, three, and four years old) spent the night so that their great-grandmother, Rhea, would not have to sleep alone. At other times during the next year the house membership changed still more. I have labeled Marina's home, which belonged to her mother, House A. (See figs. 2.6a–d.) The residents of House A changed a number of times during the first two years that I was a guest in Gambell. For at least six months, only Marina's nephew lived in the house. I lived in House A for almost five months while Marina worked in a distant mainland village. I lived there with Marina's mother, Rhea, with Marina's nephew mentioned above, and, from time to time, with the various great-grandchildren who kept Rhea company.[19] The residents of House A were closely related to House B, where I also lived with Rhea (fig. 2.6e). This flexible residence pattern with a composition based on patrilateral (or patrilineal) kin is characteristic of not just this one family, but of other families as well. While a house with husband, wife, and small children may remain the relatively stable center of many households, additions and subtractions of kin happen all the time.

People move from one house to another for reasons that include crowding, family conflict, lack of money to buy stove oil for the furnace, adopting out a child to grandparents or another childless couple, and adopting in a child because of personal need, crowding, or family stress. Marriage, too, was a reason to move. Men moved to their wife's home to work for their prospective in-laws for one year. Later, women moved to their husband's family home.

On that first day, Marina greeted her grandnephew,[20] then six years old, in Yupik. The language of the home remains St. Lawrence Island

19. Figures 2.6a–2.6d and 2.7 show movement of family members in House A between 1987 and 1988. For most of 1987 and 1988, Marina lived in a distant village where she had taken a job.

20. Indicated as (E) in figures 2.6a, 2.6d, and 2.6e.

2.6a HOUSE A (April 1987 - May 1987)*

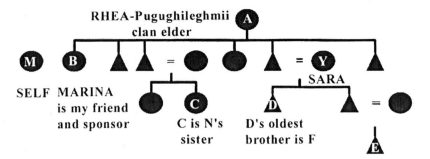

* Only a few family relations are shown. A's children except for B were married with their own families in 1987. B married in 1989, after her mother's death in December 1988. Y died in May 1987. E's parents live in House B.

HOUSE A occupants: A, B, C, D, (E), M

2.6b HOUSE A (October 1987 - January 1988)

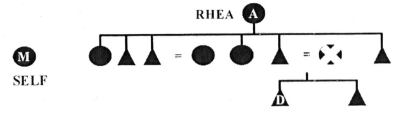

HOUSE A occupants: A, D, M

KEY

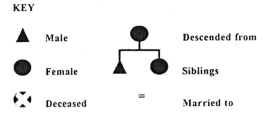

2.6c HOUSE A (February 1988 - April 1988)

D lived alone at this time

HOUSE A occupant: D

2.6d HOUSE A (End of April 1988 - June 1988)

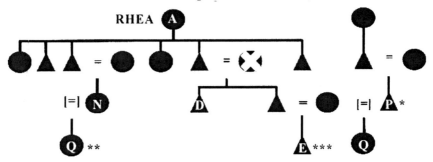

* P belongs to the Aymaramka clan. He moved to A's house to begin "groom's work" for N's family, after his clan "bought" N in a marriage ceremony. P and N are Q's parents. P and N lived with A instead of N's parents because there was more room.

** The diagram shows Q's relationship to her father's patrilineage and to her parents' temporary household membership in the home of Rhea, her maternal great-grandmother.

*** E split his time between Houses A and B during this time.

HOUSE A occupants: A, D, (E), N, P, Q

KEY

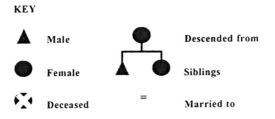

▲ Male	⬤	Descended from
⬤ Female	▲ ⬤	Siblings
◈ Deceased	=	Married to

2.6e HOUSE B (February 1988 - June 1988)

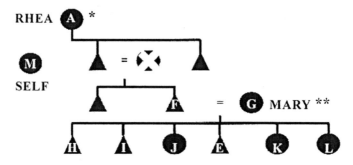

* Rhea (A) moved back to her own home, House A, at the end of March. M remained in House B.

** F and G had six young children living at home.

HOUSE B occupants: A, M, F, G, H, I, J, E, K, L

KEY

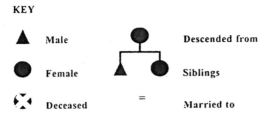

Yupik. The language of the school and business with outsiders is English. As an English speaker I found myself automatically relegated to a by-stander's position, a position reinforced because, in the beginning, conversations in Yupik were seldom translated. Occasionally someone tried to teach me a few isolated Yupik words, but it was apparently assumed that my inclusion in an exclusively Yupik world was either unnecessary

or undesirable.[21] It may also have been assumed that I would have no
great desire to speak the language, since few non-Natives attempt to learn
the language.

Food was obviously very important. My place in the family was marked
by my treatment during meal time. The kinds of food consumed by a
Gambell family and the manner in which food is served are considered
to be at the heart of being Yupik. "Real" food (*neqepik*) comes from the
island itself or from the Bering Sea surrounding the island.[22] There is actually a fairly large number of such food items, in the form of meats, fish,
migratory water fowl, sea plants, crustaceans, berries, barks, roots and
leafy greens; these constitute the traditional diet and make up the category of "real" food. All else is considered *laluramka* food. In 1987, most
of the families I ate with still served their meals in a traditional manner.
Food was prepared by the women of the household, who sat at one side
of a large tray (*qayuutaq*) and spread out the food after cutting it with a
woman's knife (*ulaaq*). Meats were cut into little pieces and, along with
any greens or sea food, placed on the tray, together with small bowls of
seal oil and soy sauce. Salt, "Mrs. Dash," and ketchup were often poured
directly onto the tray. Northern hunter-gatherers have always been described as flexible and adaptive. It seemed to me that dipping one's walrus or seal meat into ketchup, or, as I witnessed later, making spaghetti
sauce from bowhead whale meat, was the essence of adaptability! Families either sat around the tray on the floor, often on large sections of cardboard which helped to insulate the sitter from the cold drafts along the
floor, or they ate around a tray placed on a low coffee table. In the past,
walrus hide floors were insulated with moss or grass to protect the sitter
from the cold. Each person took what he needed from the tray, one piece
at a time, dipping pieces of meat into the seasonings and sauces. By con-

21. When I returned to Gambell in the fall of 1987, several children began my Yupik
education in earnest, teaching me words that were bound to embarrass me, or so they
thought. One of my first words was *leq*, which the children told me meant "hello"—
of course, it meant "fart." Another word that the children found hilarious was *aneq*. It
means "feces." Even today, the family chuckles over my first Yupik lessons.

22. Hughes (1960) asked men to keep food diaries in 1954 and 1955 and the
Dorothea Leighton, M.D., Collection (1982) contains several food diaries. The *St.
Lawrence Island Curriculum Resource Manual* (Walunga 1987) contains a compre-
hensive list of island subsistence resources.

trast, *laluramka* foods usually are served from a bowl or a plate, and eaten with silverware. To eat comfortably, one usually sits at a table.

My first meals in a Yupik household were remarkable for two reasons: first, I was served separately on a plate, while the family ate from a tray; second, I was told to sit on a chair at table while the family sat around the tray on the floor. I was clearly an outsider: I couldn't understand most of the conversation and I ate by myself.

Two events helped to break down these initial barriers. The first, the taking of a bowhead whale, occurred within a week of my arrival. It thrust me into the center of the most positive of all local events. The second — the unexpected and tragic death of Marina's sister-in-law, the wife of her older brother — was even more significant, because of its long-term impact on Marina's family, where I was a guest. Each of these events not only placed me in the midst of family interactions, but also introduced me to the many family members within Marina's family (patrilineage) and the larger membership of the Pugughileghmiit *ramka*.

First, I describe what happened when the whale was struck and later I describe the death of Marina's sister-in-law. Both events had a profound impact on my own life within the community and the shape of what was to come.

The whaling season, more than any other, provides the symbols from which the community draws its identity. Whaling occupies two months of the year at most. Large leads (areas of open water) appear in the ice in April, and in April and May the bowhead whale migration occurs close enough to the island for hunters to take advantage of their presence. By the end of May the whales have moved too far north to be hunted safely, however, and by consensus the whale hunters turn their attention toward walrus, which are hunted with rifles.[23] Other, smaller whales are taken throughout the spring and summer months (beluga, minke, grays), but it is the bowhead to which people refer when they speak of whaling. It was this hunt that Marina had invited me here to witness. On April 21, 1987, Gambell took a bowhead whale. The story of that April whale follows.

In the spring of 1987, Gambell had been assigned three strikes by the International Whaling Commission (IWC). The first, a small one, had al-

23. The noise of rifles disturbs the extremely sensitive whales.

ready been taken before I arrived. Under the IWC rules, only two more strikes, whether successful or unsuccessful, were allowed. The next was greatly anticipated, and each day the weather was the most important topic. Would it be clear enough and calm enough for the men to hunt? A wind of more than twenty knots renders the *angyapiget* (split walrus-hide boats, equipped with sails) unsafe. Storm, of course, or dense fog, common in the spring, meant no hunting. On clear days, high school boys eagerly waited for calls from their male relatives to the high school secretary saying that they were needed on the beach. Hunting season had caught up the whole community and young people found it difficult to concentrate inside in classrooms whose windows face the sea. On my visits to the high school, students constantly talked about the blue of open or ice-free water and the level of cloud cover (a storm/fog/open water indicator). Almost every house kept a CB radio turned on, waiting for the calls to get ready or comments from Savoonga relatives about ice conditions on the north side of the island. Old men clustered on the beach right after their morning tea or coffee to discuss the day's possibilities. Women, as I learned later, were not expected to make an appearance on the beach "for no reason." (The following autumn, my interest in the men's activities on the beach led to a rumor that I had come to Sivuqaq to look for a husband, a rumor that my own husband wasn't sure he appreciated!)

On Saturday the twenty-first of April, most of the Sivuqaq boat crews were out hunting (there were 22 boats and crews in 1987 and 1988). CB radios were turned on. I don't remember who was "playing" that day, but early conversations over the CB included reports of NBA (National Basketball Association) scores to the men at sea. Later, a small boy managed to get on the open channel and talk to his father, by now far to the south of the island, about what his mother was preparing for lunch. A woman's sharp reprimand to him to get off the line reminded those of us who listened with amusement that whaling is a serious business. Radio conversations also reminded me that this is a contemporary community, in many ways far removed from its past.

At 1:30 P.M. that afternoon came the call: "We have a strike!" I can hardly convey the excitement that followed this simple announcement. Marina screamed "Praise the Lord" and then began to cry. She hugged me enthusiastically and began to dance around the room with me. The next moment she was on the telephone, notifying her close relatives in Anchorage, Fairbanks, and Denver, Colorado, of the news. With phone calls completed, she asked those of us in the house—her mother, her nephew, and me— to pray. A "strike" does not mean the whale has been killed, only that it has been hit. Whale hunting is an extraordinarily dangerous undertaking, and everyone was thinking of the men confronting *aghveq* (the bowhead whale) out at sea.

I would not understand the full significance of that "we have a strike" message for at least a year. At the time, I thought "we" meant the village as a whole. I had not yet learned to think in *ramka* terms. Perhaps my first concrete observation was to note that whatever traditional sentiments and beliefs were evoked at the news of a strike, the family turned to Christian prayer to give thanks and to ask for help in securing the whale. I recalled, too, that in one of my first conversations with Marina, she had explained that "we have always been Presbyterian."

As the initial excitement wore off, Marina suggested that I dress warmly and proceed to the beach. The beach, it turned out, was approximately a mile from the house and was absolutely vacant. It remained so for many hours. Occasionally, an old man ventured out, stared at the horizon, and disappeared into the village. Elder John Aningayou appeared briefly on his three-wheeler and horrified me with bloody stories of harpoon gun accidents; then he went back home where it was warm. I spoke enthusiastically about the whale strike to a non-Native family enjoying the winter sun on the beach until I realized that this must be the Seventh-day Adventist minister and his family, who were vegetarians!

When I finally left the beach and went "home" by myself, I learned that the initial strike had become a kill. The boats were far from shore, mired in ice floes and confusing leads (open channels through the ice). The whale was said to be large indeed, 55 feet (as I learned later). The family began to prepare for a walk to the home of the striker (the crew member responsible for hurling the harpoon that had struck the whale) for an all-night vigil. This house belonged to Rhea, too (see fig. 2.7). In fact, Marina had grown up in it. It was the home of the striker, Marina's nephew and her mother's grandson, who was also the son of the boat captain, Jonah[24]

24. Pseudonym.

2.7 *This house, built with money originally generated by trade in arctic fox pelts, belonged to Rhea and her husband. It has been occupied by their descendants since the 1980s.*

(Marina's oldest brother). The striker lived in the family home with his wife, their two children, and the striker's unmarried brother. We entered a three-room downstairs apartment (bedroom, kitchen, and sitting room) en masse. Family members had already gathered. At various times that night the space held Marina; Rhea (oldest member of this large patrilineage); Marina's uncle (her deceased father's brother from Savoonga); Rhea's sister's daughter; Marina's older sister; two of Rhea's granddaughters-in-law; two of Rhea's granddaughters; four of Rhea's great granddaughters; three great grandsons; and me, the visiting anthropologist. With the exception of Rhea's mother's sister's daughter and Marina's older married sister, those who appeared in the house were all members of Rhea's husband's lineage and therefore all Pugughileghmiit members.

This does not mean that the married women were no longer members of Pugughileghmiit at all, but their daily lives were devoted to and very much a part of their husbands' families and the traditions and activities of their husbands' *ramket*. It was among the members of the Pugughileghmiit *ramka* that I found myself.

Within moments of stripping off their heavy outer gear, the adults formed a prayer circle. The prayers were both audible and individual. Each person prayed aloud. Quiet interjections of "Praise the Lord" or "Thank you, Jesus" punctuated the prayers, which were in Yupik. Children did not participate, although they were subdued and respectful. Adults, including Marina's uncle, wept openly. This was a serious occasion. At that time, I had not considered fully how dangerous and difficult the work of whaling is. It was not simply the honor of the family that was at stake here. Everyone was thinking about the health and the safety of the men out in the boats. After prayer, tea was served, to the old people first, and then to all, along with fried bread, which the striker's wife was in the process of cooking on a small electric burner in the middle of the living room floor. (Later, the striker's wife became a close friend.) Over the long hours of waiting, we consumed many cups of tea and doughnuts of "fry-bread." Children came and went. The weather was decidedly cold and dark clouds obscured the night sky. At one point, perhaps a dozen children piled in hastily through the outer entryway. Adults on the beach had noted a polar bear wandering at the beach's northern end, near the village dump area. Eventually, all became sleepy and lay down on the floor. Rhea lay down on the sofa with one of her small great-grandsons. Rhea's brother-in-law slept in the bedroom with another of the small great-grandchildren. The rest of us stretched out on the patchwork linoleum floor of the living room/kitchen, and the striker's wife went quietly around covering us with blankets, towels, and jackets. The CB was silent. The whale had been taken almost twenty miles out to sea, and it would be 4:30 A.M. (fifteen hours after the strike) before the crews finally brought it to shore.

Sleeping on the floor with the women, children, and old folks of the *ramka* and later being present for the distribution of shares after the landing and butchering of the whale not only allowed me to witness the family engaged in activity considered most significantly Yupik, but also allowed members of the *ramka* to meet me most definitively on family turf

and on their own terms. The event gave me initial acceptance, not only
as Marina and Rhea's guest but as a guest of the family.[25]

During the next forty-eight hours, men from the extended family continued to butcher the whale while other members of the family and the
community and I watched with interest. Later, women who had been
present that first night extended invitations to me to visit them. In addition, men related to Marina's household took notice of my presence
within the context of their own lineage and clan. *Laluramket* have been
regular visitors in Sivuqaq since the late 1800s. They are accepted as outsiders, persons different from the Sivuqaghhmiit. Some are "more different" than others. In my own case, I was accepted as outsider, as guest, as
friend, and most definitely within a gender-based framework. As a woman
guest, it was assumed that I would speak and consort with women as well
as find occupation and entertainment among women. To do otherwise
would be to suggest my own "availability."[26] I was asked to baby-sit, to
cook (although only those foods considered to be *laluramka* foods, such
as canned corned beef hash), to sew, and to be ever ready to be occupied
with women's talk. This first event, then, opened me up to clan acquaintance and located me within the female realm. I was perceived as somewhat different from other outsiders in the community because I lived
with a local family (an uncommon occurrence) and was more than willing to eat local foods. Nevertheless, I was basically an unknown quantity
and was received cautiously into the context of Marina and her mother's
family situation.

The second event (described in Chapter 6), the tragic, accidental
death of Marina's sister-in-law, who was only 54 years old, fixed me, as
such events sometimes do, among those who belong, however peripher-
ally, to the family group by virtue of having witnessed and shared in the
family's sorrow. After the sister-in-law's funeral, I was welcomed into
many households where I had hardly been known before. And, in some
houses, women said to me, "Come over any time. Just come in. You're
one of the family now." In Yupik households, those with family status do

25. I did not realize then that Marina's family belonged to one of the largest lineages in the two major *clans* in the community—a circumstance that would have a
profound effect on my life there.
26. Hence, the rumor mentioned earlier.

not knock to announce their presence before entering a house. After this event, I did not have to announce myself, either. I could simply come in, sit down, and eventually make my needs known if I wished—or even depart without saying a word.

REFLECTIONS

The context and general limitations of my work with the community residents were established during my initial visit.[27] Fortunately for me, Marina, the president of the Corporation when I had first contacted the village, was a sympathetic woman who graciously invited me to visit Gambell. She belonged to a large family in one of two major *ramket* (clans) in the community. By entering the community under her sponsorship, I, in effect, came under the protection of her family. In the years that followed, many of the contacts and relationships available to me were dictated by the connection to her family, the lineage itself, and the *ramka* to which the lineage belongs, the Pugughilegmiit. The family was large and well established. Through them I was able to make friends with many people. In recent years, I have visited many more families in the community who are members of other *ramket*, and I now have working relationships and close friends among the other major clan, Aymaramka, as well as several smaller *ramka*. There are some rivalries between clans and families, and I have had to "tread lightly" and politely among my many acquaintances, taking great care not to offend people inadvertently by ignoring the differences and loyalties among them. My own personality and scholarly interests have also been a factor. I originally came to study religious history, especially Christianity. Christian faith is very important here and many people opened their homes to me because of my interest in their devotion. It turned out, too, that I have a passion for Yupik food. Food is central to identity in the community. To refuse to eat the products of the land and sea is to reject part of what it means to be Yupik. Because of my sincere interest in local food, several women took delight in feeding me, and it was only with great restraint that I could

27. For example, I received permission to interview community members, but I could not read local Presbyterian Church minutes.

keep from eating five or six meals a day when I first arrived in town. As a guest within several Yupik households and as pseudo-family member in some, I have seen the value placed on close family, lineage, and clan relationships in the community. It was only natural that when it came time to relate my experience of this community, I would focus on faith, food, and family.

CHAPTER 3

Early History

In the warm days of late spring, when Gambell turns from whaling to walrus hunting, men and women trek to the archaeological sites that cover most of the town. It is a joy to go outside without heavy winter clothes to dig in the ground and to contemplate the past. The community is so old and so rich in ancient resources that even twelve- and thirteen-year-olds may spend the afternoon digging for ancestral treasure.

The landscape around Gambell is littered with dozens, even hundreds, of excavated holes, mini-archaeological sites that have already been explored or await further exploration. During the spring thaw, some holes fill with icy meltwater, and parents warn young children to stay away from the array of ancient house sites, grave sites, and abandoned *siqluwat* (underground food storage) sites. Occasionally, a new building, inadvertently placed on an old grave site, disturbs the spirits of the deceased that linger here. The sounds of formless spirits in the modern prefab structures remind the listener of Gambell's antiquity.

This interplay of ancient and present is a conversation that embraces both resident and visitor. Walking the village, the gravel, and intermittent tundra, decorated with dozens of pockmarked digging holes, overwhelms the senses. From June to August, the depressions often hold diggers eager to find the few marketable resources that the island now furnishes its residents. Inhabitants use the same methods and techniques that their grandparents first learned from the archaeologists and collectors who searched these sites from 1912 onward. In the spring of 1992, for example, I saw evidence of the sophistication of the would-be discoverers as two women passed by me on the road that runs behind the high school and along the flanks of Sivuqaq Mountain before it heads up and over the

edge and across the tundra. As they ambled past Mayughaaq, once excavated by archaeologists Hans-Georg Bandi, Henry Collins, and James
Giddings, they paused beside a family digging diligently into a small em-
bankment. One woman unfolded an ivory harpoon fragment from a
cloth in which she had wrapped it, remarking that it was probably an Old
Bering Sea piece. She mused aloud that finding an Okvik[1] piece would
have been better, because it would bring a better price from art dealers.[2]
Occasionally, an *ulaaq* (woman's knife) appears, complete with a finely
shaped slate blade and a carved ivory handle representing a polar bear or
whale. More often, the digger fills a sack with the cast-off teeth of walruses consumed long ago. These and fossilized ivory walrus tusks can be
sold to the community Ivory Co-op and will eventually be used by Native
artists all along the northwest Alaskan coast. St. Lawrence Island is a
major walrus ivory supplier. By 1997, the Gambell IRA had begun meetings with Savoonga and Shishmareff to discuss ways to preserve their
unique bone resources and artifact heritage, and village leaders wrestled
with the difficult problem of managing these resources, which are both a
source of income and a record of their past.

Sivuqaq history includes much more than these ancient sites. Island
history is constructed of the interwoven voices of many people, past and
present: islanders, Siberian immigrants, explorers, U.S. revenue officers,
sailors, ships' captains, missionaries, church workers, schoolteachers, and
early and contemporary archaeologists and anthropologists (myself
among them). Their voices speak from letters, diaries, journals, and personal narratives, and from them it is possible to construct a portrait of island life.

Sivuqaq is an old, old landscape. Evidence of its earliest inhabitants
dates to approximately 500 A.D. or before (see Dumond 1998). The stories
of its beginnings are numerous. The first stories are those of the elder
storytellers from the island and from the shores of Chukotka on the Russ-

---

1. Bandi claimed that "Okvik" was a clumsy English rendering of a Yupik term
meaning "place where walrus are found" and was used originally by island men who
worked with Geist in the 1920s.

2. Morningstar Gallery in Santa Fe, New Mexico, showed an "Okvik Ivory Harpoon Thumb Rest," c. 100 B.C. to 100 A.D., for $450, in its spring 1999 catalog. Some
early pieces have sold for $35,000 to $50,000 to private collectors.

ian side of Bering Strait. Their stories put the island on the map, situating it in mythic time and space. On the next few pages are stories from Ungazik (labeled Chaplino on Russian maps, Indian Point on U.S. maps) and from Native island historians Paul Silook and Willis Walunga. They offer an intimate and personal view of island history. These origin stories, whether told by islanders or others, reflect the time when they were told, the political allegiances of the storytellers, and the different scientific, social, familial, and religious perspectives that the speakers bring to their storytelling.

In May 1901, while on St. Lawrence Island, Russian ethnographer and exiled revolutionary Waldemar Bogoras recorded this story, told to him by Ale'qat, who is identified only as an Asiatic Eskimo man:

THE CREATION OF ST. LAWRENCE ISLAND

When Creator was creating the earth, he made at first the shore of Unisak; then he made the Russian land, after that the American land. Then he felt tired, and lay down to have a rest. The sun, however, had not set, and he said, "It is still light. Let me create something small." So he stretched out his hand, and took from the bottom of the sea a handful of sand. He pressed the water out of it—and therefore our island is called Cibukak ["pressed out," "wrung out"],—and put it upon the ground before himself. Then he picked up a few small pebbles and put them in various places on this mound of sand. These were men. They were weak and without enterprise.

He said to them, "You must take your food out of the water. I shall not give you reindeer. They are too good for you." They sought food, and found a walrus, a thong-seal, and a ringed-seal. Still it was not enough, and they were starving. All the people died of starvation; only an orphan was left alive. He was covered with scabs; his skin had large ulcers, and in some places hung down in tatters. He had no food for nearly a month. So he lay in the cold sleeping-room, unable to rise. His body was covered with an old coat of bird-skins without feathers. He lay shaking with cold, and asking for a speedy death.

He wanted to sleep, but could not. So he prayed to the Sea-God, if not for food, at least for a little sleep. But the sleep did not come.

Then he prayed to the Upper-God for a little sleep. The sleep did not come. But the Sea-God had compassion on him, and sent a walrus. The walrus came roaring, and emerged out of the ground near the house. Then it plunged back, but left behind a few jelly-fish. Some of them were right in the sleeping room. The boy felt around with his hands. He found one jelly-fish, and swallowed it, but his stomach was so little used to food, that he died of cramps. The Upper-God had compassion on him, and brought him back to life. He ate five more jelly-fishes and died again. The Upper God brought him back to life another time. Now his stomach was stronger. He ate plenty of jelly-fish, and felt better. Still he had no sleep. He prayed again to the Upper God, who had compassion on him and sent him sleep.

He slept three days and two nights. Then he dreamed. Six women— one old one and five young ones—entered the sleeping-room. They put everything in good order, cleaned away the rubbish, spread the skins, and lighted the lamp. Then the room was warm and tidy. He wished to move nearer the lamp, and then he awoke. The sleeping-room was dark and cold, as before. He prayed again for sleep, but without success. Three days and two nights he was there, trembling with cold, then he dozed off and had the same dream. The women came and put the sleeping-room in order. The old woman said, "We are the assistants of the Upper God. We must not waken him till everything is ready. Now prepare the food!" The younger women brought a dish filled with fish, walrus-meat, and seal-blubber. There was everything except whale-skin.

He was awake, but felt afraid to stir, lest the happy dream should vanish, as before. Then the old woman nudged him, "Get up! The meal is ready." He ate. Then the old woman urinated into a chamber-vessel, and rubbed his body all over with urine. Instantly, he was healed of his sores. She blew upon him, and he became strong, like a walrus. Then he copulated with all five of the younger women, one after another; so that his name after that was The-One-Copulating-with-Five-Divine-Women. After that he went out and set off, journeying towards the sky. He came to the Sun-Man, and said, "Give us reindeer!" Sun-Man answered, "I cannot do so. In the world above me there lives another God greater than I: he would be angry. Instead of that I will give you something large and oily, a great mass of food. Keep it as your property." He took two handfuls of small pebbles. "Take these, and when you come home, throw them into the water." The young man descended, and threw the stones into the water. They turned into whales of various kinds. After that he lived on the surface of the sea. He walked about with the walrus. In the end the people of Kukulek killed him by mistake. When dying, he said, "Such are you, and such shall be your fate. When you go out to sea, you shall be drowned. When you stay ashore, you shall die of starvation. When you have food enough, you shall be visited by the tornaraks of the disease." After that he died. That is all. (Bogoras 1913:433–434)

Twenty-seven years later, archeologist Henry Collins came to the island to work for the fledgling Smithsonian Institution. He wasn't the first researcher to come to Gambell. He had been preceded by physical anthropologist Ales Hrdliĉa and his associate Riley Moore, and by the sometime adventurer and self-taught German archaeologist Otto Geist. Both Geist and Collins, who were often on the island at the same time, hired islander Paul Silook. Moore, too, had employed Silook. Collins spent many evenings in his tent visiting with Paul after a day's digging. Occasionally, he visited Paul in his home. The two men would sit and smoke and talk. Collins asked Silook about his community and penciled Paul's answers into small notebooks, using his own personal shorthand so that he wouldn't miss too much of what Paul had to say.[3] He recorded this version of the island's creation from Paul in 1928. Silook's version omitted some details that identify his people (the Aymaramket and Kukulget) and other island residents as walrus and whale hunters. Still, it offers one explanation of the long tradition of wearing dance mittens, perhaps to acknowledge human debt to the Creator.

Silook was a Sivuqaq resident whose relatives and ancestors hailed from Ungazik and from Kukulek, the settlement mentioned in Bogoras's story. Kukulek is on the north side of the island, near the modern community of Savoonga. This is significant, since other versions, told by clans other than Silook's, may differ, just as Bogoras's version differs in many ways from Silook's.

CREATION — ST. LAWRENCE

The Creator thought it was lonesome between these two big countries [Alaska & Siberia] and so he put his hand down into the depth of the sea and took a piece of earth from under the sea, squeezed it and placed it

3. Paul Silook's notebooks are housed in the Henry Bascom Collins Collection, National Anthropological Archives, National Museum of Natural History, Smithsonian Institution, Washington, D.C.

between these countries and called it Sevookuk [Sivuqaq] [that which is squeezed]. Gambel also called Sevookuk. When he had done it, he took a journey and dropped his pair of mittens on this Island which turned into humans. Then after several [days, weeks, years?] these men became lonesome and they went to the Creator and asked for wives. The Creator was surprised to see these 2 men he did not know and asked from where they came from. They answered that they were from Sevookuk and remembered about his mittens he had dropped. He found out that they were his mittens. Then he gave each a wife and they brought them to Sevookuk and multiplied. (Henry Bascom Collins Collection 1982)

In January 1989, elder-historian Willis Walunga told me this story, which also explains the shape of the island. It ties together present religious understanding and past tradition. He said that at one time a large village called Siquvek was located on the south side of the island. According to tradition, this village was so large that smoke from its lamps would blacken the wings of a sea gull flying across before it reached the other side of the village. The village was washed away by flood, caused, some say, by the curse of a man who did not receive his share of walrus meat. According to Mr. Walunga,[4] people now realize that when the flood occurred and Noah took the animals into the ark, God must have taken a small portion of land, squeezed it out, and set it where a few deserving people could survive. Sivuqaq means "squeezed out dry." Before men could fly over the island , no one could tell that the island seemed to be shaped by a giant hand—even though that is the meaning of the island name—because they could not see the whole island all at once. When he finished his story, Mr. Walunga expressed a quiet amazement that his ancestors should have passed on the knowledge of an experience that is recorded in the Bible.

While island tradition and legend suggest that the great hand of Kiyaghneq[5] placed the island between the two continents in a time out

4. There are two reasons for referring to Willis Walunga as "Mr. Walunga": first, as a mark of respect toward an elder; and, second, Walunga is both a first name and a last name and indicates another person when used alone.

5. Bogoras identified Kiyaghneq as the "Sea-God." Today Kiyaghneq is an acknowledged name of God. Apa is another acknowledged name of God. I use both terms frequently throughout the book.

of time, geologists account for the island's origins in this way. St. Lawrence Island is the uppermost section of a volcanic ridge that stretches along the continental shelves between the Asian and North American land masses. Twelve to fifteen thousand years ago, during the last great ice age, the island was integrated into Beringia, or the Bering Land Bridge, which covered an enormous expanse—from Bristol Bay in the south to the Arctic Ocean in the north. As the ice melted and the waters of the Bering Sea rose some six to seven thousand years ago, the gravel, rock, and tundra terrain of St. Lawrence Island took shape. Geologically speaking, too, one could say that the land was "squeezed out"—dried out as it emerged from the sea.

Near the beginning of the Christian era, immigrants from the north Asian mainland established small, isolated settlements along the island's shores, sustaining themselves as maritime hunters and gatherers.[6] Recent immigrations from Chukotka to St. Lawrence Island, from approximately 1880 to 1948 and since the reopening of the Russian-American border in 1988, continue this pattern. The evidence for early occupations comes from layered middens that dot the shoreline of both St. Lawrence Island and the Punuk Islands, east of St. Lawrence Island's Southeast Cape (see fig. 2.1). Island history, which may well stretch back to a time when island shores were indistinguishable from the lands of Beringia, is considered an important prehistoric component of the movement of Paleo-Siberians between the Asian and North American continents (see Fitzhugh and Crowell 1988, for example).

To walk on the island, then, is to sense the ancient quality of the land. The ground is crowded with past burials, and on foggy days the air itself seems filled with the ghosts of generations past. Occasionally, someone from Sivuqaq will comment that it is unwise to speak loudly at the foot of Sivuqaq Mountain,[7] for the dead, buried along its slopes and across its top, are easily disturbed. Graves cover the bluff above the village as well as the rock and tundra sides that stretch westward from the edge. The western side of the bluff, down almost to its foot, holds many graves of the

---

6. Don Dumond (1998) has reanalyzed Collins's data and suggests a later date, closer to 400–500 A.D..

7. While the community identifies the 610-foot rise as Sivuqaq Mountain, it is in fact a long, high bluff.

recently deceased. Beneath and among these are the bones and, sometimes, the belongings of those who lived near the mountain over the last
several hundred years. Each grave is a silent reminder of the nearness of
death, as well as the many names found among the rocks. The names of
the dead are also the names of the living and the presence of these names
is a powerful source of continuity and identity in the community (see
Chapter 4). Even in the ten years since I first visited Gambell, many elders have gone to lie among these rocks. Some have rested only briefly
before contributing their names to the newborn. Others have yet to reappear in the community. Perhaps it is this intimacy between those who
now live and those who once lived that has caused some families to worry
that the boisterous basketball games played in the high school, which sits
below the mountain, will cause the dead to stir.

There is some disagreement about how many people once lived here.
Community historians believe that 5,000 people lived along the shores in
the late 1800s. Anthropologists and early explorers suggest a more modest
1,500 for this same period and perhaps an even smaller population before
that.

Life in the late eighteenth, nineteenth, and early twentieth centuries in
Sivuqaq can be inferred from numerous sources. These include archeo-
logical studies of the island and its neighbor, Chukotka; eighteenth- and
nineteenth-century logs, diaries, and journals kept by the crew members
of expedition ships, whaling vessels, trade ships, and revenue ships; and
the traditional stories still remembered by island elders. The outlines of St.
Lawrence Island prehistory were explored by several researchers.[8] Local

8. Riley Moore worked in Gambell in 1914 under Aleš Hrdlička's direction; in the
late 1920s and 1930s, sailor-turned-archaeologist Otto Geist of the fledgling Alaska
Agricultural College (later the University of Alaska at Fairbanks) excavated sites near
Savoonga. He relied on Paul Silook to record cultural information. In the 1930s and
1940s, Henry Collins, J. Louis Giddings, James Ford, and Moreau B. Chambers of
the Smithsonian excavated more sites. In the late 1950s and early 1960s, Hans-Georg
Bandi of Bern, Switzerland, continued that work. In the 1970s, Robert Ackerman was
probably the last to conduct extensive archaeological research on the island. In 1984,
Aron Crowell, with the aid of Paul Apangalook, surveyed still unexplored sites. In
1997, Don Dumond reexamined Collins and Giddings's work. Finally, in 1998, Allen
McCartney and James Savelle, with the assistance of elder Conrad Oozeva, examined whalebone remains for evidence of long-term subsistence whaling patterns.

men provided the substantial labor required to excavate archaeological
sites. In cases such as Paul Silook's, they also mapped the sites and kept extensive written work diaries. Some who made major contributions to the
archaeological research were Paul Silook, James Aningayou, Steven
Aningayou, Philip Maskin, Moses Soonagruk, and Nolan Silook.[9] J. Louis
Giddings, who employed Silook in 1938, said of him: "At Gambell, I engaged helpers, one of whom, Paul Silook, introduced himself in surprisingly good English. . . . We no sooner began to dig at the edges of older
excavations at Miyowagh [near the northwest foot of Sivuqaq mountain in
Gambell] than I realized I had been chosen by the right man. . . . Paul
was . . . clearly an archaeologist at heart . . ." (Giddings 1967:168).

Between 1928 and 1967, archaeologists uncovered much of the heritage of these northern peoples. Evidence of their presence is found in
their remarkable tools, their middens, which reached depths of sixteen
feet or more,[10] their scattered burials, and their house remains. Their
houses were of two semi-subterranean types, square and circular. Sergei
Arutiunov and William Fitzhugh note that the remains (Okvik and Old
Bering Sea) of the earliest settlers indicated fully developed cultures
when these immigrants reached the island some 2,000 years ago. The
roots of these cultures, and, indeed, of Eskimo cultures themselves, date
back at least 4,000 years. Before that point, "the trail of Eskimo origins
vanishes in the Bering Sea fog" (Arutiunov and Fitzhugh 1988:121).

Early residents probably relied as much on walrus meat as on whale
meat for their livelihood, a subsistence pattern similar to that practiced by
present residents. At times, the walrus may have been even more important than whales. That seems to be one message of the creation story
recorded by Bogoras and it is certainly true today, although the destruc-
tion of the great bowhead whale herds by nineteenth-century European

---

9. Paul Silook's work diaries give a feeling for the work day that these men put in
as employees of the archaeologists (see Appendix C). The earliest archaeologists
carted off hundreds of skeletal remains, and islanders are still coming to terms with
this wholesale disrespect for their ancestors. Not until 1997 did the Smithsonian return
hundreds of bones for reburial. Understandably, the islanders have been reluctant to
allow further archaeological research on the island.

10. Punuk Island middens were at least that deep. So were the mounds that Geist
excavated at Kukulek.

and American whalers probably changed the hunting patterns of this community forever. Today, walruses are the staple meat, but whales offer the successful hunters a special prestige and respect and provide a food valued as much for its spiritual, ceremonial, and festive qualities as for its sustaining virtues.

The earliest peoples, those who lived here near the beginning of the Christian era, included a succession of cultures related in their living practices, although significantly distinguished by artistic designs engraved on harpoon heads and amulet figures and on tools such as sewing kits, lice-mashers, sled runners, and knives. Their tools were beautifully made of finely carved ivory and slate.[11] Some groups possessed baleen buckets, fine leather garments, weaponry and armor, and a wide range of hunting gear including walrus-hide boats.[12] Archaeological research confirms the marine adaptations of the community, especially the consistent use of whale bones[13] for dwellings and the interior surfaces of underground storage units, and walrus ivory for tools and ceremonial objects.

Islanders lived in *nenglus*, which depended on the whale for their structural support. They used its massive bones to hold their whaling boats; and, according to early twentieth century descriptions, women became symbolic emblems of the whales the men sought each year to nourish their families in body and in spirit. At some point, whaling became a central feature of the religious system as well as a major subsistence food. The small village settlements were situated in places from which it was easy to see the annual whale migrations and vast herds of walruses, before the indiscriminate slaughter of the walrus by Europeans and Americans.

Old housing sites in Gambell alone suggest at least six different waves of occupation in the last 2,000 years, each reflecting a shift in the beach shoreline at Northwest Cape. In 1980, elder Lloyd Oovi described the disappearance of houses that once sat on the western beach:

11. See Collins 1937; Geist and Rainey 1936; Giddings 1967; and Fitzhugh and Crowell 1988.

12. Their artifacts, once buried in the Punuk Islands, in Mayughaaq, Siqluwagh, and other local sites, can now be found in the auction houses of Sotheby's and Park Barnett galleries in New York and London.

13. The term "whalebone" can be misleading, since commercial whalers referred to baleen as whalebone, although it wasn't bone at all.

When I became aware of the surroundings around me as a child [around 1900], all the houses were made out of walrus hide. I don't know how the *nenglus,* underground homes, were made because I was born after everyone had already made and moved into houses that were made out of hides. But I saw the ruins of several of them that were partially damaged. One of them was where my oldest brother, Waamkuun, was born.

There were lots of houses made out of walrus hide. Some of them are under the sea now, especially two of them that I know belonged to the Tungiyan's and Anangti's. Anangti, who raised Paanga. . . .

At that time the beach was farther down and there were no erosion waves back then. At least the waves did not go beyond the banks of the beach. (Apassingok et al. 1985:11)

Other house sites have also disappeared. In 1917, schoolteacher John Coffin recorded his escape with other villagers to the slopes of the mountain when waves swept across the western beach and carried off several houses. Such shifts continue. Between 1987 and 1992, for example, Gambell residents tried to keep the north beach from eroding into the sea, using bulldozers to shore up its disappearing gravel and sand embankments; and, periodically in the spring, waves threaten boat racks on the west beach, a contemporary reminder of the inconstancy of arctic shorelines. The gradual erosion of the airport runway (described in Chapter 2) is yet another example.

For several centuries at least, St. Lawrence Island has been a rich cultural mixing pot. By the end of the nineteenth century, the island was apparently home to ten or more small groups of people, who lived in settlements that were probably named for their specific geographic location (if present practice is any indicator). Ethnohistorical accounts of the island by Europeans, and later still by Americans, date from the first Russian explorations into the area in the eighteenth century. Early nineteenth-century explorers noted that the small groups of people located at several different sites appeared to have great cultural similarity (e.g., in clothing design, tattooing, housing).

One of the first outsiders not native to the area to have entered St. Lawrence Island waters may have been the Russian Cossack explorer Semeon Dezhnev. In 1648, he supposedly traveled from the mouth of the Kolyma River on the Chukchi Sea, south through Bering Strait, and into the Anadyr River, which flows into the Sea of Okhotsk. To do so, he must have passed the island, although he could easily have missed it in the ever-present summer fog. Two Russian sources, an atlas published by Remezov in 1700 and a map drawn by cartographer Ivan Lvov in 1710, are apparently based on Dezhnev's information. Lvov's map shows two rather undistinguished island masses, one of which could have been St. Lawrence Island (Ray 1975). We can only assume that there had been much traffic between the island and the Asian mainland for many centuries before, although it is no longer possible to document these passages of Siberian and St. Lawrence Island Natives. Some traffic must have been for trade among relatives, some for trade with strangers, and some for the purposes of war and aggression. Accounts of conflict between the two shores and between various settlements on the island abound, both in stories told by elders about Siberian raiders and in ethnohistorical reconstructions (see, for example, Iutzi-Mitchell 1989; Bandi 1995). And, in the notes of Henry Collins, Paul Silook relates that Siberians used to "steal island women to sell to the Chukchi as slaves."

Like other Alaska Native peoples, the St. Lawrence Islanders have several stories to explain the arrival of white strangers (*laluramket*) on their shores. According to local tradition, an important shaman named Agigseghaq first foretold the coming of non-Natives. The story has various features that assure the listener of Agigseghaq's authority. Elder Nelson Alowa recounts the story:

> Our ancestors, Maranga, spent a winter at Siberia and started to come down to the island. (We are of the Maranga clan.) As they were boating, they saw the mountain to their left and turned toward it. They had almost missed it. [They were near Pughughileq.][14] They landed there. There were people there. They spent the winter there. When winter started, they got tired of them and the Pughughileq people said they were island people and took them north to Kenliqaq. Kenliqaq was somewhere by that big lagoon over there, offshore of the outlet of the big lagoon. It was a small island. It came up out of the ocean. You can see the breakers in the water where it used to be. The Tapghaq people went out to see it because they thought it was a dead whale. When it was just starting to come

14. Words in brackets indicate explanations by Deborah Apatiki, who assisted me.

out of the water. When they got to it, it was land. This was before the Marangas came. That is where the Pugughileghmiit took them. And they lived there. They made a *nenglu* there on Kenliqaq. As they were living there they noticed it was getting smaller. So they moved to Penguqusiq. That island sank. Then they settled down at Penguqusiq.

The descendant of the Maranga was Agigseghaq. He prophesied. He put up poles. (This is how I hear it—some of it I don't know.) He would put up poles at night, talking loudly. In the morning the poles would have *pakestiya* [sail rigging]. This was before they had ever seen ships or sailboats, way before. There was a crow's nest in one of them. Sometimes when he came down [from the crow's nest where he was looking out], he would be very unhappy. Other times, he would come down, he would be very happy. He would tell them that he was not the only one doing this, looking out like that. Somewhere out there others were doing the same thing. Maybe he was the same age as Noah. Maybe when Noah was around, Agigseghaq was also living. Because he was prophesying all the time.

He had a daughter. Their *nenglu* was two story [a lower and an upper one]. She had a doll, a big wood doll [child-sized], Paperrqu was her name [the name of his child]. When he did well [prophesying], the doll would move. The arms would move, of this big wood doll. He was in command [control] of the weather, when he wanted to—not when somebody asked him to. When there had been a long period of nice weather he would scold the weather. And just as soon as his words ended, the weather would grow stormier. It would stay stormy for a while and he would go out and scold it, and it would be nice again. He was some kind of a man. His daughter died. He told them not to cry for her; they would give her a bad journey. That she was going into the future. A certain time of year they would go to Gambell for boat hunting—and people being curious would bother him, for him to scold the weather. And he wouldn't. He probably did it when something [inner calling] told him to do it.

One of the times he was here, he told them that he was going to die that day and he was going to go up. That they should look to the south, and they would see smoke. They would see something like what he had made [the rigging poles]. And he died. And maybe one year after he died—there appeared black smoke in the south. Everybody was running around because of the thick smoke coming. When the men from the ship had come on shore, they were having some kind of ceremonies for praying and for protection. When the men got on shore, they would get off, bow down to the ground and kiss it. They came to land by boat and they were handing out all kinds of things like bread and dried meat. And they let them go on board too and looked around on their ship. (Alowa 1985)[15]

The earliest undisputed non-Native account of the island comes from the Danish sea captain Vitus Bering. Bering, who sailed under orders from the recently deceased Peter the Great of Russia, sighted the island on his first venture into the sea that now bears his name. He named it St. Lawrence on August 11, 1728 (Gregorian calendar), on the occasion of the saint's birthday—but left no description of its inhabitants. Later maps suggest some confusion about the island's geography. The island is reported as one, two, or even three small land masses. Sir James Cook observed the island in 1779, but also did not land. He named each "part." He called the northwest, which he attributed to Bering's discovery, St. Lawrence Island. The mid-section he called Clerke's Island, after his second-in-command. And, the eastern end, identified today as the Punuk Islands, he named Anderson Island after his midshipman, who had died of consumption during the journey. However, Cook was aware of his error. On one ship's map, Cook's officer, Bligh, wrote that they had made a mistake—there was but one large island. In 1816, Otto von Kotzebue ventured ashore on the island, describing what he saw and the people he encountered in some detail. Was Kotzebue's the ship foretold in Alowa's story? It is impossible to say. Other Russian ships made brief visits, and then, six years later, Sir Frederick Beechey did the same. The island is mentioned intermittently in ships' journals over the next hundred years, although no major reports describe the inhabitants. In August 1874, Henry Elliott, who landed on the south side of the island close to the Punuk Islands, had this to say about the people he saw just a few years before the epidemic and famine of 1878, which wiped out almost the entire population of the island:

> The Innuits, living here as they do, some three or four hundred in number, are great walrus-hunters. They enjoy a location that enables them to secure these animals at all seasons of a year. In winter the sea-horse floats on big ice-fields; but during summer-time the "aibwook" hauls up to sun

15. See also Aningayou, DLC 1982:11–13.

and rest his heavy body in and on the inviting peace of those beaches of
St. Lawrence. (Elliott 1896:444)

The comments of Kotzebue, Beechey, and others, along with the
sketches and drawings of their ships' artists, become brief glimpses into
the life of island people in the nineteenth century. Their comments, biased by their European and (later) Euro-American perceptions of Yupik
culture, are the only written descriptions from this time. Island memory,
while substantial, focuses more on genealogies and more recent historical events than on a past that can only be imagined. Still, taken together
with islanders' descriptions of their distinctive homeland villages, we can
envision life as it must have been in the late 1700s and 1800s.

From objects collected by Europeans in the late eighteenth and nineteenth centuries and from written descriptions, it would seem that island
life had changed but slowly. Most ethnohistorical documents describe
local dwellings and the generally small populations in the various sites.
One significant aspect of these early European-Yupik contacts was the
constancy of trade. Both Otto Von Kotzebue, who landed in 1816, and
Frederick Beechey, who followed him in 1826, engaged in bartering. This
seems remarkable when one considers that Kotzebue is thought to be the
very first European the islanders had seen. When Kotzebue came ashore,
he was greeted by men who swayed between interest and fear. The
women and children had been hastily hidden outside the settlement, so
he had little opportunity to observe them. The drawings of the ship's
artist, Louis Choris, reveal people whose distinctive tattooing and hair
arrangements suggest the presence of meticulous artisans. When Frederick Beechey entered St. Lawrence Island waters in July 1826, following a
brief visit by Shishmaref's ship in 1820, a skin boat carrying men and
women came to trade with his ship.

Both Kotzebue and Beechey remarked that the islanders were experienced traders. They expressed a preference for objects of iron, blue
beads, and cloth. Kotzebue says that the small band of island traders even
bit into the beads to make certain that they were glass and not valueless
wax. And everyone commented on the islanders' demands for tobacco, a
habit that must have developed in the early 1800s. Wendall Oswalt and
Dorothy Jean Ray have noted that tobacco did not become a common

trade item in the Bering Strait region until after 1800. It became generally available only after the establishment of the Anyui trade fair on the
Kolyma River in western Chukotka in 1789 (Ray 1975).[16]

Kotzebue, who put ashore with members of his crew on June 27, 1816,
gave the first detailed European account of the island. From his observations of the shoreline and description of his ship's position relative to the
island, it seems likely that he first landed at Southwest Cape. He would
have encountered the Pugughileghmiit people, whose descendants live in
Gambell. He recorded his thoughts about the inhabitants in his journal:

> June 27th . . . We observed people and tents on the shore; and the wish of
> becoming acquainted with the inhabitants of this island, who had never
> been visited by any navigator . . . induced me to pay it a visit. . . . At a
> small distance from the shore, we were met by a baydare (boat), with ten
> islanders, who approached us without fear, calling aloud to us, and mak-
> ing the most singular motions, holding fox-skins in the air, with which
> they eagerly beckoned us. . . . After some salutations, according to their
> custom, which consisted in stroking themselves several times with both
> their hands, from the face to the belly, their first word was Tobacco!—of
> which I had some leaves, handed to them, which they immediately put
> into their mouths. I afterwards saw them smoking out of small stone pipes,
> about the size of a thimble; they repaid my presents with different articles
> of their workmanship. . . . We landed opposite to the tents. . . . This place
> appeared to us to be visited only in the summer, . . . as we perceived no
> settled dwellings, only several small tents, built of the ribs of whales, and
> covered with the skin of the morse [walrus], which indicate only a short
> stay. . . . We observed several European utensils of iron and copper. Every
> islander is armed with a knife, an ell (two feet) long, and adorned with
> large blue and white glass beads.
>
> . . . The island is called by the inhabitants, Tschibocki; and the coun-
> try to the east (America) Kililack.[17] . . . The arms of the islanders, which
> they use fore the chace as well as wear, consist of bows, arrows, and
> lances; the two latter are furnished with a broad, well-wrought iron head;
> these, as well as their other European utensils, we afterwards learnt they

16. See Ray 1975 for descriptions of trade developments in Alaska and Siberia between 1650 and 1850.

17. The nearest Yupik approximation to this word is Kiyalghaq, the name of an
abandoned village site at Southeast Cape.

received from the Tschukutskoi. They do not appear ever to have seen any European, to judge by the amazement with which they beheld us. (Kotzebue 1821, 1:189–93, quoted in Collins 1937, 96: 19–20)

. . . On the evening of the 28th of July[18] . . . At ten o'clock in the evening, when it was rather dark, three baydares approached us . . . we now had a lively barter.

July 29 . . . at daybreak saw the northern point of St. Lawrence islands.

Kotzebue's entry also gives the first written description of the site that would eventually become known as Gambell. "The promontory is distinguished by a high rock, rising perpendicularly out of the sea[19] a little more to the south, a low tongue of land extends to the west, and has a very singular appearance arising from several jurtes (Subterraneous [*sic*] dwellings)." (Kotzebue 1821, 1: 195–96; also quoted in Collins 1937, 96: 21)

Following Kotzebue's 1816 visit, the island was again visited by Russian explorers in 1820. The expedition under Vasil'ev included two ships. One of them, the *Good Intention (Blagonamerennyi)*, commanded by Shishmaref, was to survey St. Lawrence Island. Upon reaching the island on June 24, 1820, the captain appointed Lieutenant Alexei Lazarev to take the ship's tender ashore at Southwest Cape in order to bury a crew member.

Beechey landed on the island in July 1826. His descriptions reinforce those made by Kotzebue and the Russian seaman Lazarev:

> At about noon we were enabled to see some little distance around us; and, as we expected, the ship was close off the western extremity of St. Lawrence Island. . . . The upper parts of the island were buried in snow; but the lower, as at Beering's Island, were bare and overgrown with moss or grass. We stood close into a small bay at the S.W. angle of the island, where we perceived several tents, and where, from the many stakes driven into the ground, we considered there was a fishing-station. The natives soon afterwards launched four baidars [boats] . . . , of which each contained eight persons, males and females. They paddled towards the ship with great quickness, until they were within speaking distance, when an old man who steered the foremost boat stood erect, and held up in succession nets, walrus teeth, skin shirts, harpoons, bows and arrows, and small birds; he then extended his arms, rubbed and patted his

18. Kotzebue landed at Southwest Cape in July of 1816 and again in June of 1817.
19. This presumably is Sivuqaq Mountain, the eastern edge of Gambell.

breast, . . . and came fearlessly alongside. We instantly detected in these people the features of the Esquimaux, whom in appearance and manners also, and in deed in every particular, they so much resembled, that there cannot, I think, be the least doubt of their having the same origin. They were if any thing less dirty, and somewhat fairere, and their implements were better made. Their dress, though Esquimaux, differed a little from it in the skin shirts being ornamented with tassels, after the manner of the Oonalashka people, and in the boots fitting the leg, instead of being adapted to the reception of either oil or infants.

The old men had a few gray hairs on their chins, but the young ones, though grown up, were beardless. Many had their heads shaved round the crown, after the fashion of the Tschutschi, . . . and all had their hair cut short. Their manner of salutation was by rubbing their noses against ours, and drawing the palms of their hands over our faces; but we were not favoured as Kotzebue was, by their being previously spit upon. In the stern of one of the baidars there was a very entertaining old lady. . . . She was seated upon a bag of peltry [furs], from which she now and then cautiously drew out a skin and exhibited the best part of it, with a look implying that it was of great value. . . . She was tattooed in curved lines along the sides of the cheek, the outer one extending from the lower jaw, over the temple and eyebrow.

. . . . With the men, tawac, as they called our tobacco, was their object; and with the women, needles and scissors; but with both, blue beads were articles highly esteemed. . . . They had a great many small birds . . . strung upon thongs of hide, [which] they sold seven dozen for a single necklace of blue glass beads. (Beechey 1968 [1831] (1):330–333)

Between 1728 and 1867, St. Lawrence Island moved from independence, with its focus primarily on the Asian shore, to Russian territory, to American territory. Given its position at the extreme periphery of both Russian and American political and economic interests, it is unlikely that these shifts in ownership or membership initially affected the island residents. More crucial were the effects of increased commerce in the region. Between 1848 and 1900, the north Bering Sea filled with enterprising whalers and traders. As the area became increasingly profitable, the Russians, using Cossacks, set up trade fairs along the Kolyma River in the Siberian interior. Near present-day Kotzebue, Alaska, on Hotham Inlet, the traditional Inupiaq and Yupik trade crescendoed every few years as

local bands and tribes bartered for goods and cemented distant trade partnerships. Whalers working in the north Bering Sea made sporadic stops
at Inuit and Yupik whale-hunting settlements, trading alcohol, weapons,
tobacco, and other items for baleen (whalebone), ivory, meat, skins, access to women, and fresh water. Captain Hooper of the U.S. revenue cut-
ter *Corwin* confirmed these trade relations for St. Lawrence Island in his
1881 report:

> They [the St. Lawrence Islanders] live directly in the track of vessels
> bound into the Arctic Ocean for the purpose of whaling or trading; they
> subsist upon whales, walrus, and seals, taking, as already stated, only so
> much as is actually needed for their immediate wants, never providing
> for the future. They make houses, boats, clothing, & etc., of the skins of
> walrus and seals, and sell the bone and ivory to traders for rum and
> breech-loading arms. . . . (Hooper 1881:10–11)

The islanders, living at the crossroads of commerce in the north, were
active traders. Elders still speak of the travels of their parents and grandparents and also of the several languages that they spoke. All of this suggests a kind of northern cosmopolitan perspective. Visiting distant communities for six months to a year was fairly common. And, intermarriage,
at least among persons who spoke the same language, was frequent
enough to be included in personal narratives. Estelle Penapak
Oozevaseuk, the oldest of Paul Silook's children, tells stories of the travels of her great-grandmother in Siberia that illustrate this cosmopolitan
character of late nineteenth century and early twentieth-century Yupik
family life.

ESTELLE: My grandmother came from Nengupagaq—Irrigoos
[family].
    And my mother had came from Aymaramket, and our own from
Kukulek.
    They call us in Siberia "Sigungpaut",[20] but we grow up knowing
about Sanighmelngughmiit—so that's a boat's named for that, too.
Their tribal name. And I'm married to a Pugughileghmiit.
    CAROL: So you're like a pudding! [I laugh.]

20. Spelling uncertain.

ESTELLE: I was thinking about myself, if I ever go to Siberia, how would I tell the older people?

I have cleaved to so many tribes!

. . . I have listened to my great-grandmother. I was a little girl. But I remember

I don't know how old I am, maybe three, three or four years old. And some of them I forgot.

My great-grandmother had traveled so much. Her father was a wrestler. He went to Siberia and down to the north side of that and right on to Wales

and he went right on to Barrow I think, or north of there.

So he knows a lot. He can talk Inupiaq language and Quiisiq [?] language.

She [Estelle's great-grandmother] tried to teach me but I never get to learn.

My great-grandmother, from my grandmother's mother. Her name is Wiya . . . .

Everybody knows her because she has been traveling.

(Oozevaseuk 1989, in Jolles 1987ff)

Such visits were not limited to trade. As more than one elder has re-called, there were wars. The scale of these conflicts is not known. At least one inter-island conflict in which the streams themselves turned red with the blood of the dead and wounded is considered part of local legendary history. Elder Gail Angi remembered her grandmother's stories about these conflicts. She followed her grandmother when she was a small girl.

GAIL: Our grandmother used to tell us stories with us sitting around her, so maybe we will keep still and listen to her. She was always watching over us. She used to tell us stories.

The ones before us, our ancestors, used to be like this, like enemies.

They used to be enemies, Gambell and Pugughileq people.

They used Eskimo slings and threw rocks when they fought.

They used bow and arrows, and slings too; that is the way they used to kill each other.

They used to really fight.

There used to be a lot of people down there [Pugughileq]. The people there really multiplied.

This here, Gambell, never used to be Gambell, there was no one here.

ONE of the women interviewing Gail asks: A long time ago?

GAIL answers her: Yes. Aghnaghlluggak told me; I knew her.

When we picked greens, she used to take me with her to Kentuqak or somewhere by it.

We sit down and eat. I listen to her—she asked me to pray.

While I'm praying, and when I looked at her, she's throwing food around and naming people that have died.

She'd name some people up to, people at Ungaziq.

SOMEONE asks: Ceremony?

GAIL: Yes, she said it was a ceremony. I asked her, "Why are you throwing food?" [Gail and her interviewers all laugh at this.]

So people that have died will eat.

I told her then, "They are not going to eat. Their spirits have gone up" [more laughter].

And then she told me that they used to be enemies.

They came from Ungazik, running away, having babies—that is the way they multiplied.

The population really grew—all along the north coast.

There were a lot of people. [On] This little island.

They used to be enemies: from Pugughileq, Northeast Cape, Gambell, Ayveghyak, Mayughaaq.

They used to be enemies always. From Ungazik they used to attack.

This area [the spit where Gambell sits today] was not land. The houses were on top of the mountain.

ONE of the women doing the interviewing asks: This area didn't have houses?

GAIL: This used to be water; [it] was not land.

When attackers came and fought she [Gail's grandmother] used to clean the space

between the walls of *nenglus*.

She used to say—so they wouldn't trip over anything, so they wouldn't get killed while tripping.

She used to tidy it real good, clean it up, so when they attacked they'd hide inside the walls.

They'd hide their wives, their children, their daughters—they'd hide them.

They'd stab each other and fight.

That is the way it happened, she told me.

There was so much blood that it reached the shins—and—[they] were wading in blood, stepping on men, slipping on lots of dead people.

Then the water started to rise. It rose and rose. It washed out all the dead people.

Then it started to go down and down. That is how Gambell came to be.

The tide went way down [so] that the water was way out.

It was really red from the blood.

She told me stories, but I didn't really listen.

They tell us not to listen to anybody, when they're talking to someone else.

So that we wouldn't think they're saying something bad about somebody else.

That is the story I remember. (Angi 1992, in Jolles 1987ff)

Gail's story suggests at least one more reason to think of Sivuqaq as a land that emerged from the sea, literally from a sea of conflict. Evidence of conflict between distant Siberian kin and island dwellers can still be found in the undercurrents of discussion about island relatives in New Chaplino, Russia, and elsewhere. Local tensions among families in the community also reflect older divisions. Often these conflicts were resolved ceremonially. For example, just after the turn of the century, William Doty, one of the first government teachers in Gambell, described a meeting between Pugughileq and Gambell people. The two groups acted out a ritual battle in which each challenged the other before joining together in several days of celebration and trading. The de-

3.1 *Estelle Penapak Oozevaseuk (seated, left) and Gail Angi (seated next to Estelle) watch Fourth of July festivities, 1997.*

scription of a trading ceremony that follows is excerpted from Doty's log book and conveys a sense of the social and religious as well as economic intent of such relations.

> Whenever the villagers from Southwest Cape visit "en masse" the people of Gambell, usually for the purpose of barter—as the former natives rarely have an opportunity to trade with whaling captains and never with the Siberians directly, . . . —they are met on the outskirts of the village and escorted to a place where reception ceremonies impress them with their welcome. [They] . . . engage in a sham fight. . . . A chaplet is worn on the head by these persons, made of strands of polar-bear fur. . . . After trading has begun one of the guests will place some dried salmon or other article of trade on the walrus skin, and he and the wife of the man

who desires to enter into the trade will dance together, the latter taking the article to her husband. Later he will, in turn, place the article which he wants to give in exchange—as some flour. . . . In all trading the dancing is as described above. (Doty, in Jackson 1900:206–207)

Ceremonies sometimes concluded with exchanges of women between the obligated parties. These relations, sanctioned by formal ritual, established extended fictive family networks that operated as invaluable alliances.

The summer months saw numerous whaling ships and other commercial vessels passing St. Lawrence Island and stopping to trade when weather permitted. Trade records kept by the first teachers between 1899 and 1911, when commercial whaling was already in decline, give some indication of their frequency. William Doty noted twenty ships between 1898 and 1899, while Edgar Campbell recorded ten or eleven ships each for the years 1904, 1907, 1908, and 1909. Thus, islanders continued to trade and to include new items in their inventory of common goods. Men hunted arctic fox and saved baleen from the spring and fall hunts for trade purposes. These exchanges continue to affect island life. Arctic fox has remained a trade item, although it no longer commands much of a price. And, islanders continue to use baleen as a kind of local currency, although it is used only for certain artistic projects. During whaling season each spring, individual boat crew members wait for their shares of baleen. These wands, giving the appearance alternately of feathered forms and hardened leather, stand in snow drifts outside doorways or lie in snow banks next to buried shares of *mangtak* (edible whale skin with a small fat layer attached).[21]

In late 1880, Captain Hooper landed on St. Lawrence Island expressly to confirm rumors of starvation. He returned in 1881 with the collector-naturalists Edward Nelson and John Muir and sent a report back to Washington intended for the U.S. Congress. He believed that at least four hundred persons had died, either from hunger or from illness and hunger

21. Since the 1980s, Gambell has been a destination site for new kinds of trade. The late Jacques Cousteau and other marine researchers have made trips each summer to St. Lawrence Island. Eco-tourism and cultural tourism are also increasing, with visitors from around the world coming to spend a few spring and fall days bird-watching.

combined, and that alcohol consumption was the cause.[22] His report reached Sheldon Jackson, a Presbyterian minister and friend of President Benjamin Harrison. Harrison later appointed Jackson as his General Agent for Education in the Alaska Territory (1885–1908). Hooper's report was used to justify direct intervention into the affairs of the Sivuqaghhmiit. In the report, Hooper presented the St. Lawrence Island case as a sad story of degeneracy and predilection for drink. In his new position, Jackson responded with a twofold solution. The first was to bring school teachers to the island, an obligation he was bound to fulfill anyway. The second, coincident with the first, was to recruit teachers with a strong Christian commitment, under the general assumption that education should have as its objective the "civilizing" and Christian conversion of the residents. The two were considered to be synonymous in the late nineteenth century. The spiritual salvation of the Sivuqaghhmiit would, he believed, assure their future survival.

Jackson's solution reflected widely held sentiments of the day concerning Native American peoples. As early as 1819, Congress had passed a bill providing funds to promote literacy and instruction in agricultural methods. The House Committee on Indian Affairs offered the following rationale: "Put into the hands of their children the primer and the hoe, and they will naturally, in time, take hold of the plow; and as their minds become enlightened and expand, the Bible will be their book, and they will grow up in habits of morality and industry, leave the chase to those of minds less cultured, and become useful members of society" (quoted in Bowden 1981:167).

Whatever the earlier population, the subsequent depopulation was devastating. Hooper had blamed the disaster on whiskey provided by commercial whalers. He believed that an unwillingness to hunt due to drunkenness had precipitated widespread starvation. This seems very unlikely. Other reports proposed this as one of several contributing factors. According to some local accounts, there was hunger all along the Chukotka shore and the famine was attributed to bad weather, which de-

22. Deaths were originally underestimated. Researchers now suggest a population decrease of 1,200 (Collins 1937:22; Burgess 1974:27–32). Islanders believe several thousand people died.

layed the arrival of winter ice and significantly affected autumn and early winter hunting. Another version points to the early arrival of winter ice, which prevented access to the walrus and seals at the ice edge. Still other local accounts note that some homes still contained food. From the poignant descriptions left by John Muir, along with local descriptions of the accompanying illness, it seems likely that disease, possibly measles brought by traders, swept the island, although it isn't possible to identify the illness.

The depopulation of the island permanently changed the living patterns and probably precipitated the later development of clan structure among the Sivuqaghhmiit. Kukulek on the island's north side was never resettled. The Punuk Islands, too, were abandoned. No one lived at Kiyalighaq, which is mentioned in several nineteenth-century ships' journals. Only those settlements where survivors remained stayed in general use. The majority of the survivors gathered at Northwest Cape. A few people remained at Southwest Cape. How many survived in other locations is not known. By 1901, Edgar Campbell, the fourth school teacher to come to the island, recorded a total island population of 230, with 149 of those living at the Gambell site.

ELEMENTS OF CHANGE: EDUCATION AND CHRISTIANITY

Major changes in Sivuqaq daily life came from these first contacts with Europeans and Americans. The first newcomers to the island expected to trade, but after the late 1800s, those who came to Sivuqaq came to teach and to persuade the Sivuqaghhmiit to become Christians. To understand what happened in Sivuqaq, one must consider both the first American missionaries who ventured here and the earlier meetings with whalers and traders. Geography, the location of the island between two continents and in the very midst of the sea highway used by whalers, was critical.

Migration and trade were obviously nothing new to the islanders. There had long been relationships between St. Lawrence Islanders and residents of the north Asian shore, particularly with their relatives from Chukotka. Archaeological evidence shows that north Asians have migrated from Chukotka to the island for centuries and that recent immigrations (1880–1937) are simply a continuation of an old pattern. Rela-

tions between the Asiatic shore and the island were apparently somewhat
testy. Estelle Oozevaseuk's and Gail Angi's stories both illustrate a pattern
of trade, inter-marriage, and, at times, conflict. Conflict included raiding,
the kidnapping of women, and armed assault. It was through local trade
that Sivuqaq first received the material goods that were eventually associated with those who came to proselytize. After all, on July 17, 1816,
Kotzebue had written in his journal that the islanders already possessed
blue and white trade beads of European origin as well as iron utensils and
copper cooking pots. He did think, however, that since the islanders regarded him with great surprise that it was unlikely that they had ever *seen*
a European (Kotzebue, in Collins 1937:20). These same items, beads and
metal utensils, had taken on symbolic importance in the settlements.
Beads were used to calm the spirits that caused disease and death. They
could also be substituted for objects that belonged to the dead and were
left at the "destroying" place, where items belonging to the dead were
placed after a funeral, in exchange for an item that a person desired to
bring home. Metal utensils could only be used under certain conditions,
lest they prevent the return of certain animals (Campbell 1904, 1:26).
Trade items, it seems, had developed local cultural meanings.

As Nelson Alowa's story suggests, the arrival of the first missionaries in
1894 surprised no one. The appearance of Caucasians, not simply missionaries, had long been prophesied (Alowa 1985).[23] Establishment of a
missionary settlement followed the catastrophic period of sickness and
hunger (1878–1880) that had earlier been reported by Hooper. Before the
arrival of missionary-teachers, the islanders and a succession of European
and American whalers appeared to interact mainly as traders. Some early
relations were apparently loosely patterned on the more formal trading
partnerships that were a critical component of the Yupik social and economic systems. Such partnerships, commonly practiced among Eskimoan
peoples throughout the Arctic with slight variations, were a way to maxi-
mize resources and to provide for the safety of families through formal,
mutually beneficial trading pacts. While it is an exaggeration to consider

23. Given the many people who traveled to the island in the early years, however
briefly, it is not surprising that the appearance of missionaries was no cause for alarm
and even fit into early prophecies.

trading relations between the Sivuqaghhmiit and the whalers in the same light as those practiced among themselves, some of the same rules may have applied. Exchange itself was bound up with many obligations to give and to receive at appropriate intervals, based on long-term need and well understood rules. Exchanges involved ceremony or ritual sanction, and the value or amount of goods offered for trade, if present practices are any indication, was a significant element.[24] Trade relations may also have developed with certain ships that wintered over or came every year in search of baleen. Again, if present practices are any indication, it must have been uncommon for the Sivuqaghhmiit to make gifts without some expectation of return according to traditional Yupik rules governing all aspects of distribution and exchange. Spontaneous giving, practiced by missionaries and teachers, tended to upset the responsibilities that anyone has who gives or shares.

The desire for these new, non-Native goods, developed over an undetermined period of time, had begun with the indirect transfer of such goods across Siberia and into Sivuqaq settlements through trade partnerships with relatives from Chukotka. Doty, the teacher mentioned earlier, had remarked on a "friendship," perhaps more accurately labeled as a trading partner relationship, between Shoolook (Suluk) of Pughughileq and his trading partner from Indian Point, Siberia. Such trade relations

---

24. For example, the entire village brings gifts to the school a few days before Christmas. Gift distribution follows a Christmas program prepared by students and teachers from both the elementary school and the high school. Gifts received are not always opened during the program. Instead they are carried home. A careful accounting is taken of who has received what from whom. About three days later, at a second Christmas program held in the Presbyterian Church, more gifts are distributed. During the second gift exchange, those gifts that were not exchanged reciprocally at the first distribution are given out. It is important to offer a gift to each person from whom one has received a gift.

Other distribution practices are similar, but they work over a longer period of time. One is obliged to give to persons of one's own lineage and clan. One should also give when someone asks for something. Once one does give, one can then ask in return. For example, one night when I was baking bread for Rhea, a family member came in and remarked, "I wish I would have some of that bread you are baking." Essentially, he was asking for the loaf of bread. If I had made a gift of bread to his family, I could then have gone to his wife and asked for something in return. But I didn't understand the convention at the time and wondered why he had asked for his mother's bread.

were also a feature of social interactions between established extended family groups or clans on the island. The description of their trading ceremony, originally recorded in Doty's log book and quoted above, conveys a sense of the complexity of these ceremonies.

Exchanges of women by trading partners established extensive obligations among the families involved. Household heads in these families had many of the same obligations to their partner's household members as to their own households. Whalers, entering the area after 1850, also established economic ties with the community. Elders have commented that modified exchange partner relations occurred sometimes between a whaler and a man desiring certain goods. Doty saw evidence of venereal disease, which may have been contracted during these exchanges, although it also could have been contracted from Gambell men who had sailed with the whalers to distant ports (Doty, in Jackson 1900:195).

Whalers sometimes wintered over on the island. According to Aningayou, Doty, and others, three whalers wintered over in 1893, and a Portuguese sailor and his Native wife spent the winter in Sivuqaq in 1896. Doty, his predecessor Vene Gambell, and others after them relied on Sivuqaq men, who had often spent many months working on whaling ships up and down the north Pacific and the north Bering Sea, to translate for them whenever they conducted business in the community or to interpret for them when they preached. Even before the arrival of teacher-missionaries, then, the islanders had some idea of Europeans and Americans and their peculiar habits.

The original task of education and Christian conversion fell to the missionary-school teachers recruited by General Agent Sheldon Jackson. Jackson considered it his Christian duty to convert the Native populations of Alaska to Christianity by whatever means available. The schools were his instrument. Following the precedent established by President U.S. Grant among Native Americans living on government reservations in the western U.S. territories, Jackson divided up the Alaska Territory among several Christian denominations and contracted with them to provide schooling to the Native peoples in the territory. The starvation and loss of life in Sivuqaq drew his attention to the island and he determined to save the people from themselves (U.S. Congress 1896:1425–1426). He contracted with the Episcopal Church in 1890 to construct a school in

Sivuqaq. In 1891, materials to build a combination church-school-living quarters were shipped to Sivuqaq and the building was constructed over that summer. The Episcopalians, however, could convince no one to travel to such a remote place. In 1893, Jackson negotiated with the Episcopalian mission offices to purchase the building in Sivuqaq for his own denomination, the Presbyterians. He convinced some wealthy patrons of the Presbyterian Church to pay for the buildings and the church itself to take up the teaching contract. He then set out to recruit the first missionary-teacher himself (Presbyterian Church of America [PCA], Record Group 98, Box 6, File 13). He found a young couple in Wapello, Iowa, who burned with the necessary missionary fire.

The arrival of the Gambells on St. Lawrence Island marked a turning point in island history. Until this date, island residents had acted as an independent society of loosely affiliated settlements. Their newly acquired membership in the United States had affected them but little. It is uncertain whether the islanders ever realized that their island was considered Russian territory before 1867; the transfer of the island from one nation to another concerned them less than the day-to-day relations with their Yupik relatives to the west and with the various settlements around the island. The outside influences upon island life to this time had been the ever-increasing numbers of whalers and traders who appeared along their shores in summer and fall. The inventory of non-Native goods regularly employed in local life had gradually accumulated. Generally, however, islanders were an independent people. The introduction of teacher-missionaries signaled their incorporation into a larger political entity and dramatically changed the face of island life.

In September 1894, Vene Gambell and his wife arrived in Sivuqaq, armed with Bibles, Sunday School cards, slates, and chalk. Their intention was to turn the eyes of the people toward Christ, to teach western ideas about individual property ownership and individual responsibility, and to promote late nineteenth-century notions of cleanliness and morality. Contact between islanders and this first missionary couple produced confusion and conflict. Gambell described a riotous welcoming from the Sivuqaghhmiit, with everyone loudly reciting the few English words they knew, a collection of horrendous and extremely colorful terms learned from the sailors they had encountered.

3.2 *The original Gambell Presbyterian Mission, right, and the nurse's quarters, left, photographed in 1955 by the late Charles Hughes. Photo courtesy of Leslie Hughes.*

Their few English words, picked up from whale-men and smugglers, were mostly terrible oaths, and still more revolting expressions. As they crowded forward laughing, they poured forth a torrent of this awful language. Of course, they did not in the least comprehend what it signified to us, and later we learned that all this was only their way of making us welcome. But you can imagine how shocked we were, and with what haste I conducted my wife to the school building. (Gambell 1910:5)

While the early teachers saw as their purpose the education and conversion of the islanders, the islanders, in all probability, first regarded these newest non-Native residents as more trading partners. In fact, the Gambells and those who followed them did not discourage such ideas. They apparently believed that their many material possessions were signs of their special relationship with God from whom all blessings flowed. The influence of later missionary-teachers upon island residents can, I think, be traced in part to this belief in the tie between the material wealth of the emerging capitalist economic system and a devout Protestant Christian world view. The new religious and economic ideas were so entwined that both the teachers themselves and the islanders thought of Christianity and the American society from which the missionaries came as one and the same.

Teachers encouraged trade, but attempted to reshape trade practices. During the months when pack ice closed around the island (November to May), teachers traded their imported canned and dried foods for skins and ivory carvings, which they later sold for profit. Unlike earlier trade goods, the teachers' goods were available in small amounts during the entire year and they were particularly welcome during lean winter times. Sometimes teachers asked a man to promise to make his children attend school more regularly or to try to hunt without performing some of the traditional prayers, in exchange for food or other necessities. No journal records state that a man tried out the new religion in order to feed his family, but teachers did tell their students and their students' parents that these new supplies, which the teachers had in abundance, came from God and would be theirs, too, if they would only believe. In the early days of the twentieth century, islanders struggled to understand this new relationship to God, influenced by the early teachers, who tried in so many ways to reshape their lives.

Vene Gambell was concerned with transforming Sivuqaq lives to resemble those of the enterprising Iowa farmers he had left to take up his teaching mission. He expressed concern over the apparent disregard for individual property rights, hygiene, the lack of indoor clothing, and the destructive power of shamans. If the articles that Gambell submitted to *The Youth's Companion*, later published as *The Schoolhouse Farthest West* (1910), are to be believed, he and his wife found themselves treated as curiosities. They were stared at, exploited for their goods, and threatened by shamans (the Yupik word for shaman is *alignalghii*) who felt their power was at risk. Nevertheless, Gambell noted in a letter to Sheldon Jackson that, after an initial period of tension, the islanders had welcomed them: "No one has shown a hostile act towards us since we came. I had no trouble keeping order neither had Mrs. Gambell when she taught. They don't know how to act disrespectfully or to disobey anyone older than themselves. Everybody is as pleasant to us as they can be" (Sheldon Jackson Correspondence, 1904–1908, 17:155).

The Gambells' goals as schoolteachers are clearly expressed in this ex-

cerpt: "The education which we are giving the boys and girls of this village is doing great good already, for it has led the boys to reject the odi-
ous superstitions with which the shamans, or sorcerers, contrive to hold
the natives in a state of slavish terror" (Gambell 1910:26).

Gambell and his wife spent three years, from 1894 to 1897, in Sivuqaq,
only to die while returning from a sabbatical leave when their ship, *The
Lady Jane Grey*, sank north of Vancouver Island, British Columbia. As far
as I could determine, beyond the regular exchanges that the Gambells
conducted with the local residents, they had little effect on the community. The traditional religious system remained intact. The Gambells left
only their names, an act for which Sheldon Jackson bears the major responsibility.

They were succeeded as teachers by William Doty and P. H. Lerigo.
Each man stayed on the island for only a year. The most influential
teachers of this early period were Edgar and Louisa Campbell. Their
lengthy tenure (1901–1911), energy, and affection for the community
made considerable difference in the political, economic, and religious
life of Sivuqaq. The records of the Campbells and their predecessors suggest that trading relations with whalers gave way to highly influential
trade of a different sort with the first teachers. While whalers had economic motivations but little commitment to the community, teachers
had personal, spiritual motivations that compelled them to remain in the
community. They hoped to persuade community members to become
"good Christians" and to resemble industrious farmers. Such motivations
necessitated stays of greater duration and active involvement in the local
community. And, while missionary-teachers believed themselves to be
acting from religious motives, their activities shaped political and economic relations within the community as well.

Many changes occurred in Gambell while Edgar Campbell was the
teacher. His arrival coincided with the introduction of reindeer into the
community. The deer had been imported from Siberia in order to create an alternative economy in Sivuqaq, one more in keeping with the
agricultural practices of the United States. Deer were delivered directly
to teachers. Sheldon Jackson instructed Campbell (and teachers elsewhere in Alaska) to select and train likely young men in the villages as
herders and to use the reindeer as rewards for those who gave up the

lumber house, or to become a shopkeeper, or to interpret for him during Sunday church services, he believed he was achieving a spiritual victory.

Part of Campbell's legacy in Gambell is the present arrangement of the village. Older wooden homes, either constructed in Campbell's day or modeled after those first wooden homes, still stand. The earliest houses, arrayed near the west beach, roughly resemble the Main Street of Campbell's dreams. The first store evolved into today's Native Co-op. The strong ties that still exist between school and church, so evident at Christmas and Thanksgiving, remind one that the two were once joined. The Presbyterian Church itself, with its system of elders, deacons, and trustees and numerous organizational features, served as an early example for later government bodies in the community and acted as a training ground for community leaders.

Campbell and his predecessors assumed economic roles in the community. Campbell and his wife gave out food as well as medical services; sometimes they traded with a man or woman and sometimes they simply gave away things for free. Campbell continued and elaborated the new ceremonies of Christmas and Thanksgiving. The handing out of missionary boxes at Christmas is a relic of that early time. Campbell's first converts, who followed his suggestions such as to stop giving fresh water to the sea mammals they had taken during a hunt, had various motives: some wished for the material goods that Campbell said would come to them, some (especially women) wished for occasional release from the pressures of home life, some must have seen the new way as an exciting spiritual and intellectual challenge, some must have wished for greater access to power, and some undoubtedly wished to express their affection for Campbell in the only way they knew, by learning the way that he had tried to teach them.

A part of Campbell's success was directly attributable to his personality. He seems to have had some of the qualities also associated with powerful shamans. He was passionate, he was a medical doctor, and he was perceived by the community as caring and generous. His passionate concern, or perhaps personal charisma, his medical expertise, and his access to imported trade goods were associated in his own mind and in the minds of his potential congregation with his relationship with a superior spiritual power (Campbell 1904–1905, 1:90; 1907–1908, 2:21). These qualities, com-

bined with his perception of the spiritual world that resembled that of the
Sivuqaghhmiit, made Campbell a well-remembered figure. Many in the
community were drawn to Campbell's church on Sunday morning. As
Lawrence Kulukhon, who passed away some years ago, put it: "There were
lots of people with evil powers then, but they go to church also when Doctor was here, while he was minister and school teacher. . . . The Doctor
taught us both Christianity and just regular school things. . . . All of Gambell people goes to church on Sunday to listen" (Kulukhon 1966:4).

Campbell asserted his own ideas about the spiritual world, doing so, in
part, by approving of some island spiritual experiences. The most dramatic of these was his acceptance of the account given by the shaman
Yugniilqwaaq of his encounter with Jesus out on the tundra (described in
Chapter 7). Campbell notes in his journal that a number of adherents to
traditional practices converted after hearing the shaman. Sacred amulets
were burned in the church stove and several boat captains publicly re-
nounced their traditional ways. While Campbell privately expressed
some doubts over Yugniilqwaaq's experience, he rejoiced in the conversions that followed the shaman's testimonial. Campbell also made efforts
to substitute Christian ritual for traditional ritual whenever he hunted
with island men out on the ice. He described in his diary how he brought
a cloth with him, which he spread out on the beach or the ice. When the
men gathered to eat before hunting, Campbell asked them to go on their
knees before God to ask for His help in the hunt. In exchange, the men
agreed not to offer sacrifices to their ancestors or to Apa (God) in the old
way. They also agreed to give up the offering of water to animals they
took.

Campbell had some success in turning people from the old ways, although he maintained privately that the Sivuqaghhmiit had been generally demoralized through alliance with the devil. He noted: "several villages on the St. Lawrence Island have all gone . . . leaving only decayed
ruins and whitening bones to tell a mournful tale. . . . one who gives the
subject thought will inquire the cause of all this. . . . the main factor is
filthiness, not of body alone, but also of the soul" (Sheldon Jackson Correspondence, 15:347).

Campbell never denied the existence of the spirit beings that people
encountered. Instead, he suggested that some of the most difficult spirits

with whom the people had to deal came from the devil. In his own way, he attempted to build a bridge between his own Christian system of meaning and the religious system of the islanders. He told his congregation that Kiyaghneq was, indeed, God. He admitted what the islanders had always known, that many of the spirit powers were demanding and often capricious. He convinced some to accept his own view, which included an expanded understanding of Apa that took in the trinity. He offered literacy. And he gave them a most powerful amulet, the Bible. The amulet quality of the Bible is still a concept in Gambell. Several consultants explained to me that having the Bible in hand, singing Psalms (or hymns), or simply calling out the name of Jesus were the surest protections against the spirits that still lurk in the village or out on the tundra.

Campbell periodically welcomed into the church those who had decided to cast away their old amulets. On several occasions, church service ended with someone throwing into the church stove either amulets or the small carved wooden figures that were kept in the home and fed regularly. This journal excerpt describes one such occasion: "Ponugook asked me for medicine for tremblings. Said she had tried the old method of tying a sinew thread about a bone post and the thread had broken twice, so she concluded the old way was no good. There was evidently more feeling than was apparent at first sight. She promised to bring her idols for me to burn next Sunday" (Campbell 1904–1905, 2:21). Campbell also welcomed those who received dream visions, admonishing them to give up the old way, and those like the shaman Yugniilqwaaq. These incidents served not only to reinforce the validity of past tradition, but also the power of the new.

Once Campbell departed, however, few villagers continued the new religious life. The language of the new religion, found mainly in the Bible, was difficult to understand. Teachers lived on the island between 1911 and 1924 only intermittently, and, with the departure of Sheldon Jackson from the office of General Agent for Education in 1907, teachers in the Alaska Territory were no longer expected to have strong religious convictions and missionary zeal. The records of the Presbyterian Historical Society show no missionary in Gambell from Campbell's departure until 1924, and again from 1925 to 1934. During the first period, elders all stated that the community returned to the old way, and services in the church came to a standstill. There is brief reference (PCA 1894–1960, RG98:Box 13) to the "spasmodic work by Reformed Episcopalians," but I have not been able to discover who that might have been. It is generally accepted that only one family, the Aningayous, remained faithful to the new religion, continuing to hold prayer meetings at home despite criticism from the rest of the community. Kulukhon suggests that even some members of this family returned to the old ways from time to time. He also says that he and three others tried the "Doctor's way" of doing things. One of the men wanted to perform sacrifices on top of Sivuqaq Mountain, with himself as a special priest-like intermediary, but the other three rejected this idea (see Chapter 7).

In 1924, missionary Roscoe Nickerson came to Gambell for approximately one year. He roused the people with his fiery sermons, regularly filling the church, but he soon fell ill in the harsh climate and his tenure was short. Perhaps as a result of his influence, several men continued in their beliefs. Between 1925 and 1934, their small prayer group began to ask Apa for a missionary (Kulukhon 1966, n.p.). They also began to pray systematically for selected individuals in the village to join them. In 1934, Gambell finally received a new missionary, Ann Bannan. The men in the prayer group reported that her arrival was God's answer to their prayers. The new missionary was remarkably effective. Like Campbell, she had medical training and was also prepared to stay in the community for an extended period of time. She participated in the life of the community. She invited elders into her home to share meals, brought pregnant women and new mothers gifts of food, and spent hours visiting families. She was well remembered by older people in 1987, and they often compared more recent ministers to her. Bannan worked with the small men's group and together they gradually increased the number of professing Christians. In September 1940, following repeated requests, the Presbyterian Board of Missions finally sent the Rev. John Youel to the island to baptize[27] converted Christians and to organize formally the Gambell Presbyterian Church. In Sivuqaq, 211 men, women, and children were baptized, and 140 adults became charter members of the Gambell Presbyterian Church. In neighboring Savoonga, 180 were baptized, and in

27. At that time, women could neither baptize nor become ministers.

the following week 98 became charter members of the Savoonga Presbyterian Church.

Just as the community had established its first church and was beginning to feel comfortable with Christianity, it was introduced to a second Christian denomination. In 1939, Frank and Ila Daugherty arrived in Gambell as schoolteachers. Ila Daugherty was a devout Seventh-day Adventist, and through her efforts a few school girls became Seventh-day Adventists, eventually drawing in their families as well. The presence of two denominations, however, was confusing and painful, both for Bannan, who felt betrayed by her friend Ila, and for families who suddenly found themselves divided over issues within their new-found faith. Nathan Noongwook, now deceased, had become absolutely convinced of the rightness of the Seventh-day Adventists, but for many months he and his wife were of two minds. Eventually, she too became a Seventh-day Adventist and their differences were resolved (Noongwook 1988, in Jolles 1987ff). The Daughertys remained in Gambell until 1945, with Frank Daugherty heading the Alaska Territorial Guard unit on the island during the war. Since the Daughertys' presence had not been planned by their home mission office, it was only after their departure that the Seventh-day Adventist Conference begin to consider Gambell a "mission" station.

In 1942, the U.S. Army asked the two white women on the island, Ann Bannan and Ila Daugherty, to leave. Members of the community moved away from Gambell, but no one else was evacuated. Elders still remember that time. Some say that the Japanese overfished the waters around the island then, emptying the near seas of once-plentiful cod. Others recall the dark nights when they endured blackout curtains because of the danger of attack. After the war, a succession of Presbyterian missionaries, occasional Seventh-day Adventist ministers, and regularly appointed teachers came to the community. The school, under the jurisdiction of the Bureau of Indian Affairs at first and Alaska's Bering Strait School District later, became an accepted feature of every child's life. A Christian way of thinking and doing was also common in the community and the number of believing Christians continued to increase. The majority appeared on the rolls of the Presbyterian Church and a minority was listed as Seventh-day Adventists. By 1957, the Seventh-day Adventists too had built themselves a small church (*North Pacific Union Gleaner*

68(1):12–13). The few who clung to the old way of doing things gradually
disappeared. The last public practitioner of shamanism converted to
Christianity in the late 1950s. In the winter of 1987, I heard a rumor that
someone had been accused of witchcraft, but even this took place within
the context of the church.

The introduction of Christian ideas and education to St. Lawrence Island is associated with the more general changes that have taken place
here. Changes in Sivuqaq that began with contacts with the whaling fleet
into the north Bering Sea intensified after the transfer of the island to the
United States in 1867 and the introduction of teachers into the community between 1894 and 1911. The first missionary-teachers to come to the
island affected not only the islanders' religious life but also their economic and social life. Isolation from much of Alaska led to a few individuals having a great impact in the community. How the community perceived its new political affiliation and the religion brought by its new
countrymen depended heavily on the few individuals who came as
preachers, teachers, and doctors. Trade altered to reflect the shape desired by the early missionary-teachers. Men were cautioned that God
frowned upon their making their wives available in exchange for goods.
Polygamy was discouraged. Both housing and clothing were scrutinized.
In fact, because religious belief and life style were understood by both
laluramkas and potential converts to be inseparable, each was eventually
transformed as a result of contact. Still, the new life style and the new
concepts brought by the missionaries were not adopted without a careful
assessment by the Sivuqaghhmiit. The end product was an assimilation
of Christian concepts and practices that incorporated much Sivuqaghhmiit spiritual knowledge into the resulting religious system.

Even though the contemporary community in Gambell reflects in
many ways the traditional society that preceded it, it should in no way be
considered a simple evolution and extension of past life. Perhaps the foremost change was the gathering of families belonging to different *ramket*
from around the island to live in permanent houses on the Gambell spit.
There is ample evidence that others have lived in this same location, but,
according to local historians, only one family, the Iyakitans, is associated
through ancestral ties with the Gambell site. The others, as evidenced by
their *ramket* names and by the names of individuals themselves, demon-

3.4 *The St. Lawrence Island reindeer herd. Photo courtesy of the University of Alaska Fairbanks Arctic and Polar Regions Archives.*

strate the dispersed character of previous settlements on the island. To envision the past, then, is to think of an island composed of extended family groups living autonomously in various local communities around the island shores. For the Sivuqaghhmiit, like other Yupik seafaring folk, the ideal spot was in sight of the sea, the source of all but green foods and the eggs of some summer nesting birds. The island interior was used generally for winter travel. For those in need, it was a source of spiritual power—the dwelling place of spirits whose force might be harnessed by hunters and others. Only after increased trade with outsiders did hunters regularly start to hunt arctic foxes, risking the cold of mid-winter in the island's interior to set their traps in order to obtain pelts to supply their families with goods available only for cash. Also, after the turn of the century, reindeer herding brought herders into the interior to manage the animals.

From the early 1900s onward, U.S. citizenship and American institutions have been the driving forces of change in the community. Children are educated in public schools, families embrace a Protestant Christian vision of the world, and the technology and material goods of democratic capitalism are everywhere present. Change has been mediated in Gambell by the villagers' strong commitment to a subsistence livelihood. Christianity, too, has been a major factor, along with an abiding concern to continue in the ways of the fathers. Finally, there is the family. Few who can stay leave the community, and those who leave come back again and again. The population is growing. Today, the population of Sivuqaq lives in two communities, Gambell and Savoonga. In June 1997, with approximately 640 permanent residents in each village, and an additional fifteen to twenty teachers and others moving in and out of the villages for business and occupational reasons, it had become one of the largest communities in rural Alaska.

CHAPTER 4

Names and Families

For centuries, St. Lawrence Island has been home to northern marine mammal hunters who settled along its shores in small extended family groups. Each group had its own homeland with its own special name, and here, as elsewhere across the Arctic, people identified themselves both by their homelands and by homeland names. Islanders today still talk about the movement of their ancestors to and from their homelands and about the defining events that once took place in them. While this topic might seem commonplace, it is also powerful. Islanders today derive some of their strength and their enduring sense of identity and personhood[1] from these settlements, even though only the oldest of the elders remember when people lived in these homelands more often than in the two large communities of Gambell and Savoonga. Homeland names have gradually assumed the status of clan names as well. When someone refers to himself as a Pugughileghmiit, for example, he means not only that his ancestors came from the south-side settlements at Pugughileq. He also considers himself one of several member families associated with the name itself. Pugughileq, or some area of the south side of the island where Pugughileq is located, is also likely to be the place where he returns each year with his family to camp: to hunt, fish, collect greens and bird eggs, and to dig for fossil ivory and artifacts.

Anthropologists have argued that St. Lawrence Island *ramka* are not "true" clans. The late Charles Hughes believed that because *ramka*

---

1. For a discussion of personhood in Central Yup'ik society, see Fienup-Riordan 1986. My own understanding of the importance of place has been influenced by essays found in Feld and Basso (1996).

names seemed to assume significance only after the 1878 tragedy, they could not be considered clans, nor did they equate with them. Others have made similar arguments, particularly for the islanders' Russian relatives living in Sireniki and Chaplino on Chukotka. One concern is the lack of exogamous marriage rules. However, my conversations with many elders seem to point to just such rules. Exogamous marriage rules prevailed among the different *ramka*, and only in the last several decades, with the cultural homogeneity introduced by public schooling and formal tribal government, have these rules been gradually disregarded. From the 1878 famine until World War II, at least, St. Lawrence Island life was dominated by *ramka* membership. Closely tied to it was the importance of lineage name and individual names.

Today, in Gambell, one could probably show that everyone, with the exception of total outsiders like me, is related. In that sense, Gambell is one huge family. Any discussion of life in Gambell has to take this fact into consideration. What happens to families *is* Gambell's story. That story embraces families, family names, individuals, and the names individuals bear. Names evoke the traditions and values that the community holds dear, and thus it seems appropriate to start with the names as they are conceptualized, remarked upon, and celebrated in the community. It is also appropriate to consider the frame that encompasses these names and the bearers of them.

On St. Lawrence Island, the traditional rules that bind humans, animals, and plants together in harmony or on a "right path"[2] invoke the respectful treatment of all things and all beings.[3] For humans, respectful treatment begins at or even before birth. In a sense, respectful treatment begins with the introduction of each infant soul into his or her family. The soul, which sometimes appears in visions as a miniature replica of the person, is honored through its name and through the incremental achievements of childhood until, finally, the child is grown and assumes

2. I rely here on explanations of harmony in Native American tradition outlined by writer Paula Gunn Allen in her introduction to *Spider Woman's Granddaughters*, 1989:1–21.

3. Ann Fienup-Riordan (1994) describes the "boundaries and passages" that link humans and other spiritual entities together in Nelson Island Yup'ik perspective. She suggests that much of the community's spiritual energy and thought is devoted to activities that "clear the passages" that connect animals and humans.

its rightful place as a parent or other respected adult, as defined by proper understanding of adulthood and the myriad responsibilities associated with adulthood.

Island celebrations of proper humanity can be traced historically from the late nineteenth century. The tremendous loss of life that resulted from the 1878 tragedy makes it difficult to consider the families living before that time. In 1874, Henry Elliott reported seeing as many as 500 or 600 people in his travels around the island's southern shores. He remarked on the general good health of the men he met and commented on the islanders' desire for tobacco and whiskey, as had others, but he saw nothing unusual in it. The practice of trading scarce goods for available goods was already well established, since islanders had traded with Siberian and Alaskan peoples for a long time. By the 1870s, trade with Euro-Americans and European adventurers had also become routine.

In 1878, however, almost every settlement became an open graveyard. By 1881, St. Lawrence Island was no longer dotted with prosperous settlements along its shoreline. Only a few settlements still held people. In 1900, Edgar Campbell[4] had found only 230 people. Stories passed down orally by elders to the present, along with the evidence of vacated *nenglus*, which still dot the island's shores, convinced local historians Willis Kepelgu Walunga and Anders Iyaaka Apassingok, among others, that a large population had once lived here. Using conservative estimates, it is likely that over 1,000 people died here within a two-year period, transforming the island's population and history. One can only imagine what it must have been like to lose a thousand individuals and a thousand unique names. In 1881, Edward Nelson described the few remaining inhabitants and the ghastly contents of the *nenglus* and "summer houses":[5]

> During July, 1881, the *Corwin* made a visit to this famine stricken district, where the miserable survivors were seen. Only a single dog was left among them, the others having been eaten by the starving people. Two of the largest villages were entirely depopulated.
>
> In July I landed at a place on the northern shore where two houses were standing, in which, wrapped in their fur blankets on the sleeping

4. See Chapter 3.

5. These may have been *manteghapiget*, a house style generally in use after the tragedy. Paul Silook believed that islanders used the new style to protect themselves against future misfortune.

platforms, lay about 25 dead bodies of adults, and upon the ground and outside were a few others. Some miles to the eastward, along the coast, was another village, where there were about 200 dead people. In a large house were found about 15 bodies placed one upon another like cord-wood at one end of the room, while as many others lay dead in their blankets on the platforms.

In the houses all the wooden and clay food vessels were found turned bottom upward and put away in one corner—mute evidences of the famine. Scattered about the houses on the outside were various tools and implements. . . . among these articles were the skulls of walrus and of many dogs. The bodies of the people were found everywhere in the village as well as scattered along in a line toward the graveyard for half a mile inland.

The first to die had been taken farthest away, and usually placed at full length beside the sled that had carried the bodies. Scattered about such bodies lay the tools and implements belonging to the dead. In one instance a body lay outstretched and almost touching the sled runners, lay the body of a man who had died while pushing the sled bearing the body of his friend or relative.

Others were found lying in the underground passageways to the houses, and one body was found halfway out of the entrance. . . .

On the bluff at the northwest point of this island we found a couple of surviving families living in round-top, walrus-hide summer houses. At the foot of the hill not far from their present camping place was a winter village, where about 100 people lay dead; the bodies were scattered about outside or were lying in their blankets in the houses, as we had seen them in other places.

The two families living in there consisted of about a dozen people; the adults seemed much depressed and had little animation. Among them were two bright little girls, who had the usual childish carelessness, and kept near us while we were on the shore. . . .

When I asked one of the inhabitants what had become of the people . . . he waved his hand toward the winter village, saying, "All mucky mucky," being the jargon term for "dead."[6] (Nelson 1983:269–270)

---

6. "All mucky mucky" could be translated as "the dead are now only bones." "Mucky" may be a mispronunciation of "*makighaaq*," meaning "to completely pick the bones." In Yupik, "corpse" is *tuqukaq* (Jacobson 1987:236).

Later, Smithsonian researcher Henry Collins wrote in his notebook what he had learned from islanders Paul Silook, Moses Soonagrook, and others:

FAMINE OF 1878

1878 (or 77) was a year of bad winds from s. & s. e. instead of the N. wind which brings down the solid ice. The ice was broken up and it was not possible to get out to hunt walrus either on foot or by boat. So none were killed and since the preceding summer & fall the game had been scarce there was no food stored away—Consequently famine followed—This seems to have been followed by an epidemic of some sort for Gambell people going to Kukuliak & S.W. Cape found some meat in the caches altho most of the people were dead.

They deny that whiskey from the whaling ships had anything to do with the catastrophe and there seems no doubt but that they are right. Say they got some whiskey, but that was nothing new to them, and thus did not go on a prolonged drunk as Hooper & Nelson so confidently state. Died all over the Island, even at Kialegak & Punuk; 100 miles & more away. Truly a potent lot of liquor. (Henry Bascom Collins Collection 1982)

Nelson's description speaks to the complete transformation of Sivuqaq society. The few adults whom Nelson saw were clearly depressed, perhaps deeply disturbed and demoralized. It is hard to tell clearly which groups that had once been important to the social community of the island had been vanquished. The great settlement at Kukulek was gone. So, too, were most of the people who once lived at Northwest Cape. At Southwest Cape, a few survived. Perhaps there were people at Northeast Cape, too, but that is not certain. The last persons to live on the Punuk Islands were gone as well, according to Paul Silook's father, Owittillin: "Paul's father remembers the last family that lived on Punuk about 40 years ago. A woman now at Sevunga [Savoonga] lived on Punuk about 40 years ago" (Henry Bascom Collins Collection 1982). Islanders struggled some years later to account for the tragedy. Some described the weather that had kept the men at home when they needed to hunt. No one gave any credit to the *laluramka* versions of people drinking while the children went hungry.

In 1940, Paul Silook and James Aningayou told anthropologist Alexander Leighton that the elders used to talk about asking Kiyaghneq or Apa for help. Although there is no record of their actions, *alignalghhiit* (shamans), who were believed also to have the power to change the weather, must have been sought out as well. Appeals to Kiyaghneq and other more controversial spiritual powers had failed. Later, the survivors gathered in a few locations to continue their lives. In fact, if island oral history is correct, the 1878 famine was only one of many. The traditional religious system provided a partial explanation for the disaster. Aningayou and others believed the disrespectful behavior of Kukulegmiit hunters had brought down the vengeance of the Almighty on Kukulek, causing the death of all its inhabitants. Apa had punished all because of the improper actions of a few.

> JAMES: We come back to Kukulik [Kukulek] now. They [the people of Kukulek] not whaling, but have lots of walrus, mostly male walrus. . . . They had one time, I guess, a shortage of meat or something. Somebody strike [somebody harpooned] a young male walrus, pull it right on top the ice. Cut it up before it died. Kind of a cruelty, having a good time cutting that live walrus. That is the way they had their fun with it.
>
> When summer came, the same year . . . they heard sounding rocks, just like an earthquake. But doesn't earth-quake, but sounding like the rocks hitting each other, in front of the village. They were scared. And a short time afterward, same year maybe, something happened to them. Nobody will [ever] know exactly what happened to them, sickness or starving. . . . That year [when] . . . somebody went over, they [the dead villagers] had water there and some meat in front of them [inside their homes where they had died]. They [the dead villagers] had little room made from deer skin, something like a tent, but when the night come two strings tied up, made from a skin, hair on it, hair inside.[7] Somebody came in from here; they

7. Aningayou describes a traditional *mangteghapik*, which had an inside living space walled off completely from its outer room with heavy reindeer skin curtains. Families slept in these spaces, their heads resting on a driftwood log shaped to serve as a pillow. It was here that the stone seal-oil lamps that kept a home warm were lit. In his diaries, Paul Silook recorded interior room temperatures as warm as 80° Fahrenheit.

saw everything ready there and thought the people were alive, just sleeping. When curtain was pulled up, all were lying down along wood pillow; you know our way lay down? Just all dead people. That is the way we found out. I guess nobody will tell exactly what happened to them. It's maybe either starve or sickness. . . .

LEIGHTON: Did cutting up the live walrus have anything to do with it?

JAMES: Some people says it was because of the walrus something happened to them, account of the cruelty to the walrus. (Aningayou, DLC 1982:36–37)

Aningayou's story could explain only the tragedy that befell one settlement and resembles in many respects the story recorded by Bogoras (see Chapter 3). The tragedy struck all, however, perhaps one settlement at a time, as the sickness moved across the island. In each location, undoubtedly elders struggled to explain it. They may have speculated upon which important forms of abstinence or acts of respect had been ignored. There were a plethora of rules of behavior: some celebrated the animals that fed people; others maintained the land or honored the elders. Occasionally, when things were not quite as they should be, the transient spirits of elders traversed the landscape apart from their sleeping bodies. Neglect or outright disobedience could and did have powerful consequences. Two years later, some of the bones of the deceased, exposed where they had died, were picked clean. Other bones still lay in the abandoned houses. It is no wonder that when Nelson collected skeletal remains of the dead in 1881, and later, in 1891, when strangers built a school house at the present site of Gambell, the intruders were not challenged. Who would have had the energy or moral strength to confront strangers in such an atmosphere of dismay? In 1894, when the first teacher arrived, a small community of persons was living in Sivuqaq. We will perhaps never know exactly what drove people to gather in that spot. We only know that many settlements held, overwhelmingly, the spirits of the recently deceased. Otto Geist, who investigated Kukulek some 40 years later, remarked on the many bodies still remaining in the homes. Small wonder that the living did not wish to stay near. There were so many dead that the appropriate traditional funerary methods, which separated the spirits of the dead from the living community, had surely been neglected. Many bodies were still clothed, and the important task of cutting away the clothing to release the spirit and to allow animals to clean the bones had not been performed. In addition, special tasks such as creating cat's cradles had most likely not been done either.

> Cats cradles used now only as amusements but formerly when someone died members of the family would make cats cradles in the belief that they would serve as a net to protect them from the spirit or spirits that caused the death of their related one, and so prevent them too from dying. Paul states that his parents scolded him when he was a small boy for making these, believing that their use should be restricted to that as outlined above. (Henry Bascom Collins Collection 1982)

Once the survivors had begun to gather in Sivuqaq, they commenced a new phase of existence salvaged from the former settlement societies or tribes. Each group associated with a particular settlement set up house-keeping within relatively close proximity to its own members on the grav-elly spit at Northwest Cape. Even today, a quick examination of the older village houses that remain from this period and the residential pattern created by them suggests that the survivors grouped according to settle-ment names and family designations.

The many words in Yupik that mean "family," "relative," or "kin" high-light the focus on relationship by blood and by marriage. Family life re-sumed in the settlement at Gambell. Ceremonies—some of which are still performed by families today to celebrate the birth of a child, to join families together in marriage, or to establish trading partners (also a join-ing together of two families)—vividly remind us of the importance of fam-ilies. All celebrated to some extent deep family values and family names. Ceremonies marked the boundaries of close family ties and led to the es-tablishment of new ties. These celebrations were performed through the 1930s and 1940s, and perhaps well into the 1950s or 1960s, but they changed to accommodate new times and new surroundings. A few were abandoned entirely. Others became even more elaborate. Still others be-came more spare. Always, however, the celebrations reinforced a new sense of community solidarity, despite the inevitable family divisions that existed.

Eventually people returned to the older settlement sites and camping spots, living at spots known for good hunting, fishing, gathering, and trapping. Nonetheless, the established living pattern had changed. By the early 1900s, bowhead whales were no longer in demand. Although baleen still commanded a price locally, as it does even to this day, the once-powerful whaling industry, which had sent such great traffic into the north Bering Sea, was in decline. Men in need of cash or credit for an ever-increasing supply of non-Native goods purchasable at the now thoroughly established village at Sivuqaq turned to trapping arctic fox, with furs the new source of wealth. After fur replaced baleen as a cash commodity, trapping provided a livelihood of sorts. Families stayed at small family base camps to give the men easier access to their trap lines. Many families returned to Sivuqaq from an entire winter in their trap line camp for the spring whale hunt. Even though baleen no longer commanded a strong position in the cash economy, *aghveq* (the bowhead whale) was still highly valued in the traditional economy and the celebration of whaling remained an integral part of the new Sivuqaq community. In addition, by 1900, the new school had become a fixture in Sivuqaq—or Gambell, as it had been renamed by Sheldon Jackson—and children attended classes whenever their families returned to the village. Some of Gambell's families stayed throughout the school year in "town," not going out to hunt foxes. The world had changed, but the new world was not without its celebrations. The ancient tradition of maintaining a harmonious universe through multiple celebrations of life, livelihood, and family continued.

In 1928, Henry Collins wrote down a list of currently or recently inhabited sites on the island. A teacher from this same period also contrived a list. Their lists record the places and the names that remained uppermost in people's minds in the 1920s.

MEMORANDUM BOOK—ETHN—1928

1. Owahlat or Koraquak—The people who dwell at the north end of the village. . . . [1. Owahlat, Paul thinks, have always lived at Gamble.]

2. Imaremket— . . . Over 100 people [2. Imaremkit, Paul thinks, is a Chukcha word, because they have none like it. They come from Indian Point, Siberia, and they were the most numerous people.]

3. Puwowellumeet—People from SW Cape— . . . about 50 people. Only one house at SW cape of this tribe—another of Gamble people [3. Name for SW Cape is Puwowelluk, usual Eskimo arrangement.] [3. SW Cape people are supposed to have come from Imtook, a short distance south of Indian Point. Language is the same as at Imtook, where some words are pronounced differently than at Indian Point.]

4. Merooktameet, . . . from an old village 3 miles east of Gamble called Merookta. James & Stephen's tribe. James boat is called this.

5. Nangopagakemeet . . . came from Nangopagak, 1/4 mile s.e. of Merookta . . . No year round residents.

[5? Tradition that these people came from Plover Bay. 5. Apovwok-meet or Poongwokmeet. There are two brothers with their families called this, living at Sevoonga. They are descendants (grandchildren, Paul Says) of the last inhabitants of Punuk. They lived part time at East Cape (Apovwok), hence the dual designation.]

6. Kinleghkutmeet or Amiqtowugut. . . . Came from Kinleghkut, 20 miles e. of Gamble. [6. Kinleghkut is now washed away. The lagoon encroaching on it about 12 years ago.]

7. Naskagomeet. 2 houses. From Naskog, about 14 miles e. of Gamble. . . . No people live there regularly.

Kiwahgomeet, come from west of Indian Point. 3 houses of these at Sevunga. (Henry Bascom Collins Collection 1982)

Through names, the island residents are also irrevocably linked to their relatives on the north Asian shore. The same Yupik settlement names that identify Yupik *ramket* or patriclan-type units are found in Chukotka and on St. Lawrence Island. Their unique *ramket* features distinguish St. Lawrence Islanders and their Chukotkan relations from other Inuit and Yup'ik groups. As already described, historically, each *ramket* took its name and identity from ancient settlements found on both shores. Descendants of at least ten settlement-derived clan or sub-clan groups live in Gambell. More *ramka* are found mainly in Savoonga, the contemporary village on the island's north shore, established in 1916.

The chronology of an individual life passage in Gambell begins with naming the newest family members and recognizing the names that broadcast family solidarity, the names of lineage and *ramket*. The process through which newborn children, deeply loved and much desired, receive and carry their names in the community underlines their significance. In the early years of the twentieth century, naming and celebrating the stages of a child's life must have mirrored older traditions in many ways. Today, while much has changed, the pattern of the older traditions can clearly be seen. In 1928 and again in 1940, Paul Silook described naming this way:

> Children named by eldest members of household, male or female. Name, besides being that of a long dead relative may be that of a brother or sister who died as much as 3 or 4 years back—Or if the old person happens to dream of some particular person (relative) that name may be chosen.

> If a child cries very much after it has been named, the name may be changed.

> If a man drowns, his name if used by relatives, must be given to a girl baby.

> If a couple lose their children they may try to remedy this state of affairs by borrowing a name from some other family, a name of a dead relative from that family. This is thought to insure the child's health & life. Sometimes the baby is adopted by the one giving the name, & for the same reason, to keep the child in health. Adoption is never practiced except in this way (except when left as orphans or if the mother dies).

> Poongook people when naming a child go outside & call out the name. Spirit of dead person is said not to look after its namesake—If names are few, a child may be given the name of a locality, such as a certain rock, cape, etc.

> Most names means something.[8] (Henry Bascom Collins Collection 1982)

More recently, Iyaaka and Kepelgu (Apassingok et al. 1989, 3:181–185) described different features of naming, including naming after someone who has recently died; naming after geographical sites; names taken from nature "if there is some sound reason for selecting such a name"

---

8. A partial list of examples that Paul Silook gave to Henry Collins: "*Soonogoruk*—mud; *Teeweree*—middle post of a house; *nukiyuk*—wants to eat—*kunuhuk*—little blood; *Emoghomet*—people of the sea; *Iyaketan*—impenetrable . . ." (Henry Bascom Collins Collection 1982).

(ibid., 3:183); choosing a name that recalls a deceased person, rather than simply repeating the name of a deceased person; naming from a vision or dream during pregnancy; and giving a shortened version of a longer name.

Name-giving is both a prayerful, sacred act and a time for celebration. Today, as in the past, respected senior *ramka* elders give names. Each *ramka* has established right and possession of names associated with its particular homelands and history.[9] Such names come from a limited universe of names that continually recycle through the community and whose "ownership" or "place" within a particular *ramket* is well known. Each time a name is given again, it calls up the history and memory of those who have held the name before. In the spring of 1997, for example, Elinor explained to me how naming works in her family. She and I had been sitting together discussing various aspects of her life, including the time that I first met her and her younger sister, Sara:

> ELINOR: Sara used to go camping with, Herbert, [our] uncle,. . . . Herbert's first wife was by the name of A———q [this Yupik name was Sara's also].
>
> CAROL: Oh. So that was the closeness there.[10] When your children were named, were they named after people in your husband's family?
>
> ELINOR: Yes. Every one of 'em.
>
> CAROL: Every one of 'em. Ah. Is that hard? [To use names drawn only from your husband's family and not from your own?]
>
> ELINOR: No. . . . Because [of] knowing my children belong to

9. These names are articulated within a hierarchical system of named persons and groups distinguished at the level of *ramka*, lineage, and individual families. Whaling-boat names and camp sites also reflect the patrilineage affiliation of the men who use them and symbolize the association of certain names with particular patriclans.

10. The connections among families follow somewhat circuitous routes. The Yupik name of Elinor's younger sister Sara, whose tragic death in 1987 affected so many people, had been A———q. Her name came from the deceased wife of Elinor and Sara's Uncle Herbert. When Sara passed away, her name went to her grandson, the newborn son of her oldest son. Thus, over a period of approximately 56 years, three people have carried the name A———q, two women and one male child. All are connected by ties of descent and marriage. The name is one that evokes deep feeling among family members.

them [to her husband's *ramka*], and *they have to name 'em. . . .* [emphasis mine]

CAROL: Who gave the names in your husband's family?

ELINOR: Ah, Walter and Andrew and Addison, I think. They counseled about it and gave names too. [For] The children. The babies.

CAROL: And now who?. . . . Conrad . . . ? [Elinor's husband]

ELINOR: Conrad. Stanley used to. [Conrad's older brother] For grandchildren. Now Conrad is doing that. You know how he is doing it? He's taking names out of the Bible and giving his grand-children the Eskimo names of the Bible words. Like Naayghagh-haq. Jodeva. Naayghaghhaq is in the Bible, little mountain, some, something happened there, in that little mountain. And then Iknaqusighhaq. He named, he named her for that, her Eskimo name is "Strengthen." Hoping that, her parents, . . . would become stronger. . . . [Elinor laughs.] He, he got reasons for naming, the grandchildren that way.

CAROL: But, . . . some groups take their names from places on the island.

ELINOR: Yes. Most of 'em. Most of 'em are from the places like, like my children's are. Baymii. . . . And Alangayaaq is from Tungiyans, Tungiyan's daughter used to be Alangayaaq. Pretty name, too. Yep. It used to be Oseuk's daughter, daughter's name. Except Oozeva has Willard's son under that name. They use names from the clans, you know.

CAROL: . . . So . . . if Conrad is giving those names, he is really changing the pattern. Changing the tradition a bit.

ELINOR: Some, . . . Yes . . .

CAROL: Some. By adding names.

ELINOR: Yes. Yes. And one little girl's name I was so happy about was, when Carson and Wilson [her sons] asked us for *lalu-ramka* names, Akulki [Conrad] and I give them the answer. He's your child, you can find an English name. So, Carson and Jodene were having a baby and they asked, "What kind of a *laluramka* name can we give the baby?" "It's your choice, you can do it." So, Carson called on the telephone and said, "We have a baby girl."

4.1 *Elinor Mikaghaq Oozeva and her husband, Conrad Akulki Oozeva, April 1999.*

Oh, I knew the name already in Yupik. Because Akulki had the name for it. "What'd you name it in *laluramka?*" "You know, Elinor, I cut my wife's name in the middle, and I cut my last name in the middle, and put those together, and they became Jodeva." Jodene and Oozeva. Jodeva! So it became a name! Oh, that's good, I am so happy, you know. And they thought of it themselves. They cut Jodene in half, and Oozeva in half. Throw away Jodene's last letters. And their last name's first part, Oozeva. So they put that together and called her "Jodeva." Yeah. [Elinor laughs with pleasure as she thinks of her granddaughter.] (E. Oozeva 1997, in Jolles 1987ff)

The conceptual recycling or re-emergence of persons through their names is well known across the circumpolar north among Inuit, Yup'ik, and Aleut societies, as well as among other Native American groups (Guemple 1972; Fienup-Riordan 1990). The concept that humans and other sentient beings are invested with both perishable and nonperishable qualities is found across the Arctic. It is often cited as a reason for Native American and Alaskan Native's respectful treatment of the environment and is held up as a model for others, particularly *laluramka*, to follow. The bounded universe of names and their bearers suggests "a scarcity of souls" (Fienup-Riordan 1994:149). That scarcity implies that "the living have lived before and the dead never finally pass away" (ibid.). While the concept of a bounded universe of names, representing an aspect of a person's essential substance or soul, is well known across the circumpolar north, how it is understood in each community varies.

In Gambell, not only do names constitute a bounded universe, but only one name bearer should properly carry a name at any time. This concept has been modified in practice because of the peculiar political circumstances of contemporary Yupik life. *Ramka* members in Chukotka and St. Lawrence Island were separated as if they had dwelt in different worlds between 1948 and 1988. Some St. Lawrence Islanders have moved to such distant cities as Fairbanks, Nome, Anchorage, and Sitka. In these instances, names have sometimes been given without consulting the elders who still live on the island; in the Chukotkan case, names parallel the naming on St. Lawrence Island. In some cases of out-migration, names have been given because the traditional prohibitions or sanctions that once kept such names from being assigned more than once among the living have been relaxed. Nevertheless, most island residents still feel it is appropriate to give a name to only one living person. Names are perceived as inherently powerful and singularly representative entities that belong to specific clans. That names are meant to stand alone also signifies the powerful autonomy of independent personhood. Names carry personality, relationship, and history. As Iyaaka and Kepelgu point out, "some people have only one Eskimo name, although most will have two or three different names, rarely more than three. These are not first and middle names as in the western tradition, like John Paul Henry Jones. Each Eskimo name stands alone as a complete name. . . . Usually, . . . only one of the names would be most commonly used" (Apassingok et al. 1989 [vol. 3]:181). The names were often given at significant moments of the person's life and stand for different things. Here Estelle talks about a name given to her mother's first husband. The name was intended to protect him from harm. "My mother's husband used to be Kelumii. Another time they called him Amaghaluk. They named him after the rocks over on the south side. Because their father was a shaman and whenever they have illness, he [they] give them names, just to appease the spirits that are bothering them. And, they all died . . ." (Oozevaseuk 1992, in Jolles 1987ff).

Bestowing names tends to affirm membership, renews *ramket* solidarity, and reminds the living of the contributions that former name-bearers have made to the *ramka* members who now reside in the community. Names recall the stories of previous generations and glue the community together in an intricate web of essential qualities suggested by the stories. Names also continue the social relationships and important kinship ties of their most immediate predecessors.

Often when a baby is born, the name of the child has already made itself known to the elders responsible for selecting its name. Today, that seems to be especially true when someone has just died. A longing for the name that belonged to the deceased is expressed by members of that person's family. This longing is even stronger if the deceased person did not die of old age. Accidental death and suicide leave an emptiness and a grief in the community that is not easily overcome. Traditionally, the name of the deceased was not given out immediately, lest a similar death befall the new name-bearer. Today, however, because community members entreat Jesus to guard the newborn, the name of someone recently and even tragically removed is often given almost immediately. On one occasion, when a highly respected elder died, the child born that very same day to her granddaughter was given her name—suggesting that she had, in a sense, not truly departed, but had given over her name to the community so that they might come to terms with her passing. Some in her family feel very strongly that the elder sensed her approaching death and had already picked out her successor. Thus, the elder's leave-taking and the respectful honoring of her departure were gratefully coupled with the celebration of her great-granddaughter's birth.

In other circumstances, elders meditate and pray for guidance in selecting appropriate names. At some point, the name comes to the elders and it is returned to the community through this prayerful act. Recently,

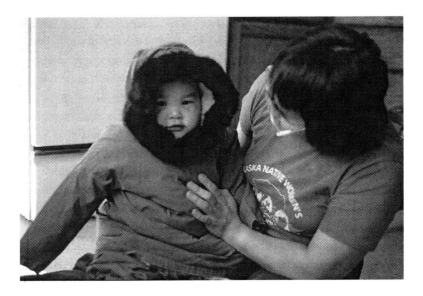

4.2 My friend Mary tries a first parka on her young son.

as the population in the community has increased, some elders have begun to create new names, drawn not simply from the island itself but from especially loved texts in the Bible or by combining English names that have belonged to well-loved individuals.

When a child grew, its passage used to be heralded by a series of small celebrations. Lawrence and Rosie Kulukhon described infant celebrations for Charles Hughes in 1955. Collins also recorded some of these: "When baby is old enough to roll over the father presents small gifts to the old men & women of the nearest houses. Same when baby first crawls, walks & jumps" (Henry Bascom Collins Collection 1982).

These celebrations gradually moved the child into the community of persons who would, hopefully, survive the unpredictable forces of disease that snatched so many infants from the community. There was always a concern that infants might become sick and die. Infant mortality rates are believed to have been generally high for northern hunting and gathering communities prior to modernization, and St. Lawrence Island would have been no different. In addition, however, St. Lawrence Island had a

history of recent and catastrophic epidemic disease. It takes little imagination to consider how parents must have felt at the end of the last century and during the early 1900s. They had seen so many children die.
Older women today, born many years after the epidemic but before the
introduction of modern medicine, speak of giving birth to as many as fifteen children, but the survivors are few. In 1988, for example, Rhea, then
83 years old, spoke of having given birth to many children, only six of
whom survived to adulthood and were living in Gambell in 1988. All too
often infants did not survive the hardships of the first year.

Quite naturally, then, parents were often fearful because their newest
child had been born to them after they had already lost several children
and endured the tearing grief of laying their bodies on the mountain. To
ensure that the child would survive the difficult period of infancy, they
took special precautions to safeguard its life. Elinor recalled that in 1926,
when she was born, her grandmother had quickly taken her, newly delivered, from her mother, rushing out into the night with the naked and
unprotected newborn. It was November and a violent snow storm raged
outside. Nevertheless, her grandmother believed that the only way to assure the baby's security was to fool the spirits of illness that had already
taken other children from Elinor's mother. Moments later, Mikaghaq's
(Elinor's) grandmother came back into the house with the infant Elinor
in her arms and said loudly to Elinor's mother, "Look what I found outside!" When Mik told me this story, she laughed and said that years later
she asked her mother why she did it. "I might have caught pneumonia
out in that cold storm!" But, parents have always done what they believe
is best for their children's health and livelihood, and Elinor's mother was
no different. One friend described her parents' grateful treatment of her
as a young girl. Her mother had lost several children before she was born.
When it seemed that she would survive, she became a *panignaq*, a favorite daughter, receiving gifts and attention from them until she left
home to marry.

Each celebration of an infant's achievement must have seemed to its
family like a small assurance that their child would indeed survive. Another protective measure was to give additional names to a sick child. New
names suggested new personhood and could deceive the spirits of sickness
into believing the child was someone other than their selected target.

Iyaaka and Kepelgu note that a "non-traditional" name or a new name might be given to a child who was ill or seemed terribly distressed. Several women, including Grace, an elder who used to live in Gambell, were given the names of men in their families who had lost their lives through drowning. It was considered dangerous to give the name to a male child again, lest he suffer the same fate. Girl children were not subject to the same danger because they seldom went out on open water to hunt.

Names, especially name changes, were a kind of insurance policy. For example, Penapak described the names that her grandmother's relative received to protect him from sickness. The concept behind the addition of names had to do with the essence of a name. Almost all sickness was thought to be caused by "disease" spirits, which in turn had their own names. These disease spirits attacked the names associated with those who had neglected or angered them. Because these were known names, it was necessary to change the names and thus the essential personhood of the child or adult, to confuse the spirits and perhaps to add the power associated with the new name.

Other actions were also taken to protect children. For example, a child's feet and hands might be splashed with urine to disarm the spirit forces. Or, as an added precaution, wide-open eyes would be drawn onto the sleeping child, deceiving the wandering spirits into believing that the child was awake and aware and therefore less vulnerable to attack. In May 1996, Estelle recalled that each night before she and her sister went to bed, they would have wide-awake faces drawn on them with a mixture of soot and oil from the base of the seal-oil lamp. Sometimes when they woke up, the eyes and mouth that had been painted on were all smeared and runny. Estelle recalled that her sister always wanted a smiling mouth for the night. The eyes were always drawn onto the forehead. Nostril marks went just below the nose and the mouth was drawn onto the chin.

The system of names was at once social and religious in concept. The establishment of Gambell first as a school site (1890) and later (1900) as a reindeer reservation area, under the jurisdiction of the U.S. Congress, set the stage for yet another transformation of St. Lawrence Island society. The families spread around the island's shores had already changed dramatically by sustaining and surviving the loss of so many family members. In some manner they had coped and had rebuilt their lives. We shall never know the details of what they endured; their stories have been obscured, perhaps because they were too painful to repeat in the time-honored fashion of oral tradition.

The appearance of a school teacher whose mandate was to instruct their children must have surprised the residents of Sivuqaq, if they understood his purpose at all. Instruction of young children was divided informally by sex and accomplished in the early years by grandparents and other older relatives. Still, after the initial curiosity wore off, Sivuqaq residents apparently accepted the new teacher and his young wife, attributing no ill will to them. It was not until the fourth of these missionary teachers that the impact of Christian teaching upon the naming system really emerged.

In Gambell, as in other Native American and Alaska Native communities, English speakers found the local language extremely difficult to learn. In 1901, the teacher, Edgar Campbell, was still somewhat ignorant of the island system of naming and its spiritual basis. For him, whatever he encountered that was unfamiliar he called "pagan," and he wrote about it to his home churches in the "south." He thought of the Sivuqaghhmiit as lost souls, burdened by devil worship and unclean practices (see Chapter 3). Not the least among their burdens were religious concepts quite unlike the Christianity of a devoted Presbyterian. Like others of his time, he equated his own social system with a Protestant Christian religious commitment. To him, it was unthinkable and surely un-Christian that a man should have no common last name with his father, his brothers, and his unmarried sisters. It apparently did not occur to him, or perhaps he was unwilling to recognize and acknowledge, that *ramket*, each with its own set of personal names, served the same purpose of identifying membership among close and distant kin. He began actively to rename people.

In retrospect, Campbell (and other missionary-teachers in Alaska and other Native communities elsewhere) acted with an audacious and biased disregard for a social system that had functioned so well for so many years. In all likelihood, he was not entirely aware of the implications of his actions. Nor, in all likelihood, were the Sivuqaghhmiit. His first act was to select men who seemed to him to head families and to take the most commonly used name of the man as the family surname, including under the surname a man, his wife, and his children. In this manner, married male siblings suddenly found themselves distinguished socially and conceptually in the eyes of the island's single governmental representative. It is not at all clear when members of the community actually accepted this imposition of last names. At least one elder stated that last names were not really assigned until the first official census, which she placed sometime in the 1930s. Census workers also divided families by household head and indicated the father's common name as the last name.

Campbell, through his special, combined duties as teacher, government representative, and medical doctor, began to assign English given names to the babies he delivered. He was required by the Congress to note and register the actual birth and death dates of community members. Thus naming itself became critically associated with the new concept of calendrical, non-repetitive, linear thinking and time concepts. To this notion was added the concept of being born in a Yupik versus a Christian world. These names would come to be known both commonly and conceptually as Christian names. Like Yupik names, Christian names participated in the sacred. As St. Lawrence Island society gradually transformed, the naming systems, conjoined both socially and spiritually, came to epitomize the processes of change in the community. Yupik names evoke history, belonging to geographical place, membership in kin groups, and the sacred turning of the social wheel. The system has been fixed in Sivuqaq society in some modified version for several hundred years. Christian names connect individuals to the inspirational and protective powers of God and his son Jesus. Sivuqaghhmiit manifest both of these systems through the names they carry, through the languages they speak, and through the social constraints they choose to recognize or to put aside. Like social change itself, systems of naming are now articulated, if somewhat uncomfortably, with each other.

Older celebrations and formal naming procedures were followed until the 1960s and possibly the 1970s. Illness, especially tuberculosis and several severe strains of influenza that swept through the United States and Canada, continued to affect community health until the late 1960s. Childhood diseases such as measles, mumps, and chicken pox also took their toll, with children particularly susceptible.

Today the health of the community is protected by access to community health clinics and mainland medical facilities. While many older forms of protection have been abandoned, names still offer some protection. In one case, for example, a child has been given a name that suggests that Jesus will protect her. Baptism too is believed to give added protection to the young. Prayers and hymn singing are used to ward off sicknesses that periodically sweep through the village.

Infants, except in unusual circumstances, now survive the first difficult year of childhood. The greater likelihood that a child will survive has not diminished the Sivuqaghhmiit appreciation for children in the house. No house is considered complete without children, and the community continues to treat children as special gifts to families, celebrating their arrival and marking down their birthdays. The older celebrations are no longer performed, but *apapaaq*, performed following the birth of a child, still announces its name formally to the community. The father's female relations stuff food gifts such as Lipton tea bags, lump sugar, Oreo cookies, and pilot bread crackers into plastic Ziploc bags and deliver them door to door by snowmobile or four-wheel all-terrain vehicle to clan elders. In *apapaaq* celebrations, the family of those who have just received a name enthusiastically feeds the older generation, which is most likely to have donated a name. Because elders usually select names from among recently deceased elders of their own generation or from others recently lost through unexpected accident or illness, the return of a name has enormous impact, profoundly affecting community members by providing a human vehicle in which to invest their emotion and to assuage their grief. When someone dies in the community, it is not unusual to hear someone say, "We really miss that name." And, with remarkable timeliness and regularity, infants appear to take up the names relinquished by the deceased, thus providing a sense of internal continuity among families and a more abstract sense of historical community among *ramket*.

While descriptions of naming may suggest a kind of abstract continuity, in practice this is not the case. In 1987, for example, within a few weeks of the accidental death of Sara, who broke through shore ice while ice fishing alone, her eldest son's wife gave birth to a baby boy. The baby, who received Sara's Yupik name, was known during his first year to its many aunts and uncles either as "Mom" or as "Naa" (Mother). For a short time, the family discussed whether the child, living holder of his grandmother's

4.3 *Cousins, siblings, and friends gather in front of the television set in House B, waiting for a birthday party to begin.*

name and thus bearer of her relationships and qualities, should go to live with his grandfather, to fill the deep void left by his grandmother's untimely and tragic departure. Had he been born fifty or sixty years earlier, perhaps he would have joined his grandfather's household. By the end of his first year, however, his family had ceased to address him with kinship terms evoking his grandmother's presence and considered him his own small person, based on the gradual emergence of his own personality. It seemed that he would remain with his parents, although his name still draws a special smile from those who knew his grandmother. Family members on occasion look for the influence of his grandmother's qualities on his character as he grows older. He is, however, regarded as his own, as distinguished from her own, self—or, perhaps, as some unique combination of the two persons and the others before them who have carried this name through the long history of the island. In the best sense, he is a walking representative of the history of his family.

Today, along with Yupik names, children receive "Christian," first, or given names, as well as the family names or surnames that families acquired arbitrarily from government representatives in the early 1900s. Christian names carry their own peculiar distinguishing power just as Yupik names do. In a sense, these names are in tension. As Iyaaka and Kepelgu point out, each Yupik name "stands on its own" and should not be regarded as a first or middle name, since each signifies a different aspect of individual personhood (Apassingok et al. 1989, 3:181–185).

Because of their history, some Yupik names have the potential to reassert ancient and equivocal spirit relationships born by their ancestral name-holders.[11] Few would wish to engage these spirits now, and some of the more turbulent moments in recent community history have been generated through battles with older spirit forces attracted to individuals who bear names of ancestors who once had powerful ties to spirits.

If Yupik names suggest the recycling or re-emergence of human essential and enduring qualities, Christian names indicate another aspect, tied somehow to what one friend refers to as *whangapik*, or a person's real or true self, taken from the Yupik word *whanga* (self) and *-pik*, an ending that identifies that which is real or true, as in "Yupik," a real or true person. Christian names are not "more" essential; rather, they are imbued with protective power that guards a person's essential soulness, a quality associated with his or her Christian character. The power accorded a Christian name derives from the nature of its categorization— that is, from the community's unconditional acceptance of the name as a uniquely Christian form—and from the overwhelming belief that if names carry power, then the name aspect of Jesus, spoken in moments of great perilous need, has the power to ward off evil. All Christian names, by extension, partake of this quality.

This acceptance is explicitly demonstrated in the village graveyard. The top of the bluff, located behind the village at its eastern edge, has long served as a repository for the dead. Traditionally, its brow or heights was reserved only for men who had killed a whale or a polar bear. Bodies of the

11. Yupik names and soul concepts suggest older beliefs in a complex cycling of social and physical relationships. Estelle compared it with reincarnation. This view is but one of several interpretations, however. Some consider older concepts incompatible with current Christian perspectives.

deceased, wrapped in skins, were laid upon the rocky ground, surrounded by objects emblematic of their livelihood or perhaps necessary for the deceased's journey to the realms of the dead. Women and children lay on the lower slopes. While name-souls hovered nearby waiting to reenter the community through newborns, bare bones constantly reminded the living that the spirits of the dead and of those for whom death was imminent did not always rest quietly. As Estelle explained to me, "They say that when the spirit leaves the body, the body dies . . . and when they buried them they tried to put the head away from the village, in case the spirit might come back" (Oozevaseuk 1992, in Jolles 1987ff).

By 1911, missionaries had not only begun to baptize infants with English, "Christian," first names and to assign surnames based on the Yupik essential names of male heads of households, they had encouraged the use of wooden coffins as well. They were appalled by local funeral practices, which included visits to the unclothed corpse to determine which animal had consumed its flesh, suggesting the form the released spirit might assume, and they actively encouraged the use of coffins. In contemporary Gambell, the deceased are lovingly placed in wooden coffins constructed immediately following a death. Coffins are distinguished at one end with hand-carved crosses made by men of the family and inscribed with the name of the deceased. Significantly, it is the English given name or Christian name that graces these crosses, along with Yupik surnames. When I asked why Yupik names were not included on crosses, I was told that Christian names were used because "that's what we are." Christian names, it seems, protect the unwary, both living and dead, from assault or distress at times when they are most vulnerable. Both names and crosses protect against spirits, which sometimes seek out familiar places or attack the unwary because of some remembered insult.

If Christian names shield the bearer from unwanted spiritual adversity, Yupik names confer important aspects of personhood upon group members, a characteristic particularly evident during birthday parties. Birthday calendars, found throughout rural Alaska, mark births, deaths, and marriages in communities. In Gambell, calendars contain an interesting mix of Yupik and English given names along with Yupik or English family names. These simple records suggest the ambiguity surrounding the assignment of names and the importance of the names themselves.

4.4 *The community cemetery, on top of Sivuqaq Mountain.*

Children's birthdays are occasions for two distinct celebrations. One conforms to children's parties found throughout the United States. The other focuses on the child's name and is attended only by elders. In the past, clans performed a series of interrelated rites designed to feed the dead and to comfort and include them, lest they feel neglected and seek retribution from the living. Offerings were thrown into the air or into a small ritual fire as the spirit's name was called.

Today, living elders are honored through birthday parties that commemorate the return of a name to the village. Birthday parties for elders are major events. Properly, *neqepik* ("real food") should be served, the same that was used formerly to feed ancestor spirits. Invited elders are served by the child's mother and by her husband's female relatives. Birthdays simultaneously express clan solidarity, as women of related patrilineages prepare food for elders from the community at large, and signify the intrinsic worth of the child's name to the community as a whole. Where ancestral name-spirits were once fed metaphorically through the transformative capacities of air and fire, today elders, the most respected name-bearers, are themselves fed most concretely by members of the next generation. Thus, a symbolic pacification of the dead has given way to celebration of the living. And, if *neqepik* was thrown into the ritual fires fifty years ago, elders now dine on substantial helpings of whale blubber, followed by chunks of birthday cake with chocolate icing. At the center of this reconfiguration is the child name-bearer, whose name until recently was carried by a member of the elder generation or by some other sorely missed, now-deceased individual.

The most interesting contemporary expression of naming and its conceptual association with soul and spirit concepts is made explicit through the written word. By 1989, local authors had published three bilingual volumes of community history for use in island schools. Some of the explanations for naming given by Iyaaka and Kepelgu have already been cited above. In their discussion of customary naming practices, the authors avoid any reference to the spiritual qualities associated with naming. While they do say that names ". . . provide constant reminders of genealogy and events associated with ancestors," they do not suggest the inherent substance that names hold. That quality of names is left to the individual to infer from local practice. Thus, textual references by local writers to naming practices refer neither to souls nor to the deeply embedded qualities of personhood that names encapsulate. The written word has seemingly been employed to reconfigure history for Americanized Yupik youth through the use of objectified forms, even as it is also employed to evoke a highly valued traditional past. Iyaaka remarks that "children now expect to find education in the classroom. Books have become the new authority . . ." (Apassingok et al. 1989). These books, which "bring the . . . wisdom of . . . elders into the classroom" (ibid.), juxtapose Yupik and English versions of identical texts, highlighting underlying tensions that are played out in the reconfiguration of history through the written word, and suggest also the divisions that inhere in separately conceived Yupik and Christian personhoods that are joined together in the same individual. Yupik and English texts authored by the same elder appear side by side in community history volumes. This is a standard technique for presenting bilingual materials. The overall effect, though, is to contrast the Yupik and non-Yupik elements of the community. Not only does the same person appear as bilingual, but also as one with two distinct names, one English and one Yupik. To the uninitiated, the two distinct names do not seem to connect with each another. This contextual estrangement is paralleled both in the spoken and unspoken elements of name-soul qualities in their Yupik and Christian forms and in naming ceremonies in which *neqepik* main courses of whale blubber and aged young walrus are followed by chocolate cake and Lipton's tea, which elders consume while retelling the stories of an ancestor whose name has just been returned to the living.

The reinterpretation and simultaneous textual representation of the past merge in daily practice with the reconfiguration of essential religious notions and the acceptance of a reformulated and significantly different post-colonial Americanized world. In this context, the "interplay of subject and object" is made explicit in the naming of children, the feeding of spirits, and the protection of the living and the dead from the forces that inhabit the external environment. At the same time, the textual representation of these experiences by Yupik scholars reminds one that the island's religious history is being transformed. As religious concepts are pulled from oral tradition and recorded, they go through significant changes, symbolized by the introduction of Christian names and the encapsulation of the dead in coffins. Older concepts have given way to historical processes instigated at least in part by local residents; at the same time, older meanings, divested of the more controversial spiritual aspects associated with names and souls, have become part of the new collection of village history texts.

CHAPTER 5

Marriage

W hen I first visited Gambell in April 1987, I was the guest of Rhea and Marina.[1] Rhea was 82 years old, a widow, and a respected elder. She was the head of her household and the oldest person in the large A—— family. Later, as I lived with Rhea and one of her grandsons, I learned about marriage from her married children, grandchildren, and great-grandchildren, who visited her house in a steady stream. Rhea belonged to the Pugughileghmiit, the people of Southwest Cape, a belonging based especially on marriage into her husband's family or "side." Sometimes a person explained this belonging to me as tribal membership, sometimes as clan or *ramka* membership.[2] Most older women I met came from a different *ramka* than their husbands, whereas younger married women were sometimes from the same *ramka* as their husbands but from a different branch or family group (*nengllugutet*). Older women told me similar stories about discovering the identity of their husbands-to-be and their feelings upon leaving their parents' home to live with their husbands' families. At first, after moving into her husband's family's home, a woman would be terribly homesick for her parents, her sisters and brothers, and the many relatives of her own familiar *nengllugutet*. These powerful family attachments were so different from my own suburban, *laluramka* youth that I was forced to

1. Portions of this chapter are based on Jolles and Kaningok 1991.
2. Strictly speaking, a *ramka* most closely resembles a patriline, a group of families with blood ties through the male side. In some patrilines, though, there is a strong feeling about the significant experiences of an ancestor with a particular animal. When a *ramka* identifies strongly with that special relationship and, more importantly, has a history of exogamy, then clan seems a more appropriate term.

5.1 Rhea, with whom I lived in 1987-88.

rethink the meaning of family and the significance of marriage in this Yupik community.

Estelle, a Pugughileghmii by marriage, is one person who taught me about marriage. In 1997, she was 76 years old. When we first met in 1987, she told me her name was Estelle. Like most Yupik people, she had an English name and one or more Yupik names. Usually a person introduces herself by her English name if she is meeting a non-Native or non-Yupik person. For a long time I called her Estelle, as I do through most of the book. As I got to know her, I found myself calling her "Penapak," her Yupik name, and sometimes I just switched back and forth. Somehow, it seemed natural to do so. Estelle has an open, generous face. She describes her life as a series of stories mixed with family history. When I think of her, I can see her hair, parted in the middle, a mixture of black and gray. Her energy constantly amazed me. In 1975, she had survived a terrible airplane crash. The plane slammed into Sivuqaq Mountain, killing teachers, children, and several local adults. Estelle survived, but her leg was horribly mangled. She was pulled from the wreckage (which is still scattered across the mountain) just before the plane burst into flames. The doctors who reconstructed her leg told her she would never walk again and should expect to spend the rest of her life in a wheelchair. They had made no allowance for her will and her faith, however. In 1997, Estelle's walk had slowed somewhat, befitting her 76 years. She still drove a four-wheeler, sat on the Gambell City Council, remained on call as a community health resource person, and kept house for her unmarried sons and daughters. In 1995, she began to baby-sit for her new grandson, who was almost three years old in 1997. And, of course, she had time to tell stories.

Sometime between 1938 and 1940, Estelle married. Her early marriage experience was a common one for women her age. Estelle helped me to understand that her preparation for marriage really started with her preparation for womanhood, when she was still a small girl spending her days in her family's home at her grandmother's side.

> ESTELLE: It seems to me like—they [older women in the family] just taught us. At first they started us with soft things, like intestine sewing and not too much hard work like the women does.
>
> As we get older they started to give us more harder things to work on.
>
> And the only thing that some of the Eskimos never taught us about—sex. So we never know nothing about that.
>
> The only thing that they told us about when we become mature enough to have a child,
>
> they told us never to mess around with boys in case we might get pregnant
>
> CAROL: But they didn't explain how it was going to happen?
>
> ESTELLE: [laughs] No, no—so, it seems like, just because of that, it's kind of scary to us and I, myself, . . . since I've been a carefree girl and . . . I thought only through kissing, the girls might get pregnant. Sometimes I [was] just scared, because I thought kissing would produce a child. Because, we never been taught.
>
> And, the first thing—when a girl became a woman—that is the

first menstruation. They just treated them like a woman who had a baby. They let them—they never lie down. They just put their legs like this [Estelle draws her knees up together and clasps her hands around her knees] and stay squatting down at least for three days, I guess, for first menstruation, just like having a baby.

I don't know why they do that to the girls, but I never do that, because my grandmother had died.

I was about eighteen years old when I first had my menstruation. My—pretty old.

So my parents were concerned about me. They thought—my mother always thought that I'm not going to have any babies, if I get married.

I was a hard worker in the family, so I got very strong from working [hard] like a boy.

When we make some meatballs, I just put one of my middle finger and just throw them out from the meat cache. [Estelle refers to large balls of walrus meat covered with walrus hide.]

Maybe that part kept me from—I think having a hard working is a cause of that [starting menstruation late], because all of my sisters had their first menstruation very early. Twelve, thirteen, only me.

And, even if I don't know what that is, my mother scares me when she's concerned about me.

But I was healthy, very healthy . . .

I was married without knowing or acquainting with the person that I have to marry, . . .

my grandparents talk about, especially my great-grandmother had choosed me for one of A——'s sons to be a wife when I grow up. So from the childhood, . . . I . . . never say anything. I try to follow the pattern of my father's character. [Estelle refers to her father's respectful obedience to his parents, an obedience which she herself has tried to practice.] He never say anything bad, even if he does not like what he's doing. When his parents told him to do [something], he does it, without any believing or liking it. Just like that.

I try to follow the pattern of his life. . . . And, maybe, . . . at that

time, seems like the way we live is changing, starting to change.
I thought to myself: we put him down too much. I'm sorry for that
all the time, . . .

    In my twentieth year, I got married—and—it's not a happy thing
to get married to the person that I never been acquainted to.
(Oozevaseuk 1992, in Jolles 1987ff)

Estelle was not the only woman to tell me initially that it was "not a
happy thing to get married." I don't think these statements should be
taken literally. Women feared marriage itself and all that it represented.
After all, these were very young women, with little or no sexual experience, who had been sheltered and protected by their families. Often a girl
still had a childhood sweetheart or teenage romance while her parents
were planning a marriage that had been arranged when both she and the
groom-to-be were babies. Parents, under these circumstances, were not
terribly interested in the passing fancies of their teenage daughters and
sons. They were thinking about family survival and doing what they
thought best. Most often, these planned betrothals resulted in strong, successful marriages and later the men and women had no regrets.

    . . . ESTELLE: I try to obey my father and uncle, [especially] one
of my uncles, John Apangalook . . . he's the one mostly. I look up
to him when something happens like that.

    And, my mother, from [my] nineteenth year my mother tried to
have me get married.

    I *never* listen to her [laughter] . . . And, it's scary to sleep with a
boy . . .

    It's very hard for me . . . . And, I thought about my father's
words, "Try to follow what we have set for you."

    That's what I'm trying to follow in.

    But he [my husband] was patient enough to tame me.[3] That's
the one thing I like from him.

    He never tried to do anything to me, until he tamed me very
much.

3. By "tamed," Estelle refers to the kindness and consideration that her husband-
to-be gave her as they got to know each other.

. . . I was twenty years old [and he was] . . . two years older than
I am.

Yes, in the future I start to see why they have put me like that . . .
[my husband] . . . never drinks.

That's a good thing—I'm thankful about that. Otherwise, I
would be beaten up or got a lot of bruises.

Maybe that's why they, the old ancestors, the Eskimos, used to
put their girls to their cousins, not women's sister's kids, not the
man's brother's kids, but sister and brother.

That's the only permissible [way] to get married, because these
sister's kids are just like blood brothers and sisters.

So with fathers, if they are brothers—they were one. The Eskimos believe that these are—these believe that they are brothers
and sisters. More closer.

But these sisters' and brothers' kids are farther . . . Mother's
brother's kid.

Because they say that two women, the sisters, are very close.

And, their brother, when they get married, the mother is different, different tribe.

[W]hen a woman is married to a different tribe, it is permissible for the brother's kid to marry her kids. [Estelle describes the
classic pattern of cross-cousin marriage found in most clan-based
societies.] . . . at first, every time when he [Estelle's fiancé]
comes in . . . we never sleep together.

At night time when everybody sleeps, he tried to get over to me.
I always run away from him. I'm always scared. (Oozevaseuk 1992,
in Jolles 1987ff)

Traditionally, elders arranged marriages, sometimes in infancy, sometimes even before birth. Estelle said that until the 1940s the preferred
marriage partners were cross-cousins. A boy or girl married the daughter
or son of their mother's brother. Elinor, one of Estelle's sisters-in-law, believed that her own father's conversations with the public health nurse in
the late 1930s might have contributed to changes in the marriage system.
The nurse sat down with her father, Albert Kulowiyi of Savoonga, and described the possible consequences of marriage to biologically close fam-

ily members. Kulowiyi, following the instructions of his elders, had already arranged for his children to marry their cross-cousins, and Elinor herself was deeply upset by this arrangement. She had fallen in love with Conrad Oozeva of Gambell, and no amount of pleading had yet caused her father to change his mind. Later, however, when he did change his mind, she believed his conversations with the nurse were a factor. The devotion of Elinor and Conrad over several years may have been another. At any rate, it is likely that the forces of change were already transforming village marriage customs. Kulowiyi and his family as well as Conrad's family were two of several families who eventually permitted their young people who "fell in love" to marry.

Even so, in the 1940s and 1950s, most families observed the older Yupik rules governing selection of a marriage partner for their children. Generally, grooms belonged to *ramket* different from their brides'. In keeping with the rules, it had been arranged that both Estelle and Elinor marry outside their own *ramket*. Several women told me that although their families had arranged for them to marry their cross-cousins, they themselves had married the men of their choice. What is fairly obvious is that certain families did tend to "get their women" from certain other families and still do. The remark, "we've always gotten our women from them" (referring to a particular "opposing" *ramket*), was repeated to me many times. Occasionally, and even more often at present, weddings take place between a man and woman who belong to the same large *ramka* but to a different sub-*ramket* or *nengllugutet* (extended family group). (See note 10, page 14.) I suspect this change is the result of the gradual integration of the community after the turn of the century.

The very last arranged marriages occurred in the early 1960s, although by this time, no one followed the strict cross-cousin rule anymore. Many young people were routinely "falling in love" while in school and then waiting for their parents to consult respective elders in the appropriate *ramka* on their behalf. This form of permission was still in use in the 1990s. In June of 1997, I spoke with Lucianna,[4] who believed that hers was, indeed, one of the very last of the arranged marriages. Lucianna, a woman in her early fifties, took pride in her domestic tasks. She loved to

4. Pseudonym.

cook and went out of her way to prepare foods from traditional recipes, which she believed should be preserved. Although in 1997 we had only a few conversations together and didn't know each other well, she was unfailingly polite and cheerful as she sat and talked with her granddaughter sitting on her lap. We talked in a back bedroom, away from the noise of the television and the traffic of her hunter sons who came in and out. Lucianna described what happened after her older siblings married without the full endorsement of their parents, just when marriage rules were beginning to change. Lucianna said that her family decided to arrange for her marriage as their youngest daughter. It turned out to be a very successful marriage.

Lucianna's experience reflects another common aspect of parental control. Parents in the 1950s and early 1960s were extremely reluctant to send their children, especially their girl children, away from home for high school or special training. Boys were much more likely to leave than girls. It was unusual for a family to choose to send away their daughters. Even without that opportunity, Lucianna spent many years as a respected community health aide until her own poor health forced her to retire. Here is an excerpt from our conversation:

> LUCIANNA: I think if I had the opportunity to go out to school I would have taken some practical nursing or nursing. But I studied on my own. My dad wouldn't let me go out to school.[5] High school . . .
>
> They wouldn't let me go out, because X——— got married . . . And [then] Y——— . . . got married to Z———
>
> And they didn't approve of [marriages that hadn't been "arranged"], so I was the target. [We laugh together.]
>
> CAROL: Ah-hah! [I laugh.] Sounds like me. I got married to somebody my mother didn't entirely approve of and my brother was the target. [We both chuckle.]
>
> LUCIANNA: But . . . it turned out very good, I've learned to appreciate [my husband]. . . . He is a strong person. Very strong

5. Until 1977, Gambell had no high school, so any young person wishing to finish school had to leave the island.

5.2 *On the north beach, at two in the morning, Mary works on a maklak (bearded seal) while I watch.*

man. And, looking back . . . .It was hard at first. As the time goes, I have learned to appreciate him. . . .

CAROL: Did [your family] pick him out for you? Was yours an arranged marriage?

LUCIANNA: Yes. . . . The last, maybe the last of the arranged marriages. And it was in the '60s. . . . He had wanted to see me, or date me, but before we even got to that point. . . . He was out [of the village] in [high] school.[6] But then he came back and . . .

6. While Lucianna speaks of her marriage as arranged, some of the changes that had already taken place are implied. Clearly her husband had conveyed his interest in her to his own family.

. . . my grandfather knew the best . . . He [Lucianna's husband]
doesn't drink, he doesn't smoke.

So he [Lucianna's grandfather] picked the first best. I was his
daughter.

. . . . Now I appreciate [what my family did for me by choosing
my husband].

. . . I've learned a lot from him. My values. I've changed my
values. Some of my values, from another family to his values. We
have our own set of ways. We are taking here and there from both
families, and kind of mixing them. ("Lucianna" 1997, in Jolles
1987ff)

Many of the values and beliefs that have shaped and sustained the
community for the last hundred years find expression in marriage. Respect for elders, marriage choices, family membership, clan (*ramka*)
membership, and obligations to family members take root in marriage.[7]
Children begin to prepare for the gendered tasks of adult life when they
are young. Values that people associate with the roles men and women
play in their families are first articulated in marriage ceremonies and in
the obligations that families assume through marriage. The great affection with which the islanders regard children and the appreciation of
women who successfully bear children are rooted in marriage.

Underlying the system of marriage is the long-standing rule that the
young should heed the advice and dictates of elders without question. According to Beda, Elinor, Estelle, Linda Womkon Badten, Nancy Uglowook Walunga, Lawrence Kulukhon, and many others, a young person
should "obey parents and always believe what they say. Obey His instructions. . . . The Eskimo way of living is like that. The Eskimo way of
living is in line with the Bible" (Kulukhon 1965:9–10). Even when a parent's instructions were painful because they went against the deep feelings of the younger person, elders should be obeyed. Here Beda describes
her own marriage:

7. The strong identification with specific patriclan units takes shape in marriage:
however, at the same time, the marriage alliances and exchanges that create or mod-
ify exogamic and endogamic rules are defined and redefined through local pragmatic
arrangements and practical adjustments to circumstance.

5.3 *Beda Avaluk Slwooko and her husband, Vernon Qaqsungiq Slwooko,*
August 1999.

BEDA: Many years ago, we never used to choose boys we like to
be our future husband. Parents, grandparents decide who is to be
our future husband.

Yeah. . . . I used to have a good boyfriend when I was a young
girl, but Grandfather picked out Vernon. He's my relative . . .
through my mother—relative.

Boy, *we have to obey* instead of refuse or [get] upset.

We have to obey whatever [our] grandfather [says]. . . .

(B. Slwooko 1992, in Jolles 1987ff)

Young people followed the rules of obedience set out by their elders
and continued to join together in alliances that glued together the various family groups spread across the island in relationships that were carefully negotiated and arranged by each family's elders. Antagonisms did
exist between *ramka,* and it was the responsibility of the elders to manipulate and arrange marriages to reduce conflict. Their methods included
the exchange of young women formally through marriage with other

ramka and through an elaborate system of trade with "partners."[8] As a result, marriage provided strong bonds that cut across inter-family barriers and inter-*ramket* ethnic boundaries. The presence of these multiple formal bonds reinforced through ceremony and celebration may have provided the secure foundation for the new, integrated community that formed gradually in the village of Gambell after 1878. Certainly, the community came to mirror the collection of smaller neighborhoods that were once scattered across the island.

As I have already suggested, before 1960 most marriages were arranged in advance. The descriptions of marriage given here suggest that, at least for young women, marriage could be a trial. It took great strength, a commitment to obedience, a willingness to learn, and tremendous endurance to enter into an arranged marriage. Estelle, Beda, and Lucianna learned to accept and appreciate their parents' and grandparents' choices for them. Elinor, who was allowed to marry the man whom she herself had chosen, had other problems. She had been raised by her father's brother, her Uncle Herbert, as a hunter, and knew almost nothing about the tasks performed by women. In addition, her husband was from Gambell, but she had spent her early life in Savoonga. When she married, she not only left her home, she left her home village.

Marriage arrangements apparently were not discussed with the young people involved until just before the first celebrations of their joining were about to occur. In many cases, the young persons had a kind of general awareness but were ignorant of the particulars of their marriage arrangement. Young men were more likely to know who had been selected for them than women were. Before the first celebrations were to

---

8. These partnerships, between men either distantly related or substantially unrelated by blood, form a second web of important social ties through fictive marriage exchanges. Many people now believe that these partnerships were formed so that a childless couple might be able to get children. However, it seems very likely that partnerships served many different purposes and that childlessness was only one of them.

While these were articulated somewhat through the established patrimony, they were also inherited relationships that passed down through generations of fathers and sons. Beda said that her husband and his brother, who often got into scrapes when they were young, used to spy on their mother whenever she was with her husband's partner (an inherited tie), giggling as they peeked through a gap in the house wall.

take place, elders associated with the boy's family approached elders of the girl's family to seek formal confirmation of the process. Once agreement had been pronounced, the boy's family members—all those of the *ramka* most closely associated with his family—began to collect gifts. In the days before the village store was filled with stacks of imported goods and the practice of ordering from the Sears, J.C. Penney's, and other mail order catalogs had become routine, the most common gifts were tanned skins of various sorts, carefully made skin ropes, sleds from baleen, fur pelts, and, always, valuable ammunition and weaponry for hunting. When enough goods had been gathered together to bring honor to the "purchasing" *ramka* and to show full respect to the "selling" *ramka*, the celebration of "buying a woman" (*tukfightuq*) began.

On a day agreed upon by both families, the combined family and associated *ramka* members of the groom-to-be gathered together with gifts piled high on their sleds and walked in a formal procession through the village to the home of the father of the bride-to-be. Today, processions include walkers and many people riding on all-terrain vehicles and snowmobiles. The procession is still grand, and the sense of two large family groups preparing to bring together their young people is profoundly moving. In the procession and waiting in the home of the bride's family, there are always the most senior elders of the *ramka*. As the families enter, they crowd into the small living room space bearing the collected gifts to present to the girl's family.

> BEDA: When our grandparents picked a boy for our future husband, then those boy's parents plan to gather, gathering walrus hide, brand new ones, skin ropes, walrus skin ropes, different kinds of seal skin, *maklak* [bearded seal] hide, *maklak* bottoms and young bearded seal hide for gun cover and back pack; hunting bag, and . . . many years ago, dried meat, dried boat food, reindeer meat, clothings.
>
> Aah, skin—aah—seal skin pants.
>
> Yeah, maybe how many skins, everything until it will be 2 sleds, wooden sleds full.
>
> Then they, whenever they had enough, they have to carry to the girl's parents, grandparents, parents.

That's the way they used to pay [for] the girl. Just like engaging.
(B. Slwooko 1992, in Jolles 1987ff)

On these occasions, even at the end of the twentieth century, the elders of both families make formal speeches, calling on God to bless the
marriage and invoking their ancestors in the name of respectful tradition.
Such celebrations are both enjoyable and emotional. In all likelihood,
neither the young man nor the young woman is present for this occasion.
Marriages were and still are to some extent agreements between larger social groups. They signify commitment and the enduring relationships between *ramket*. They express alliances and renew friendships. Through
marriage, a young woman's name passes from her family for the duration
of her life and into her husband's household and the buying ceremony is
the first stage of a process that will remove her from the social realm of
her family and move her to her husband's realm.

Once the speeches are finished, the gift giving begins. Often elders
from the boy's family carry special gifts intended for the most senior elders
in the girl's family as expressions of respect, friendship, and affection. On
the occasion of one buying ceremony that I attended, L——, a senior
elder of Aymaramka, presented Rhea, her counterpart in Pugughileghmiit, with a new blanket, and one of L——'s sons gave Rhea a carton of
pilot bread. Marina received a microwave oven. The pile of gifts filled the
floor space in the living room where the ceremony was held. On another
occasion, again one in which Aymaramka was "buying" from Pugughileghmiit, the gifts included a pair of new hunting rifles, which went immediately to the father of the bride and his older brother. Camping stoves,
food, jewelry, small kitchen appliances, and many other items filled the
room on that occasion. Before the presentation of gifts began, the oldest
men of these two *ramka* asked for God's blessing upon the young people
and called on God, in the name of tradition, to protect and preserve everyone present. Once the major gifts had been presented to the elders, the
buying *ramka* left and the rest of the family began to select among the
stacks of gifts for things to take home. Today, the young couple looks forward to the buying day, even if they feel a bit shy about it, but in earlier
years it was often regarded with conflicting emotions. Here Penapak describes the day in which the gifts were brought to her house: "When I
came back from—we used to just play ball—and play tag and all kinds of

things out there, hide-and-seek. When I came back, our outer room was filled with *all* kinds of things. And I know that I feel bad to see them" (Oozevaseuk 1992, in Jolles 1987ff).

The "buying a woman" celebration signals the next long phase in the marriage ceremony, "groom's service." The young man begins to work for his father-in-law–to-be and the rest of his fiancée's family. At a time designated by the elders, he actually moves into his father-in-law's house. In the past, eventually, after much embarrassment and tribulation, the young couple would sleep together, consummating and signifying the true beginning of the marriage. Rules about engaging in such intimate relationships used to be quite strict. Elinor remembered her father's stern warning to her clearly:

> I got married June five and I had my baby June twenty-one, a year later, yeah. And one of my kids asked, "You got married June five and had [the first baby] the twenty-first?" "No [Elinor replied], a year later I had him". . . . A good way, very good way. . . . Daddy used to tell me, "If you get pregnant without a husband and if that baby comes, if I see who the baby looks like, I'll take it and bring it over to the maker." I used to tell my father, in my mind, "Daddy, you're never gonna do that." [Elinor laughs] (E. Oozeva 1996, in Jolles 1987ff)

Today, in Sivuqaq as elsewhere, the young people may have begun sleeping together well before the actual commencement of the marriage ceremonies. Still, whether the young persons have slept together or not, the work of groom's service is a regular part of the marriage procedures. Today, by village law, "groom's work," as it is known, lasts no more than one year. Beda described groom's work and the struggles of the young man to get together with his bride when she was a girl. Her audience was a group of women who were working on a community history project with me. Beda is a wonderful and most expressive storyteller, and it was hard not to laugh when she made funny faces to go along with her stories or used a particularly appropriate hand gesture to illustrate a point.

> Right after when they were paid, the boy, young man, who is her future husband, start working. Like, hauling water, shoveling off the heavy snow from the doorway area outside.

And whatever they, or whenever they caught a seal or walrus or *maklak* [bearded seal), they took it to his in-laws. For 2 years I think they work like that 2, 3 years.

Then, afterwards, through the order of the older parents, older people, especially grandparents, grandmother, the boy starts, starts sleeping in the girl's tribe, *ramka*, girls. During the night he would wake up and tiptoe to the girl's sleeping area. The girl that's supposed to be his future wife. Then lay beside her nicely. Whenever the girl woke up, she have to hurry up, move away pretty quick, [Beda laughs]. That's the getting—try to be acquainted with [the] girl—during the night—During the night maybe four or five times. [Everyone laughs.] . . .

Then, finally, sometimes the boy trap the girl, completely.

Never, because too much, keep doing that, boy, finally the girl give up.

And she sleeps with the man completely. That's the way they getting used to one another.

Right after, 2 or 3 years of working hard, that young man.

Then sometimes lady got pregnant, the young wife pregnant while they were still living with her parents, with a boyfriend [the groom]. . . . Then after year or so parents had to plan for marriage or something. (B. Slwooko 1992, in Jolles 1987ff)

The actual consummation of a marriage could take tremendous patience and endurance on the part of the young man. Beda continued with a description of the hilarious experience of her own father- and mother-in-law.

When [Amy Slwooko, Beda's mother-in-law] . . . was starting to getting an acquaintal with her husband, [her] future husband, Charles Slwooko, during the night, before too late, two girls and Amy, that's Vernon's mother [Beda's mother-in-law], they had planned to guard, to [stand] guard as a guard; Nita Campbell [would stand] as guard for Amy. They planned, [to] settle up everything before midnight or something.

Whenever Charles, young man Slwooko, try his best to tiptoe and try to completely, try to lay with Amy, there somewhere, Nita stand up real fierce looking! [Everyone laughs.]

Boy, she really scared [him] away; she really scared [him] away, Charles. [Everyone laughs.]

Can't stand beside Nita. With looks like that. Try to be an enemy. Ha, ha, ha, ha!

Boy! She really—Charles Slwooko used to tell us those some, sometimes before he died, when he was still living. As Nita got a guardian to Amy. [Everyone laughs.] (Ibid.)

After a marriage was finally consummated, the couple's families waited anxiously for the first grandchild to appear.

Although marriages are no longer arranged, Gambell is still a community where almost everyone marries and children are the delight and the responsibility of all. Even the youngest brother or sister knows how to change a diaper, to hold his infant sister, and to feed her when she's hungry. Rough-looking young hunters melt into smiles and the universal language of baby talk when they see their youngest brothers and sisters or their sisters' babies or the young nieces and nephews of their bride-to-be. Grandparents hope to have a grandchild or two to share their bed at night. And no house is thought to be complete without the patter of small feet and the laughter of young voices. Consummation of the marriage was also a signal to the young man's family that it was time to organize the return gifting ceremony, one that Beda refers to as the "marriage" ceremony. *Nengughte*, "to marry," literally means to populate, as in to fill the home, to be in a way as to create a family (Jacobson 1987:134). It was accompanied by the "stepping on" ceremony (*tuutkaq*, or "something that is stepped on"), performed by the bride as she entered her husband's home for the first time. As a result, the young bride finally joined her husband's family. In 1997, the very last ceremony of all was the church wedding, held in either the Presbyterian Church or the Seventh-day Adventist Church.

> BEDA: Many years ago, they have marriage ceremony, too.
>
> . . . the parents have to keep skin hides, different kind of seal, bearded seal, adult bearded seal, walrus hides, skin ropes and a skin clothing and some food, and some knives, aluminum pans and whatever they brought from the sea—ships' crates.
>
> Many years ago during the days of my grandfather, steam ships and whalers used to come to St. Lawrence Island every spring.

They caught a whale, share the *mangtak* and meat to them.
They save the blubber. . . .

So that's the time they put shotguns and another guns and pans
and pots and flour, sugar, tea, pilot bread.

That's the time they brought these sales [objects purchased or
traded from the store or from the traders].

And those traders used to boat, lots of hunting boats, some of
them clear up to here, some short ones and seal skin pants, seal
skin parkas.

Trade it and baleens [whale bone].

Many years ago, baleens are very expensive, baleens and white
foxes.

$85 a pelt for fox skins.

Already made clothings.

Whenever they got enough, maybe 2 loads or more than that,
then the young lady moved away to her in-laws.

Those in-laws came to gather that man and his future wife.

That's the time they settle up the day [that they] were wife and
husband. . . .

Some girls give up easily, some girls are stunned for long while.

But some other young girls easily give up, maybe too much
wake up here and there.

Especially ladies who don't have guardian like Amy [laughter]

. . . . Ah, that's the time, that's the sign when they were start
sleeping together.

Parents, parents now settle that in their mind that their daughter
is completely become that young man's wife.

When the young girl give up moving here and there during the
night,

When the young lady give up, stay together during the night,
sleep together,

That's the time parents were settled up in their minds.

Now our daughter completely become his wife. . . .

The first time, I remember myself.

When my in-laws made up their minds to move me away from
my parents to become their family,

one of the ladies came over to my parents' house and settled up, talk to them, settled up everything.

Time for me to become their family.

Without engagement right after when 2 or 3 years or 1 year, working hard.

Then they gathered up maybe 1 or 2 loads of skins, sleds, everything.

Whatever they bought from white people and Eskimo stuff.

Then that's the time like . . . seventeen or more people came along with the lady to in-laws' house.

Then, whenever they get them to the inside front room those lot of stuffs.

The young lady was called to step on every stuff, whatever that comes along with her from parents.

Stepped on every piece.

That's the way I did, too. So we won't have a "heavied" or "something like covered by these."

That's the law. So we won't get underneath those stuff; always on top. . . .

That's the only thing I remember—so you won't get overload or covered by the stuff—[the] ones that came with you.

Just step on . . . everything. So [you] will be on top of everything—safe and sound. Something like that, I think.

Safe and sound. . . . So we won't [be] burden [ed] [by] these stuff.

Yes, that's the way I understand.

So, you won't be burdened by these stuff, the ones that come along with you.

You'll be top—in good shape. Something like that. . . . So you won't be burdened or something.

People [will] always be healthy or something. On top of something like that.

The way I understand, I should have asked that. [B. Slwooko 1992, in Jolles 1987ff)

Once a woman moved to her husband's home, she worked for her parents-in-law and learned the ways of her husband's household. This could be traumatic indeed, for she had little experience outside of her own family. Estelle tried to describe how she felt in those first days after she had joined her husband's household.

Hmm, but, when they're taking me to my husband's home, the one that always is there, who is married, and they give them something to carry, to give to their father-in-law as soon as he comes in. I think in some tribes it's different. They have given me a big—you know those big planes that they use to shave [carpenter's tool used to shave or plane wood surfaces]?

And, my grandfather's cousin, told me to: "Give that to your father-in-law."

So that's *very* hard. I feel embarrassed . . . but I give it. . . .

Since that, when I get used to staying with them,

My brother-in-law, the older one, [they're my cousins], he always says . . .

"Did you see your gift to your father-in-law?" He tease me all the time [laughter]—and, that's very bad.

It seems like when I get into their home and when I sit among them, it seems like everybody is looking at me—aaghh—it's very bad, I don't like that.

I always tell my daughters . . . "You have a good luck, you choose the ones you love and that's easier."

Because we never even visit to our in-laws—before we moved.

Mostly meals are the ones that are the hardest things for me.

And I never liked fish eggs that is mixed with fish flesh and all kinds of things like that.

Mixture of fish eggs, yes, *eslevagaq*. That's one I hate.

But, I tried to eat it because nobody knows me. . . . My mother-in-law gives them because . . . since I was little girl she's related to a distant cousin to my father.

She took me out for green[s] picking and sometimes for digging.

She always took me so I got used to her . . . but I never told her that I never like that *eslevagaq*.

After, when we done eating before we have tea, I ask her,

"Shall I go and dump this wash basin out there?"—*just* to throw up.

And then at the end, she said, "You never like that kind?" And, I said, "I never like that kind."

Now, I like it [laughter]. I tried and tried since my boys [have been] getting some and I tried to eat them.

I like them now. I always make some for them. (Oozevaseuk 1992, in Jolles 1987ff)

Marriage still unites families across *ramket* divisions, and the celebrations and duties accompanying marriage carry many of the traditional characteristics of past marriage. Any number of writers have said that there was little ceremony marking Eskimo marriage, and that divorce was as uncomplicated as marriage among Eskimo societies. While this might be true elsewhere, for at least one hundred years, marriage on St. Lawrence Island has been of such significance that the actual coming together of a man and woman could take years. During that time every care was taken to instruct the marriage partners in the family ways of the potential wife's household and of the potential husband's household.

Divorce, before the 1960s, tended to be quite rare. Few separated. Only the absolute inability to produce a family or ill treatment or total incapability on the part of husband or wife was considered grounds for permanent separation. In the past, choice did not enter into the decision-making process. In fact, the partners themselves were least likely to initiate divorce. It depended primarily on the young wife's parents in consultation with the elders of her *ramka* and to a lesser extent upon the young husband's parents and *ramka* elders to suggest separation. According to Beda,

Sometimes when after year or so when the lady was mistreated by her husband, some young boys many years ago make big bruise here or there—for some reason, mistreat—the parents took that young lady, moved her away to their own place. Even if she got married, they let the kids stay with the in-laws.[9] Many years ago, whenever someone mistreated.

But sometimes those families, young lady's parents who have peace in their heart, whenever the lady start coming, because I'm not having mistreated, I don't want to stay. They always [have] her

9. According to patrilineal descent rules, children belong to the father's family.

going back again with some kind of little gift along with the daughter, with their daughter. They gave her some skin or some meat or
some very nice piece, like clothing or something, not too big.

[They] sent her away, [saying] "You don't have to make trouble
between us and your in-laws, we don't want you to move to our
side." Some courageous peaceful parents started acting like this.
Sent their daughter away to her husband, "So you don't have to
make trouble between here and your in-laws. We want to be
friendly."

Maybe someone has talked to the in-laws, she don't upset. But
sometimes [the] young lady can't stand [it, and] keep coming
[home to her parents] whenever her husband mistreat her, [and]
those parents finally made up their minds to take their daughter
back. . . . (B. Slwooko 1992, in Jolles 1987ff)

Estelle, sitting comfortably on the sofa as her small grandson slept
nearby, also remembered divorce from her growing-up years as rather unusual:

ESTELLE: I think the divorce is not happened too often.

It is not too familiar to the Gambell Eskimos long time.

Only the divorce took place when the husband beats the wife for
no reason, for every little thing.

The parents done that, got her, just took her away from that.

The girl never complains or said anything bad about her husband, whenever they knows about this.

That's the only time. The girl's parents made the divorce.

They [the girl's parents] just talked to the parents, the boy's parents, about how the boy is treating that girl.

They just took her home, because the boy's parents knows about
that, too.

Some parents are very honest about that. They were sorry about
their boy.

While they [the boy] are doing that to the girl, they felt sorry for
this girl.

It seems to me like there's no animosity [toward the girl].

(Oozevaseuk 1992, in Jolles 1987ff)

Since marriage was not simply a joining of two people, unraveling the fabric of their relationship could be a complicated process. The families belonging to the boy's clan had given many presents to the girl's clan members, especially the respected elders in the girl's more immediate family. If the boy had actually completed his groom's service duties to the girl's family, her family might have given gifts to his clan as well. At stake was harmony in the village. In earlier days, another consideration would have been harmony between settlements. Even today, animosities between families can be traced back to an unfortunate marriage or, as is sometimes the case, to a family's unwillingness to give their daughter to a particular young man.

Even though the boy's family had already "bought" the girl, according to Estelle, gifts didn't actually have to be returned in every case, although in some cases they were.

> Some of the tribes do [return the gifts]. It depends on the—it's tribal custom.
>
> . . . It seems to me like, they take back whatever they have only when the parents, girl's parents, ask them.
>
> And some times, I hear that nobody ever ask for whatever they have given for exchange for the girl,
>
> Because it had been shared by the relatives already, and they forgot what they are, I think.
>
> —in some tribes—but not in some other tribes, [the family has to give back new things; but in others] . . . they just forget about [it].
>
> [If there are children] . . . the custom, the custom we have is the children belongs to the husband.
>
> That's our custom.
>
> Because the woman, when she intermarries with the other tribe, she never belongs to the parents any more.
>
> She belongs to the in-laws, became just like a daughter to them.
>
> So, if she has to leave her husband, she just left all her children there and only she herself go back to her parents. (Oozevaseuk 1992, in Jolles 1987ff)

The joining together of families through marriage was and is at the heart of traditional island culture. Through marriage one can trace the older patterns of exchange, the distinguishing features of the *ramka* system, the differentiation between men's and women's roles, the patrilineal basis of households, and the extensive and complex celebrations holding all these together.

On St. Lawrence Island, as in other arctic villages, gender relations, how men and women behave toward one another and how they perceive and perform their individual roles within the community, are structured both by the local hunting economy and by the kinship system around which hunting is organized. As in most hunting communities, elders have the greatest authority here and are thought to be most deserving of respect. Among the Sivuqaghhmiit, senior men in particular, and older persons generally, have authority over the young. Children learn to respect elders, including their own older brothers and sisters, as they grow up. In households, for example, an hierarchical "scrapping" first establishes who should respect whom. Older children regularly exert control over their younger brothers and sisters whether it be to demand their younger siblings' shares of candy and gum or to employ a young sister or brother to perform a household task that was originally their own responsibility. As children grow older, boys gradually assert dominance over girls, with fewer household chores demanded of them and greater freedom granted to them. Parents seldom interfere unless it looks as if an older brother or sister is being too rough with a younger sibling. Overall, the system bestows greater authority upon men than it does on women (Jolles 1989:16). This pattern is reinforced by the community's patriclan social organization.

The *ramka* system shapes gender relations. It suggests the relative authority of women once they leave their family home—where they have been subject to the supervision of their parents, grandparents, and their father's brothers and sisters—and go to live with their husband's family (Hughes 1960:247; Shinen 1963:205–206; Jolles and Kaningok 1991; Jorgensen 1990:228). In marriage, a woman still conceptually transfers her "belonging" to her husband's family. As a girl grows up she routinely asks permission first of her father; later she asks it of her husband when she wishes to engage in some activity, whether it is a serious step such as a trip to the mainland for medical treatment or accepting a job as a wage earner outside the home, or simply taking a ride down the beach or going to visit someone in her free time (Jolles and Kaningok 1991). It seems very likely that as long as St. Lawrence Islanders settle in Gambell and Savoonga, the age-old marriage customs and the relationships between men and women that they sanction will continue. The groom's family will honor the bride's family with a buying ceremony in which the groom's *ramka* collects gifts to be presented to the bride's *ramka*, particularly to the members of her lineage (Shinen 1963:201–202; Jolles and Kaningok 1991). The two largest *ramka*, Pugughileghmiit and Aymaramka, will continue to intermarry. Most men will work for their brides. During the groom's work period, the young couple will live either in the bride's parents' home or the home of one of her father's close relatives. After the groom has completed his year of groom's work, his family will organize the return[10] gifting ceremony and the two will begin their lives as a married couple in the groom's family. Sometime later, the families will raise the money to be wedded formally in church, the final sacred seal upon the couple's bond. In all likelihood, by that time they will already have been married legally by a local magistrate if there is one in residence. The completion of these many social and religious duties finally releases the young bride, now a wife, from her father's household, and she becomes a member of her husband's household in every sense of the word. Her name, once included among those in her father's line, is added to the roster of names in her husband's lineage. She is expected to accept instructions from her mother-in-law and her husband's patrilateral aunts (unmarried sisters of his father and women married to his father's brothers). Her husband's family assumes that her girlhood friendships and close ties with the female relatives of her father's side will diminish in importance and that she will choose her friends from among his unmarried sisters and his sisters-in-law. When she receives meat from her husband, the women of her husband's lineage are the ones to whom she distributes it first.

Marriage, then, is intricately articulated with the patrilineal system that prevails in Gambell. Both linguistically and in practice, patrilineal associations and terminology distinguish among members of the nuclear

---

10. In the 1930s, the Gambell IRA voted to limit groom's work to one year because a few senior men were taking advantage of their daughters' suitors, exploiting the suitor's free labor and then, later, rejecting the suitor.

family (*nengllugutkullghiit*), close relatives (*ilakwaaq*, especially the *atalgun* or persons of the father's side), and more distant kin. Cousin and sibling terms denote sex, age, and descent lines. The same is true for father's brother and sister versus mother's brother and sister. Only grandparents and grandchildren are labeled with terms in common. Patrilateral parallel cousins sometimes blur the few distinctions between them and refer to each other as brother, emphasizing the closeness of the male line.[11]

Marriage contracts symbolize a woman's transfer from her parents' home and control to that of her husband and his family. In marriage, women make new friendships and form new work relationships with their husband's family. Men continue to live and work among their own kin. This arrangement strongly suggests that in the early phases of married life, in-marrying women have little established authority and few allies. Elinor, for example, said that during her first year of her marriage, when she had been in Gambell only a short while and hardly knew her husband's relatives, she depended on her father's older sister, who lived nearby, when she needed something. The stage is set, initially, for a marked imbalance in male/female relations played out in marriage.

While the kinship system and the gender relations which embody it indicate an asymmetry in the relative authority of men and women, marriage itself affects the balance of authority. The longer a woman stays in her husband's household, bearing children to her husband's line, the more consideration and respect she receives. If she lives to old age, her husband's family members will consider her an elder of their line. If she outlives her husband, she may even be regarded as a senior elder in her husband's lineage, with the authority to select names for the newest members of the family. Jorgensen (1990:231) says: "In at least one clan, a woman who gained membership through marriage is the clan's steward, or leader." For example, until shortly before her death in 1988, Rhea was certainly regarded as a senior elder or steward in the A—— family. Important issues and family decisions were always discussed with her. At the very end of her life, as the family recognized that she had grown tired, her oldest son grad-

11. For more discussion of St. Lawrence Island kin terminology, see Hughes 1984:266–270, 1960:227ff and 1958.

ually assumed the role of senior member of the family.[12] A woman does not have to wait until she is old, however, to gain the respect of her husband's family. Respect comes from her proper and skillful handling of subsistence work, her willing attention to the distribution of food among her husband's relatives, her generosity, and her management of family celebrations.

Men spend their working lives side by side with the men of their father's side, especially their grandfather and his brothers, their own fathers and his brothers, their siblings, and their parallel cousins. These men generally work together as members of boat crews. Senior men are the captains of the all-important *angyapiget* (walrus hide boats) employed during spring whaling.[13] Even now, when many families use aluminum or fiberglass boats for hunting, pairs of hunters will most often consist of patrilineally or patrilaterally related men. In January 1990, Mary used her "permanent fund"[14] dividend and that of two of her younger sons to buy such a boat. Her husband, her father-in-law, her husband's brothers, and other men in her husband's family use it. When I asked her once if she planned to use the boat herself, she just laughed and said that maybe the family would take it to camp, neatly sidestepping the intent of my question.

Kinship, marriage, and most activities (whether practical work or formal religious duties) are articulated through a subsistence ideology that rests on a well-established system of obligatory giving and receiving. These exchanges, found at every level of Sivuqaq society, are potentially capable of generating bases for respectful relations between men and women. Giving and receiving is a contractual relation between individuals and groups. Both giving and receiving (or asking) imply the value or respect accorded the participants. While marriage is a buying ceremony,[15] for example, parties to the marriage are valued precisely because of their proper and will-

12. The term "leader" is somewhat misleading. Most leadership responsibility in Gambell is distributed among elders who consult each another. While there is no single "leader," elders are respected and their counsel sought out.

13. Whaling descriptions are based on interviews with whalers, personal observations and descriptions by Paul Silook (DLC 1982); Hughes 1960:254–255, 1984: 270–273; Boeri 1983; and Apassingok et al. 1985, 1987.

14. Permanent Fund dividends are investment dividends resulting from oil and other nonrenewable resource revenues that are returned to Alaska residents each year.

15. See descriptions by Shinen 1963:201; Jolles and Kaningok 1991; and Boolowon 1997.

5.4 *Triumphant boat crews return from a successful bowhead whale hunt, April 1996.*

ing participation in the contractual arrangements. Although marriages are no longer arranged and young people marry "for love" these days, marriage is initiated through a customary formal request. Elders of the young man's lineage or *ramka* travel to the young woman's parents and to the senior elders of her family to ask for her. Such requests are critical—not only the marriage itself depends on this request, but social ties between the two families will be shaped for years to come by the reply. Regardless of the wishes of the young couple, the woman's family can choose to reject the young man at this point, if the elders consider the young man to be too young or if they have other concerns about him or the household in which the daughter will eventually make her home.[16] Once permission is

16. Between 1988 and 1990, for example, elders from two different families rejected suitors in this fashion.

given, the young man's family begins the expensive task of purchasing gifts for the buying ceremony to confirm the contractual arrangement. Gifts given to a woman's family imply not only the respect with which her family is regarded, but her own worth as well. The groom's work performed by the man also indicates respect. A man works for his wife because her family will miss her, both as a worker and as an important participant (in body and in name) in her family's life. Once she leaves her father's house, she gives up her primary allegiance to her natal family, an event of major significance in her life. In all likelihood, when she leaves, she will carry, or may even have given birth already, to her first child. Sometimes, that first child is given to her parents to take the place that she has left empty and to bring the sounds of childhood back into a home grown quiet. The contractual arrangement is completed after her extended family escorts her to her new home carrying many gifts to give to her husband's family. Thus, exchanges honoring the participating patrilineages and the young couple are the foundation on which marriage rests (Jolles and Kaningok 1991).

Marriage provides a physical structure for all that goes on in the community. It is not as if the community would disappear without marriage, a concern here as elsewhere as teenage girls increasingly have children out of wedlock, but it acknowledges and continues a system of meaning in a community where almost everyone is related to everyone else. Individual families may choose not to support marriage of their children on occasion for serious personal reasons, but overall marriage is seen as the objective for one's children, even if there is talk of further education. In the long run, most parents would like to have their children and grandchildren near them. This very old support system is called into question by new practices such as housing for nuclear families, but it has not yet been seriously challenged, even with a rash of teenage pregnancies since 1995. Marriage remains a joining of families, not simply a matter of romance among the young.

CHAPTER 6

Life Passages

In 1928, fifty years after the 1878 tragedy, the abandoned *nenglus* and *manteghapiget* at Kukulek and Kiyalighaq still held the bones of those whose untimely deaths kept them forever entombed in their homes. The original survivors and their descendants, cautious and respectful of the restless and sometimes angry spirits of the dead, had left them to themselves—mourned, feared, and untouched.

Elsewhere, along the slopes of Sivuqaq Mountain and in the high outskirts of the island's other small settlements, occasional slanted poles remained. Once the grim foot markers of the deceased whose remains had been properly disposed, they were dug into the tundra at south-facing angles to keep contract with *aghveq*, lest that great beast be offended by the actions of men. The first James Aningayou had told Alexander Leighton in 1940 that the whaling ship crews out of Boston and New York sometimes ignored traditional rules which the islanders followed to assure the return of the whales. One such rule involved the burial stakes:

> Sometimes those whaling ship people never went back to their ship for a long time, too busy to go back to their own ship. Just building a fire on the beach and having a lunch there.
>
> A long time ago we used to carry dead people up to the grave yard [situated on Sivuqaq Mountain], rolled up in a deer skin and lashed, with a stick in front to keep [the] body from bending. After [they] lay [the body] in the grave yard, [they] pull off the deer skin and cut it up, cut up the lashing rope, cut up the clothing and leave the bare person there on the ground. That stick drive into the ground close to the feet, straight up but kind of leaning away from the body. That stick [is] called Erryoduk. White people [whaling ship crew members] burn those [sticks taken from the

grave yard] near the beach. Oh, how people don't feel good about burning that! They believe driving all the whaling game away. Then I heard
about people saying long after that, they says whale never come near
again, on account of Erryoduk burning near the beach. Maybe sometimes
happen like that here about the whaling. (Aningayou, DLC 1982:52–53)

When pain or hunger or misery weighed too heavily upon someone, he
or she still sought release in death. The decision to end life this way was
very hard for the family. Death came only after the person pleaded with
relatives at least three times to end his life. The person hoped to find honorable release and a place in the realms of the dead through suicide. Relatives hung the person on stakes which they held upright until life ended.
Often the person was already dressed in readiness for his own funeral.

When dearly beloved children succumbed to the capricious forces of
disease spirits, some men sacrificed themselves, believing when they did
so that their afflicted child might live, once the voracious appetite of
these evil spirits had been satisfied.

Young couples, saddened by the cheerless prospect of a childless marriage, toiled up the long rock-strewn slopes of Sivuqaq Mountain to make
offerings to spirits, which sometimes seemed to bring infants into barren
households. Later, the couple returned and the wife went dutifully and
hopefully to the bed of her husband's hunting and trading partner. These
and other age-old practices were used to fill houses grown unusually
silent following the epidemic and famine of 1878. Paul Silook told Henry
Collins:

> On the top of the hill back of Sevugenuk, the old village about 2 miles
> from Gambell, is a fallen-down stone structure or enclosure, mainly the
> remains of a wall with a small enclosed space. . . . [It] was a place where
> barren women came with their husbands to ask for a baby. A small sac-
> rifice was made. . . . Immediately after that the woman was sent to some
> other man in the village . . . [in hopes that a] child might result.
>
> Afterbirth is kept until the mother is able to get up. She then gives it
> to a woman who has not been able to have a child. This woman buries
> it. Purpose to help her have a child.
>
> There are records of women suckling puppies. Paul's [Paul Silook]
> mother did it when several of her children had died, thinking to avert
> more deaths. . . . (Henry Bascom Collins Collection 1982)

Estelle discussed some of these practices with me, which her father once described for Henry Collins.

ESTELLE: You know, when women had a baby? The people, in their own traditional way, they keep the placenta for five days in the house until the woman is strong enough . . . because, that time before the doctors help them, they . . . stay in one place,

[The mother] . . . squatted down [and the midwife and her assistants] make a ball of either skin or cloth, and let [the mother] . . . sit on there for five days. Just squat there for five days—for boys.

CAROL : Very uncomfortable!

ESTELLE: Uncomfortable. My mother had that. I watched it. For the girls, three days is enough. [If the baby was a girl, the mother "sat" on the ball for three days.] And, when it is over, they [the midwife and her helpers] let . . . [the mother] up, and the woman who had delivered the baby had taken her [the new mother] out [out of the house] and goes around the house clockwise, just once. And when she comes in, they let . . . [the mother] bathe in the small basin [kept just for that purpose]. Cleanse, cleanse them.

But [the new mother] never touch the hunting clothes [clothes worn by the male hunters in the woman's family] until the bleeding[1] is cleared. They thought this woman is unclean. Then the animals wouldn't come near to that hunter, if they have done something with that. . . .

And the placenta—so many times the old ladies took me out to [the] dump. And I'm scared and laughing [from embarrassment] all the time! [Estelle laughs as she remembers.] And, [they] took the placenta out . . . away from [the village] . . . we were living down there [near the West Beach] in that old village, and when we get over here [closer to where many of the new houses now sit], we just make [a] dent in the ground, and they laid the placenta, [with] the cord [pointing] toward the village. And they let us pee [Estelle laughs again as she recalls her embarrassment so many years ago].

---

1. Estelle refers to the extensive menstrual bleeding that follows the birth of a baby.

Why they do that is . . . they laid the cord facing to the village, [so that a] . . . baby [which had been lost in childbirth] again might come back to the mother. . . . And, they took the young girls with them, in case that young girl would not get any baby, so they can have an access to get a baby if they pee on that![2] Ah! That's so scary! I don't! I couldn't, I couldn't pee on that, and I started to laugh!

CAROL: [Laughing] You started to laugh?! . . .

ESTELLE: I thought . . . that thing might come alive and get me! I'm always afraid!

And, one time I remember that one of the old ladies, who is an oldest lady that had helped my mother when she delivers . . . me . . . they let her take me to her home, and let me stay there, because when women had delivered a baby, they pointed to that woman as "godmother." Being a godmother to them. [In other words, the woman who had helped bring Estelle into the world became her godmother.]

And, Uwhaawen, [Estelle's godmother] one time my mother had a baby. . . . And, when she [Uwhaawen] delivers the baby, she cut about one inch from the cord. And Jane,[3] you remember Jane? She never [was able to] conceive any [children]. She would like to have a baby. . . . She [Estelle's godmother] gives a little piece and told her to just, put that in her womb. . . . Into her vagina! . . . What happened to it I don't know. . . . Just to have her conceive.

Another thing for the barren woman, too. They encouraged them to adopt the baby, because . . . if she have to nurse[4] them, this baby will reward them with another baby. . . .

From ancient times, they always do that when they couldn't

2. Estelle explained that both women who had suffered miscarriages and young girls who had yet to conceive could become pregnant through the power residing in the afterbirth of a newborn infant.

3. Pseudonym.

4. Estelle may refer to two different behaviors here. One is that nursing a baby, even if a woman has no milk, may comfort it. The second is the more general act of caring for the baby. The idea that imitative behavior may actually encourage the desired object such as pregnancy is found in many cultures.

conceive, they adopted a baby from somebody. Especially I think from their own tribal, tribal relatives. (Oozevaseuk 1992, in Jolles 1987ff)

As in most foraging communities, on St. Lawrence Island the greatest threat to survival came in the first years of life. Because babies were so susceptible to illness, parents took uncommon care to protect them from the disease spirits that threatened them. James Ford, who worked with Henry Collins, spent many hours with Estelle's father, Paul, and wrote down these notes based on their conversations.

NOTEBOOK OF JAMES A. FORD: SILOOK'S CHARMS

2. Cont[ent]s: Dried frag[ment]s. of a kind of starfish called by Yuit "Wrestler with the waves."

Direct[ions]: Sewed onto baby's clothes. As the sea never breaks up the star fish these are supposed to give unbroken health to the child. Association of ideas.

Note: The bones of Young Murres are used as charms for babies. They are sewn on their shoulder strap and as the young murres often fall and hurt themselves, why shouldn't their bones help the babies from falling and hurting themselves.

8. Parts of the halibut. Tied onto a baby by a string around neck or waist. Used to keep away sickness.

Some of the people get a stone, about as big as the fist, from their ancestral homes—Maskin and Silook got theirs from Sevoonga [Savoonga], near Kukooliak [Kukulek]— which is hung either inside or outside the house. This charm protects the people from sickness.

The connection is, accord.[ing] to Selook [Silook], that sickness is like a storm. That when sickness comes it will tear down the human body like the storm rends the house.

The stone is to keep the people safe, whole and well. . . . (Henry Bascom Collins Collection 1982)

To thwart sickness, mothers and grandmothers tied beads and small packets of amulets to their children's clothing. The leather bands that girl children wore as ornamentation were heavily laden with beads, which created a protective armor of prayer around the girl. Each bead was burdened with its own particular message and served as a barrier across which disease spirits would not travel. Older women, especially those who were somewhat sickly in their youth, describe these ornaments with some distaste. Here my friend Ruth[5] talks about growing up in her grandparents' house, where she was often covered with beads.

> I had plenty of beads over my ankles, my waist, my arms, my wrists, my neck, my hair. I think that was to ward off the evil spirits. I don't know [Ruth laughs] or that I was that important to them. Because I was the only girl and they don't have any other children other than Reuben.[6] And I hate those, I hate jewelry for that reason because they are so heavy. I used to be very sickly and . . . when I had high fevers they were so cold and I feel so miserable: they [are] heavy and cold. I think they were to ward off the evil spirits or I don't know. . . . They over-decorated me [We both laugh together]. ("Ruth" 1992, in Jolles 1987ff)

These and other practices that were designed to bring children safely into the world, to protect the newborn, to heal the sick, to regulate relations among the living and the dead, and to maintain harmonious discourse with marine creatures, who regularly gave themselves to hunters, were gradually modified or abandoned in the late twentieth century. Nowhere are the changes of the last hundred years more evident than in the customs and practices surrounding these most fundamental events: birth, death, and healing. In each case, religious concepts, scientific-medical knowledge, and concepts of legitimacy have affected how members of the community deal with them.

PREGNANCY AND BIRTH

To understand birth, pregnancy, and protection of the newly born as a physical process and as a source of deep meaning, I turned to several older women. I relied particularly on Elinor and Estelle, who were community midwives for many years. Elinor was trained in Savoonga

---

5. Pseudonym. This pseudonym was originally used in Jolles 1994.
6. Pseudonym. This pseudonym was originally used in Jolles 1994.

6.1 Ruth with her beloved grandfather, 1955. Photo courtesy of Leslie Hughes.

under the watchful eye of Polly Waghiyi and the Savoonga public health nurse; Estelle was trained by retired midwife Alice Yaavgaghsiq of Gambell. Estelle, Beda Slwooko, and Nancy Walunga all discussed menstruation and the ideas that men seemed to hold toward menstruation, pregnancy, and birth.

In the 1920s and 1930s, a girl truly became a woman after menstruation began. For Estelle and perhaps for other young girls, the onset of menstruation was traumatic. How it would begin and its overall significance were seldom discussed among the women of the household. As Estelle said, "the one thing they never taught us—about sex" (see Chapter 5), and sex included the mysteries of menstruation. Even in a household of sisters, an aura of privacy surrounded the events of the female body. It's not that young women didn't "know" about menstruation, but, like knowledge of the young man to whom a young girl might have been betrothed since birth, it was knowledge in the abstract, a distant knowledge, hardly realized and often deliberately avoided or ignored in daily life. The changes likely to occur in a woman's body were seldom openly discussed. Even today a girl may feel too shy to tell her mother and aunts that she has begun to menstruate for the first time. A few years ago I visited with a friend and her close female relatives. We all sat on the friend's living room floor. The friend's teenage daughter was sitting with us. Suddenly, one of the relatives noticed a spot on the floor near the daughter and realized that it was blood. Immediately, of course, the women focused on the young girl, asking if she had, indeed, just begun her first period. The girl responded slowly that actually it had begun several days before. The girl's aunts chided her gently, but it seemed obvious that she had felt very shy about this change in her body and had not wanted to tell anyone about it.

In the past, once a young girl menstruated, she was cared for by her grandmother, mother, and any of her father's sisters who still lived at home. Nancy Walunga recalled that in one corner of the interior room of the house, a girl drew up her legs, which were then bound with grasses, and remained almost immobile for at least five days. In some families, the girl held a small doll, representing the children she would bear someday.[7] She could eat only certain foods. Restrictions on foods were not limited to first menstruation, however. Estelle remembers that, at least during pregnancy and when a woman was nursing a child, she was not to eat old meats and certain other foods. No one seemed to remember exactly how a young

---

7. Like the nursing behavior that Estelle described, this type of imitation was thought to promote fertility.

girl's diet might have been restricted during first menstruation or there-after. They agreed, though, that her time was uncomfortable. Estelle's father told Henry Collins that "at first menstruation the girl's hair beads and those around neck are taken off. Leave hair uncombed until period is over. They must not sew on clothes to be used by hunters, or prepare food for hunters. Same applies to older women during menstruation, except that a middle-aged woman who had a number of children would be allowed to cook" (Henry Bascom Collins Collection 1982). She was carefully kept away from the active hunters in her family: her father, brothers, and uncles. She could touch no food that they might eat, and she was not allowed to perform her household chores. Later, when she had passed through her first menstruation, she followed the same restrictions although she no longer sat immobile in a corner. She and the other women of her house would be careful of the foods they ate and keep away from hunters.

> —Boys & girls are not supposed to eat the sea weed (red) that drifts in on the west side. North side is all right.
> —Pregnant women must not eat baby walrus (baby walrus is generally aged before it is eaten), rotten meat (any kind), young big seal, young cormorants.
> —If she became pregnant, she would keep herself away from the beach, but a menstruating woman could still go near the beach. This seemed to represent no problem. (Henry Bascom Collins Collection 1982)

To care for herself during menstruation, a girl followed the older women in her family in the late summer and fall to collect grasses and mosses to line the neat leather pants that she wore in the house. Even after women gave up these garments and wore calico dresses, they followed the same procedures.[8] The same kinds of materials were used to line the insides of a baby's all-in-one snowsuit when he was carried outside. Beda Slwooko described how to prepare these grasses and mosses so that they would be soft and absorbent.[9] The women pounded the grasses

---

8. One must remember that feminine hygiene products were only introduced during World War II, and they were not routinely available to women in the Arctic for some time after that.

9. A rougher grass was gathered at the same time and used as a kind of scouring pad to clean utensils.

and mosses until the material made a soft, smooth mass. Pounding also killed any insects that might have lingered in the plant materials.[10] Once processed, the materials were carefully dried and stored in leather pokes in the cool outer room of the house, for use during the year.

Even though a young girl had begun menstruating, she did not expect to marry for several years. Her family watched her carefully. Ideally, her behavior was quiet and passive. Even the courting games that she played on the beach with young men once she reached her teens were not meant to lead to marriage directly—that would happen later when she had been bought by the family of the groom-to-be. The children she bore were intended for her husband's family, so her first pregnancy ought to take place in the context of her arranged marriage.

When a young woman became pregnant, her life changed, because having children made her a woman, much more than beginning to menstruate. Just as she was protected from physical and spiritual illness by the beads and amulets hung on leather strands across her body, so too was her unborn child. During the birth of her child and in the days just preceding and following it, she was attended only by women. Unless she was terribly ill, women of her husband's household were likely to care for her at this time. Sometimes a woman with special skills in midwifery was called in to help. Sometimes, an older woman who had assisted in a birth prophesied about the baby's future or identified a name that the baby was meant to carry. Often a child had a special relationship with this woman who had helped in its delivery, akin to the godmother relationship, which Estelle described earlier (see Chapter 5). In the summer of 1930, Henry Collins wrote down what Paul Silook and James Aningayou had to say about women and childbirth: "Child birth is relatively easy for Eskimo women. May keep to bed as much as 5 days with first baby but after that the period of confinement is usually not more than one or two days" (Henry Bascom Collins Collection 1982).

Despite the pronouncements of the two men, sickness and death did visit women in labor. If the birth was extremely dangerous, a woman's family called in an *alignalghii* (shaman). The *alignalghii* might perform

---

10. An old story tells of a woman who forgot to pound out the grasses and died from the fatal invasion of her body by insects.

a healing ceremony in which the pain or illness suffered by the young woman, believed to be spiritually led or owned, was brushed onto the body of a dog, which was then killed. Still, young women sometimes died in childbirth. Elinor, reflecting on her years as a midwife, spoke of the pain sometimes borne by women in labor and of those whose lives were jeopardized by internal bleeding. In her experience, women turned to God for help at these moments.

Although the time of wrestling directly with antagonistic spirits had passed from Elinor's life and the life of many others by the 1940s, ancient forces still occasionally intervened and women sought assurance in spiritual matters from men and women of faith. Elinor herself had such an experience. In the days soon after she started working as an errand girl for her community's midwives, she began to hear newborn babies crying in her house. This sound in her ears seemed to herald the arrival of a baby. So powerful was this message that she would ready herself for the birth of an infant either that night or the next day by laying out her clothing and any other necessities when she heard it. She said it always was a true indication that a baby was on the way. And, when she had a ringing sensation in her left ear, it signified that something bad would happen. The same sensation in her right ear signified that something good would happen. She asked one of the wise women elders who guided her about this sense or awareness. She was told that if she had been brought up the old way, this would have been her special gift. The elder told Elinor to pray to God about it. If the gift were from God, then she would keep it. If it came from somewhere or something else, she would lose it. Elinor prayed and prayed—she lost her awareness (see Oozeva 1994, in Jolles 1987ff).

By the time Elinor began to work with expectant mothers, women generally gave birth lying on their sides or backs. Older women recalled that a woman often gave birth in a sitting or kneeling position. The woman caring for her pressed down on her from behind. The baby was born onto a special leather cloth laid upon the ground. Afterwards, as Estelle described, she sat on a leather ball for three to five days. The ball, pressed up against her bowels, was supposed to keep her from sagging and becoming distended or disfigured. The three to five days seemed to parallel the time which she had spent sitting quietly during her first menstruation. At the same time, her legs and stomach were bound with a seal intestine to keep her body "together" and to prevent stretching.

Estelle's first experience with childbirth began as a teenager when she was asked to help her own mother give birth. Her experience was not one designed to instill confidence. Although Estelle laughs about it now, it must have upset her as a very young woman:

> ESTELLE: And, I never know about [childbirth], even if I have watch my mother so many times.
>
> My mother, I help her one time, just before I got married. She had one of the babies.
>
> And I was so afraid!
>
> We [Estelle and her sisters] tried to avoid her all we can.
>
> My mother had gotten Willard's mother, the old lady, to help her with the baby.
>
> And, she [the old lady] called me and [said], "Come here and take this!"
>
> When I look, she [is] clean[ing] a big diaper pail! A big one!
>
> And still the legs were about this high, and I think the water is still in there [inside her mother, waiting to be born].
>
> And she ask me to "come and pull this out" [pull the baby out from inside of her mother].
>
> And I was so scared of the baby!
>
> She [the old lady] put a little piece of reindeer skin right under her [mother's] legs.
>
> And on this side I took the baby—and every time when I try to pull [the baby out, it was] very slippery!
>
> . . . It just slip from my hand and bump its head on [the bucket]!
>
> [Estelle laughs as she recalls what it must have looked like— almost like an old Laurel and Hardy movie.]
>
> I got started to laugh while I am [trying to help].
>
> [The old lady said:] "You might hurt her!"
>
> And then I grab, pulled very hard on the wrist and on the ankle and just brought her out.

And I couldn't! [entirely pull the baby out]

What's that?! [Estelle asked the old lady]

"Ah you!" [said the old lady]. She said that she always told me simple things.

I didn't know that the [umbilical] cord is attached! [Laughs]

. . . And I put it [the baby] right on that little [reindeer] skin thing, and the baby start to gurgle.

And she told me, "Put your finger in and poke out the excess water from [its mouth]."

That was a girl.

I put my finger in and it was very smooth and warm in there!

And I [said to the old lady] . . . "You do it by yourself!" [Estelle and I both laugh.]

CAROL: How old were you then?

ESTELLE: I was seventeen or eighteen years! [Estelle laughs.]

(Oozevaseuk 1996, in Jolles 1987ff)

In 1934, when missionary Ann Bannan, who had some medical training, came to Gambell, she attended young mothers. Perhaps it was at this time that women began to give up some of the older birthing customs. Of course, Bannan didn't talk about such things in her letters to her church supporters back in the "States." In those days, menstruation and birth were not things a *laluramka* woman could discuss in a public forum. Rhea once told me how pleasant it had been when she received a gift of fresh oranges from Ann Bannan after the birth of one of her children.

Elinor and Estelle both say that in their years as midwives and in training to become midwives they learned much about medical procedures from the public health nurses who had come into their villages. While Estelle still remembers women sitting on the leather balls, Elinor, who is a few years younger than Estelle and grew up in Savoonga, learned only the ways of the public health nurse and the wise older midwives who worked with the nurse. Later, when Elinor herself married and moved to Gambell to join her husband's family, she worked with Estelle, her relative through marriage, and with Irene Reed, another midwife, under the general instruction of elder Alice Yaavgaghsiq, among others. For both Elinor and Estelle, helping a young woman to give birth to her child was a gift: surrounded by the prospect of new life, midwives kneeled down together before they began work and asked God to help and guide them. In this atmosphere, the mother began the age-old business of pushing out her baby. Elinor described how she cleaned the baby, listened to its breathing, and placed it beside its mother. It seemed best, she said, to place it with its head a bit down, until its breathing was fully adjusted. While both boy and girl infants were welcomed into the family, boys were much desired. Boys were seen as the salvation of their families, because they would bring home the food that made life possible. Elinor describes boy children this way: "Our food is very important to us because from long time ago it has been our food, for one. That's why they take care of their boy babies, watch 'em very carefully as they grow up, because they're supposed to be our food for tomorrow, you know, our hunters for tomorrow" (Oozeva 1988, in Jolles 1987ff).

Elinor, like Lucianna (see Chapter 5), had wanted to become a nurse. As a young girl growing up in Savoonga, she nursed a doll given to her by her school teacher, Hazel Troutman. Like many girls of her generation, she wanted to go to school but was only allowed to finish sixth grade. Her father had said, "There's no use for girls to learn." Her boundless energy and intelligence were later taken up with becoming a midwife. Here she describes how she became a midwife:

> ELINOR: I was best in arithmetic and spelling in that class in that big room.
>
> And then when I was around sixteen or seventeen I didn't know, I didn't think of it, but then one time my father came home from the store and told me, "Elinor, the councils have chosen you to be the errander or runner for the midwives."
>
> So it was the councils who have chosen me to run around.
>
> So, we had a box full of things needed for delivering babies, everything.
>
> We didn't always have a nurse around, so it was kept in the clinic. . . .
>
> [W]hen somebody's in labor they used to let me get that, bring it up and that's how they started.
>
> They used to let me take care of the babies, give them a bath

and help mothers who doesn't have anyone to wash their diapers or whatever you know, let me do that for one week. Every day I'd go over.

But then when mothers were in labor at first, they used to keep me there with them.

I used to sit in the corner, cover my ears, you know. Until somebody said, "Elinor, you better do this"—or something like that, you know. . . .

There was this one nurse, and she taught me *laluramka* way
—Not really teach me—we didn't sit down and talk,
But she taught me how to fill up that box we have with the stuff she needs.

She put everything away and one afternoon let me come and then just by my memory I fill it up.

So I passed that way, *laluramka* way.

And then she let me watch a baby being born.

Ohhh, I couldn't sleep for three days, three nights—close my eyes and see the baby coming—Ohh.

The very first thing: you know what I told my mom?

"Mom, I'm never going to get married."

"Why?"

"Because I'm never going to get a baby" [Elinor laughs and I join her].

. . . But then I learned to deliver babies. Even alone. Oh, I love to do it, you know.

When somebody comes around, wakes me up, when it's almost time, I get everything ready: my clothes, and everything.

When I know somebody's pretty big—all ready to have a baby any time. . . .

When somebody wakes me up, it was a thrill, you know.

It always was a thrill. Something I love to do. I love to do it.

The miracle of a baby being born. Talk to the baby, talk to the mother and I just love it.

We hardly had difficult births, hardly had stillborns.

I didn't even see twins being born, nothing.

But, we had mothers who bleed to death when I was over there.

One, did. One did.

But after three days she came back.

She's an old woman, she's a miracle.

She's still alive today.

Doctor Gregory flew over Savoonga and dropped plasma and there was this little nurse who, maybe a year ago [before this delivery] or so [had] let me watch a baby being born.

And, I told her, "I quit, I'm through, I don't want to do it again."

But then she told me, "All mothers aren't going to be that way."

. . . I was scared after that, [but] she talked to me, she talked to me and finally I said, "OK, I'll do it again."

So, I did.

And just before I came [to move from Savoonga to Gambell], we lost a woman again.

Oh, that was something.

I went to the teacher to report her condition because he was talking to the doctors over the radio.

I'm always running in those days all the time.

I ran down, I ran up, the minute I opened the front door, I heard noises.

I went into the inner door, opened it and lots of noise.

I remember walking in, but then the windows just closed in on me and I was out. [Elinor fainted.]

So, I was brought home.

But then I begged my mom and dad to bring me over. I was going to take care of that woman, you know.

So they brought me over by sled. I must have insisted, in my condition. [What Elinor is not saying is that she was very pregnant herself.] They brought me over. When I, when I got in she was, everything was already taken care of. Another time I was so scared was that.

CAROL: Did you learn a lot from working with those older ladies?

ELINOR: I learned a lot from working with those older ladies . . .

Especially from . . . Polly Waghiyi.

She knows, she uses her hands, her eyes and her ears.

She hears the heartbeat of a baby and when she's examining a mother [she says], "In three days you'll have that baby"

And, sure enough!

I didn't learn that. . . . She taught me that, but I didn't learn that.

She learned to tell when that baby's going to come. . . .

. . . so once upon a time I was in [the] Anchorage hospital, waiting to have a baby.

I had a roommate who had twins, just before the one she was carrying.

The doctors thought she's going to have another twins.

And the doctor asked me, they know I was a midwife, [the] doctor asked me, "If you feel it, how do you think it's going to be? Twins or only one?"

So I came over, feeled around, [and] I said, "There's only one big baby, that's all."

So the doctor went out, "We'll see, we'll see."

They think it was twins. And that baby was one, big boy.

[Elinor laughs with pleasure at the recollection.]

. . . So I didn't learn to use instruments at all. Nothing, no. Just my eyes, my hands and ears. That's all.

. . . When the baby first comes, you grab it by its ankles on both sides, pat it, get the mucus out, with your fingers, you know, nothing else, with your fingers or with cotton and then when its breathing gets normal or crying gets normal, get 'em down.

And for first two or three days, we used to put that baby head down a little bit, so that mucus would run out . . . .

CAROL: [And the baby just] stayed with its mother . . . ?

ELINOR: Every baby stays with its mother. . . .

[And] Whoever delivers the baby would cut the [umbilical] cord.

And then, when I started delivering babies, I cut the cord and give it to my assistant or whoever was there, to take care of the baby to take care of the mother, the afterbirth and clean up. . . .

I was taught to examine that afterbirth, every time when it

comes up, out, because of the bleeding that women have, in those days, to see if every part of it is out. . . .

Because some part of it [might be] torn and stays in there [and] it causes bleeding. . . .

I learned all that, too.

So, Polly Waghiyi and I, we examine it, everything.

. . . We had real wide cloth with a strap in between but we tie them as tight as we can, especially up here [above the uterus].

Sometimes when a mother is bleeding, we roll something, put up here above its uterus And just tie the whole thing, real tight. So, the uterus won't come up, filling with blood.

And then this keeps massaging it when it tries to move around so it keeps it down, you know.

And those things I learned from Polly [the midwife who trained Elinor in Savoonga].

. . . . Now, today, they [the village health aides] learn doctor's way, the other way.

I told the doctor, I don't know how to use instruments.

I learn the Eskimo way, but the doctor told me both ways is good ways, you know. (E. Oozeva 1993, in Jolles 1987ff)

In the late 1960s, women began to go out to hospitals to have their children and, as Elinor says: "Most all of the mothers go out [to a mainland hospital]. Whether they like it or not, they have to. . . . Some of the ladies, . . . [were upset] . . . only the ladies who the doctors think are going to have problems. But then every woman started going out" (ibid.).

Birth itself was such a powerful process that any element associated with it was originally thought capable of disrupting the hunt. Silook told Collins in 1930 that in the early spring, when hunters prepared to honor the Giver of whales and other sea mammals before the spring whale hunt, they worried so about it that

two or three weeks after their ceremony, "offering to the whale 'moon worship,'" the captains and strikers take turns in watching the whale boats to see that no one tries to put in a piece of human bone or articles belonging to dead people, or a knife that had been used for a severing a

baby's umbilical cord — the baby dying subsequently. This would frighten
the spirit of the whale that they are going to kill. This is not observed so
rigidly today. . . .

   If a whale is struck within sight of land a pregnant woman must not
look on. Her husband could go hunting but must not touch any of the
weapons used in the whale hunt — Women at menstrual period free to
look on — applies only to pregnant woman. . . . (Henry Bascom Collins
Collection 1982)

Even today, some men prefer not to have women along in a hunting
boat. Women might keep marine mammals from showing themselves to
hunters. So interwoven into the fabric of local tradition are these ideas
that discerning where concepts and practices concerned with birth, healing, and death leave off and those concerned with providing food to families begin is difficult.

   The differences between the ways that children are brought into the
world in the 1990s and how they once entered the world in the 1930s and
1940s are great. Perhaps the greatest is that the child, much desired and
often expected to take a dearly loved name, is now born many hundreds
of miles from the village. Because Gambell weather is highly unpredictable, a woman may fly from Gambell to Nome as much as two weeks
before her baby is expected. If any complications are predicted or develop
during the later months of pregnancy, she may give birth at the Alaska
Native Medical Center in Anchorage, over 700 miles away. At the very
least, she will give birth at Norton Sound Hospital in Nome, 200 miles
east on the Alaskan mainland. With her will be *laluramka* doctors and
nurses, not the quiet voices of women she has known all her life. So birth
has been removed from the village. That most intimate and most celebrated of all human experiences has been taken outside of the community. On birth certificates, these babies have as their registered birth
places cities of the outer world. No longer are they St. Lawrence Islanders
in that most fundamental sense. But St. Lawrence Islanders they are, in
name and in spirit.

   Both pregnancy and birth, still celebrated and awaited anxiously, are
monitored by community health aides, trained through the public health
system of Norton Sound. The aides, who keep constant telephone and
computer contact with doctors in the Nome hospital, are the ones who

tell an expecting mother when to depart for the mainland. Many of the aides who run the clinic and care for pregnant women are devout Christians. They combine medical knowledge with prayers for spiritual guidance and protection. Sometimes a woman receives medical instruction in the clinic followed by prayer, perhaps with a health aide and a local minister present, in her home.

In the past, the names a child received at birth, the restrictions his mother observed following his birth, and the amulets and beads attached to his small body shielded him from the spiritual dangers waiting to assail him and perhaps to make off with his fragile and vulnerable soul. Today, prayer, baptism, and powerful names, both Yupik and Christian, protect newborn children. The celebration of the child through multiple birthday parties (described in Chapter 4) continually refocuses the life of the community on its children. A cycle of birth and rebirth infuses Gambell with a sense of historical and physical continuity.

Children are so important that every attempt is made to fill homes with them. As a result, children are adopted into the families of relatives for a number of reasons. When a couple is childless, it is not at all uncommon for a sister who already has several children to give up her newborn child to be raised by her sister or brother and their spouse. Other circumstances, too, result in adoption. Living in Gambell is about living with families, learning about the intricate web of family connections, and sorting out who considers himself related to whom and why or why not. Probably the only persons who are not related are the outsiders, *laluramka* like me and the mainland Native people who were adopted into the community in the 1930s and 1940s or have married into the community. Outsiders amount to a very few men and women. In a few remaining cases a baby has been adopted from outside, but outside adoption is the exception, not the rule. On the other hand, so many children have been adopted within families that figuring out actual relationships is not always possible. Such relationships are sometimes as confusing to children as they are to outsiders. Consider my own experience.

In 1987, the almost-new John Apangalook Memorial High School was one of three sources of running water that everyone could use and the only place in the village to get a free shower. Consequently, winter intramural basketball games at the high school drew crowds of people who

6.2 *One of Mary's sons plays with his cousin from within the safe confines of a cardboard box.*

came not just to watch the game in the gym but also to take a shower. It was a great place to see relatives and friends, a real community gathering place. There were only five showers in the girls' bathroom and usually at least one of these managed a mere driblet of water. Women and their young children, teenage girls, and whoever else wanted a shower lined up each night the gym was open, sitting on the benches on one side of the bathroom or just "hanging out," talking with each other while their children played.

Soon after my own arrival in Gambell, I joined this line-up. I was a curiosity, the only *laluramka* to use the women's showers. One night, I remember, a group of children sat on the bench in front of my shower stall, eagerly waiting for the chance to see a real, naked white lady. I was terribly conscious of the small size of the bath towel I had brought with me, and partly to distract my audience, I asked one little girl, who was about ten years old, if the little boy whose hand she was holding was her younger brother. She thought very seriously for a moment, stared at him intently, and then frowned. "He used to be my brother, but now he's my cousin." Later, I learned that this little girl's parents had given her to their brother-in-law and sister to raise as their own. Ten years later, the same girl, now a young woman, has given birth to her own children. One of these was given to her adoptive parents to raise as their own child. In all likelihood, that child will think of her mother as her sister. Probably, the mother herself will eventually refer to the daughter she has given up as sister, at least some of the time.

Examples such as this one are repeated again and again throughout the village, tying people together in an ever-tighter web of family as daughters become sisters, sons become brothers, grandparents become parents, and aunts and uncles become mothers and fathers. Children, as Beda and Estelle so eloquently put it, belong to the father's side. This is the case if the family has already requested a young woman from her family and the family has agreed to the arrangement. A first child sometimes goes to the girl's parents to take her place. Now, however, as girls become pregnant before the young fathers have joined the family of their in-laws to fulfill "groom's work" obligations, or, as young girls increasingly become pregnant before finishing high school, the number of grandparents raising their unmarried daughters' first children seems to be growing.

The messages of *laluramka* society interpose themselves, too. Several years ago, a young mother with small children was widowed. For a while, she continued to live with her deceased husband's parents, raising her children within their home. But then the inevitable happened. She fell in love with someone and they married. Her former parents-in-law asserted their patrilineal rights to their son's children in this community where membership is determined through the father's side. Reluctantly, the young mother gave up her children to be raised by the babies' paternal grandparents. In a similar situation, arising out of the separation of a married couple, the family again supported the paternal rights of their son, but the daughter-in-law turned to the American court system, where a mother's rights often take precedence over a father's rights, and succeeded in keeping the baby with her. Thus, traditional rules and the American court system conflict in ways that can pit families against each other. Today, the children who were the foci of these debates spend time with parents and grandparents from both sides, but never quite enough time with either.

One more example: the teenage daughter of a friend recently had a child. Like many other families in the community, her parents plan to adopt their grandchild. In this way, the daughter will be able to finish school while her child is well cared for in her parents' home. Although the daughter and her young boyfriend appear to be very much in love and spend hours of every day together, they have not discussed their future with anyone. The young man was raised partly by his grandparents, highly respected elders. The elders would probably like the young people to follow older tradition and begin the formalities of the buying ceremony, but in the 1990s it is much more likely that the young people will prefer to seek education and training as a means of ensuring their future success before settling down. In recognition of the feelings of these elders and to honor and respect them, the baby visits his great-grandparents often.

SICKNESS AND DEATH

In stark contrast with birth customs and adoption are those which once healed the sick and protected the community from the fearsome spirits of the dead. At the beginning of this century, healing was a matter for *alignalghiit*, those who had obtained extraordinary powers through a visionary encounter. Most of those who trafficked in spirits were men, but some women also had spirit assistants and healed in that way. Often, a person who possessed unusual powers or extraordinary sight healed through touch or by licking the wounded or infected spot. Estelle's grandfather was such a man:

> ESTELLE: . . . my grandfather sings. He can foresee what's coming. But he never brought any spirits. Never even, just like ordinary sing[ing] he does. And after the song, he was silent for a while and he told us about what he had seen. That is *all* he does.
> CAROL: So he had a gift of sight?
> ESTELLE: Yes. And also he used to have a gift of healing for wounds—just by putting that [wounded place or cut place] in his mouth. And the wound heal[ed] up. . . . And, one time I tried to find out how he's doing that. Because that amazes me. And, he said, "It's not—you don't have to point that to shamanism. That's

our gift from our ancestors, because we were taught to use our mouths in a good way."

Never to say anything bad about the others or anything that is forbidden, that is not good. I know that these taboo things are not good for our life. It's really not superstitious.

I can see that when I became [a] health aide, some of the food had been forbidden to some people, that is, the woman who has babies and other things like that. And, for the sores sometimes the older people told them not to [eat] any sour things. . . . when I became a health aide I uses both of them in the clinic when I work. I can tell that whenever a person with lot of sores in his body or head, if they have eaten some sour things like *nunivak* [roseroot] and other things, the sores starts to ooze some water. I know that sour things makes them.

And also salty things. It does show, because it goes all through our bodies. And they're good. I admire them for that. . . . I always like to learn more about why they had tabooed this and also my mother used to have a drinking from a meat broth that willow greens had been boiled in. And it's kind of sweet and bitter taste. And they taste so good when I put my finger in. Tries to see what it's like when my grandmother used to boil some fresh greens, willow greens. And, I ask her why she's drinking that alone? I *would* like to taste that. That's why. And she said to me, "That's for her healing," because she had *big hurt* inside. I didn't know that's how she got the babies. I thought she always cut her up and get the baby out. And, she explained to me that is for inside healing. (Oozevaseuk 1992, in Jolles 1987ff)

In the past, when such pragmatic methods failed, however, an *alignalghii* healed by using both ritual and various forms of spiritual travel — to the moon, to the underground, to the sea — to restore health to members of the family or to convince animals to give themselves up to the hunter when there was hunger. In his conversations with Alexander Leighton, Estelle's father noted several complex ceremonies designed to turn illness or other misfortunes away from the family. These were performed inside the home by Estelle's grandparents and eventually in-

volved many members of the family. A segment of one such ceremony
follows:

PAUL SILOOK: . . . After when the worshipper comes into the
house, the wife puts that lamp off and puts another bigger lamp.
Then she sets the other lamp away. Then she lights both sides, and
after she lights it, fills it with oil up to the rim. After the lighting of
the lamp, the worshipper sets up the post just behind the lamp.
The top is grooved all around. He puts the string around it and fas-
tens it four ways, so it can stand steady. And also he puts a rope
around the posts that support the roof of the house, and hangs
these circles with the little stick in the middle, all above the lamp,
and hangs down that image of a bird above the lamp. Before setting the lamp in its place the worshipper pours that salt water at
the place where the lamp is going to be placed. And after setting
up all these things, the worshipper takes the four pebbles and
throws one to each corner of the house and puts one behind the
lamp. You have seen these little strips of sinew that my wife is
twisting? The worshipper takes a little piece of sinew and grabs the
standing stick. He believes by grabbing that stick, sickness will
keep away from him. Then he ties that string around that post.
Then his household does the same way, each ties a piece of string
around and grab it for a few minutes. . . . So also the guests do the
same way. Each brings a piece of sinew from their own homes.
Then when every one of them ties up his piece of sinew to the
post, the wife of the worshipper brings in big platters filled with dry
meat they have saved for that worship, and sets it on the right-hand
side of the lamp. The guests also had brought a dish filled with
some kind of meat, any kind, and all the guests' dishes are placed
on the left-hand side of the lamp. Then the worshipper takes his
drum and begins to sing. Then after his song, he puts his drum
aside and begins to sacrifice this meat.

ALEXANDER LEIGHTON: What are the words of his song like?

PAUL: Something like about the worship they are having; they
mention some kind of a game, especially to bring them good luck.

ALEXANDER: Game?

PAUL: Animals. And, by the way, these little circles represent seal holes and the stick in the middle represents a seal. [Paul draws a diagram for Alexander Leighton as he speaks.] After throwing—he always throw toward the lamp—he names some spirits, spirits of all kinds of sicknesses and some of the ancestors. Also every time when a person is going to have a worship and older people are present, the worshipper asks one of the older women to give out all the meat. The meats are cut into small pieces, and the women distribute them, but spare some for the worshipper. . . . all go up to their houses. . . . Then next morning, when all the guests come to the worshipper's house . . . the worshipper takes a paddle in his hand and runs to the same houses that he saw before. . . . These people know that the worshipper is calling them, . . . so the wives of these men go to the worshipper's house with the dishes filled with meat. . . . Then the men and women walk around the lamp; the man puts his arms around the woman while they walk around. These cousins walk with the wives of their friends. . . . Then when they finish that, the women go back to their houses again. These wives exchange their meat; they take out the meat from these dishes and put in their own meat. . . . When two persons do that, they especially are called brothers. . . . Between the men cousins and also between the women. And later these men used to trade wives. . . .

These ceremonies are held five times, once each year. Then after having it five years, they stop, and burn all the things. But if any trouble comes, an emergency, they call back the worship again and hold it five times. (Silook, DLC 1982:41–44)

Sometimes simple precautions could prevent sickness. Estelle was told by her aunt to stay away when it seemed that one of her close relatives might die in childbirth or might lose her infant in childbirth; otherwise Estelle might somehow find that her own unborn child had been hurt:

ESTELLE: Often times my auntie, . . . She sent me out [away from the house] to do things out there. And one time I ask her, "Why are you sending me out?" "She [Estelle's relative who was ready to give birth] might die [while you're here]," [her aunt replied].

"What's the reason for that?" [Estelle asked].

[Her Aunt answered:] "You might have a hard time with your baby, delivering your baby, if she dies while you're here."

ESTELLE: . . . My mother never even taught me that.

And, the funny thing that I do is—there were so many crabs washed ashore. And the people used to go to the beach and gather some and come back. And sometimes we brought in some and thaw[ed] them and eat.

My auntie said, "Don't eat those things! That's your first baby. You might have a very long labor, because the contractions would be weak." Also the baby, . . . she would walk sideways like crabs [if you eat crabs now, while you are pregnant].

And I never believe [her]. I like to eat! Whenever I have chance to go to my own house, before I go in, I took some crabs with me in the house [from the outer kitchen area where they are usually stored]. And I started to eat them! [Estelle and I both laugh.] Nothing happens. Nothing happened. . . . And, I have [my first daughter]. And I'm always afraid that some of my kids might be deformed like that [but they weren't]. (Oozevaseuk 1996, in Jolles 1987ff)

In truly bad times, men prayed directly to Apa or Kiyaghneq. Remote and unattainable, surrounded by barriers of extreme respect, Apa was thanked when food was plentiful and when *aghveq* or *nanuk* came to the village, but he was beseeched only when meat racks were bare and the *siqluwat* (underground storage units) were empty. As the late Samuel Irrigoo explained, those who spoke to Apa were usually men of standing in the community, boat captains and hunters. When the village was hungry, boat captains might exercise their privileged position to pray for family and community. On the other hand, a small child might be told to pray—a person so pure that Apa could not take offense at the child's presence or prayerful request. The community turned to Apa only when all else failed. Somewhere near the village was a large pole, possibly located in the old village of Sivuqaq near the west beach. Certain chosen individuals dressed themselves in a special *qaliq* (parka of treated seal gut) after having purified themselves carefully. They climbed the pole which stood some eight or nine feet above the ground. From this position, they asked Apa to help (Oozevaseuk 1989, in Jolles 1987ff).

Elders did not recall whether these prayers to Apa were offered on behalf of a single family, a patrilineage, or an entire *ramka*. Walter Wongitillan recalled this experience in 1988 as he sat with Elinor and me in the kitchen of the Presbyterian Manse in Savoonga:

> I was eight years old when my father died. The following winter [The period to which Mr. Wongitillan refers is 1920–1921.], there was hardly any food. Just about famine. When the weather became good at last, men went out hunting, by dog team. As I was going out, as I reached the shed, my great-grandmother Wiya came out after me: "You children are very pure and clean. The great Apa will hear you." Then she taught me how to pray. She taught me this way. And these were the words: "Grandpa, I am very hungry today. Please give us something to eat." And then, when the hunters came home, my uncle Kulowiyi brought home some walrus meat [that same day]. And since then, when I was only 8 years old, my uncle Kulowiyi accepted Christianity because of that.
>
> . . . What I heard from my parents were that, long time ago there used to be wars, too. And when they're going to have a war, then that's the time, too, when they're going to call on the great Apa. (Wongitillan 1988, in Jolles 1987ff)

As the community depended more and more on modern medicine and medical practices, the older forms of healing or curing disappeared. What remained, however, was the recognition that when the scientific-medical world failed, the spiritual power resident in an almighty God might prevail. Many people in Gambell rely on God to heal them when medical practitioners cannot. In 1987, Belinda,[11] a woman in her mid- to late fifties, suffered a serious attack of gallstones. Gallstones are extraordinarily painful. The pain Belinda must have experienced added to the powerful effect of her story. In late November, I was present at the evening church service in the Presbyterian church when Belinda began to talk about what had happened to her.

11. Pseudonym.

Belinda came forward during the testimony of faith period, which comes toward the end of the evening service, to announce that she had been miraculously cured of gallstones. At the beginning of the week she had been in severe pain, so much so that she was flown out to Nome to the hospital under the direction of the village health clinicians in consultation with the Norton Sound Hospital staff. She went with her husband, very sick, with her head lying on his lap and her eyes closed. As she lay in the plane, she thought back to the previous week when she had asked her friends for their prayers during another church service. When she and her husband arrived in Nome, she went directly to the hospital where she was examined by doctors. The doctor who examined her said she would need an operation in Anchorage. The Norton Sound Hospital was not equipped to perform the operation that the severity of her condition required. While she was being examined, Belinda suddenly felt sick to her stomach, as if she would vomit. She did vomit, three times—large amounts of water. Belinda's description of what happened next conjured up an image of an active fountain. Belinda was then a heavy-set woman with black, short curls framing her face. With her hands she made gestures which resembled somewhat a carved baroque figure gushing water. Belinda considered that her vomiting up large amounts of water was unusual. She had, after all, had no liquid to drink. Where had it come from? As she spoke to the congregation, she suggested that it was a sign that God was working. Then, she related, she had had to go to the bathroom. She was still feeling quite ill. She excreted a large amount of material. She went back to the doctor, who wished to examine her once more before her trip to the hospital in Anchorage. Following his examination, he told her in astonishment, "Mrs. ——, you have experienced a miracle. Your gallstones are gone!"

At this point, Belinda stopped and looked out over the congregation, saying, "Praise the Lord." Her head nodded, as if to encourage a response in those around her. And, with the skill of an accomplished conductor, she drew forth a series of answers—around me men and women murmured "praise the Lord" and "thank you, Jesus," along with prayers in Yupik. Into the miracle was interwoven a vision as well. Belinda "saw" or "felt" a light. She was aware that the light came from Jesus. She opened her eyes and saw the robe of Jesus. It resembled a great brightness. She reached out her hand and touched it. In her words, "I touched it, my friends, I touched it. It did not feel like silk, it did not feel like cotton. It was the wondrous light and love of Jesus. It was the wondrous light and love of Jesus. It was a miracle, my friends. They were gone." She placed her hands on the right side of her abdomen and circled it with her hands. Once again she repeated the sequence of events in which she discovered that her gallstones were gone, ending with the words of the doctor, that she had made a miraculous recovery. Then she moved away from the podium at the front of the church toward the few persons seated in the front pews. She held out her hands to them, and said, "Touch them. I have touched the robe of Jesus. And, it is your prayers which have helped me. It is a miracle."

As I listened to Belinda's story in church that evening, I realized that the articulation of physical and spiritual healing processes that she described and that others in the congregation both understood and accepted depended on a world view with roots in the traditional medico-religious system; it was premised on the idea that the body and the soul are not separate in a metaphysical sense. A woman who placed her faith in God and Jesus should not be amazed to find that physical healing occurred as a result of divine intervention. I resolved then to ask Belinda to tell me what happened in her own words, on tape.

When I arrived at Belinda's house, she was busy soaking and softening a polar bear skin in a large galvanized iron tub filled with household ammonia, in the comfort of her living room. She was extremely pleased to talk about the polar bear, which one of the men in her family had taken, since taking a polar bear is considered a great achievement. Her story, told as she worked, follows. The only portion not included comes at the very last, when Belinda asked to sing for me a poignant rendition of the Lord's Prayer, the tune for which she had "received" as a spiritual gift.

Around 2:30 the real big pain wake me up, real big pain, and then I get up. I couldn't get up. There was real big sharp and dull pain or something, and then I go to the bathroom and then when I look there in the mirror my face was just pale. My face was just pale and when I see my hands, they were just pale and no veins. Real sick.

And then I woke my husband. My husband knows me I was just ouch, ouch, you know, hurting. [He] said, "Honey, you look pale." I told him I was sick and then he call the nurse aide and the nurse aide, they didn't come over on time. They sleep instead and then later on Lawrence[12] called again and he notice my face. I look real sick. And then she [the nurse aide] took my temperature and blood pressure. And then that nurse aide said, "You have attack from gall stones." And my back was just hurting. So the doctor [via telephone conversation with the aide] tell me to go to Nome [site of the nearest hospital on the mainland]. And the doctor saw me. They see me.

And then three times I vomit. I didn't drink water. Three times clear water with sour. I could notice the sour in my mouth. I vomit three times. And, I was thinking, "Where's—where did that water come from? I didn't drink water. Where did that water come from?"

And, the doctor said, "Your gall stone—it went bowel movement. You already—" [When did you go to the bathroom? I asked.] That time. That time I went to the bathroom and vomit at the same time. And I was in the bathroom too and the doctor said, "Your gall stone is gone. And I couldn't believe because I was having still pain. I didn't believe the doctor because I was still having a pain. And then, later on, Dr. Olson came to me and said, "You want to go to Anchorage—you need a operation to remove that gall bladder. I'll talk to the doctor first." "OK," I said. "Wait there, sit down and wait." It was painful. And then Dr. Olson came to me and said to me, called Lawrence and me and said, "Your gall stone is gone. In Anchorage the doctor don't want to open you because there's no stone, no way of opening you. There's no stone in there, but your gall bladder is swollen in there. That's the one is swollen, is making you sick, cause the stone go out."

I said, "Praise the Lord." And the doctor said to me, "Mrs. B——, you can say, 'Praise the Lord' again." And then we went to the Kristiansen's [Presbyterian minister] house and the telephone ring. It was my daughter and she said, "Mom, I talked to the three doctors."

12. Pseudonym.

"What did they say?" "The head doctor said, 'Your mom has a miracle. The gall stone is gone.' It's a miracle. Praise the Lord."

I struggled along the way, cause I still have pain. And then, Satan tried to doubt me, heavy doubt on me, put heavy doubt on me. I still have pain, the doctor give me pills and my husband said to me, "Put your faith in God and look upon and who's there? It is Jesus. Your mind is foolish. Your heart is deceitful. Throw those away and walk in front. You walk. You have already healed." I was just struggle away yet. And, then—he opened the door, he opened the window, so I'll have fresh air.

And, then, I had a dream. First, I dream about when I was real sick. Look, you always plant flowers, you always plant flowers. Look at what Satan plant is. Look at it. And, then, I look down. There was—the first thing I see was group of women right there. And the name of it was right there, gossip. Ladies were gossiping. And over there they were doing that, young people, drugs. Other one—drinking. Other one smoking marijuana. Some of them—crash. Car crash. Dirty. Satan's plan. And, then, the voice came to me again, "Turn around and look this on your right." And, when I look right there, I saw few Christians—people. Here they were feeding needy, that are hungry. Some of them were making little crosses out of yarn, that lady was making lots of crosses. And the other ones were putting clothes on the needy ones. And they were letting them drink clear water to them, help them. Some of them were hugging the other people, praying for them, praying for sinners, to receive Jesus Christ as their personal savior. And, then, I woke up.

And then I dream again. When I woke up I dream again. I saw my Savior's hand, big hand. And the nail was there, it was taken out. The nail—and in the circle the love was written. Love, on that scar, the love. And his garments, sleeve, his sleeve's garment. And, then I said to, in my dream, I said, "The lady had bleed for twelve years and then she touched the garment and she was healed. The sinner was healed. I can do it too—I'm gonna be healed." So, I reach for his garment. It wasn't the cotton, not cotton. Not silk. It's the glorious glory garment from His Father. That's when I wake up. And then I believe I am healed. . . . ("Belinda" 1987, in Jolles 1987ff)

Belinda's healing, together with her vision of Jesus, was only one of the more dramatic instances in which the spiritual energy and power of God were sought out in the midst of a medical emergency. On several occasions I joined a family prayer for someone who was sick or hurt in an accident. Once, a little boy had a high fever and the family asked his father's uncle or grandfather (in Yupik kinship terminology) to come to pray for him. During the prayers, the little boy lay bundled up on his grandfather's lap. His mother gave the family Bible to the grandfather, who allowed the Bible to open at random. Then he searched the open pages until his eyes fell on a verse that he felt was significant for the child's recovery, and on this verse he centered his prayer. Afterward, the grandfather went home. It was around three o'clock in the morning. The family breathed more easily, believing that everything possible had been done to return their little boy to health. Soon after, he recovered.

In the past, whenever someone in the community sought help from Apa, there was an implicit awareness of Apa's unimaginable power and of his unpredictability as a spiritual force. Prayers of supplication were delivered in reverential whispers. As center of the ancient spiritual ensemble, Apa stood apart from other spiritual forces. He was stern and exacting, and, in contemporary descriptions, deemed ultimately and perfectly good, but very difficult to please. Misunderstanding his requirements or unwittingly offending him could result in his unleashing spirits that could wreak havoc upon offending individuals or entire families. Thus, Apa was directly associated not only with life and healing, but death. The arctic world is filled with dangers. Survival in that world was dependent on more than a deep knowledge of the land and its resources. Those who lived there were expected to maintain the rules that governed all living creatures as well as the complex relations that regulated interactions among those creatures. Not to maintain those rules could result in sickness or death.

In 1989, a tragic death occurred, which illustrates what could happen when someone inadvertently trespassed against the old rules governing human-animal relations. Some men had gone out on snow machines in search of polar bear. Their hunt was unsuccessful and they turned toward home. Their way was blocked suddenly by a snow storm, which reduced visibility to zero. Nevertheless, the men continued on their way at a good speed. The first driver used his compass to find a path through the blinding snow. The way lay perilously close to high cliffs along the sea. Then, without warning, the compass failed, and the first man plunged off the cliff to the rocks below, receiving a mortal blow to his head; the other sustained injuries to rib and arm. The two men were well regarded in their community. The death of the first man affected almost everyone on the island. The military funeral held in his honor during extremely cold temperatures across Alaska and Chukotka (the thermometer registered 37° below zero that day) was attended by many. Within days of the funeral, however, some worried that depending on technology such as a compass when the weather was so perilous had somehow offended ancient forces and caused the accident and the death. Some even worried that the use of such a device together with the search for polar bears had somehow been disrespectful of those animals. According to island tradition, polar bears "give" themselves to men. When they are ready to offer themselves, they allow themselves to be seen by the individual destined to receive them. For this reason, the first person to "see" a bear is its owner, even if someone else kills it. To go out in search of a bear might contradict this principle. These two men were by no means the only ones to have sought bears in this fashion and certainly not the first to use sophisticated technology when hunting. Thus, the suffering of the two men was meant as an example for all. What happened seems to fit with Paul Silook's remarks in 1940 about the character of Apa: "God is in heaven, is a perfect person, and the creator of the earth and the giver of animals and other things . . . and he accepts only the successful hunter's gifts, sacrifices. He is very merciful, but on the other hand he may punish those who do not do exactly what he has instructed" (Hughes 1953:243).

The elders reiterated that it was the duty of a man of stature to ask Apa for help. According to Samuel Irrigoo:

There was one God that the Eskimos and the white people worshiped. With us Eskimos, God up in heaven — we couldn't even say his name, in general, it was too holy. God, who has a son, only the boat captains, in those days, were allowed to talk [pray][13] to him. They would go out at night and go under their boats, and ask if He could give them some food,

13. Explanations provided by Deborah Apatiki.

when the weather was good for hunting. . . . So when good weather came they would get food, walrus, thanks to God [because they had prayed]. When they got walrus they would give food to everybody, *awalightuq* [to bring over food across family lines as a sign of friendship]. (S. Irrigoo 1979)

According to traditional disease concepts, spirits caused illness of all sorts (Murphy 1964). Sometimes, an intrusive item, placed there by witchcraft or by a spirit, could be withdrawn by a powerful shaman with the assistance of that person's spirit helper. On many occasions, however, death seemed imminent, and a loving parent or other relative might be propelled to act, believing that only through substitution of a sacrificed human spirit could the assault be stopped. Thus, a person took his or her own life in exchange for that of a sick relative, often a beloved child. On other occasions, a dog was sacrificed, and the sickness "swept" into the animal, whose belly had been slit open and then sewn up and disposed of in an appropriate place. In the example that follows, Doris Uglowook describes for Lucy Apatiki and me a ceremony that she remembered had been used to heal her sister, who was very sick. She added afterward that she had not understood what was happening at the time. Only after seeing and hearing of a similar performance in a videotape did she realize what she had seen as a child. In Lucy's translation, she refers to Doris in the third person:

> LUCY: She remembers as a little girl her older sister was sick, very sick and they probably thought she was going to die. So they took this healthy dog, killed it outdoors and slit it open and they brought her sick sister near the dog and brushed off her sickness into the dog. And they lifted out its intestines and that—the dog took the sickness. The girl was healed. The dog took—she died—the dog died in place of her.
> CAROL: Does she remember was it an *alignalghii* who told them how to do that or was it someone else in the family—how did they come to the decision to do that?
> LUCY: She doesn't know if it was in the family or if it was with the shaman's assistance or knowledge. (Uglowook 1988, in Jolles 1987ff)

Later, Estelle described this type of healing for me, adding her own analysis of what took place:

Yes, we have different types of like purifications and just like that, something like sacrifice.

We have nothing, no animals here, . . . the only animal that lives with us [are] dogs.

So, the people use it for it.

They say that they use [dogs] when the person is so sick. They place their disease on that.

Just put their hand on that animal and let the elder kill that animal.

They have some words to say to that; like transferring the disease to that animal—and —

Just like replacing that sick person [with] . . . that animal

And get that well one.

So that animal dies instead of that [person]—just like sacrifice—instead of that sick person.

They believe that and just like we do with the faith.

When we pray, we pray with faith to God, because without faith we can't get anything from God just like that.

The Eskimos believe what they're doing and this person will [get well if the dog is sacrificed in their place].

So I always try and explain that to the pastors and the missionaries—that's faith they're using.

They have faith. (Oozevaseuk 1989, in Jolles 1987ff)

Sacrifice of a living creature (being) was not always required. An item of value might be offered to repay a spirit. Here, Paul Silook describes how his parents offered a pair of binoculars in exchange for his health.

As I have said before about my father's old custom, he used to be very superstitious about some things that the other people had to do. When I got sick one time he let me lie over a small field glasses which he had bought for me from one of the trader. He tied a small piece of baby seal hair dyed in the red bark to the glasses and took it out and shove it between the skin lashing which holds the walrus skin covering of the home.

I got better, but, I do not go out for a while, until I am able to walk around in the sleeping room. So one morning he and Mother took me out. I carried a walking stick in my hand, while Mother bringing out a flame of fire built on a piece of board and set it on the ground, right side of the entrance way but some distance away. Father brought the glasses and take the dyed hair from it and burned it. He let me put my feet on the glasses as though I am stepping on it, one foot at a time, first my right foot, then the other foot.

He pretend grabbing from the metal and throw it up into the air, and break the glasses and put them on the fire and pretend to shake me over the fire and then quench it and threw it away, board and all. His belief was that he pays for my life from the spirit that is trying to take it from me. (Silook, DLC 1982:6a)

When someone died, the spirits that caused illness, traumatic accident and pain triumphed over the living. Their presence, always acknowledged and apparently greatly feared, had to be reckoned with, in order to give to the deceased respectful treatment and safe passage from the world of the living to the land of the dead. On St. Lawrence Island, gravel-strewn, rock-surfaced, and frozen for much of the year, the dead could not easily be buried. Every precaution had to be taken to create insurmountable barriers between the living and the dead. The spirits of the deceased had been known to reappear to catch the souls of the unwary living—draining the spirit of life through sickness. Sometimes a spirit, jealous of its living spouse or other dear persons, tormented its relatives, allowing them no peace. In the 1920s and 1930s, when the horror and numbness associated with the epidemic had somewhat abated, care of the dead was a regular concern. If Nelson's experience was typical, in the time just after the disaster, when the dead so outnumbered the living, the living went about their lives scarcely lifting their eyes to the presence of the dead except to comment on the condition of their wretched bones.

Upon death, several ceremonies were performed through which the estranged condition of the deceased person was recognized through formal reversal of outer garments—both among the living relatives of the deceased and among the deceased as well. Through these ceremonies the dead were separated both in mind and in practice from the living. Parkas and outer trousers were turned inside out. Hoods were turned up and backward. Across the nose, a strip of grass was fastened and strands of reindeer fur were hung. The ornaments that accompanied these ceremonies were similar in form but not in content to happier celebrations in which people greeted and welcomed visitors into their settlements. In the home of the deceased, no one stirred for at least five days. Absence of movement was in stark contrast to other celebrations and rites. Men performed many of the duties, and the concern of all was the possible contamination of the nearest relatives by the dead, a contamination that might lead to their own death. Almost immediately upon death, at an appointed time, close male relatives came to move the body; their dress signaled symbolically the body's transformation to the other, that which has been turned against its "self." The body was tied to a driftwood pole and carefully carried to Gambell's graveyard grounds on the sides and slope of Sivuqaq Mountain. Here the body was put down, with its head pointing north. The pole was driven into the ground facing south. Around the body were laid rocks, ringing it entirely. These, and subsequent rocks and stones, would become symbolic mountains across which the spirit could neither climb nor penetrate. The dead became separated. One day, Estelle told me what her grandmother had told her about those who had died:

> ESTELLE: [This is what people believed.] Before we become Christian. I was just a little girl. And, she [Estelle's grandmother] told me that there's two places to go [when you die]. The good ones goes to the north, travel to the north. And, the other ones, the ones that are not good in their lifetime, hang around here. And, often times the spirits come back to the village. And, but they can't go into their own home. As soon as they [come] near their own home, they go down to the ground, until, under the house, they go and come up way far from it. They couldn't go into their own home.
> CAROL: Now, is that why, when somebody dies, they lay, they used to lay them so that the head is towards the north.
> ESTELLE: Yes! In case they, their spirits might return. [They are placed] Like that [so that they will travel away from the village]. (Oozevaseuk 1996, in Jolles 1987ff)

On July 10, 1940, James Aningayou told Alexander Leighton about the funerals he remembered from his youth. As he talked, Leighton typed his words on a portable typewriter.

JAMES: When a person died, before the body got stiff it was washed, starting from the feet and up to the head. Then put the clothes on. This is before we wear any socks, when we have skin socks; the men's are short and the women's are long. . . . On a man they put deerskin pants, hair side out and the skin side in. The parka the same, skin side in. A woman has a kind of a romper, like, with long sleeves. They slide it on from the feet and pull it up, and the arms go through. That is the real old way. A deer skin is laid flat and the dead person is put on it; sometimes two deer skins, if the person is tall. Then another one is put over him. Then they cover the face and everything, put the hood on.

LEIGHTON: Where do they get the skins?

JAMES: From Indian Point people. It is used just like a coffin, that winter skin, heavy hair. Then put a stick on top. No boots, just the stockings, hair out. The deerskin just come to the ankles, not come to the feet. But the head and face all covered. Then they lash up from the feet to the head, with that stick on, to keep from bending the body. If it is a boat or canoe captain, then they use steering paddle instead of a stick. I forget which way, maybe the blade side toward the face, or down lower. Then they use walrus skin rope, split in two. . . . [because it] Makes it easier to tie up, smaller size. They make loops on each side, not all the same size, some longer, some shorter, fixing the body that way for the men to carry by.

When somebody begins to get tired, he says stop, and all put hands on the ground this way, or that way: (*sic*)[14] They trade sides then, and start again. They do that a few times as they go (points toward the mountain), I don't know how many. That was in the real old times, before any white people stay around with us.

The dead person's family, wife or children or somebody, close

14. Words in parentheses are notes by Leighton; words in brackets are notes by the author.

family, take some kind of a plant that grows around the village here, *reeghlook* [*ggilleq* or woody core of edible willow leaf], that smells strong, and tie it up with maybe two or three blades of grass, and put it across here underneath the nostrils. . . .

LEIGHTON : All of the relatives do that?

JAMES: . . . that is the way I saw the custom. We used to wear sealskin pants outside and deerskin pants inside, and sealskin pants had the hair out. That is the way the man [was] dressing. But that time when one of his family die, sealskin pants turned hair inside, and the outside parka changed, too, skin side out, nothing but skin out. . . . (The deerskin pants were) Not changed. I don't know really what that was for, must be to show that it was their sad time. Even that leaf, over one side [of the] (nostril), leaving one side open, and tie up back (of neck; all these additions he indicates by gestures). They wear those things to that first place to stop, and carry some things that belonged to that person, going to be destroyed there. They carry that pot or something to wash with, and wash that dead person with soles of grass from inside his boots. Another string of grass that long (2 feet) is fastened to that dead person. Then when they come to that first place they are going to stop. . . . (in order to) destroy the old clothes or whatever the dead person had, woman or man. Then [they] cut up there the old clothes; stick one knife over that dead person, slide on the lashing of a skin. That knife they are going to use to cut the rope and the clothes when they get to the mountain.

. . . I think they emptied that pot what they washed with, and the oldest person in the family picked up that pot which they wash with and call by from the older person. (By gesture and words he [Aningayou] shows that the oldest member, man or woman, of the deceased's family takes the pot and makes a sweeping motion with it down the front of the next oldest, from head to near the ground, over the dead person. then turns to the next oldest around does it to his back. so on down the line of the family in chronological order and does it to himself last, or has some one else do it for him.) I think that means sweep off sickness on that dead person from the whole family and let it all be buried with him. . . . Then, about that straw: When the first one came he held the end, and that sweeping man cut with the knife just a little piece of the straw for that person. Then when the next one come, he take another little piece off, and so on until the end. Then himself cut and held the last piece. Then that little dish or pot . . . he destroy; and the old clothes, cut it up with that same knife, everything they had destroyed there. . . . Sometime they carry up on mountain on back. Sometimes the helpers get a little bit of thread, if a woman, or a scraper or something, they bring it home. I did that myself twice; I bring home a scraper when I was a helper. . . . If [the item was] used for a long time, they destroy, but if new, in good condition, better keep home. . . . [The places where the goods were destroyed] We call those the destroying places; and still have left some extra split rope (from carrying up the body), that rope is brought up to the destroying place and then they bring it back again.

Then when [they] get up the mountain, and when high enough, we [are] looking for a place to lay that dead person. When we come to a level place, if somebody had been there, [we are] not allowed to lay over again that place. . . . Then turn the head toward the north, the feet toward the south. . . . then cut up the clothes, I think from the feet up. . . . But only one knife, the same knife all the way from the house, the same knife cutting up old clothes. I saw older person leading coming home; just moving lips and whispering some kind of prayer as we coming. Then we follow his steps. Then pick up little bits of gravel, he lay across, spit on it, and step over; then we follow . . . every step he makes. . . .

So they told us to pick up something, old seaweed, just a little piece of it. . . . The man leading us says, "When you get home, take a bath, wash yourself. That seaweed rub into your wash basin." Then we come right straight to the dead person's house. When we close enough, somebody lighted a fire, out of doors. Then each one who carried that dead person come to the little burning fire, and smoke up gloves or mittens over the fire, or (his) body (by leaning over the fire). Then each person has a little piece of skin rope given us . . . This goes to old meat racks . . . hung on to the old whale jaw. Then put that piece of rope, slide into the crack. Then everybody goes home. . . . [T]he family [of the deceased] . . . they tear down the string (of grass) on the nose, then burn it. . . . They says, if you are careless (about observing these rules), in a short time something will happen to you. . . . [T]hey themselves in a very short time will get sick and die. (Aningayou, DLC 1982:82–87)

After an appropriate time passed, the soul was invited to return or perhaps let it be known that it was ready to return through the naming process, already described.

As the village responded to the new religious ideas brought by the missionaries, the ways in which the community cared for the deceased changed. One of the first physical changes already mentioned was the introduction of imported lumber, which could be made into coffins. It is hard to imagine the effect of lumber coffins on the community. Certainly the community continued to use the destroying place. The custom, once common, of including a special cup for the deceased continued for a long time. Older graves, weathered with the strong winds and storms that batter the slopes of the mountain, sometimes reveal the outline of a cup within a coffin from the 1940s or 1950s.[15] Today, the coffins of the deceased are filled with gifts from relatives to give comfort to the deceased in their long rest. Blankets, pillows, and warm clothes, along with items the deceased might have cherished in life, are thoughtfully tucked into the coffin.

To understand death in its modern context, let me describe two intimate experiences involving the deaths of persons who were much loved and deeply valued in the community. Both were devoted members of the Presbyterian church; thus, the descriptions of their funerals and the circumstances surrounding them are colored slightly by that particular religious denomination. The deaths represent two aspects of community response to death: one was an untimely death—totally unforeseen and accidental. The second was no less untimely—but at the same time anticipated.

15. Other practices, such as placing small stones with the body of the deceased, sometimes on the abdomen, are much more difficult to determine. The dead remain for the most part undisturbed.

The death of Marina's sister-in-law, Sara, a devout Christian woman, shook the community to its core in the spring of 1987. She was an active woman who liked to be busy. She was known for making gifts of food and clothing to young mothers. At the high school, whenever she worked as a cook, her fried bread was always anticipated by the students. When she met visitors, she was likely to feed them, as she did me, and then to describe enthusiastically her love of Jesus. Sometimes she joked—as when she compared the new gray hairs showing on the top of my head with her own dark hair and suggested that I must be becoming an elder. She was at least ten years my senior. She loved to be outside and more than anything she loved to be out on the ice on a calm clear cold day, dropping her lines for Alaska king crabs. On the day of her death, she went crabbing. She may have died because, in her enthusiasm, she forgot the warnings of her husband that the ice was no longer entirely safe. He had taken her to the north beach, where everyone goes to crab, on that Friday afternoon. Crabbing usually stops when the shore ice leaves in the spring. Her husband had told her not to go far and pointed out the weak places—and that is where she was found. She went through the ice and managed to pull herself partially out. She was in the water at least an hour. Her husband found her when he went to bring her home. She was no longer conscious and was suffering from severe hypothermia. She never had a chance. When her husband, a well-respected hunter, called Rhea with the terrible news, it was 9:10 P.M. Marina was at that time employed at the high school. It was prom night and she was preparing to supervise the high school prom. When she heard her brother's news, she turned pale and exclaimed a startled "Praise the Lord." Then she made a few rapid telephone calls to direct people to the beach to help—and rushed to the sofa to tell her mother of the accident. She had to shout because her mother's hearing aid was out of batteries and there were none available in the store. Then Marina asked her mother to pray. Her mother, tiny and deeply shocked, began to pray in a strong firm voice, while her daughter beside her prayed also, repeating again and again "Thank you, Jesus" and "Praise the Lord," as they wept. The spiritual process of accepting God's will had begun.

And then followed frantic moments of deciding what to do and changing into outdoor clothing. As a visitor, I was assigned the task of taking

Rhea, my elderly hostess, across the drifted snowy walk space that separates her house from that of her grandson, son of the stricken woman, and
his family. By this time, Rhea had changed into a yellow-flowered calico
parka and had her purse and her cane in hand. Together we made our
way between the two houses as Marina took the granddaughter-in-law's
three-wheeler to the beach. I could see other machines racing across the
snow and gravel from all corners of the village, converging somewhere
along the north corner of the beach below the mountain. The sky was a
deep thick gray stretching from horizon to horizon, giving no hint of the
day to follow.

At one end of the village, the prom was beginning to go full force.
Dozens of children played on the steep-sloped, corrugated iron rooftops
of the laundry buildings near the high school. It was May and already the
nights were shorter. At that time, Sara's daughter-in-law was in her ninth
month of pregnancy. She came outside in snow pants and T-shirt to call
loudly for her children to bring them inside. It was the first time I had
ever heard her raise her voice.

Three little girls gathered near the north entry to Rhea's house: two
great granddaughters of my hostess, one of them Sara's granddaughter,
and their close friend. Their talk turned to ghosts. The friend said that
they had one at home. They all agreed that there were ghosts on Sivuqaq
Mountain that could be heard and sometimes seen. In the discussion that
followed, the two little girls assured the young granddaughter that her
very dear grandmother would be an angel if she was indeed dead. I
brought the girls inside and gave them tea and toast. It would become the
first of many feeding and baby-sitting tasks I carried out in the 36 hours
after Sara was found.

Between 10:30 and 11:00 P.M., the prom was dismissed. High schoolers
with bags of dress-up clothes trudged sadly through the snow. One of
Sara's nieces, who had spent the day decorating the gymnasium, came in
with her boyfriend, weighted down with the knowledge that her aunt
might be dead. Finally, Marina returned, saying that Sara had been
brought to the clinic. There was prayer and then Marina sent home
many of the children who had gathered in the house. From time to time
she went next door to check on her mother. Long after midnight, following the arrival of a doctor from the mainland, Sara was declared officially

dead. We received the news first from a niece and then from Marina; again, there was much prayer.

Some time during the long night that followed, Marina and I dragged mattresses from the bedrooms into the living room so that we might all sleep together. No one wanted to be alone. Much later still, I found myself wondering what it would have been like had this tragedy occurred in 1887 instead of 1987. Would we have gathered in fear of the spirit of the deceased? Would all normal activities have stopped? Who would have cared for Sara's poor body? Or would she have been left there on the cold shore ice?

In the morning, very shortly I found myself alone with children. Briefly one or another of Marina's nephews and nieces came in and left again. Marina went to the clinic, where women of Pugughileghmiit, and especially the extended family of John, Sara's husband, had gathered to dress the body. Eventually, she was warmly dressed in new long underwear, warm new pants, parka, and other clothing. When she was finally dressed, she was taken home wrapped in a large tan blanket and laid carefully on a single iron bedstead with a red, plastic rose placed across her bosom. Men gathered in the church to construct the plywood coffin, and her oldest son carved the cross bearing her name and the dates of her birth and death to be affixed to the head of the coffin once it reached its final resting place.

Some of these events I know about only in their retelling. As they transpired, I was already engaged in one of the two tasks that were to occupy me most of the day. A constant stream of children collected in Rhea's house. They made pictures with crayons, talked, sat, drank "juice" (a term covering everything from Kool-aid to Tang to sweetened tea), ate pilot bread crackers, teased the dog tied up in her corner, and went back outside. These were Sara's grandchildren; their mothers and fathers and older brothers, sisters, aunts, and uncles had already gathered to mourn. As the number of visitors cycled in and out, I realized that I had become caretaker by default.

In the early afternoon, Marina returned and suggested that it was time to make up bread dough to be turned into "fry bread." As I fried the dough into individual doughnuts, others began to drift in—among them were some of Sara's sons and their girlfriends and two of her daughters.

Someone came to collect the first batch of bread. A nephew brought me more flour and, with the help of two of Sara's young granddaughters, I cooked more bread.

It became clear that the funeral would be that evening and that more and more people were gathering to keep company with Sara's husband at their home. The coffin was being finished in the church. Once, one of Sara's younger sons sat down to tell me that he suspected foul play in the death of his mother; there may have been someone or something supernatural seeking revenge on him and using his mother as the vehicle.

Finally, with a granddaughter as my guide, I made my way to the house of mourning with the last of the bread. The house was almost the last on the southwest side, facing the lake. A collection of snowmobiles and all-terrain vehicles were scattered around it in the snow. As we came into the entrance way, we passed through a small group of smokers. Coming into the house, I offered the container of still-warm bread to Marina, who had risen from the floor where she and others were seated quietly, eating reindeer ribs and walrus. It is not quite clear to me now who actually took the bread from my hands. I do know it was taken into the short section of the L-shaped room. This section held a number of women managing food and drink.

I could not tell what to do next. My young guide was already gravitating toward the food. I could see some of her cousins playing outside. A voice murmured a thank you for the bread. I heard a second comment about what a lot of bread I had made. Even as the bread was being put into a large bowl mixed with cookies and rolls, Marina told me to please come in, that there was a place for me right next to her mother on the seat by the window.

The funeral service was held in the late afternoon. It was powerful both in its restraint and in its emotion. Members of the family gathered in the front pews of the church. At their feet the coffin lay with Sara inside, dressed in the warm clothing donated by her closest friends and relatives. Behind the first rows, I sat with Rhea, who was, of course, Marina's mother and Sara's mother-in-law. She was grief stricken but restrained. As the brief funeral service came to an end, the powerful singing of hymns was accompanied by raised hands, signifying symbolic release and submission to the will of God. Afterward, the community paid its respects to the family.

Then, the coffin was tied securely to a large sled behind a snowmobile to be pulled up the long road to the graveyard.

Once the funeral service ended, the community escorted the deceased woman to the top of the mountain. I sat with my elderly hostess and many of Sara's grandchildren while the rest of the family joined the long procession that took the daughter-in-law to her final resting place on top of the bluff. There the bereaved said good-bye to her once again with Christian prayers and hymns atop the cold stony rise, a place where once only men were laid down. Her coffin was adorned with wreaths of plastic flowers, her name clearly marked upon the cross at the head of her coffin. Even today, coffins are placed, if possible, facing north. Around the coffin is built up a cradle of stones to keep it firmly ensconced in its place; the stones too are reminiscent of another time.

The second death, in 1987, was of Nathan Nakanek,[16] well known as a teacher in the elementary school. He had been employed for many years as a bilingual teacher's aide, first by the Bureau of Indian Affairs and, in 1987, by the Bering Strait School District. The students called him Mr. Nathan. By 1987 he was also becoming a respected elder in the community. For many years he had served as a Session elder in the Presbyterian church; he was a member of the Eskimo Walrus Commission and a former member of the Eskimo Whaling Commission. His wife, my friend Ruth, worked part-time as a translator for the Wycliffe Bible translation project. Husband and wife together were known as believers and generally described by others as devoted Christians. They had brought their five children up according to strict Christian principles and with a strong grounding in traditional practices. Ruth was known for her skill at splitting walrus hide for *angyapiget* and her work was in demand during the summer months. During my stay in Sivuqaq, Ruth was teaching her younger daughter the techniques for managing a traditional household. Nathan had trained his three sons in the methods of traditional hunters. At that time two of his sons were members of the high school wrestling team. Wrestling, a traditional athletic activity formerly used to resolve disputes, is extremely popular, not only on St. Lawrence Island but in

---

16. Pseudonym. This pseudonym was created originally for Nathan's life story, *Eskimo Boyhood* (Hughes 1974).

other Alaska Native communities as well. At the same time, Nathan's oldest son (and Nathan himself, at one time) was an active member of the Alaska Army National Guard. Both parents expressed great pride in their eldest son's achievements in the Guard. On Sundays, the whole family could be found in church.

In the winter of 1987, Ruth's father, Reuben, had died. He was the adopted son of a man who had been in his early life an accomplished shaman, but who became a Presbyterian in his later life. In fact, Ruth had been raised by her grandfather, and, in her own words, she had witnessed "frightening things" when she was young. According to some, Reuben had also "been bothered by" traditional spirits, although he was believed to have rejected them in his later years. One of my friends told me that she had once heard Reuben pray and that his prayers were really "good," that is, good in the sense of both Christian and strong.

Before Reuben died, he struggled in the last stages of a disease that seriously impaired his lungs. His labored breathing was undoubtedly painful. Smoke and smells bothered his breathing and no cooking was allowed in the house; thus, the women of the household cooked outside in the *saayguraaq* in temperatures well below zero. As Reuben's condition worsened and his physical suffering increased, he railed against the "new way," which prevented him from taking his own life and releasing him from pain. He spoke harsh words to Ruth, who for a time symbolized the restraints imposed by the new faith upon his suffering physical body.

The tensions surrounding the stages of Reuben's dying grew in the days before he succumbed. Everyone in the village knew that he had been extremely hard on his oldest daughter and had created emotional havoc among the other members of his family. He had never been known as a particularly peaceable man and it seemed his leave taking would be anything but quiet. Then, shortly before his death, Ruth came to him, prayed for him, and asked to sing to him. Remarkably, he agreed, and she sang "Amazing Grace," a hymn whose translation into Yupik, she explained to me, she had been "given by God" some years before. Ruth, with other close members of her family, prayed together to combat the fearful spirits that had gathered to harass her father in his last moments, when he was most vulnerable to the older forces that had once figured so prominently in his life. Through communal prayer the family created a "wall of peace" around the dying man. Even as he died, Ruth and the others could "feel" the spirits trying to cross the wall in a last attempt to wrest Reuben from God. And, in the end, Reuben remained peaceful, and according to Ruth, without pain and "happy in the Lord" until he died.

Reuben's funeral was a major event. As many as 300 people crowded the small church. The old man lay on a soft cushion in his new coffin, dressed in a warm parka, a cap on his head, and covered with new blankets, gifts from the many relatives who had come from Savoonga, Nome, Anchorage, and Fairbanks. He clutched a red plastic rose in one hand, which lay crossed with the other on his bosom. His funeral service, it soon became apparent, would be a platform for testifying to his final faithfulness; in death he would follow others who had placed their faith in the Lord. There would be no doubt as to the appropriateness of placing his Christian name on the cross soon to be firmly affixed to his casket when he reached his final destination on top of the mountain. He too would enter Heaven. The service lasted much of the afternoon as each relative got up to speak on his behalf. And, finally, at the end, his daughter Ruth stood up to sing "Amazing Grace" to him, a last farewell and a powerful statement of the relationship between traditional and Christian beliefs.

In the spring of 1988, just as the family was recovering from Reuben's death, the seemingly healthy Nathan was stricken with terminal cancer. In a matter of a few months, he was gone. In an attempt to prolong his life, he was flown to a mainland hospital and was no longer on the island when he died. I visited him before he was taken out to the hospital, and Ruth told me that he needed a cross. He had lost his cross on his travels as a whaling commissioner. Among the items I had brought to the island was a small pocket cross that had once belonged to my grandmother. I gave it to Nathan. Later, Ruth told me that it "had really helped him." When he died, it was sewn onto the outside of his *qiipghak* (parka cover) as a protective talisman and was buried with him. His body was flown back to the island to be buried.

Nathan's funeral, too, was a major event, but it was without inherent conflict. Wallace Ungwiluk, an elderly uncle of the deceased with much prestige in the community, was the first person to speak to Nathan's memory. After the elder had prepared the way, person after person got up to recall Nathan's faithfulness, to remember his many contributions to the community, or simply to reminisce about a particular moment when they had enjoyed Nathan's company. Anders Apassingok spoke of his many contributions to the children. The *laluramka* minister, Agnes Brady, described Nathan in her brief sermon as one of the most saintly men she had known. Ruth's impassioned statement stood out from the rest. She began by thanking God for imposing the pain that both Nathan and the family had had to bear. She compared the wrenching apart of man and woman joined together to the separation felt by God at the loss of Jesus. She spoke of her husband's suffering and death, but said she believed him to be in heaven resurrected. She assured the congregation that in spite of this terrible pain inflicted upon her by the Lord, she had not given up her faith. Then she tried to encourage the congregation in their own faith, promising to continue to proclaim the gospel over the CB radio when the men were out hunting in the boats.

As the service drew to a close, the congregation began to sing hymns that Nathan had liked, volunteering song after song as if reluctant to relinquish him. Arms were raised high over heads as the congregation symbolically surrendered both themselves and Nathan to Apa's will. Finally, it was time to load his coffin onto a large sled, attached to two snowmobiles, and the long funeral procession set off through the snow. One of Nathan's cousins held a large wreath. Nathan's wife and son held the cross with his name on it. When the procession reached the top of Sivuqaq Mountain, the final words were said by the minister after the coffin had been carefully placed by Nathan's relatives. The cross bearing his Christian (English) name was nailed to one end of the coffin, and the flowers were firmly attached so that the strong winds that sweep across the bluff, which holds many centuries of the community's dead, could not dislodge them. Quietly, the procession reversed its direction, following the long, sloping path that comes round at last to the south end of Naayvaq. It was almost dark, and the lights of the snowmobiles marked the return of the funeral party once more to the village.

A few days after Nathan's death, Ruth carefully gathered up all of his clothes and took them outside, where she burned them. While Nathan's soul had found rest with God, protection was still needed to assure that the spirit associated with death did not return unheralded and unwelcome to take up residence in Nathan's house or to disturb Nathan's family, drawn by his once-familiar garments.

The story of Nathan and Ruth illustrates the power that Christianity holds for individuals in the community and the depth of its influence on their understanding of life and death. At the same time, Ruth and others have accepted that certain protections must be taken against the older powers, which might take advantage of the unwary person. Thus, traditional beliefs and newfound faith together are employed to assure the spiritual and physical safety and success of the Sivuqaghhmiit.

Nathan's life in many ways epitomized the values that the Sivuqaghhmiit hold most dear. He was passionately attached to his island. He was a skilled and enthusiastic hunter. He expected his wife and family to fulfill the obligations of persons for whom family and clan come first. He believed that many of the traditional rules such as those involving formal marriage exchange, groom's work, and absolute respect for elders should be maintained. He extolled the virtues of traditional meat-sharing practices and believed they should be continued. He was mindful of the many forces in the environment that can plague a man and his family if he fails to respect the subsistence creatures on whom they depend for food.

As one who had received a bride from a family once known for its powerful shamans, he was aware of the dangers that the spirit world holds. He chose, as have many in the community, to turn his life over to Apa in His Christian form, relying totally on the mercy of Apa, on Jesus, and on the visitation of the Holy Spirit to protect him and his family from attack from the more equivocal of the traditional powers. Thus the faith that he professed included within it an acknowledgment of the traditional spirit world but at the same time accepted the proposition that these spirits were ultimately subject to Apa's power. The Apa in whom Nathan placed his faith was the personalized Apa of the New Testament.

Nathan, like others in the community, took pride in his Sivuqaq identity and heritage. As a bilingual aide in the elementary school, he actively promoted his native language and culture among the next generation. He took his role as subsistence hunter seriously also, teaching his sons the necessary skills at home and fulfilling his obligations as an elected member of the Eskimo Whaling Commission in the outside world. Like other respected whalers in the community, he had traveled to other parts of Alaska in connection with his duties. In his travels, he carried a Bible and a small cross for purposes of protection and meditation.

6.3 *Shortly after the death of Ruth's husband, Nathan, his family "got" a whale. As a reminder, this mandible rests near the house of Ruth's relative.*

As he lay near death, he told his wife that life would still hold many pleasures for her. Apa would see to that. That spring, following his death, his relatives took a whale and his wife served traditionally prepared *nunivak*, frozen sour greens mixed with seal oil, to those who gathered to wait. When I spoke to Ruth that night on the beach, she repeated that the Lord would provide for her and that Nathan had known this, too. The gift of the whale, symbolic of the traditional past, is considered the finest of the gifts that Apa bestows. Thus, Ruth understood that when Nathan comforted her before his death he must have had in mind, or perhaps have envisioned, this great presentation of food, whose harvest is only possible through the combined efforts of all members of the family, an effort in which her own sons, their uncles, and their cousins would be the major actors.

CHAPTER 7

A Religious World View

In Gambell, all institutions and occupations—birth, naming, marriage, death, care of the sick and injured, and traditional and non-traditional work—embrace some form of religious thought and practice.[1] At its heart are the deep religious philosophies and concepts that have supported people in the community over the last 150 to 200 years. It is a world view divided between older traditional religious concepts and more recent religious concepts. The former concepts depend on ancient teachings about the ancestors and the spirits present in the environment. The latter concepts depend on experience with Protestant Christian teachings since the end of the nineteenth century. Together, these concepts center on several related and articulated systems of religious thought and behavior. At the base are the enduring principles and practices known informally as "respect for the elders." Both Christian tradition and Yupik tradition rest on a reverence for the elder. This includes elder thought, elder persons, and that which is metaphorically elder, that is, Apa or God.[2] Spiritual and physical kinship join in religious concept and practice here.

As the most important members of the physical community in Gambell today, elders are celebrated in the dance songs and praise songs to which women dance when the voices of men and drums blend together, recalling songs once "given" to a father, grandfather, or great-grandfather. They are celebrated in the birthday parties prepared for elders to honor the return and rebirth into the community of a name whose presence

---

1. Portions of this chapter appeared originally in Jolles 1989 and 1990.
2. The long form of Apa is *Apaghllak* or possibly *Apaghyughluq*, the great-grand-father.

7.1 *Women dance at one of many community celebrations, 1997.*

evokes the history and memories of all those who once bore the name. They are celebrated in quiet summer picnics when families travel to the top of Sivuqaq Mountain to repair the coffins of the deceased, to place new memorial wreaths, and to pray together in remembrance of the departed; they are celebrated through traditional dance festivals held in their honor in the high school gymnasium, Qerngughvik, and the City Building. Elders themselves offer thankful prayers when the community takes a whale, and they supervise the important distribution of whale meat and *mangtak* in the festival atmosphere that prevails on the beach once a whale has been brought to shore. When marriage ceremonies begin, elders most often deliver the speeches. They invoke Apa, the most powerful elder of all, God, the grandfather, the Creator, whose presence is at the core of respect for elders and the honoring of ancestors who once graced the community and whose name and spiritual being remain.

Ultimately, the religious system rests on Apa, once personified in two separate spiritual forms. Apaghllak is described as unreachable, remote, judgmental, generous, and unknowable, while Kiyaghneq[3] is identified as the master of weather and creator of the world and of men. Possibly, in traditional thought, God, in his Kiyaghneq aspect, was the creator of animals—walrus, whales, and seals. As I noted in Chapter 3, ancient stories handed on from Ungaziq on the eastern shore of Siberia suggest that Kiyaghneq was once thought of as a giant, colossal figure, who created the island from the squeezed-out sediments of the sea's bottom grounds and, through his absentminded loss of his mittens, created humans—two men. Later, in response to the pleas of these first humans, he created female companions.

Today, under the multiple titles of Apaghllak, Kiyaghneq, Ulimaghista, and Ataneq, Apa is both God as described in the Bible and as described by elders, whose stories knit together older and newer understanding. It is clear, however, that Apa is ultimately a father, whose generosity in allowing his son to give his life for humans is overwhelmingly appreciated here, in a world where the deeds of men on the ice provide food for families and the loss of a hunter-son is an immeasurable loss. Out of respect and awe,

3. See C. Hughes (1959) for a translation of Voblov's descriptions of Kiyaghneq in Siberian Yupik society.

Apa is addressed humbly and in purity of thought. Much ceremonial life was directed toward Apa in the past; today, in the conventional prefabricated buildings where most Gambell folk now live, people continue to speak to Apa in daily prayers given at meals, whenever a family member is confronted by illness or other threats, and whenever men at sea face the dangers that northern hunters have always faced.

Viewed from the outside, an implicit religious or spiritual perspective seems to support most contemporary life in Gambell. That perspective derives from an ancient tradition in which the networks of ties among land, subsistence, and family—those championed by the Alaska Federation of Natives—continue to be central. Religious life in the community includes both the old and the new, that which characterizes a primarily Yupik world and the contemporary global system within which the community is situated. While many if not most folks in Gambell identify themselves as Christian, it is also true that the present form of Christian thought and behavior is built upon the older religious system that was shaped by religious concepts derived from an unpredictable environment and a dependence on subsistence hunting. The place of tradition within the contemporary community remains strong and tradition serves as a continuing source of moral strength and values.

In the late nineteenth century and perhaps before, a tri-part religious philosophy supported the various settlements on St. Lawrence Island. One aspect was a well known and perhaps quite ancient attention to family, both living and deceased. Most evident were the attention and respect owed to ancestors and to elders, whose age and wisdom set them apart from others. Less obvious perhaps was the parallel attention and recognition given to newborn children. All ceremonial life included ceremonies that marked humans' entry into and exit from the Yupik world. Paralleling this system of respect was a spiritual hierarchy with Apa at its apex. Apa was a patriarchal figure of superabiding strength and supernatural power who was responsible for all life, for the weather, for the seasons, and, indirectly, for the appearance or absence of animals.

Precontact religious belief and practice on St. Lawrence Island drew also on a well-known shamanic tradition prevalent across Native North America and Northeast Asia. Belief in a world filled with spirits was at its base. Manipulation of those spirits through the intercession of an *alig-*

nalghii was but one aspect of it. According to the men and women consulted by Otto Geist in the 1920s and 1930s and by Alexander and Dorothea Leighton (DLC 1982) in the summer of 1940, imploring spirits of various sorts constituted much of the religious activity on St. Lawrence Island and took a number of forms. In some cases, invoking spirits occurred within the family, in others it was a matter of individual choice, and on still other occasions it was the special function of a shaman. The kinds of spirits approached were quite various as well. Although it is no longer possible to reconstruct in its entirety the cosmology of this earlier religious tradition, due both to the loss of knowledge of some earlier practices and to the discomfort that some elderly members of the community express when called upon to speak of it, it is possible to suggest its general form and the identity of some of its actors.

At the zenith of the supernatural realm, as noted above, was a being considered at the time to be two separate and powerful figures, Apa and Kiyaghneq, who perhaps were two facets of the same being or deity; it is difficult to know.[4] In mainland Alaska and Canada, one powerful, male spiritual being was thought to control the weather or air and land mammals, often from a home in the moon, and a female spirit being controlled the sea mammals from a place of seclusion under the sea. On St. Lawrence Island, men and women acknowledged Apa/Kiyaghneq as the most important spiritual being, and he took precedence over all else. Other spiritual beings held in their hands the responsibilities for the commonplace activities of land and sea mammals. On the one hand, a keeper of game beneath the sea does appear in some stories, but seems much less important than on the mainland. In island stories, on the other hand, there were beings or forces known for their important local tasks: they managed the animals on which each individual *ramka* community depended for subsistence. Thus, when male walrus gathered on the north side of the island, they were under the local jurisdiction of a male walrus spirit, an old man. When female walrus collected on the south side, they were under the control of an elderly female spirit, an old woman. Consistent with concepts of respectful and careful relations among humans and

4. Presumably Apa originally corresponded to similar beings noted across mainland Alaska. See, for example, George Marsh (1954) and Margaret Lantis (1947) for discussion of Eskimo religious life.

the animals on whom they depended for food, respectful behavior was required whenever humans encountered seals, walrus, whales, and polar bears. Fox spirits too were given respectful treatment, although they were apparently regarded with some ambivalence. Unlike other creatures whose contributions to subsistence were of major importance and whose spirit nature or spirit state was regarded as positive and powerful, fox spirits were unpredictable. Some said they were sought by *alignalghiit* to assist in the difficult tasks of managing the health and social well-being of families. Consistent with the patrilineal and hierarchical nature of St. Lawrence Island society, Apa exercised power over all, including humans.

In addition to major spirits defined by their animal representatives, there were said to be numerous spirits, both good and evil, that frequented the island in the settlements and out on the tundra. Care was taken not to disturb them, or, alternatively, to make use of them after a specific encounter in a dream or vision. Along with animal spirits and the undefined spirits mentioned above, the spirits of the dead were a presence in the community and great care was taken to feed them and to include them in all celebrations. If dissatisfied, they could cause endless hardship. Thus, they were fed and addressed at regular intervals, both publicly and privately. Each spirit of a major type was worthy of ceremony. If elders' recollections recorded in 1940 (Dorothea Leighton, M.D., Collection 1982) and Paul Silook's words (see Dr. Otto W. Geist Collection c. 1916–1961) are any indication of older traditions, then religious performance was an important feature of daily life.

Paul Silook, James Aningayou, and others discussed local religious ideas and practices with Henry Collins in 1928. (In fact, Silook and Collins became good friends and corresponded with each other after Collins left the island.) Collins wrote down these notes one night after talking with the two men:

> Spirits of health and sickness *To ho na hat*—spirits which cause sickness and death. Not spirits of dead persons. There are two kinds of these spirits, one good & one bad—The former are guardian or tutelary spirits, teaching the people certain ceremonies, and appear to them in dreams in which they advise action to be taken along various lines, bring success in hunting, wealth, etc. The evil influence of the latter are averted thru sacrifices made to them at the ceremonies.

Spirit categories: Sorcerers have some of the *To ho na hat* as helpers. Some have also spirits of dead persons and of animals. When a person dies his spirit (*tagh ha nagh hot*) turns into a bodyless [*sic*] spirit (*to ho na hat*). . . . Dead persons' spirit or soul become a "*to ho na hat*" but a good one, one that does not work evil on the people. A man not a sorcerer may also seek the assistance of spirits, going to some secluded place and waiting for the arrival of a "good"—*to ho no hat*—a good one always appears from in front or from the right: a bad one from behind or from the left. On its appearance the person might become unconscious and during this state would receive instructions from the spirit to perform some ceremony, how to treat a sick person, what payment to receive. This latter is illustrated in the payment given the shaman which is always a stipulated amount of certain things, always the same. If there is variance from this the shaman's helper would cause his (the shaman's) death. (Henry Bascom Collins Collection 1982)

Probably the most important religious cycle focused on bowhead whales. It featured rituals to honor the spirit of whales taken the previous spring and included prayers to Apa or Kiyaghneq. The prayers ensured that the whales would return. They[5] were performed regularly by each *ramka* group.[6]

Much has changed in the last several hundred years. Nevertheless, whaling ceremonies together form the most complex religious cycle and still provide the most obvious traditional symbols of identity. Similar ceremonies were performed around the taking of polar bears that had offered themselves to hunters, but they were not so elaborate or so regularly performed. In the spring of 1988, as she sat with Lucy Apatiki and me in

---

5. Hunters today sometimes have thanksgiving feasts before the whaling season begins. These same men are devout Christians. Parallels to ceremonies once held on St. Lawrence Island occurred in Russian Yupik settlements in Chukotka. Russian Eskimos recommenced traditional whaling only after a long hiatus. Russian Natives were given official permission to whale in the fall of 1989 (Arutiunov, personal communication, 1989). Russian Yupik whalers continue to observe some older ceremonies.

6. The constitution of these groups and their counterparts on the Russian shore as patriclans distinguishes Asian Yupik societies from other Yupik and Inuit societies. (See Moore 1923; C. Hughes 1958a; Fitzhugh 1988; Krauss 1988; Jorgensen 1990; Schweitzer 1989, 1992; and Krupnik 1983 for further discussion.)

7.2 *My friend Mary's little boy poses with the head and skin of a polar bear taken by his father.*

Lucy's home, elder Doris Uglowook described what she remembered of polar bear ceremonies that had been performed in her childhood. We had just finished eating a delicious meal which Lucy had prepared featuring frozen clams taken recently from a walrus stomach, *manguna* (walrus meat), and frozen *ququngaq* (willow leaves). Before Doris spoke, we stopped quietly so that Doris could pray. She felt safer talking about the past after she had prayed.

DORIS: When a person got a polar bear, the people would come and congratulate him and gather together and tell stories and that is the way they would express their joy.

LUCY: Did they do anything special with the polar bear after he was killed?

DORIS: They might have done something with the heads—when we went to the place where they made the sacrifices there were a lot of polar bear heads and I can't tell if it's the same altar they used for the whale or it's different. (Uglowook 1988, in Jolles 1987ff)

Polar bear heads were brought into the home, symbolically fed, and entertained with stories for three to five days. Walruses received similar treatment. The taking of walrus and polar bears was celebrated with other ceremonies, too, including annual religious services to give thanks for having received these animals as well as the careful, respectful disposal of their skulls that Doris described. Bones of seals were returned to the sea. Some families were known to have special relationships with certain animals. In such cases, the family might have a ceremony, which was used to confirm that relationship and to ensure that the animals would come to that family. In the following example, Silook describes to Alexander Leighton[7] a ceremony belonging to Iyakitan's family, which was used to bring in walruses:

LEIGHTON: What about *Terre sek?*

PAUL: That means something like Calling in Sea Animals. Simply means so everybody can have good luck. . . . Aiyakitan (Iyakitan) held this ceremony. There was nothing decorated for it in the house, only he has one of these dippers filled with salt water, and he has his harpoon and its head; something like ready to strike, he put the head right on the harpoon. He took that harpoon to the shore in the evening and set it upright in the gravel, and leave it there. Then he let some of guests make a walrus hide tube, about

7. Alexander Leighton interviewed the men in summer 1940, and his wife, Dorothea, interviewed the women. The Leightons later divorced, but in 1940 they were still married. Thus Alexander Leighton interviewed Paul Silook, James Aningayou, and Jimmy Otiyohok (C. Hughes, personal communication, 1990).

two or three inches in diameter. Then during the night he sings, sings about these sea animals. You know, some of the songs has words about walrus, and the grunt is in the song. As soon as he mentions that word, we put that tube into our mouths and begin to grunt like the walrus. The next morning he stays indoors, facing toward the sea. They said that the first evening the worshippers were supposed to go into the water to bring all the female walrus near the land. The worshipper never lies down to sleep; he just sits and sleeps there.

LEIGHTON: What does he do at the sea to bring in the female walrus?

PAUL: He goes just to the beach and he thinks that his spirit will go out and get the female walrus and bring them in.

LEIGHTON: What does he do when at the beach?

PAUL: Just he goes and shakes that harpoon. He thinks that when the walrus see it they might come. Then every evening he sings. Every time when he is to sing he brings that dipper filled with salt water and puts it by him. That dipper is always set in the outer room, in the center of the big room. . . . This dipper is covered with a piece of intestine; . . . when he brings that dipper into the inner room, the cover is removed. Then he sings. . . . he believes that dipper filled with water will shine clear to the bottom of the sea, something like dig a hole in the earth clear to the bottom of the sea. And also any person that is going to have some kind of trouble, will show himself in that dipper of salt water. The worshipper does that about ten days, facing toward the sea; sleeping while he is sitting. Then at the end of ten days he goes out in the evening with his dipper and pours that salt water away, and fills the dipper with fresh salt water. . . . Ten days he faces the sea, west, never goes out doors in the daytime. On the eleventh night he turns toward the east. The idea is that while he is facing toward the west, his what you call imagination is that he is travelling out from the land. Then on the eleventh night he turns toward the east, he believes he is turning now toward the land. . . . I heard that this ceremony was inherited from their ancestors. . . . I heard that one of their ancestors often goes with the female walrus, every fall, and

then comes up in the spring when the female walrus comes up to
the north. Then after several years his people can see hair growing
from his body. Then perhaps two or three springs after that they
never see him any more. So when Aiyakitan's people were living,
they were the best walrus hunters. (Silook, DLC 1982:72–73)

A second group of ceremonies focused on the welfare of ancestors. According to present-day elders, these ceremonies took place annually in
summer and included food offerings and general feasting. At other times
during the year, respect was paid sporadically through individual and lineage offerings made simply by calling upon the ancestors in question and
either tossing the food into the air or placing it in the fire. Paying respect
to ancestors occurred in several contexts, both in conjunction with hunting or procuring good fortune and in other enterprises that could assure
that the spirits of the dead would remain satisfied with their lot. Here,
Paul Silook describes a hunting ceremony:

> In summer my mother gathered some greens and filled a seal
> poke. First she fermented it in a barrel, let it get very sour, then
> put the greens in a poke, and put this poke up on the rack. . . .
> Then in time, when the Siberian people come around here my fa-
> ther gets some deer fat, especially the internal fat of the deer. . . .
> When he buys a box of tobacco he saves a pound of that, too. In
> time of cod fishing, he dried some up and save them for that pur-
> pose. So he waits for the time. Also he saves some green extract, for
> another little ceremony, which takes place in November. So when
> he start, in November, to have this little ceremony I go with him
> to the boat. He opened this, the other poke—sometimes my
> mother fill two pokes—then when he open the poke, he cut little
> pieces from the contents of the poke, and we go to the boat to-
> gether. This takes place in the mornings. He has a little wooden
> cup. He puts the green into this cup. Then he begins to sacrifice
> by the boat. The way he sacrifices, he just throw little pieces up
> into the air. First, he name the name of the moon, then afterward
> while he throw little pieces, he name some of the old people that
> have died. This means it will bring him good luck during the win-
> ter. (Silook, DLC 1982:28–29)

Still other ceremonies were meant to keep sickness away, to protect families in times of hunger, or simply to thank the spirits when the family had survived a time of hardship. Such ceremonies could extend over five years, with the giving of gifts to invited guests who had been asked to participate in the ceremonies. These ceremonies, which involved many people, might end with the exchange of women by men who had formal trading partnerships with one another (see Silook, DLC 1982:67–70). Silook recorded several ceremonial exchange scenarios. Another, quoted in Chapter 6 (pp. 174–75), had as its objective the prevention of family misfortune, including hunger and illness.

Many other shorter ceremonies were also performed. These depended on the visions or dreams of a single person, usually a man, and, rather than appearing with slight variation within every lineage, were usually performed only by the man and his family or lineage. Beyond all such ritual performances were acts to secure or restore health with the assistance or involvement of a shaman.[8] And, finally, extremely involved ceremony surrounded the disposal of the dead.

These ceremonies and many others divide into several categories. First, there were the ceremonies of thankfulness performed out of respect and gratitude for the marine mammals that people hunted every year such as whales, polar bears, walrus, and seals. There were annual and periodic prayers and ceremonies held to pay respect to ancestors (usually in the form of inviting the ancestors to partake in specially prepared foods given them through the transforming faculties of fire), and there were many smaller ceremonies that marked unanticipated but commonly experienced events within the family, such as birth, naming of a child, first contributions of game and vegetable foods, killing of a whale or polar bear, marriage, death, and disposal of the dead. In times of need, separate ceremonies and prayers dealt with extreme hardships such as severe weather, war, sickness, and famine. Most ceremonies were performed either by individual households or by members of the same lineage or *ramka*. The ceremonies belonged to the families involved and were most often directed and carried out by lineage heads or boat captains and their

---

8. For an extensive discussion of shaman types and shamanic performance, see J. Hughes 1960; Murphy 1964.

wives. In times of trouble, the ceremonies and prayers were more likely to be conducted by a shaman and, depending on the seriousness and extent of the emergency, might even be performed for the entire *ramka*, rather than within the family. Often, husbands and their wives were the most important actors. In times of trouble, however, a shaman was called upon because of his or her special powers.[9]

In most cases, religious practices involved invoking, addressing, and appeasing spirits, which were thought to be everywhere in the Sivuqaghhmiit world. Supplicants tried to placate spirit presences, to acquire spirit assistance or power, and to manipulate the spirits across a somewhat random cosmological spectrum. Researchers found the spiritual world in Sivuqaq confusing.[10] To a degree, cosmology appeared as a two-tiered structure, in which ". . . lesser spirits underpin events and processes in the microcosm of the local community and its environment, whilst the supreme being underpins events and processes in the macrocosm—i.e., in the world as a whole" (Horton 1975:219). However, Estelle Oozebaseuk recalled in 1992 that as a little girl, an elderly relative tried to heal her after donning special gloves so that she could pray to the spirits of the third heaven. Estelle did not know exactly what the spirits of the third heaven were, but the concept of multiple heavens seems to suggest that traditional thought embraced a complex religious universe whose dimensions are now lost or have been absorbed into contemporary religious thought. A more general relationship between the spiritual and physical worlds is accepted today. In 1940, Paul Silook and Alexander Leighton discussed the important role played by animals in human survival, the re-

9. See, for example, Moore 1923; "Notebooks of Paul Silook," in Dr. Otto W. Geist Collection c. 1916–61; C. Hughes 1953, 1959, 1960; DLC 1982; Apassingok et al. 1985, 1987, 1989.

10. Both Alexander and Dorothea Leighton (in C. Hughes 1953) and Charles Hughes (1953) saw little structure in island cosmological concepts. Hughes thought that an overriding concern with spiritual solutions to imminent physical dangers had kept the islanders from formulating an elaborate cosmology. I believe that a definite cosmological structure is evident and that cosmological concepts on the island reflect the general egalitarianism of northern foraging communities and the island's patrilineage system, in which elder men figure importantly. The two structures are interwoven in traditional cosmology.

spectful treatment of the animals that Apa required, and the consequences if Apa's demands were disregarded.

> LEIGHTON: What makes the rheumatism here?
>
> PAUL: These animals are somewhat harmful. People think that if they do not treat them correctly, then the giver of the animal will cause this kind of harm.
>
> LEIGHTON: What is the giver?
>
> PAUL: The giver is God. People especially call it Grandfather, and the Maker.
>
> LEIGHTON: Three different spirits?
>
> PAUL: All one spirit.
>
> LEIGHTON: What connection has this God with the moon?
>
> PAUL: In the story, I heard that the moon is in the house of God. There is a little house in the center of the main big house, where no one ever peeps in. But once a stranger who was forbidden did peep in, and saw half a little woman, half all the way down [indicates a longitudinal section], scraping a deerskin. God was away from his house, but even while he was away he realized that things were happening there. That stranger caused a moon eclypse [*sic*], by trying to peep in. (Silook, DLC 1982:167)

In most instances, religious life was concerned with the community's most basic needs: food, shelter, harmonious relations within households and *ramka*, and health. Calling on the major spirit beings appears to have occurred particularly during times of trouble and in thankfulness once trouble had passed. Apa was invoked as part of the whaling ceremonies and in times of extraordinary hardship. In the example below, Lincoln Blassi, one of the last men to practice the whaling rites, describes them. They differ little from earlier descriptions recorded by Voblov (C. Hughes 1959) and Otto Geist.

> We are going to talk about whaling time. Every time a hunter strikes a whale, the boat captain gives a whale-catch cry that sounds like this, "*Wu-hu-hu-hu-humeng!*" When this was done, the other boats would come and the crews would start working on the whale, some attaching the tow line, others cutting a token share of *mangtak* [skin with blubber].

They then attached a pair of sealskin pokes to both the front and back end of the whale. When they started the towing the whole crew of the boat that caught the whale would give the whale-catch cry together, "*Wu-hu-hu-hu-humeng!*" They did this again halfway home and just before they landed.

When they landed, they worked on the whale. The boat captain would get the first share of *mangtak* and fill a fresh sealskin poke with it.

The captain who caught the whale would then take the baleen from one side of the jaw. The baleen from the other side of the jaw was given to the captains of the boats which harpooned the whale the second and third time. Some of the remaining baleen was given as a gift to village elders and women of the captain's clan.

From the time of the kill on, the boat captain and the striker wore a sealskin visor. When the work on the whale was finished, the striker would cut a small piece of *mangtak* (for ceremonial purposes), and take this along with the steering oar and the killing spear to the captain's home.

The steering oar was stuck in the snow in front of the captain's house, paddle side up and slanted toward the ocean. The killing spear was strapped upright to the north side of the doorway.

During the previous summer the boat captain's family had gathered roseroot and packed it in a sealskin poke. In the winter, the top part of the frozen roseroot poke was cut off and buried in the snow for use in the whaling festivities.

Now this special portion of roseroot was brought into the captain's house and cut up into bite-size pieces equal to the number of the crew still waiting at the boat. Meantime, the captain's wife would take a tuft of reindeer neck hair and tie it onto her braid [as a symbol of the whale taken]. Some of the roseroot with blubber was cut up for the crew, some was put with a little water in a small pail made of wood or baleen. Then the captain's wife would take this down to the beach.

Meantime, the boat captain and the striker would fetch paddles from the boat rack on their way back to the boat. When they got in the boat, they drew the bow right up tight against the ice where the captain's wife stood facing the boat.

Then they rocked the boat five times from side to side. After the fifth time, the captain and striker raised their paddles to one side—the wife held up the small pail to the same side—and gave the whale-catch cry.

Then they did the same thing again, but on the other side of the boat.

The cry was "*Wu-hu-hu-hu-humeng!*" Then they would take a portion of the whale's tail, right at the back crease, about half a foot wide and two feet long, and fastened it to the bow of the boat. Then the wife splashed a little water from the pail on it and handed the pail to the striker.

The striker took his share of the roseroot and the blubber, took a drink of the water, then passed the pail on to the rest of the crew until everyone had tasted of it. The captain was the last one to take his share.

When this was finished the striker would take the striking harpoon and throw it into the snow between the feet of the captain's wife. I myself have done that four times, so I too have had that experience. (Blassi, in Apassingok et al. 1985:217–219)

Kiyaghneq, who is addressed in the prayers cited above, is almost synonymous with life itself.[11] Such prayers were usually made without actually giving his name, out of extreme respect; it is as if the prayer were directed into a void, or were mediated through a particular sea mammal, especially the whale. This seems to be the case in these prayers, excerpted from Blassi, "Prayer Song Asking for a Whale":

The time is almost here.
The season of the deep blue sea . . .
Bringing good things from the deep blue sea.
Whale of distant ocean . . .
May there be a whale.
May it indeed come . . .
Within the waves (Apassingok et al. 1985:215)

The same prayer was repeated for bearded seals and perhaps for other sea mammals as well. According to Blassi, "The boat captain would sing these songs in such a low reverent voice that you could hardly make out the words. Especially before the whaling season began, the songs of petition were sung to God in a prayerful pleading voice" (Apassingok et al. 1985: 215). Elders' descriptions of the relationship between man and God seem to parallel the patrilineal configuration of family groups and each lineage's

---

11. The word *kiyaghneq*, when used in the lowercase, can be translated as "to be, to live, way of life, and to support or provide for" (Jacobson 1987:101).

7.3 *Clan members work long hours to butcher a bowhead whale more than fifty feet in length.*

view of itself as a separate ethnic entity, with its own rites and spiritual relationships.[12]

The power that individuals acquired through establishment of a spirit assistant relationship was theoretically open to all. Some regard this type of relationship as a connection with intangible powers ultimately subject to Apa. Others understand it to be contrary to the wishes of God and church. In practice, the act of taking a spirit into oneself (*tughnegh-nakutqa*)[13] was reserved for those strong ones, such as active hunters and shamans, who needed added power to hunt or to heal. Family cere-

12. Boat captains were early converts to Christianity. They sought new power to employ in the business of survival. Today, they are often elders in the two churches.
13. Spelling of this word is not certain.

monies pacified spirits that might harm individual family members and did not necessarily require a spirit assistant relationship.

Elders described communication with Apa through a spiritual intermediary as an institutionalized feature of Sivuqaq life. Such communication was effected through offerings and rites directed toward God himself as well as to the most noble of the subsistence creatures. "Showing" the offerings to Apa, which were intended for ceremonial use following the taking of a whale, was a characteristic of several clan whaling rites. Boat crews "told" Apa that they had taken a whale while still at sea, using formal rituals and prayers such as those described by Blassi.

These ceremonies are difficult to analyze today. There is no consensus about the meanings of the ancestors' actions. One interpretation is that all actions not directed specifically to Apa were inspired by and meant to pacify the devil. For this reason, many are reluctant to speak about shamans, because they regularly dealt with so many spirits. A second interpretation is that offerings to various animals and ancestral spirits were made in order to keep from offending Apa and to avoid disobeying his rules. A third suggests that such marks of respect, seemingly directed toward subsistence creatures and other spiritual forms, were a way of thanking Apa without speaking to him directly, an abstract spiritual teknonymy, if you will. Christianity has played a role here and traditional beliefs are understood differently now than they were in the past.

Because the Sivuqaq nonempirical world was filled with spirit entities, life itself seemed to be hemmed in by spirit encounters. Since illness and hunger were the most pressing concerns, each *ramka* utilized a wide variety of religious activities to prevent them. Individuals also had rituals and prayers that had come to them in the form of dream or spirit visitations that were used to avert illness and hunger.

Only a very few stories describe misuse of spiritual powers, or witchcraft, although several elders agreed that certain persons did engage in these dangerous practices. Fear of witchcraft may even have accounted for the extreme care that people took always to appear on good terms with others, especially elders. A common form of witchcraft was to obtain some item associated intimately with another, such as hair, a piece of clothing, et cetera, and to deposit the item in the place reserved for disposal of the dead, under a skull. When the item had completely decomposed, the victim would die. Estelle, who always managed to find a way to get into trouble when she was a little girl, recalls going with one of her siblings to the graveyard and removing some remnants of cloth or hair from underneath skulls. She wondered ever after who the victims were meant to be and whether she would become a target for having interfered. Murphy (1964) also recorded examples of shamans who were tempted to cause harm rather than good with the help of their spirit assistant (*tughneghaq*). Once done, according to tradition, the shaman was then unable to reverse the process. This practice is not necessarily witchcraft but simply malevolent behavior (or sorcery), according to my consultants. Some believe that a skeleton uncovered by archaeologist Hans-Georg Bandi was the body of such a person. As the story goes, the community tried to kill this dangerous man, shooting him or spearing him at least sixteen times. He was finally vanquished when urine was spread in a circle around him, effectively disarming the power of his spirit assistants. Up until that moment, each time he was shot, he would simply get up again. As noted earlier, present-day accusations of witchcraft seemed to occur within a Christian context and apparently referred to those who perhaps willingly consorted with the devil, a concept introduced by Christianity. Formerly, spirits were considered variously good, evil, or simply unpredictable. Today, people recognize an undetermined number of spirits as the earthly manifestations of Satan.

Death itself was regarded differently before conversion to Christianity. At one time, for example, suicide was relatively common.[14] Today, those who choose to take their own lives are regarded with tremendous sadness. The Christian view of the sanctity of life is nowhere more evident than it is when community members must reflect upon a life ended prematurely. In the early 1900s, however, suicide was used to save the life of a child and was also an acceptable way to leave this life. In other words, suicide was both a way to end life and a way to cure. According to tradition, those who died a violent death would find themselves in a slightly more comfortable afterlife than those who died through ordinary means. At

14. See Alexander Leighton's interviews with island men in 1940 (DLC 1982) and Leighton and Hughes (1955). See also the description, "Putting an End to Life," by Estelle Oozevaseuk in Apassingok et al. 1987:165–167.

least two afterlife dwelling places were thought to exist, one above the ground somewhere in the sky and one beneath the ground. Though similar, that under the ground was crowded and less pleasant than that above the ground.[15]

At the back of the village, near the foot of the mountain, was one of several spots known as a "destroying" place.[16] A potential suicide might ask his relatives to take him to this place, along with a post from which to hang him. He assumed the appropriate dress for those who were taken to the *lliivghet* (graves).[17] In the past, as we have seen, enclosure within a coffin was not part of the funeral procedures. Rather, the dead were laid upon the frozen ground. As James Aningayou described (see Chapter 6), their clothing was slashed free of the body to allow the spirit to leave, and elaborate precautions were taken to prevent the spirit of the dead from returning to harass the living. These practices were common not only on St. Lawrence Island, but also on the Asian shore. The belongings of the deceased, except for a few items kept by the immediate family, were broken—hence, the "destroying" place.

Much distress was associated with funerals. Only highly respected hunters were placed on top of Sivuqaq Mountain, which was reserved for those who had killed a whale or polar bear or had had long lives as esteemed boat captains and hunters. Others were laid on the lower slopes of the mountain, and babies might even be placed at the foot. Rhea told me of the agony of seeing a recently deceased baby dragged back into the village, partially devoured by dogs. Death held much horror for the living, and fear of the spirits that wander the night is still common in many households. Rhea had borne many children, only six of whom survived to adulthood. For her, the memory of tiny bodies laid upon the frozen ground was a vivid one. It is no wonder that she occasionally asked me to share her bed on nights when her grandchildren had gone home to sleep.

15. This concept finds parallel elsewhere in the Arctic, including Chukotka and the Canadian Arctic; however, it is not at all clear to me whether the concept is indigenous or was influenced by contact with Christian missionaries. I am not aware of any research on this point.

16. See Chapter 3 for descriptions of beads and other items left at destroying places.

17. From a base meaning "to put or set somewhere" (Jacobson 1987:107).

At night, the spirits of many who have not returned to the village through rebirth into the family crowded in.

Murder stood outside the rules governing proper human behavior. Those who committed murder, according to Estelle, were publicly shamed. They were shaved all over and had heavy walrus skulls attached to their feet. They were compelled to drag these skulls along with them in public acknowledgment of their breach of proper behavior. Eventually, murderers were purified and allowed to return to common life.

Death is always hard. While it might seem that the dead should be avoided at all costs, the names of those who die do return to the community. With the names of those who have died comes some immeasurable part of their spirit. The cycling of souls within the closed social context of St. Lawrence Island resembles concepts elsewhere in the Arctic. While little direct information about past naming concepts is available, there are some similarities in the present. Each name represents a separate individual, and while a person can and often does have more than one name, these names should be carried by only one person at a time. Many of the names belong to *ramka*, and permission must be given before a name can, for any reason, be bestowed outside the boundaries of a given *ramka*. Names carry the weight of soul presence. Once a name has been granted to an infant, it is felt that the essence of the deceased has manifested itself once again in the community. Relationships which were once associated with a deceased person are believed to operate in modified fashion for the baby.[18] These relationships seem to be especially important during the early months of a baby's life, before she develops a strong personality of her own. As the baby begins to show signs of her own personality, comments on her behavior and her namesake represent a way of remembering the person whose name she has taken more than a reference to the reincarnation of the previous name holder. Charles Hughes and several other outsiders have commented that naming provides a way for people to deal with their grief (C. Hughes, personal communication, 1988). I agree that this is one of the major features of naming practices. In my own experience, families who lost someone through an illness or accident waited anxiously for a newborn to take up the

18. See Charles Hughes (1960) for an analysis of naming in 1954 and 1955.

beloved person's name. The infant is then doubly welcomed into the household, both for its intrinsic worth as an infant and for making it possible to "materialize" the name of one recently gone. Relatives of the recently deceased addressed newborns as "mother" or "father" or "uncle" or "brother," depending on the situation. And, the potential for retaining certain names through the appearance of newborns reinforces the culture's strong love of children.

What I have tried to suggest is the character of religious beliefs as they might have existed in the early years of this century and to show, where appropriate, how these beliefs have carried over into the present. It seems clear that in the past, all major social institutions included some type of religious activity. Economic life and livelihood were sustained through religious action. Health was assured, and good weather, that is, good weather for hunting, was secured through religious action as well. Boat captains, the society's most prestigious individuals, reinforced their status through prayer and sacrifice to major deities. Travel through the various settlements was made difficult or easy through rites performed and precautions taken to avoid or calm the many spirits that occupied the environment. Personal power could be positively enhanced by taking on spirit assistants and fearfully extended through the misuse of these same assistants or through witchcraft. Family security was reinforced through the reappearance of beloved individuals via the naming process, and fear of the dead was softened through this same process and through rituals that nourished and sustained ancestor spirits. Through manipulation of one's spirit power, events could be foretold and the social universe managed. Social relations between lineages and *ramka* were also reinforced through rituals and ceremonies in which the relationships between man, animal, and abstract deity were symbolically represented. The Sivuqaq world was, in many respects, a socioreligious universe in which all else was embedded.

CHAPTER 8

Believing

A t the turn of the century, both islanders and the *laluramket* who came to the island accepted the premise that religious thought, behavior, and life style were interwoven. All were eventually transformed in the community, although the new life style and the new concepts were adopted slowly.

The community gradually incorporated a set of new beliefs that community members understand to be complementary to older beliefs. Apa is still the being who is most revered. His place in the cosmology is supreme, but Apa has become a more personal God. The suffering that Apa is believed to have experienced at the loss of Jesus has been an effective means of personalizing this once-remote figure. Christian religious practices have replaced many traditional practices, but in situations where the former do not suffice, either in concept or in everyday practice, the latter provides answers. The two systems have been integrated to create an indigenous Christianity that acknowledges both the old and the new.

Two Christian denominations—the Presbyterians, the larger of the two, and the Seventh-day Adventists—have permanent homes in Gambell. The Presbyterian church has been part of the Gambell community since the arrival of its first missionary in September 1894, although formal organization of the mission into a church did not occur until 1940.

In recent years, the Presbyterian church has not been entirely self-supporting. A portion of its budget has come from its parent body in Alaska (the Yukon Presbytery), the regional supervisory body in Seattle (the Synod), and from the tithes of some of its non-Native resident supporters. For example, Agnes Brady, the Presbyterian minister from 1987 to 1994, made regular, substantial contributions, and the Wycliffe Bible translators, a husband and wife team who have lived in the community since 1959, have also contributed heavily to the church (Brady, personal communication, 1988). The Seventh-day Adventist church was introduced into the community through Ila and Frank Daugherty, the village teachers from 1939 to 1945. These two sought to introduce by example the beliefs of their particular Christian denomination. The small group of believers did not have a church building of their own until 1957. Membership in the Seventh-day Adventist church remains small but devoted. Membership in each church divides generally along nuclear family lines, but it cuts across clan lines, except where clan membership is very small. While large church attendance has not characterized village life for at least ten years, the two churches are an accepted part of village structure. Names of those who rarely, if ever, attend church remain on the membership rolls, and they consider themselves as "belonging" to the congregations. When I first entered the community, some who seldom attended church still continued to tithe. While in theory the beliefs of the two church groups ought to distinguish them, in practice this is not always the case.[1] The two churches seem especially similar in those times when members of the church community take responsibility for the services. The two churches have often been without pastors or ministers. For example, during the 1987–1988 year the Seventh-day Adventist church was without a resident minister, as was the Presbyterian church during the previous year. In 1997, neither church had a permanent minister. During these times, services were led and sermons preached by members of the local congregation. The structure of services in the two churches during my first year in Gambell, October 1987 to June 1988, was nearly identical. It followed a general sequence of hymns, prayer, gospel reading, sermon, hymns, collection, doxology, prayer, and closing hymn and prayer. Usually after opening prayer, time was set aside for prayer and hymn requests. Morning services in each

1. Conflict characterized the two denominations in the early 1940s and 1950s. However, a quiet tolerance prevailed in 1987–1989, when I lived in Gambell. In 1990, I was told that the Seventh-day Adventists were considering opening a school in the village, perhaps to address local education problems or issues of religious conviction (Brady, personal communication, 1990). However, the school has yet to appear.

case tended to be formulaic and lasted the designated hour described in the church bulletin. Churches and the services they provide are significant elements in shaping and supporting contemporary religious concepts in the community.

My own observations are based on my attendance at services in the Presbyterian church over the years on a fairly regular basis. From time to time, I also attended services in the Seventh-day Adventist church. Both churches have evening prayer services and Sunday or Sabbath services. Friday evenings among Seventh-day Adventist families are often set aside to prepare for Sabbath-day, but I was never present for one of these preparation times, nor did I attend Seventh-day evening prayer services. In 1987 and 1988, when I lived in Gambell for the entire year, the Presbyterian church, under its new minister, the Reverend Agnes Brady, regularly held both Wednesday and Sunday evening prayer services. These were conducted by individuals or by husband-and-wife pairs who had volunteered to lead. In contrast to Sunday or Saturday morning services, these were of varying length, and their content depended entirely upon the individual leader and contributing participants. Apart from regular services, special services were held in conjunction with Thanksgiving, Christmas, New Year's Day, and Easter. Bible study was a regular feature of both churches, as was Vacation Bible School, held each summer for approximately two weeks. In addition, there were *ad hoc* Bible study and prayer groups as well as a Presbyterian women's organization, which attempted to meet once a month in the years when there was a regularly appointed minister. Trustees were responsible for church maintenance, and deacons sorted through clothing donations and kept track of families in need and of women soon to have babies who would need baby clothing.

In a community of 640 people, each activity makes an important contribution to social and religious life. These activities also serve as arenas in which community leaders gain training and experience. These generalizations, however, do little to convey the tenor of religious life and the expression of faith, so I will describe several aspects. I begin with a typical Sunday morning as I observed it in the late 1980s from within my own household, and then move to a description of Sunday services.

Rhea, with whom I lived in 1988, was a deeply religious woman who went to church whenever her failing health and the weather allowed.

Sundays began for her as did each of her days. She got up sometime after ten o'clock in the morning and made her way slowly into the kitchen. At 83 years old, partially blind and deaf, she moved with great care. Because of her infirmities, I laid a place for her at the kitchen table each morning with everything she needed at her fingertips: Sanka, a teacup inside a large dessert bowl, lump sugar in a special box, and a small plate of toast or pilot bread. Once Sanka had been poured and duly dosed with many lumps of sugar, Rhea prayed. This prayer was not simply a "grace" but a thanks to God for bringing her to the beginning of another day. She blessed family members, asked for guidance, and invited God to come into the house. These prayers could last a few seconds or many minutes. Those also awake in the household usually grew quiet during this time, sometimes repeating their own prayers. Although the prayers were spoken softly and were always in Yupik, they eventually became very familiar to me.

On Sundays, following breakfast, we assessed the weather, just as we did on every other morning. On this day, however, good weather meant that getting to church was more likely. On the other hand, men might be going out hunting, making use of Hondas and snowmobiles. Dressing was not completed until someone actually volunteered to take Rhea to church on one of their machines. The church was almost a mile from Rhea's house, much too far for her to walk, even on a good day. Once a commitment had been made by one of her children or grandchildren, others might also prepare to "hitch a ride" on the vehicle. As in most things, decisions usually affected more than one person. Eventually, as many as four or five people (or even more, if a sled was attached to a machine) would make their way to the eleven o'clock service at the Presbyterian church.

People arranged themselves in church based on family, lineage, and *ramka* memberships. No one ever sat in the front row of pews except when there was a funeral. Children who came with their parents and grandparents roamed freely in the aisles or gravitated to the back, where crayons, chalk, paper, and scissors (materials used for Sunday school) were kept. Little attempt was made to discipline these children except through offerings of candy, gum, or an occasional Sunday school reader, illustrated with cartoons. Once, a small child rolled under the pews among the feet of the congregation, coming to a stop between my feet, and silently offered me a piece of candy already a bit "used." When I shook my head "No," the child continued his silent journey. Throughout the service, children's noises created a quiet background for the service. The same thing happened during evening services. People came to church because they were believers. Especially for an elder such as Rhea, whose ability to discern the specific content of services was severely limited by deafness and language facility, the main reason for attending church was her long-standing faith and the sense of well-being that church attendance gave her. No particular status appeared to be attached to those who actually were present on Sunday, and election to church office had no major attendance requirements. Thus, religious leadership was not directly related to regular church attendance.

The services themselves, or perhaps more accurately, the church presence, seemed to provide a unifying and validating structure in the community. They were utilized on occasion, but were always a point of reference and a bit of defense against the forces of darkness thought to frequent the environment. From the church emerged the following spiritually based (or supernaturally inspired) activities, which seemed to bind the community members together in supportive fashion: individual prayer, group prayer, speaking in tongues, receiving praise songs, receiving "visions," encountering spirits or experiencing miracles, enacting or explicating supernatural events, expressing deeply felt emotions, and receiving sympathy and comfort within a spiritual context. These are but a few of the actions that appear to derive directly or indirectly from the church presence and contribute to the Sivuqaq world view and to individual faith.

People pray often, not surprisingly. Prayer was familiar in the past, long before the community became formally Christian, although then it appears to have been done in a more public way than it is today. Prayer has been important in the private lives of individuals for a long time as well. Both in stories passed on by Otto Geist (Dr. Otto W. Geist Collection 1927–32) and in the autobiographies Alexander and Dorothea Leighton collected in 1940, there is a suggestion that prayer was a regular feature of late nineteenth- and early twentieth-century religious life. In the past, according to at least three of the Leightons' consultants, most formal requests were for purposes of healing or to assure hunting success. Many elders with whom I have spoken agree. Broadly construed, these prayers were meant to invoke as well as thank spirits. Prayers were addressed to Apa, usually in moments of great stress. Thus, asking to be fed in times of famine as well as thanking Apa for the gift of a whale could equally be considered prayers. Interpreted in this manner it is possible to say that the reasons for praying and the general content of prayers may not, in fact, have changed much over the years. However, prayer performance and the architecture of prayers has changed to accommodate the community's Christian perspective.

From 1987 to 1997, prayer was the most consistent and most noticeable expression of faith that I saw and heard in the community. In Rhea's house, prayer opened the day. In February 1988, when extenuating circumstances forced Rhea and me to move next door to stay with her grandson and his family, prayer continued to open each day. Prayer or hymn singing was often the last sound I heard at night, as Rhea's granddaughter-in-law soothed a wakeful or crying child. In times of sickness, within the family context, family members prayed for health. As a flu outbreak and a rash of ear infections swept through the village, prayers for the health of many individuals became a focus of the evening prayer circles held in the church on Wednesday and Sunday evenings.

On occasion, the return to health of family members was seen to be a miracle. Often such occasions were marked by special messages believed to have been sent to an individual by God through the pages of the Bible. These messages, received in the context of prayer, were considered miracles themselves.

Past practice seems to indicate that certain prayers were once regarded as individual property, their power obtained through personal visions. Care was taken to hide the content of prayers, even from other family members, especially female children, who could be expected to marry out of the lineage and possibly out of the clan. Several autobiographies in the Dorothea Leighton, M.D., Collection (1982) describe prayers delivered in such a way that the specifics of their construction were difficult to determine.

Prayers no longer need such protection. Nevertheless, prayers made in public are spoken very quietly, at least those in which the congregation is the audience. Prayers involving two or three persons are, in my limited experience, more clearly enunciated. There may be other factors involved: to step forward in any public gathering is to assert oneself. Even though individuals would probably agree that praying before others, that is, praying on behalf of the group, is not the same as taking responsibility for another or directing another's activities, some people may still feel hesitant to stand before the group. Old men, now quite devoted to the new way, grew up under the older religious system, where prayers addressed to the spirit(s) were muted. Often, given the deference paid to them, these older men are asked to pray by the minister or whoever is leading the service.

Prayer is conducted differently in prayer circles than when prayers are offered among a few persons in a household context. For the latter circumstance, my experience is limited to those situations in which someone with me wished to pray, which occurred for several reasons. First and most often, people prayed with me to affirm our friendship. Prayer was a way to express emotions and sentiments which, under ordinary circumstances, would have been awkward to express. In my experience, with few exceptions, those who pray do so out loud. It is not clear where this practice has its roots. According to the Reverend Alice Green, who worked in Savoonga in the 1950s, praying aloud was uncommon then. It is possible that this new habit of prayer comes from the experience of several church members of both denominations with the Assembly of God churches in Nome, Fairbanks, or Anchorage. Unfortunately, I could find no definitive answer to this question. Be that as it may, a person wishing to express strong emotion may take it upon him or herself to hold hands and pray. In the course of the prayer, Apa is asked to care for the prayer partner and his or her family. Or Apa will be thanked for allowing the friendship to develop or for having made that person available as a comforter. Such occasions often bring tears.[2]

In church, people gather together in prayer circles. Although holding hands with a partner can be thought of as "forming a circle" and certainly joins people together physically, it is nevertheless an informal action.

2. Prayer is personal, so I have not included most of the details of prayer communication. I prayed together with people who belonged to each major lineage and clan group.

Prayers shared with individuals occur more or less spontaneously, and such prayers are usually conducted wherever one is sitting at the moment. Prayer circles conducted in the church, however, function as events in themselves. They are, in fact, formal rituals and have their own settings, actors, and special features (Turner 1982:79–82). While they may occasionally be used to respond to events such as the striking of a whale, prayer circles most often occur in evening church services. Technically, they are meant to "close" the service, but often the circle itself is the most important event of the evening. Circles have their own structure, postures, specially designated roles, and an inclusive number of actor-participants. Structurally, they have a distinct beginning, middle, and end. In the context of the circle, the deeply felt concerns of those gathered (usually representatives of the two largest clans and several others as well) are laid metaphorically on the prayer table, visible to all. Here these concerns are first presented; they are brought up again as those who have been selected to lead the prayers begin to take them up and weave them together in a request for assistance. At the same time, thanks are offered for those whose previous requests are believed to have been granted as a result of prayer. Simply to refer to a time for prayers, or joining together in a prayer circle, does not begin to describe religious performance in the context of prayer circles.

Prayer circles form at the very end of the evening church service. The service leader indicates the end of the service by saying "*Yughaa*" (to pray, as in "it's time to pray"). Those in attendance lay down their Bibles and hymn books, whatever they have been using. An evening service can consist almost entirely of passages noted for the congregation and read aloud. Such passages are often believed to have been "given" to the speaker or leader during the previous week. The comments of the leader, or of people called upon by the leader, constitute the body of the service that precedes the prayer circle.

As the prayers begin, the entire group of participants, anywhere from four to 40 persons, gathers at the front of the church between the pews and the altar (prayer) table. Everyone sits on the floor or in the first row of pews so that everyone can hold hands. Small children who have accompanied their parent(s) do not participate directly. Instead, they move about through the church. As on other social occasions, children's voices are the counterpoint against which serious adult concerns are played out. (Their levity is a constant reminder to parents not to become swept up in the emotions of the moment.) On one occasion that I recall vividly, adults were praying with great intensity, voices were high with emotion, some men and women were audibly sobbing, and several had broken into the special rhythmic speech called "speaking in tongues." Suddenly the giggles of three little girls who had joined the circle near their parents broke in with, "Slap me five." There were squeals of girlish laughter. "No, you slap *me* five!" The intense activity of the grown-ups subsided as if air had been let from a balloon with a great sigh. Prayers continued, but the high level of emotion had dissipated.

When people pray together, a prayer leader, chosen by the service leader(s),[3] usually guides the prayers. Everyone prays together, a muted choir of voices and a chosen vocalist. As each person sinks deeper into prayer, the intensity increases and there is also noticeable movement within the circle. Sometimes a person will raise her hands gradually to a position outstretched and above the head. Sometimes there is a rhythmic movement of the arm (generally from the elbow to the hand) from side to side; and sometimes speech "collapses" or is telescoped to the degree that vocalization of prayers is transformed to accelerated, incomprehensible, repetitious sound. Often these actions occur together. Certain kinds of speech are referred to by many people as "speaking in tongues." The speaker no longer recognizes her own words and understands the sound to be that of a language bestowed on her by God. Such movements and speech changes are interpreted within the religious community to indicate having been touched or filled with the Holy Spirit. Speech performance alone is interpreted to mean speaking in tongues. Receiving the spirit and speaking in tongues may occur simultaneously or independently. The intensity that attends these ritual performances varies. Nevertheless, after the fact the occurrence of spirit visitation is invariably described as "wonderful, joyous," and "unlike anything else" the person has ever felt.

Experiencing the spirit of God can occur as a result of sudden inspiration or intense prayer. Its manifestation in these instances is apparently

3. The person or persons assigned to lead evening worship services.

somewhat more subdued than seemed to be the case when the spirit en-
ters a room filled with many people. Regardless of the circumstance,
however, the experience is generally described as individual. It marks the
individual and spurs that person toward inner growth, or rebirth. It appears to parallel what Kenelm Burridge (1978) refers to as the experience
of *metanoia*. Through the act of speaking in tongues, receiving visions
(such as that described by Belinda in Chapter 6), and receiving songs, a
person is continually reborn and reaffirmed in her spiritual life. Further,
while these experiences are understood to occur for the individual, they
also unite group members. These experiences can occur at a very early
age. Any sign that an individual is potentially one of those destined to receive the spirit is strongly encouraged within the family. On one occasion
I was shown a photograph of a five-year-old child. To my untutored eye,
the child had a small shadow reflected on her forehead. The snapshot
was shown me specifically to illustrate that the child had been specially
marked by God. Each person in the room pointed out the reflection as
the mark of the cross. I was told that not long after this had transpired, the
child had received her first prayer song, a further sign believed to come
directly from God. The child had been the object of much supportive attention. The family celebrated her song gift, and it was written down so
that it could be sung in church. Others, older than the child mentioned
here, had similar experiences. Individuals called each other to confirm
these spiritual encounters, which were taken as proof of God's presence.

Receiving the spirit while in the act of prayer happens when a person
is alone, too. Publicly, however, receipt of the spirit by one person acts as
an igniting spark, and it is not uncommon for the spirit to "move" around
the prayer circle. As if orchestrated by an unseen conductor, each person
touched by the spirit is borne up on the swelling sound of prayerful voices
(each engaged in separate prayer) while his or her own prayer request becomes the center of sound concentration. In my experience, although
both men and women became the center or focus of the prayer circle,
women were more often released into a speech form unlike normal
speech. Men, however, were stricken with tremulous sobs which subsided once the moments of focus had passed. It was normal during this
time for both men and women to weep silently as the prayers progressed.

If the language used here to describe prayer and prayer circle experi-

ence seems almost sentimental, I can only say that I have hardly addressed the deep emotional content and feeling associated with the most
intense prayer experiences. In fact, prayer itself, because it is used as a vehicle for the transfer of strong sentiments and spiritual concerns, almost
never is performed perfunctorily. Prayer is itself a source or locus of
meaning for many persons in the community and through it, individuals
expressed belief, as I saw in the homes where I was a regular visitor and
in the two churches. Prayer seems to be used to change the circumstances of those burdened by the ordinary exigencies of life. Missionary
Ann Bannan remarked (ca. 1940) on the preference among her parish-
ioners: "All of the people on the island have not accepted to date [Chris-
tianity], but prayer is the one thing which they have accepted and use.
Every Christian native would rather have his friends pray for him when
he is in trouble than do anything else because he has proved the pwr. [*sic*]
of prayer" (PCA 1894–1960: RG 98: Box 6, File 32).

Prayer is presently the ritual of choice for those engaged in subsistence
activities, when employed individually or as a hunting unit before, during, and after the hunt. In the spring of 1987, Ralph Apatiki prayed to
God for a whale and promised not to keep any for himself if he should be
so fortunate as to receive this gift. When he did take a whale, he gave all
of the meat away. In April 1988, as the result of confusion over when and
where the appropriate elder should lead the prayer of thanksgiving following the taking of the first whale of the season, people on the beach
quietly registered their distress. A public remonstration would have been
inappropriate, since any remark implying either directly or indirectly that
elders were at fault would have been considered disrespectful. A prayer
was offered eventually, once all of the boat crews had returned to shore.

There were at least 25 or 26 boat crews in Gambell in 1997, and on a
good day to hunt whales the majority were in the water, working together
to bring a taken whale to shore. The crews unite both through the se-
quencing of hunting events that are designed to make the harvesting of a
great bowhead whale possible and through the prayers that acknowledge
the gift of the whale. In the past, such prayers took the form of loud calls
and ritual movements of paddles, as boats circled the whale in a clockwise direction. All measures were designed to inform Apa of the gift of the
whale while at the same time paying respect to the animal whose body

had been given over to the community (see Blassi's description above). Currently, in prayers offering thanks to God for the gift of a whale, the entire island community is united through CB radio transmission and the men themselves are drawn together as each crew receives its share of fresh *mangtak* (edible whale skin and fat). On one occasion that I witnessed, fewer people than usual participated in butchering a whale, and the whale was left earlier than usual for any person (women) to come to take an unclaimed portion. The matter was complicated. The whale had been female, a 50-foot animal. She aborted her calf as she was struck. Both mother and baby had been brought to shore. The baby was never touched and was finally returned to the sea. According to Rhea, in the past, special ceremonies would have been held for the infant. I can only speculate, given the delicate nature of the events, that participants, unable to pay full respect through prayer and other means to the whales, were less than aggressive in pursuing the butchering and distribution tasks that normally follow a successful whale hunt. The remains of that whale were left on the beach. When a second whale was taken the following week, everything was "done right," not a scrap remained of the whale, and a generally festive mood prevailed. Performing prayers that are demonstrably Christian after the taking of a whale is perhaps the most eloquent indication of acceptance by the majority of the community of a Christian world view.

Prayer is also a major component of decision making. In my limited experience in the community, decision making of all kinds began and ended with prayer. Through the process of careful listening and translation, I concluded that problems were transferred from the shoulders of the individual to Apa. By doing so, a person could then take action to deal with the problem of the moment. The hand of Apa is said to guide individual action. Those who invoked Apa waited for answers expectantly. The results of prayer, both for the purpose of deciding on individual action and for other purposes, are everywhere apparent. On various occasions I was told that prayer had carried someone safely through the day, had ensured that food was supplied, had cured the sick or had changed the weather, enabling those at sea to return home or those who needed to go out to hunt to depart. Material objects were sometimes the focus of prayers expected to protect and extend their physical lives.

The most dramatic example of continuous prayers occurred in the spring of 1988. At the beginning of June, two boats holding seven men who had gone walrus hunting were lost at sea. Departing shore ice and heavy fog combined to drive the boats away from the island and make it impossible for them to determine their location. Two days after the boats were reported missing, I left Gambell, having finished my initial work in the village. For a total of 22 days, the boats were lost. During that period, I spoke every few days to Mary, my close friend, on the phone. As Mary described it, the community seemed metaphorically to hold its breath. A deep anxiety gripped the community. Few went out to summer camp and few engaged in hunting. Family members and relatives gathered periodically to pray. At the same time, the churches continued to hold regular prayer sessions, with the missing men always at the top of the agenda. When the men were found, still alive despite much hardship, many to whom I spoke when I returned in February 1989 believed that prayer had been a significant factor in bringing them safely home.

All of my elderly consultants and most of my younger consultants preferred to begin and end taped interview sessions with prayer. Older persons, especially, believed that Apa directed all activities and that his hand was guiding my study. (The purpose of my original work in Gambell had been to reconstruct the history of Christianity in the community, and many of my consultants believed that writing this history was inspired and directed by Apa.) Once, when my tape recorder failed to work, my consultant grew fearful, interpreting the mechanical failure as God's message to her telling her not to cooperate in the taping. In the interval before our next meeting, she prayed several times and came to the conclusion that the devil was interfering with my work and must be overcome. In the session that followed, she took some time to praise me as a "good" person with a special ability and gift to communicate. It was clear that praying over this issue had included within it an assessment of my character. Her final conclusion, however, was to give God all the credit and responsibility.

Perhaps the most spectacular result of prayer was a special visitation of the spirit or, in some cases, of Jesus himself. These events, which stood out in the minds of individuals, did not occur in my presence. However, I was present shortly after such an occurrence on several occasions. In addition, several consultants did not hesitate to relate events in which they believed they had either experienced a miraculous visit from the Holy Spirit, had been saved from certain death through heavenly intervention, or had seen Jesus through a dream vision or dream encounter. These visions and visitations impressed themselves vividly on the minds of those who experienced them. Certainly there was no question that for the individual, these encounters with what might be labeled the non-empirical realm were real. Such experiences reinforce belief in the efficacy and power of Christ. In the examples that follow, the power and the emotional quality of these encounters is most apparent. Such experiences, unlike some encounters of the past, are not kept hidden. Those who actively profess themselves to be believers have taken to heart the Biblical message not to "hide one's light under a bushel."

In this example "Susanna"[4] describes receiving the Holy Spirit:

> I was attending college . . . for six weeks; I lived on the campus. . . .
>
> My husband, I appreciate [his] letting me go, all those weeks, which usually doesn't happen around here.
>
> Anyway, I always attend the little chapel below the campus.
>
> I even learn how many steps there is in that ladder in Fairbanks [which leads from the campus to the chapel].
>
> I get homesick, but . . . you can use the steps down and then walk to the road and get to the chapel. That's where I attend church services. . . .
>
> It was my first experience managing my money, cash, with me, you know. I was scared.
>
> I didn't know how to manage it, you know. . . .
>
> My first experience . . . paying for my meals which I never experience in my life.
>
> Out there [away from Gambell], you have to pay for everything. So, anyway, I always give my tithe.
>
> Ever since I learned, ever since I was made aware, [of] tithing, 10% is to go back to God in tithes; even one dollar, I give; fifty cents, I give. Ten cents, when I earn.

4. Pseudonym.

And, that time I was worried.

But I attended one evening service, I guess it was Wednesday, or Sunday service.

The offering plate was coming up. I reach into my money and I pick out some and confess to the Lord right there, not saying it, but within me, I prayed.

As much as I can give, I drop it.

As soon as I drop it I feel someone touching me twice on my back.

On my head, right below my earlobes, touching me so. It didn't scare me.

Twice I felt it and then I looked back like this.

There was another bench way back there, beyond reach.

There were my friends and some ladies sitting back there.

And then I asked, "Did you touch me?" My friend, I asked my friend.

She said, "No."

And right there, I was full of the spirit, power of the spirit,

And I stand up and my hands went up and I uttered in another language. Right there.

As soon as I was done, I sit down and there was another woman on the other side of the aisle.

She stand up right away and she started saying,

"Behold I come, and my reward is with me to reward every man according to his works." And there was another verse, too, which said, it's in 1st Thessalonians 4:17; it says something about reward-ing people when Jesus comes back.

I was real happy, unspeakable joy was overflowing. I feel it. It was with me.

I was full of joy and then later on, my friend who is spirit-filled too, asked me,

"Have you confirmed?" or "Have you proved the interpretation of the spirit's utterance?" she asked. I didn't know. I didn't know. I told her, "No."

"I have found them. First one is in Revelations 22:12, and the

second one is 1st Thessalonians 4:17." She told me the addresses
[locations of the verses] there.

I look them up, too.

We were taught to prove because of some deceiving spirit,
which sometimes we have to be alert, watch ourselves.

Always stay to the Word of God. Be in line with the Word of
God at all times.

Whatever we hear, we have to prove from the Word of God, the
Bible.

If it's there, then it's our message written there in the Word of
God. ("Susanna" 1988, in Jolles 1987ff)

In the second example, Steven Aningayou describes how God saved
him when he was in danger:

When I used to go hunting by foot on the ice, I have had a
miracle.

When I used to go out on the ice, you know, sometimes the ice
is pushed in.

Even though it was moving hard that way, a big ice boulder kept
pushing it in; it causes the ice to pile up.

Then when we pray, it suddenly stopped. It's a miracle.

When the ice moves in, it's very dangerous . . . That's how
much He took care of us.

He takes care of us—I would say the same . . . as [a mother taking care of their children].

I believe the way we live is a miracle.

When you're not thinking of anything, and perhaps an older person might see a child doing something—the great Apa is listening.

And so we stop what we do [conscience].

I heard it that way. He [God] is the one who doesn't speak. . . .

When they talk about Him, long time ago, they say:

"We make our Creator very happy." They say that way.

When they talk about Him, God, the Creator—which is Apa,
they say when they are having hardships also, you know, whatever
it is, even the shortage of food, they say,

"We have Someone who watches over us, who takes care of us, the Creator."

From long time ago this comes. You and I know about it now.

Now we know Him through this book, the Bible. Amazing.

From a long, long time ago. They know about him.

They wouldn't say to you, "Listen, listen, the Apa is listening to you," if they didn't know about Him.

They say to us, "Listen, listen, the Apa is listening to you.

He's watching and he's listening."

They say to us that way, even though they have not read this Bible—Our Watcher is going to be happy right now. Because we talked about Him.

They say He is happy when we talk about Him. (Aningayou 1988, in Jolles 1987ff)

My own experience as a researcher in the community was that prayer was a constant in the lives of many villagers. As a replacement for traditional rituals, it has become a common feature in many Sivuqaq families. Whenever I shared a meal in someone's home or was a guest at one of the many "birthday parties" given for elders to honor small children whose birthday it was, the meal always began with prayer. These prayers appear to correspond to an older tradition as well: no food, whatever its source (the land, the sea, or the Native store) belonged to the individual. It is believed to come from God and must be shared among all present. Acknowledging the giver through prayer just before a meal, however, appears to be the result of introduced practice. One friend commented that Siberian visitors in the village (following the opening of the borders to Native peoples in 1988) just reached for the food without waiting for thanks to be offered. My friend Mary remarked, "Those people [the Siberians] are just like those ancestors in those books that you brought."[5]

Prayer has its own language, which is derived from Biblical texts. Because prayer is so prevalent among numerous families, it creates a channel of communication, engendering a special intimacy among individu-

5. She refers to copies of diary entries and other correspondence from the early twentieth century that I brought to the island in 1987.

als because the language employed suggests concern for and preoccu-
pation with spiritual life. For example, expressions such as "Praise the
Lord" and "Thank you, Jesus" are markers of those engaged in religious
introspection. "Giving it (i.e., a problem or a decision) to the Lord" is
another. These three commonly employed expressions refer directly to
prayer. Other activities, such as attributing causality to spiritual intervention of some kind, combine with prayerful meditation to create a
kind of language of spiritual cognition and perception. After some
months, even the most objective researcher is likely to find, as I did myself, that they have begun to use Biblical language as a form of communication, and even dream of spirits (both demonic and otherwise). Immersed in a world view permeated with spiritual explications and
motivations, eventually even a researcher finds herself peering through
a different set of lenses.

This world view and the position of prayer within it were evident in
public gatherings in the grade school and high school, where special
events and celebrations always began with formal prayers conducted by a
minister or a respected elder. The communal Thanksgiving Day meal,
Christmas gifting program, honors banquets for graduating students,
Yupik Day celebration, and athletic awards presentations were all occasions where prayers initiated the proceedings.

Another significant expression of religious sentiment and belief, already mentioned above, is the experience of the supernatural.[6] Encounters with the supernatural appear to come in two forms in Sivuqaq. In the
first, there is either a vision-dream experience or a direct visit from the
Holy Spirit. In the second, which seems to derive from traditional experiences, a supernatural entity whose *raison d'être* stems from the traditional culture confronts someone. The affected person then interprets
this entity and deals with it through Christian ritual actions, which em-
power and protect him from the entity or rationalize that experience in

---

6. I do not intend to argue the validity of religious experience or encounter with
the supernatural, but rather to document the richness and prevalence of that experience. What is real and meaningful to one person may seem suspect to another, but
to challenge the validity of supernatural encounter would be disrespectful to any culture in which supernatural encounter is deeply embedded within the presently understood context of religious life.

Christian terms. Examples of this type of encounter with ancient spirit
powers abound.

As I have noted several times, spirits are everywhere in the Sivuqaq environment. In 1940, Alexander Leighton reported that evil spirits were felt
to reside in the village, while good or wild spirits could be found out on
the tundra. Spirits were and still are believed to be unpredictable and difficult to control. Although shamans no longer practice openly, the invol-
untary acquisition of a spirit assistant (*tughneghaq*) remains an unwanted
legacy for the descendants of some powerful shamans. Those meant to inherit their ancestors' spiritual power are not wholly protected, even by
conversion to Christianity, and they may be pursued relentlessly by potential spirit helpers.

One consultant told of a case in which a spirit helper, expecting to establish a spirit relationship with the second son in each generation of a
particular lineage, attempted to do so in a family now Christian. When an
older man refused to accept the relationship, turning to prayer in order to
withstand the power of the spirit, the spirit turned to another, a young boy
who was the nephew of the former, causing illness and a violent response.
According to my consultant, the young boy lost all control—rolling his
eyes up inside his head or twisting his ears shut whenever he perceived
that anyone near him was attempting to pray. This unusual behavior
continued for almost a month; finally, two Christian ministers who lived
in the village were able to rid him of the spirit. The required exorcism ritual was so unfamiliar to the ministers that they had to contact the main
Presbytery offices in Seattle to find out exactly what to do.

During the entire time, the family had been tormented by the spirit,
which had entered the house. At one point, the family tried to work out
a strategy to remove themselves from the house and leave the spirit behind. They intended to enter another house and to pray and somehow to
rid themselves of the unwanted presence. The spirit outmaneuvered
them, however, slipping into the second house ahead of them, where-
upon it entered the body of a young girl. One person tried to help "that
little girl" and called the spirit. It departed the child and made its way in
the form of a black, shadowy essence into the person's boot. The description of the spirit clearly identifies it as something very ancient. Once
situated, its presence could immediately be felt throughout the body.

What happened in the intervening period is unclear, although it must have been a terrible time for the family. Eventually this thing was banished through the exorcism, which included listing certain qualities or characteristics of the spirit on a paper and destroying the paper. The list remains secret, because, according to one of the ministers, the possibility exists that by reconstructing the list one might also reintroduce the spirit.

In the next example, which took place in the early 1960s, the difficult relationship between a man and his spirit helper was believed to have interfered with a man's departure from this world. According to my consultant, an older man, formerly a shaman (but at the time of his death a Christian), found himself prevented from dying by his spirit helper, which insisted that he reinstate it and pass it to one of his relatives before he would be allowed to die. As one of the old man's relatives put it to my consultant, he could see the spirit, a fox, running up and down the old man's chest, and he did not want to take it. The fox spirit, by tradition an extremely capricious and difficult spirit that would have been pacified with special rites in the past, continued to plague the unwilling relative. It would appear suddenly as a loose skin turning like a wheel alongside the man's sled as he traveled out on the tundra or emerge from behind some projection at unexpected moments. Eventually, the relative was obliged to take up the spirit to relieve the dying elder. My consultant believes that only prayer and the Holy Spirit were responsible for the spiritual health of the burdened relative.

Other examples of spirit encounters or supernatural experiences are more difficult for members of the community to categorize. These encounters involve spirit powers now identified as positive and retained more or less within their former traditional spiritual framework. Interactions with these spirit forces are sometimes interpreted through a Christian filter; at other times, they are interpreted entirely through traditional means. They include relations with animal spirits and ancestor spirits, both relations of extreme importance within the traditional culture and embodied in present constructs of identity. Two specific experiences are detailed here. They illustrate the relations between man and animal and the importance of mutual respect between man and the creatures upon whom he must rely for his livelihood, and the critical relationship between those who are living and those who have died.

The first example illustrates man-animal relationships and man-animal respect, along with the way in which professing Christians in the community sometimes understand unusual events within a Christian framework. In May 1988, Elinor and her brother John related the following event to me:

> ELINOR: I remember every time he's getting ready to go to hunt, I remember him telling us . . . I see a fox under the bed or someplace in the house. Or seal. . . . And he comes home with it. . . . There was something telling him all the time what he's going to get today he sees in the house. He was that kind of a boy.
>
> JOHN: One day I was at camp with [name deleted] and family . . . and lots of time when I started to seeing animals in front of me before I get 'em, I went over to the point where I would go seal hunting always. I went to the blind, I set down, took off my rifle. Just before I took out my rifle, I saw blood in the water out there, before I shoot even. It was right where I'm gonna get seal there's blood all over in that spot where I saw it. . . . And I saw a seal coming from the west side, and it came out right where I saw that blood in the water. I shot it right there too and killed it, and the blood was right there. That appeared before I ever got it there, so when I'm going to get fox, I know how many I will get home. There's something speaks to me, I don't know what, it's good. It's God speaking. It's not the devil, it's the Lord. (J. Kulowiyi 1988, in Jolles 1987ff)

I left Gambell in June 1988 and did not return for almost a year. Sadly, Rhea, with whom I lived during that first year in Gambell, had died in December of 1988. I had become very fond of Rhea, whom I had tried to care for as best I could, preparing her meals, doing her laundry, and sometimes sharing her bed. As an elder in one of the largest lineages in one of the two largest *ramka*, she had great prestige and she inspired much affection. When she died at the age of 84, she left behind more than 80 children, grandchildren, great-grandchildren, and other close relations. As one can imagine, she was sorely missed. Within days of her passing it came to be believed that she had known that she was going to die and, further, that understanding how much she was going to be missed, she had been made aware of her successor, that not-yet-born person who would return her

name to the community. It so happened that on the very day she died, a
baby girl was born to one of her granddaughters. This child was given both
Rhea's Yupik name and her English "Christian" name. Thus the return of
her name to the community was assured within hours of her passing. To
further illustrate the power of this spiritual conception, a few months after
the baby's birth, her mother considered moving to the mainland. The
baby's grandparents and (to use American kin terminology) great-aunts,
great-uncles, and others were worried by this decision. They felt strongly
that their mother's name should remain in the community. This second
example illustrates relations between the living and the deceased. All of
the examples related here pertain to circumstances where spiritual relations underlie hunting, health, and the stability of the family—the most
basic elements of the traditional life.

Certain spiritual encounters, which fall within the realm of the traditional culture, remain equivocal because their nature cannot be explained as subject to the positive spiritual power which can be marshaled
by calling on the name of Jesus or Apa, nor do they fit easily into a positively identified power category from the traditional world. Beings such as
seal people, yetis, giants, or the small beings that occasionally surprise
people walking after dark do not appear to harm anyone, nor do they help
them. They are simply present. Although under certain circumstances
they may become dangerous, they are not easily categorized.

In addition, sometimes a conversion or spiritual rebirth occurs or a vision appears or healing or some other miraculous event transpires that is
interpreted wholly within a Christian framework. These conversion experiences divide into two kinds, those that involve conversion from traditional belief to Christian belief and those in which a person long since
nominally Christian, that is, having a decidedly Christian world view, is
reborn. The first constitutes a series of spiritual encounters passed on in
narrative form by the descendants of those who originally experienced
them. In some cases these experiences were also recorded in aural or
written form by the person himself. Together these form a set of "testi-
monies" in the Biblical sense; at the same time, they illustrate the process
through which the old and the new have been mediated and articulated
one with the other.

Dream and vision experiences are complementary to and inform a person's spiritual reality. The personal universe is one in which the spiritual essences of the past and the present are interwoven. Animal and human and other less easily defined presences intermingle. Coping with this complex reality requires a grasp of the world that is both pragmatic and spiritually aware. Thus, not only must a man be a skilled technician of hunting, a weather forecaster, and an informed naturalist-zoologist, he must also be attuned to the interior spiritual reality of his environment. The man who could envision or was presented with a spirit assistant of some kind during a vision quest increased his own ability, and consequently his family's ability to survive, by adding spiritual power to his natural abilities. It is not surprising, then, that some of the most startling examples of this type of experience occur within the context of becoming Christian and acquiring what is understood in the community as the most potent spiritual power. A graphic illustration is the case of Yugniilqwaaq, a shaman from Pugughileq who ventured onto the tundra apparently in search of spirit power. Yugniilqwaaq's story is recounted with slight variations by several early consultants and one of the early missionaries. The most detailed version comes from Lawrence Kulukhon, who recorded the story both for Willis Walunga, village historian, and as part of his "History of Christianity in Sivuqaq" (1966). The second version is that of Edgar Campbell, missionary from 1901 to 1911. The two versions differ somewhat in detail. Kulukhon's version was recollected many years after the event, but he heard about it and it was included as a part of the original series of events because of his own father's involvement as a powerful shaman at the time. The greatest contrast between the two versions is in the differing perceptions of reality they offer. For Campbell, the shaman's experience is a vision, subject to question, but nevertheless to be exploited in the interest of its potential for converting the traditionalists in the community to Christianity. For Kulukhon and others who also make reference to the event (including present community members), the shaman met, struggled against, and finally succumbed to the physical presence of Jesus. Campbell's version (which was most likely translated for him by his interpreter Anenga) comes from his journal:

> January 19, 1910. After the Usual Wednesday evening service, Ugunalskwok [Yugniilqwaaq] of Poowowaluk [Pugughileq] came into our

kitchen and told he had had a vision. Oningou [Anenga] interpreted. We had it taken down in shorthand later and typewritten. The main points were. He saw Jesus—long robes as in the Sunday School charts—Jesus hit him on each side of the face with Bible—"Why don't you believe my word. I am stronger than all devils just the same as a handful of rocks to me. Do not half way believe. Those who half way believe are a curse to believers. Do not laugh in meeting."

"All believers should be like brothers. Go to Dr. Campbell and get robe, Bible and a chart picture." I told him to go tell Shoollook [Suluk] and Ifkowan. He was much impressed and I notices [*sic*] when he prayed, he began "O Jesus, God." We pray that many people may be led to forsake their idols and come to Jesus.

January 20, 1910. In answer to our prayers, God has sent bad weather, so Ugunalskwok [Yugniilqwaaq] has been retained to talk to others. Much interest.

January 22, 1910. Fine comet in west. People scared. Helped Ugunalskwok [Yugniilqwaaq].

January 23, 1910. Best attendance we ever had on Sunday. After the usual gospel talk, Ugunalskwok [Yugniilqwaaq] was asked to speak to the people. After a little preliminary embarrassment, he did very well. Intense interest. Many old men present, and asked questions.

January 26, 1910. Nupohuyu has brought all his idols, fetishes and charms, forsaking them all for Jesus. Told all present of his decision. Booshu and Koonooku have also surrendered. Weyu brought her last stick which she trusted in. Pooniyook hunted over her things and found some more charms. She and Poowook brot [*sic*] a drum. Much serious thought in the meeting.

January 30, 1910. A great day for St. Lawrence Island. Burning of the idols, fetishes and charms brought. After the usual services, including a lesson on the example of Asa, king of Judah in destroying idol worship from his kingdom, the stove was heaped full of gods made with hands, while we sang—"Praise God from whom all blessings flow."

The following questions were read and carefully explained:

1. Do you now renounce hate and forsake all worships but of Jehovah God?

2. Do you promise not to make, accept, use or permit any one else to use for you, any of these things or anything like them in the future?

3. Do you now tell all these people here that you want to follow only Jehovah God and Jesus his son?

4. Do you want to keep on learning God's way thru his son Jesus, until you are ready to be baptized?

Others who had previously made such renunciations, stood up with those who came today, so there were 41 who stood up. (Campbell 1910 [4]:48–50)

Lawrence Kulukhon recorded this version with interviewer Willis Walunga, when he was an old man:

LAWRENCE: And then he was a minister too. Anenga was a man, a very devout Christian. He had become a Christian too, then, but he went back when the others went back. They come from Savoonga and then they come back, fishing, maybe. And then as were living that way, at Aningayou's, in his house, a man came in, he came in. Aningayou welcomed him. He really welcomed him. He was Yugniilqwaaq. He was from Pughughileq. He wasn't a young man, he was a man [meaning a grown man]. We've heard about him, Yugniilqwaaq. This man. He was a shaman. He was very powerful. He had it all. There was nothing too hard for him to do, we heard, down there. He came in, sat down, talked to Aningayou, saying, "How is it if you have your Sunday if I could be there? I have something to say to everyone and tell everyone to be there. I'm going to talk the way of the believers. I was a very power-ful *alignalghii* [shaman]. As I was out trapping, my eyes were drawn away by a man dressed in white telling me to come, "Come, come to me," he [the man in white] said. Instead he [Yugni-ilqwaaq] would sing to it [the spirit] [in hopes of bringing him in]. "As each evening came I would sing to it to have it enter me." When he [the man in white] appeared.—He was gone.

And then again as I went trapping I saw him and he was coming to me, saying, "I am not the devil, you will not *tughneghighh-naqutka* [come into me—like a spirit assistant]. I am not the devil; I am your Lord. I had mercy upon you and I have come to you [to tell you] that what you are using is no good. Take it away [put it far from you]. Believe. And then go to Sivuqaq to talk so that every-body can believe." And then he [Aningayou] said, "Yes. Go ahead and talk Sunday." And then he told me [Lawrence Kulukhon] too, to tell everyone. That's what I'm going to talk about. And I told everyone. Come to Sunday. Yugniilqwaaq will talk there.

And then Sunday came. We do go to Sunday. When he wasn't there. Everybody used to go to Sunday. The whole Sivuqaq. Come to listen, even non-believers.

WILLIS WALUNGA: What was the year?

LAWRENCE: I don't know, but it was before he [Edgar Campbell] left, anyway. 1906—somewhere there, 1907. And then everyone came to listen. It was evening. Down there [in the west] big star grew. By coincidence at the time he was going to talk, the big star showed up [in the west], showed up down there, shining down there it seems. Shining down and it seemed to have a tail. The shining of it, it seems to be the tail. They all went [to the church], everybody filled up the little school. And then, he [Yugniilqwaaq], he came in from the other room wearing Jesus' clothes, all white. He came in. And he talked there then. Before he [Edgar Campbell] could preach. And this is how he told it. *Tughneghighhnaqutka* and when He appears: "I am not the devil," He warned. "I am not the devil. Instead you come to Me," He kept saying. And He gave him [Yugniilqwaaq] words to say, to bring here. He has come here to say, "To convert those who want to believe, let them believe, and those who don't want to, don't." And this is the way it is. This is the end [the result]. Jesus. That which comes down to me is Jesus. "I am the Savior. Sinners I will save. If you confess your sins, if you believe." He [Yugniilqwaaq] talked and talked and after that, he [Edgar Campbell] preached. But then he [Yugniilqwaaq] forgot some of the words, he said. He called Aningayou and said, "How, how am I supposed to do it?" [In Lawrence Kulukhon's opinion] See, he did it some way, he made a mistake.

—And then they went out, they went out [the people]. I kept hearing. They're going to believe.

WILLIS WALUNGA: And then?

LAWRENCE: Night fell, there was pounding at the door at my house, there. Outside there was pounding, getting louder and louder. Someone said to me, "Go open the door. Someone's out there." I went out to open the door. Yugniilqwaaq was there saying,

"Where's your elder one. Go ask him if I could come in. Ask him if I could come in, if he will not allow me to come in."

He was *alignalghii*, my father. I did tell him. "He can't come in. Today he talked, saying he's never going to do it this way again. So he can't come in." He came in. He put his head through the outer curtain wall.[7] They talked there. He wanted to come in. He really wanted to come in. "I [Yugniilqwaaq] have done wrong." [In L. Kulukhon's opinion, instead he said, he has done wrong. Coming for advice to show him what he should do.] "I [Lawrence Kulukhon's father] will not show you what to do. Instead you will get deeper and deeper into the wrong. Everybody's going to believe, I heard. Everybody's going to believe. They're going to follow you. How else are you going to do."

He would cry and cry, but he left because he was rejected. And then, they said that he had left. He left. Yugniilqwaaq. He went back to Pughughileq. And then, eventually, as we were living, someone arrived from Pughughileq. He was worried about him. He came here. Yugniilqwaaq was still gone. He had left days ago. He's still gone. He hasn't arrived. And then, they [Sivuqaq people] were worried about him since they said he was gone. Soonagruk came from Tapghaq. Yugniilqwaaq was already dead. He told Yugniilqwaaq was already dead when found. Over there near Tapghaq he found him in a *iinwaak*. His dogs made him [Soonagruk] find him. He died with his feet inside his parka, frozen. He left a trail of blood up to his sled, dripping with blood. His gun was out of its cover. I don't know what happened, if he accidentally shot himself or if he committed suicide.

And that's the way it was told. He was gone and that was the end of him. Him. Yugniilqwaaq. And then everybody started believing, Sivuqaq. Burning their things, confessing their sins, to the doctor they confessed. Everybody believed, but from there everybody believed, going to Sunday and then when the doctor left

7. Early homes had one large interior room (*aagra*), which was enclosed by heavy skins. It was quite warm and the scene of all household activity. The outer area in front of the entrance way was used to store food and other items and as a workplace.

there was no more. We lost our teachers too at that time. The next teachers were out-of-order [not what one would expect]. No wives and some were even women. Those after him there's no more. (Kulukhon n.d.)

What is particularly intriguing about this spiritual encounter is its structure, which rests on two quite opposed contextual bases. If we assume the "facts" of the encounter consist of a meshing of the events as they are variously related—that is, that the encounter included both the dialogue between Jesus and the shaman (Campbell's version) and the shaman's attempt to exercise authority over the figure of Jesus by making him into a spirit assistant (Kulukhon's version)—we are presented with an extraordinary event, in which two systems of meaning that are derived quite independently are suddenly integrated through ritual performance. On the one hand, the shaman behaves in a manner quite in keeping with his own religious tradition. He identifies Jesus as a spirit of substantial power. He knows who the spirit is because it has been described in some detail in the church services that he has attended. As Campbell points out in his journal, Yugniilqwaaq sees Jesus dressed as in the Sunday school illustrations on display in the church. Yugniilqwaaq's response to this confrontation is to appropriate the spirit entity and make it his own. What follows is an extremely interesting series of actions, in which the process of making the spirit into an assistant is turned on its head. In traditional Yupik society, when a boy became a man—that is, took his first *maklak* (bearded seal) or other large sea mammal—the men in his family, usually an uncle or his father who had accompanied him, went to him while he was still on the beach and struck him down—usually across the face—first on one side, then on the other. The boy's first kill was given away and he was considered a young man and no longer a boy, a new person ready to take on the responsibilities of adulthood.

In the encounter, Jesus strikes the shaman on both cheeks. There are strong similarities between the ritual actions that mark the move from physical boyhood to manhood and those that marked Yugniilqwaaq's move from one set of religious beliefs to another. It is as if the move marks a change from spiritual childhood to spiritual adulthood. The event fits well into the framework of social drama once proposed by Victor

Turner (1982:61–82) and also fits into theories of spiritual rebirth such as Burridge's on *metanoia* (1969). Campbell's presence and indeed his persistence pushed at the boundaries of religious belief. The missionary not only introduced the theoretical possibility of access to greater supernatural power, but also offered a whole array of material goods and technology that he connected with that power. He created a conflict situation, challenging the understanding of power and who could gain access to it. Through Campbell, the presence of God began to be felt in ways associated in the past with older spirit powers. It was, I suspect, only a matter of time before an actual encounter took place, one either cast as a physical confrontation or as a vision experience. Turner suggests that in such cases one ought to be able to discern four distinct phases, which he labels "breach, crisis, redress and either reintegration or recognition of schism" (1982:69). Yugniilqwaaq's case is particularly noteworthy. Not only does it illustrate a progression through the three stages of breach (he has clearly found himself on the traditionalist side of a religious community dividing along traditionalist-conversionist lines); crisis (he has confronted the new power in his own empirical and non-empirical territory); and redress (he gives in to the new power after failing to incorporate it directly into his own religious system), but, interestingly, he has also gone through both aspects of the fourth stage. At first it would appear that Yugniilqwaaq has become integrated in spiritual terms into a new system, one which includes the major spirit powers outlined in the newly introduced global religion. Then, however, he is assailed with doubts, going first to one religious leader (a new convert) and then to another (a powerful shaman). He is rejected by both and, in an unusual move, leaves the village to make his way to Tapghaq, a small settlement on the north side of the island. He goes alone, apparently tormented and thrown backward into the depths of his crisis, and he does not re-emerge. Various versions, all very similar, indicate that he died a tragic death, alone, near Tapghaq. One version suggests that he was eaten by his dogs. Another relates that he killed himself with his own gun. In another, he freezes to death. In the last, most controversial version, he is murdered. The end result is always the same. He dies trying to come to terms with the spiritual dilemma that faces him, and he dies tragically.

Successful conversion in Sivuqaq can be explained at least in part through examining in greater detail the conversions of some of the first Christians. The accounts of Yugniilqwaaq's experience demonstrate how stories of conversion were integrated into the oral history of the island. The formation of this oral history, like any other historical process, is selective. It is noteworthy that of the many conversions that have occurred on St. Lawrence Island over the last 50 or 60 years, only certain conversions are savored, often repeated, and passed on, even to visiting anthropologists. That these conversion experiences are not alone in dramatic content became clear to me as I listened to individuals tell me of their own conversion experiences. Nevertheless, the stories first volunteered were not those of my consultants, but those of their parents or grandparents. Tellingly, these first stories are generally of the same persons, men who were either shamans (*alignalghiit*) themselves or those who "had power" or were beginning to be approached as avenues to power ("to feel or know the power of the drum"). Their conversions are significant, even spectacular. Their stories serve as spiritual markers and have become mythic in character in the few years since they occurred.

Even before these conversions, the arrival of non-Natives had taken on significance of a quasi-religious nature, because of the prophesies associated with their coming. By embedding these stories within a non-empirical context, the events themselves gain in both stature and authority. Agigseghaq's prophesy, related in Chapter 3, was the first to foretell the coming of non-Natives (Alowa 1985; Aningayou, DLC 1982:11–13). The story seems designed to reassure the listener of Agigseghaq's authority and power.

Although the story does not include a suggestion that the strangers who would come would carry with them a powerful new spiritual concept, as it is told now, it does suggest an awareness of new beliefs. The importance of this prophesy lies in how it frames subsequent events. It also suggests, as many elders now are wont to believe, that the expectation of strangers who would bring the "good news" has long been part of island history. Thus, there are references to Agighsehaq's age, to his being as old as Noah. With the early prophesy having set the stage, let us turn to significant conversions that followed the arrival of the early missionaries, Edgar Campbell in particular.

Several early conversions significantly affected the community, among them that of Yugniilqwaaq, which I have just related, and those of Apan-

galook, Iyakitan, and Kulukhon. Also important was the final turning of
Nanghiila of Savoonga in 1946. In the first decade of the twentieth century, while numbers of persons in the Gambell community were swayed
by the message delivered by Edgar Campbell, two tales stand out. The
first, told over and over again, relates the unwavering belief of the young
James Aningayou, and the second is the transformation of Yugniilqwaaq.
Other often-told conversion stories from this period and from the second
period of missionary activity, when Ann Bannan was missionary, include
the dream vision of Iyakitan, another well-known *alignalghii*, the conversion of John Apangalook (after whom the school in Gambell is named),
the collective struggles of Kulukhon, Silook, Sunaaghruk, and Aningayou,
and, from the neighboring community of Savoonga, the account of the
miraculous rescue and conversion of Nanghiila in 1946. In addition comes
the story of the sudden restoration of sight to Kulukhon's young son.

These conversion histories have in common several features. First and
most obvious is that these are men's stories. I believe that is significant.
Campbell's journals describe in some detail efforts by both him and his
wife to instill greater respect for women and to establish a woman's right
to choose Christianity for herself. Several examples can be cited of
women, especially young women, struggling to free themselves from the
traditional bonds, including enforced relations with known shamans.
Joined together with religious choice was, apparently, the opportunity for
greater individual expression associated with the new schooling.
Women's conversion stories, however, are seldom recited.

That men are protagonists in much of the oral history of Christian conversion can probably be attributed to the social organization of the community. The *ramka* system (C. Hughes 1958, 1960), which was first noted
in 1912 by Riley Moore, a young associate of Hrdlièa (Moore 1923:340–
341), and described in great detail by Charles Hughes, persists to this day.
The system, built on patrilines and patrilineal descent rules, was characterized by political authority, to the extent that it was present at all, vested
in senior men before any others. Respect for men, especially elders and
men who command whaling crews, remains a primary value in the community. Senior men officiate at marrying ceremonies, give consent before
women and children may undertake many activities, and are consulted in

all serious matters affecting the family and clan. In the past, to provide more effectively for their families, men sought spiritual assistance through individual vision quests and spirit encounters. The power of a shaman increased through numerous quest experiences or through the acquisition of inherited powers. Boat captains and "strong men" also acquired powers. All of them exercised authority through the patrilineal structure. Thus, conversion of any one of these men had major repercussions within the family. These men probably did not try to influence their elders, but they undoubtedly did exert influence on others in their families through their own example and because of their position within the family hierarchy. In the family of James Aningayou, the grandmother placed considerable faith in the old ways. One of Aningayou's children was raised by this woman, while the others grew up more directly influenced by their father. Christian commitment in this family has predictably divided along the same lines. The allegiance of senior men to one or the other of the two belief systems seems to have been critical to the conversion of others in the early days of Christianity.

Equally important was the process through which conversion occurred. Each of the conversions I have noted assumed a form that was paralleled structurally in the older tradition. Thus, the validity of the new experience appears to have been rooted in traditional conceptions of the structure of spirit power relations. Individual experiences may vary, but they have in common a transcendent encounter that also characterized earlier relations. These encounters either occurred within an interpreted dream/vision framework or were understood to have been miraculous interventions. Thus, Yugniilqwaaq met and challenged and succumbed to Jesus; Anenga, Campbell's translator, prayed and found himself more successful as a hunter than his peers committed to the old system; Iyakitan "saw" his soul in a dramatic dream sequence; and, after an intense period of prayer, Apangalook was confronted with a brilliant rainbow that illuminated the night sky. And, together, a nucleus of men (Kulukhon, Aningayou, and Silook) attempted to renew their Christian commitment at a time when the island had long been without a missionary. To do so, they reestablished contact with Apa, in his Christian form. Kulukhon tells the story:

I was thinking hard then. I want to become a Christain [*sic*]. . . . I read a verse where He [Jesus] healed the sick and made the blind to see. The more I want to become a Christain. I did not know how to pray even if I want to pray. . . . Then I prayed right there. . . . When I prayed I called Him as Great Great Grandfather as we Eskimo's do. . . . "Great Great Grandfather please help me, please make my sons eyes to see. I trust you." . . . Then I wished I could ask some one to pray with me. . . . I went to Paul Siluk. . . . "I am going to become a Christain," I said. I have heard he does not want to be Christain. When I asked him he said he would become a Christain with me. We started out to the top of the mountain. When we got to the top we prayed our own way. We prayed for someone, to be our third person. And I asked him to pray for my son whom I prayed for. We did not know how to pray when we prayed, but we prayed that way and called Him Great Great Grandfather. We went down the mountain and came home and went to James Aningayou and told him, oh boy, he became a Christain with us. He quit being a Christain once. [At this point in the narrative, Kulukhon describes how his son miraculously regains his sight.]. . . . I was for sure a Christian because of that. . . . Again we prayed for some one . . . to be Christain with us. [Several men join the group, and they travel through the village as a self-appointed prayer and recruitment committee.]. . . . At that time not all of the people were Christains. When we went from home to home some of them became Christains and they were strong Christains then we were. Then Sunaaghruk prophesied again. He prophecied [*sic*] in a different way, he called people to himself for them to repent and become Christains to him. The kind which have gift. For us to get rid of our sins through him. Even if he kept calling me, I did not go to him. He took me to top of the mountain and asked me questions. . . . He was going to make an alter [*sic*] on top of the mountain. A snow bunting and baby walrus for offering. Bird which are the first to come. Light a fire and throw the bird into the fire and confess and be free of their sins if we could believe his way. I said to him up at the mountain, "I am not going to believe you, I am not going to follow you. Your way is far different. I have already became a Christain. I have seen strong power which healed, He healed my son who was blind. He caused him to see again. And he opened my ears which were closed, . . . And besides they tell of God's son who died and rise again so that any one can believe on Him and not be lost but have eternal life." When I told that to Sunaaghruk, he was in deep thought. We came down and came

home. Then he started following me around. He forgot about his way of
salvation, instead he told me he would become Christain and follow us.
(Kulukhon 1966:8–15)

In the 1970s, when Nanghiila of Savoonga finally turned to prayer he was
led safely to an empty cabin in the midst of a blinding snowstorm. He was
found by a search party looking for his frozen body in the spring of 1946.
He had existed for almost two weeks in the cold, with little food and no
fuel, according to Clarence Irrigoo and Alice Green (Green 1989, in
Jolles 1987ff; C. Irrigoo, personal communication, 1988). In each case,
the path to conversion held familiar landmarks: an initial period of doubt
(in the instance of Apangalook, a period of mental instability, referred to
as "nervousness"), accompanied with a period of wandering outside in
the care of an older brother, and in the case of Iyakitan a period of "restlessness"; a concentrated period of thought or reflection (similar to peri-
ods of solitary meditation in the more traditional questing); and finally
the validating experience of spiritual transcendence through spectacular
displays of God's power. While it is not possible to follow the stages exactly, enough of each person's conversion process is known to allow for
some generalizations. The account of Yugniilqwaaq's conversion has already been given above. The accounts of Aningayou, Iyakitan, and Apangalook follow. Here is James Aningayou's story:

I . . . asked why James had given up the old Eskimo religion. He said on
account of Dr. Campbell telling them a better way. He could see all the
prophecies in the bible coming true. I asked him which ones. He
stopped apparently to think for some time. Then he said, "The prophecies of wars, and change, things always changing. But even before the
missionaries came, the Eskimos knew about God. When they first heard
the missionaries speak they knew a lot of what he said about God was
true."

I asked James again why he became Christian. He said it was the
promise of life after this life. I asked, didn't they have that in the old Eskimo way. He said no, "nothing to compare." He told again the story of
Yunillqwah. He said that he, James, found it hard to believe that Christ
really appeared to him. That was not in accord with the teachings of the
Bible. The rest, he said, seemed true. He wanted to dress like his vision.

8.1 *Steven Aningayou, elder, August 1998. Steven's father, James, is often mentioned as the first "true" Christian.*

Dr. Campbell didn't say he believed in it, but he told Yunillqwak to go ahead do what he liked. So he dressed himself in white cheesecloth. He told people to decide to be Christian instead of sorcerer. Pretty near the whole village turned. He made his house a church, at Southwest cape, and preached. He talked to the people the "religion way." He never read the Bible, yet some things he said just like the Bible. "We was surprise of him." He told James after he had backslid that "maybe something will happen to me before I am ready." (Aningayou, DLC 1982:163–164)

Many years later, in the spring of 1988, James Aningayou's son, Steven or Kiistivik, recalled what he had been told about his father's acceptance of Christianity.

> ELINOR: Do you recall how your father became a Christian?[8]
>
> STEVEN: From those, just by listening. By listening to the translated ones [the translated words of the Bible]. I think, He [God] causes the ears to open. I don't think he himself [without the help of God] became Christian. God Himself talked to him in his inside.
>
> ELINOR: Was there a lot of struggle when your family was Christian and nobody else was Christian?
>
> STEVEN: . . . Yes. It causes strife. Some people were against us, but we were strongly told [not to return evil for evil]. Our father strongly taught us that. Not answer them [in a bad way]. God Himself will cause them to understand. He is a miracle. (S. Aningayou 1988, in Jolles 1987ff)

While Aningayou's account gives little hint of the inner struggle that accompanied his conversion, Campbell describes the struggles experienced by Oningou (a contemporary spelling would be Anenga), another of his translators:

> Oningou said he was very tired the other day as he was returning from hunting, dragging a seal over the rough ice, so he asked Jesus to help him and he soon came to some young ice, quite smooth so the pulling was easy. And when he got home, he did not give his seal water as the heathen do. His mother and wife asked him why, and he told them, he was going to try the other way. (Campbell 1905, 1:85–86)

My interpreter was sent to me one evening to ask about the Christian life. He sat very uncomfortably in his chair for quite a while, we patiently

---

8. Brackets show Elinor's explanations to me.

waiting the time we knew would come when he should tell us what was troubling him. At last he asked me if Christians in America used tobacco. As I told my views on the subject, his eyes filled with tears and when I had finished he drew a heavy sigh and said "I am sorry, but I can not help it; my mother taught it to me when I was a little boy." After some future conversation other topics, he went home and I thought no more of the matter until some two or three months afterward, when I was visiting him on account of a sickness that he had learned that he had given up tobacco after a hard struggle that he had made him sick for more than a week.

A boy that can do that can do many other things. Still he was a lonesome example. (Sheldon Jackson Correspondence 1904–1908:366)

Steven Aningayou also described the conversion of Iyakitan, a man known in the community for his commitment to the old ways and his spiritual strength:

STEVEN: That Iyakitan, as time goes on, he was in labor.
When he delivered a baby, the whole baby was black, completely, Iyakitan's.
So that way he was born again. Iyakitan took a close look at the baby he delivered.
It was all black, a black baby. The one he delivered.
I think that was what caused him to really think. That baby caused Iyakitan to think.
It was all black and it was Iyakitan himself. So he thought about it. So my father . . . caused him to understand, that baby was Iyakitan's own spirit, dirty, unclean, black.
So when he understood, he turned and became a believer.
Malewotkok followed [joined]. That way he did. Iyakitan was in labor and he delivered a baby.
ELINOR: Was Iyakitan an *alignalghii*?
STEVEN: Yes. He was a very strong *alignalghii*.
Elinor: Was he strong [did he have great ability] with the evil spirits?
STEVEN: Yes. But great God had power over him, by showing him his spirit [through the baby]; it was Iyakitan's spirit. He caused

him to deliver that baby and show it to him. So, Iyakitan refused
that baby because he understood it was Iyakitan himself. Because
he worshipped the evil spirits of the world.

ELINOR: Then where is that baby?

STEVEN: It was in his dream. It was only in a dream that he saw
it. God, when he wanted to show Iyakitan's spirit to him, that spirit
was no good [to Iyakitan's eyes].

And so he [Iyakitan] told it [his vision] to Lawrence Kulukhon
and Samuel Irrigoo, and to my father.

And my father caused him to understand that [baby] was his spirit.
It didn't look like Iyakitan.

As they were telling him [about the Bible], he turned to God,
because he was revolted by that spirit [his].

So, he became a believer since then. (S. Aningayou 1988, in
Jolles 1987ff)

In the winter of 1990, Larry Aningayou recounted yet another segment of
Iyakitan's story:

> When Edgar Campbell was here Iyakitan announced that he
> would never change.
>
> He was a shaman and had great power.
>
> Mr. Campbell said that he would pray for him no matter where
> he was.
>
> A couple of years after Campbell left, Iyakitan called Lawrence
> Kulukhon to him.
>
> He was sitting with an open Bible and the pages were glowing
> with their own light. Iyakitan asked Kulukhon to help him read be-
> cause he couldn't read at all.
>
> Some time after that Iyakitan dreamed that he became pregnant
> and gave birth to a small human, very dirty.
>
> He went to James Aningayou for an interpretation of the dream.
> (L. Aningayou, personal communication, n.d.)

Ann Bannan's mission correspondence records the same event as
follows:

Mr. J. E. Youel, of Fairbanks, Alaska, came here August 29th [1940] to
baptize the people of St. Lawrence Island and then to organize a church
in each village. At Gambell we were to have the installation of officers
and Communion on Sunday afternoon. All who were able to come to
church had arrived and we were ready for the service when in came the
chief sorcerer of the village. I think everyone but Mr. Youel was surprised. When the invitation was given, to those who wished to be baptized, to come forward, up came the sorcerer, whose name is I-yak-e-tan.

Mr. Youel did not know the man, of course, and I disliked to say anything about him there before the whole congregation. During the service I noticed Iyaketan picked up a child and played with it not paying
attention to what the interpreter said. Before we were mismissed [sic] I
suggested to Mr. Youel that he ask Iyaketan if he has anything he wished
to say. He said "I came to day because my son urged me to; he wanted
very much to have me baptized."

Later Mr. Youel said he could not refuse anyone who wanted to be
baptized and he believed that good would come of that baptism.

Along in October the deacons called in to "surprise" me. They said
they had good news for me which I'd never guess, so they proceeded to
say "We believe that Iyaketan is truly converted." This is their story:

After he had been baptized he could not sleep. There was something
the matter; he was restless and bothered. Now he is certain God was
back of all this. Then one night he was lying awake and he had a vision
which impressed him very much. He thought about it for days and kept
wondering about his restlessness. Then came a period when he thinks he
came to the turning point and he received Christ as his Savior. The three
deacons just dropped in one day to see how the family was and they
found their host ready for them. He told his story and then said "Now [I]
want to learn about Christ; I cannot read. I do not know how to pray;
teach me that. I do not want the old way any more; I am done with it."
(PCA 1894–1960: RG 98, Box 1, File 11)

John Apangalook's story is told first by his older brother, Paul Silook:

My brother John Apangalook was so nervous in 1928 or 1929. At that
time my father was a boat captain, still having his old custom. As John
was so nervous, I enquire of him to think about what to do. He did not
answer me right then, but as I bringing up some of our old religion he
refuse to have it, but when I say about Christian way of doing he did ac-

cept. So from that time we gave up our old custom. Even we are trying before that but living in two way of religion. (Silook, DLC 1982:13a)

A more detailed version was told to me by John Apangalook's daughter, Susanna:

> SUSANNA: His real life story is converting to Christianity, [it] is [an] uncommon happening, you know. When the missionaries were around there was hardly any knowledge of Christianity really. In those days. But, there was one family, Aningayou family, who was first converted to the teachings of the Christians, you know. . . .
>
> So, probably, my dad heard about it, but then, something unusual could happen to him in his lifetime. For some time he was, how shall I describe? He wasn't at the right state as a normal life, you know, he wasn't at the right—he felt real bothered or, anyway he tells us about that as we were growing up; And he wouldn't go into the house, too. Something bothered him spiritually,
>
> And then they consulted whoever is, you know, any people, one they think is wise or has knowledge of, probably want to know what's happening. And then, but none [of the advice which he received] worked out. They didn't know what was wrong with him and they didn't know what was wrong with that situation. But, they had Aningayou, Mr. Aningayou, pray over him, too, that helped. That helped ease up what he was going through. His nose even were plugged up, he was real full. He's talk like this, and, there was a . . . shaman, John Walunga, I guess he was. . . . He wasn't a Christian, but then they probably consulted that, whoever they think would be of help. To ease up. But this John Walunga told him that anyone have to let him be because it's Jesus, God's son, is doing this to him. And even at night time, in mid-winter it's real cold, at night time, even if I don't fully understand, but it's really happening,
>
> He was at the beach and then somebody else was with him at all times, going with him, going around with him and then he point toward the west.
>
> It's the power of God.
>
> And then the rainbow appeared, at night, in the dark.

CAROL: It must have been frightening. That's a lot of power.

SUSANNA: It is some kind of power. I don't know how he really understand that.

He was supposed to heal the sick, raise the dead, with the power. But he probably wasn't, this was new to him.

He didn't know how to handle it, probably.

But Aningayou and his wife always pray for him. That's the only help, ease him up you know, only help he receives, praying over, praying over him.

And eventually, my mom was pregnant with me. I'm their first child. But then anyway we got over this, probably, with prayer. He probably got understanding, too. When my mom was in labor, she had a real hard long labor with me, you know. She always tell me.

And Dad went down to the beach with the Bible, He carried the Bible, he had the Bible with him and went down to the beach to pray over my mother having a baby, having a long labor. Real hard labor. I wouldn't be born.

But then when he prayed his answer was that, not of Mom, of myself.

He was told—the answer was different.

His prayers, requests, answer, his answer from his prayer was when I'm born I'm going to be standing on the Word of God. . . . There was no answer about Mom. But his answer was that, that I would be standing on the Word of God. Finally I was born first. . . .

When I think back, it's supernatural, the knowledge that he might have.

The power . . . ("Susanna" 1988, in Jolles 1987ff)

Many of the most important conversions among the community's early Christians, were, like Yugniilqwaaq's, the results of a vision or a supernatural encounter, and they, too, draw on an older understanding of confrontation with the supernatural. In the case of John Apangalook, the conversion to Christianity appears to parallel the path that would normally have been followed to become a shaman. He became ill. His family was concerned and one of his brothers was assigned to be his companion. He stayed outside most of the time waiting for a crisis. Essentially, he found resolution after receiving a miraculous vision of a rainbow that illuminated the sky in the middle of the night. At this time, he had already discussed his unrest with his brother Paul and had determined to become Christian.

In this last set of examples, Walter Wongitillan first describes an encounter experienced by his great-grandfather. In the second, he relates a vision or dream that he himself experienced. Whether an experience is interpreted as an encounter or a vision may be the result of generational differences.

I have heard about our great grandfather Ataata. He died and he rose up the third day.

They were waiting for one of his brothers or relatives before they bury him, so it took them three days.

But three days he came alive and he was stiff all over.

They have to help him bend his arms and legs probably and his tongue too.

After he came alive, he told the story that, here—just recently when he died, he didn't know anything, but he woke to find himself. He became conscious again—out in—outside. When he became conscious again out there, some place, it was real calm weather, no wind, no nothing. With a light of a few twinkling stars. And then he stood up and walked and he came to a river. Then he heard a paddling sound on the water. Then a boat came. And told him to get on top of the boat. Then he took him across the river. Then after he crossed the river he saw a real big road, wide and real hard. And the other road he saw were real narrow, following the river. The grass was real tall, and he followed that little narrow path. And on the way he met his aunt. And his aunt said to him, you will never reach that white place over there. Then his aunt turned him the other way and brought him back. The wide river that he recently just crossed was just only a small creek.

And then when he reached to his house, his home, his aunt showed him his body. Oh, it was very filthy, very filthy body. And then she told him, take a look at your body—it's very filthy. You try to go to that bright light over there. Then his aunt instructed

him to raise his hands towards Heaven like that. And pray early in
the morning, and pray every morning and evening. And then she
told him, after five years, he would die for good. So, this is what
I tell about in a testimonial. (Wongitillan 1988, in Jolles 1987ff)

After Walter finished talking, he said that just as had been prophesied,
Ataata died after five years.

In the next example, Walter relates his own vision experience:

Next thing is how I myself, at my age, God helped me. I was
baptized in 1940. We were at camp and one of my sons, seven or
eight year old son, was very sick of whooping cough. But that real
sick boy often say to us, his parents, that Jesus would heal him.
Yeah, then he was healed by Jesus. And at the same time I lost
eight of my dogs. But I often pray about them. Very early in the
morning around 4 o'clock, I walked to look for my dogs. One night
I had a dream. In my dream I was walking around Temnek's Naayvaq [lake]. I climbed up Tsemahaks to the top. *Then on top I saw a
white cross*[9] [author's emphasis]. Then as I kneeled down to pray, I
saw a Bible verse, 1st Peter 3:9.[10] And the next day, I had a dream
again. In my dream the family was in a circle, and I had my Bible
with me and we were gonna pray. As I was getting ready to pray,
somebody, a voice from behind me, talked to me: "You are a
Christian. Your fellow Christians will come and help you fight,
even if somebody can kill you." Then the following day I got six
dogs from Savoonga people and then I left. I went on top of the
mountain; I got on top. I saw four dog teams. Those are my fellow
Christians who came to help me. And so, today, I honestly trust
the Lord (Wongitillan 1988, in Jolles 1987ff)

In each of the cases, men probably held most of the authority within
the family, with the older men taking precedence over younger. Older

9. Until this point, Walter had been speaking in Yupik. When he spoke of the
cross, he used English.

10. "Not rendering evil for evil, or railing for railing: but contrariwise blessing:
knowing that ye are thereunto called, that ye should inherit a blessing" (1st Peter 3:9).

men quite naturally held an allegiance to the more traditional system of belief. Campbell's journals, and the more recent conversion accounts in Bannan's correspondence and mission reports, seem to suggest concerted attempts to reach men whose reputations were just being formed or would soon be the heads of families. The implicit dialogue between the older, more conservative generation and the younger, more adventurous men continues in the present. On several occasions, in stories collected by Alexander Leighton or Dorothea Leighton, a man comments that he himself would continue to hold to the old way but expected that his children would adopt the new. Kulukhon also records similar remarks. Today's older generation is now committed to Christian belief and practice. The strong regard for elders remains. As James Aningayou commented, in the summer of 1940, "our custom is, when we couldn't think clear about something, we had to come to older people" (DLC: Aningayou 1982:93). The sanction of elders, even those who remained steadfast to the old way, was important. Regard for elders includes elements of both respect and fear. Elsewhere Leighton recorded the following:

> I asked James if he ever heard about people who could harm others with some sort of prayer. He said he had, some people were very much afraid, especially older people. . . . Some people are very much afraid; just like a knife pointing at them. . . . Said this is the reason why people are very friendly to each other; always be kind to that kind of person who can harm them. It is worst over in Siberia, a lot of that kind of people there. (Aningayou, DLC 1982:164)

In this same context, Estelle once commented that older people themselves commanded respect because of the power they were thought to exercise. Young people did not speak much around them for fear of arousing their ire.

This combination of respect and reliance, combined with a fear of the consequences of disrespect or disagreement, suggests that at one level there could be no significant religious change in the community until some of those acknowledged to have access to considerable spirit power—that is, elders—had made the change. At the same time, the converts mentioned above were not necessarily the oldest members of the community. They represent a cross-section of young and middle-aged men who would later become respected Christian elders. Their parents, the elders of that time, offered a limited sanction through remarks such as those by Kulukhon's father. He told his son that the son would become Christian, that all of the people would eventually become Christian after the older ones were gone.

In his journal, Campbell suggests that some of these early converts were the brighter and more innovative and aggressive of his older students. These were young men who apparently associated the new power (Christian power) with the knowledge and material gifts brought by the missionaries. These were also men who traveled to the Alaska mainland and experienced, as did Aningayou, the life style and especially the medical expertise of the Americans settled in Nome. These men then become effective links between the traditional and the new world view.

Yugniilqwaaq's story is particularly noteworthy because he was firmly identified as one with a great deal of power through his participation in the traditional belief system. He belonged to a large clan group; his story reflected an obvious desire to acquire new power; once he had established a relationship with the new power, he began to tell his story to others in the community; and, his experience was endorsed by the missionary. He even asked Campbell if he could wear robes that symbolized his new relationship with Jesus. According to Aningayou, Nancy Walunga, Nick Wongitillan, and others, Yugniilqwaaq taught about his new religious commitment for quite some time before his tragic death. He built a small church at Pughughileq and preached on Sundays. He was challenged by the spirits he had abandoned, however, according to Nick Wongitillan. His drum would appear out on the beach and in other mysterious places. His drum was once his way to call the spiritual powers to himself. Before his death, Yugniilqwaaq persuaded a number of men to give up the old ways. Aningayou, Kulukhon, and Campbell all speak of his influence.

The stories of Iyakitan and Apangalook, while from a later generation, are directly linked to the circumstances of Aningayou's faithfulness. Iyakitan, especially, was as influential for his generation of unbelievers as Yugniilqwaaq was for the earlier generation. Throughout, the calm resolve of James Aningayou and his family was held up as an example for others. As

James assumed the position of elder, the new generation of men sought him out for advice as they came to terms with the problem of spirit power relations.

Members of the community gave a number of reasons for seeking a new religious faith. Aningayou and others commented that the new way was "easier," that is, more predictable and less likely to leave one subject to the whims of recalcitrant and often difficult spirits. It was less problematic as well. With the new understanding of Apa, one did not have to go to such extreme sacrifices as exchanging a life for a life. A third often-stated reason was that the new way was ultimately more satisfying because the prospect of Heaven was equally available to all.

Other reasons for embracing the new religious concept included greater access to the miraculous healing power now more available at the hands of a sympathetic Apa or through his Son. Kulukhon was persuaded to accept the new system after the miraculous restoration of sight to his son Allen; physical rewards in the form of increased access to Euro-American material goods were also a factor here. Apangalook's story suggests that his new faith was an important element in the safe delivery of his first-born child.

The new spiritual life was considerably less complex and exacting than the old. Certain rites surrounding hunting were abandoned altogether. Campbell pressed the men whom he accompanied on hunting trips to give up the practice of offering fresh water to slain animals. At the same time he substituted a general prayer of thanksgiving when an animal was taken. When the islanders discovered that those who abandoned the older traditions were as successful as the traditional believers, or even more, they interpreted this as proof of the efficacy of the new system.

Simultaneous with the conversions came a convergence of certain concepts drawn from each tradition. I believe this transformation of concepts was critical to the whole process, because it provided for the eventual embedding of the new tradition within the various facets of Yupik culture. At the center of this process was the reinterpretation or new conception of Apa. Silook's description of Apa, given in Chapter 7, neatly describes the old concept. Apa was a powerful spirit being; He was synonymous with life as it was lived in pre-contact times; His house might have been the moon. Through Him the weather was controlled and animals

given. Apa could unleash powerful forces whenever a person failed to follow the rules. He was awesome. Most elders say that Apa was always
known, but before the coming of the missionaries they had not known
how to pray to him; now, the Bible taught them the right way. The new
conception of Apa maintained his powerful weather spirit attributes, his
controlling hand on the great sea mammals, and his critical role in the
matter of life after death. The name soul/life spirit dichotomy was amal-
gamated with the Christian understanding of the soul as an eternal aspect
of humans that moves to a heavenly plane after death. This concept is
merged with that of angels. The divisions among these various concepts
are not at all clear, and different aspects are emphasized depending on
the context. At present, perhaps the most widely understood and assimi-
lated concept is that of the son of God. Unfortunately, there seem to be
no early discussions of this concept. Quite likely, the community's ready
acceptance of the notion of a son who came to sacrifice himself for the
people is in part due to the high value it placed on men. A strong relationship between father and son is the ideal. That strength, and the respect that is a part of the father-son relationship, is illustrated in Hughes'
Eskimo Boyhood (1974), the autobiography of a well-known Gambell resident. Not only is the bond between father and son idealized, but the suicide of a man so that his child might live is a remembered practice. Although apparently such suicides no longer occur, people still understand
that this bond demands of its two participants the ultimate act. Thus, the
islanders' acceptance of a son of God who sacrificed himself at his father's request is not difficult to explain. Men and women alike are usually in tears when they describe the agony that they assume was felt by
God when He was forced to make this request.

   More difficult to accept was the Christian dichotomy between the
human and non-human world. Many community rituals consisted of gestures that signified respect for the spirits of the animals. These actions
were bound up with all aspects of subsistence as well as with the social
institutions associated with subsistence practices. Such rituals were, and
continue to be, a major aspect of the world view of the people. They
served as channels through which individuals exercised their power and
authority. Here missionary action intervened. The missionaries opposed
ceremonies that directly contradicted conventional Christian teaching.

They attempted to dissuade hunters from offering fresh water to slain animals, and opposed ceremonies involving wife exchange. These ceremonies apparently continued to be performed into the 1940s, but only intermittently, and care was taken to keep church officials from attending. Contemporary explanations of such activities usually suggest that people did these things only as a last resort. Today, the importance of these ceremonies in combating illness and famine or other misfortune may no longer be understood. Respect to ancestor spirits is no longer maintained through direct nourishment of the spirits. Instead, this traditional sentiment has been overlaid by a more generalized respect for the dead. Summer is a time for traveling to the top of the mountain to repair weathered coffins and to pray in the presence of the deceased. Feeding the spirits as an acknowledgment of Apa's hand in allowing mammals to give themselves to the hunter, for example, clearly falls outside the usual bounds of Christian teaching. As a result, many of the rituals associated with the non-human world have undergone an evolution in form.

The conduct of Christian prayers to acknowledge Apa's generosity and to pay respect to animals which have given themselves to the community as food is still the responsibility of lineage heads and boat captains. Perhaps the greatest difference is the shift that is implicit in the acceptance of Protestant Christianity—from actions performed by and for the *ramka* to individual salvation. This suggests a shift in the power relations that obtain in the village and reflects what Kenelm Burridge refers to as the "pain of the millennium [which] belongs only to man. It is why he is man, why, when the time comes, he has to make a new man" (1969:3). Burridge discusses shifts in power relations in the context of millenarian activities and associates these activities with the more general search for truth in which humans appear to engage endlessly. He remarks:

> Religions . . . are concerned with the systematic ordering of different kinds of power. . . . because a religion is concerned with the truth of things, and reaches out to discover and identify those sorts of power which, though sensed and affective, are currently not wholly comprehended, its rules about the use and control of different kinds of powers are grounded in an interplay between experience, working assumptions, and those more rooted assumptions we call faith. As experience widens and deepens, some of the rules and assumptions will be qualified, and others

abandoned altogether—a developmental process in which received truths or assumptions give way to new truths, and in which the new truths become in their turn the received assumptions of future generations. These assumptions are community truths, truths which command a consensus. From them are derived the sets of moral imperatives, obligations, and rules of conduct to which men, because they live in community, subject themselves. (Burridge 1969:5–6)

St. Lawrence Island has little history of prophets, generally, or of unusual religious movements. Instead, its religious history moves gradually from traditional practices to those introduced by the missionaries. Nevertheless, the world of 1850 was not the world of 1900, and certainly not the world of 1920 or thereafter. What Burridge refers to as a widening and deepening of experience fits the changed world of the Sivuqaghhmiit well, a world that included foreign whalers, explorers, teachers, and missionaries. Such a world did not fit easily into the old categories; it needed explanation. As Burridge notes elsewhere, when people are confronted with technology that has never been experienced before, they must come to terms with the new world that is suggested by it. In Gambell, for example, when the first elders saw an airplane, some of them tried to imitate it, hoping that this unexplainable thing would leave them alone if they appeared to be related to it. Burridge describes this phenomenon:

[They had to] absorb and explain [this new phenomenon to] themselves if they were to continue to retain their integrity as men. Aware of themselves in the terms of one set of assumptions, they had now to become aware of themselves in terms of assumptions that included something more. A new kind of redemption was offered, and to take advantage of this a certain reorganizing of political relations seems to have been entailed. (Burridge 1969:35)

For St. Lawrence Islanders, the world first changed suddenly when so many died in 1878–1879. But later, it changed by degrees. With the exception of Agighsehaq's prophesy, explanations of the changing world were contained within the pragmatic conduct of everyday life. At the same time, accumulated change did have to be explained. The individuals who converted struggled with the new world. Some never converted but gave permission to their children to make the change. Men like

Aningayou, Kulukhon, Silook, and Sunaaghruk actively sought to assess and reshape religious practice by seeking out Apa and applying to Him in new terms—that is, they sought to redefine their world in the light of the collective changes that had taken place. In this process, they explored new avenues to power individually and together.

It is no coincidence that these men were all respected persons in the community. If St. Lawrence Island did not have many prophets, it did have new men of unusual faith. These men took it upon themselves, in Burridge's terms, to

> take departure from their own local or greater traditions . . . to be communicable to the indigenous audience they must be cast in a traditional mould. Both in this and a deeper sense [they] . . . take on themselves the task of renovating tradition, of seeking into the familiar and accepted in order to reach into the new, of so phrasing the new that it emerges as a more appropriate expression of what had always been agreed to be true. . . . in the attempt to rediscover and remold the traditional sources of authority and power, [they] . . . , by digging new channels for tradition, also allow the new to flow in. (1969:32)

Adoption of the new faith and the establishment of new avenues of spirit power relations depended fundamentally on a familiarity with the structure of power relations as it had been manipulated in the past. Conversion depended not only on knowledge and acceptance of the newly conceptualized Apa and his remarkable son, but on utilizing specific forms of meditation, reflection, and interpretation of visions in order to embrace the new religious system.

CHAPTER 9

Men, Women, and Food:
A Subsistence Way of Life

To us Eskimos, hunting is our life; [It] very much keeps our bodies alive. Since long ago, hunting has been [our way of life] with nothing to stop it, no law [from the outside] to it. It was just as people catch animals. [It] Has been [that way] since long ago until today. In my time, now, the only thing is that since 1969, the Marine Mammal [Protection Act] limited the killing to so much. . . . In my time, the limit came. . . . From [during the time of] our forefathers, our grandparents, our parents, there was no limit to catch. The catch was as much as they can carry, as much as they [can] eat. . . .

When their month¹ arrives, they celebrate. . . . It is as we do when we have potlucks. It is like that. The boat captain notifies his clan people that they are going somewhere to eat of his catch [from] the year round.

It is like giving thanks to God. When it becomes one year to them [when one year has passed], the boat captain notifies his people and [they] have a feast of what he caught and feed[s] his people [of the choice food]. In the same way it is giving thanks. Us, we celebrate Thanksgiving now, it is like that. . . . It is like that—to show thanks at the end of hunting season to people and it is to God also. (C. Ungott 1992, in Jolles 1987ff)

Sitting down together to share food, which family hunters have brought home from the sea or which men and women have gathered from the cliffs, the beaches, and the tundra, is the enduring

---

1. Mr. Ungott refers to the month when families gave thanks for the food already received in the previous year and the food they hoped to receive during the new whaling season.

symbol of Yupik life, and it embraces all within it.[2] Almost all conversations eventually turn to food. Men discuss hunting for hours at a time. Women often think about the meat in family meat storage boxes and in freezers. When men go out on the land by snow machine or four-wheeler or put out to sea by boat, it is usually to hunt. When women visit their husband's relatives, as often as not they check the family meat racks and outdoor food boxes for food. When women chat, they consider whether this or that meat is available and speculate aloud about what they plan to cook for dinner, or they talk about food for which they have been longing that comes from the beach or the land.[3]

The foraging year or Yupik calendar begins in July, after the whaling festival, according to elders like Pelassi, who died in 1985, and Anders Apassingok. This is midsummer elsewhere, but late spring in Gambell. As Pelassi noted: "People thought of the end of the (hunting) rituals as the end of the year. All of these celebrations, festivals, and rituals were usually over by the end of June. So when I think of the month of July, I think of it as the beginning of the new year; the time to start collecting roseroots (*nunivak*) and other plants" (Blassi, in Apassingok et al. 1985 1:245).

This is the time to go to camp: to fish, to gather eggs, to net birds, to collect spring greens. It is the time of "summer" whales, like the minke and the grays, who "hang around" in the warmish summer months. In late spring and early summer, as the land begins truly to emerge from the snow, migratory birds arrive to nest. The very first sign of spring, in late April and May, is the return of the snow buntings. No one eats these small black and white birds, but many women put out oatmeal for them just to see them fluttering and clustering on the snow near a window. They are reminders that other birds are not far behind. Snow geese, sandhill cranes, and many other birds follow the buntings.

Spring brings the light. Just after the winter solstice, the days grow longer. By April, the light lingers until 10:30 or 11:00 at night. By midsummer, there is no "true" night, only a few hours of deep twilight that

2. Portions of this chapter were originally presented at the Oral History Association annual meeting, Anchorage, Alaska. See Jolles 1999.

3. Often when I visit someone, they ask me to help preserve the hunting life way by explaining to others how important hunting is here. My Yupik friends say that they cannot imagine life without local food (*neqepik*).

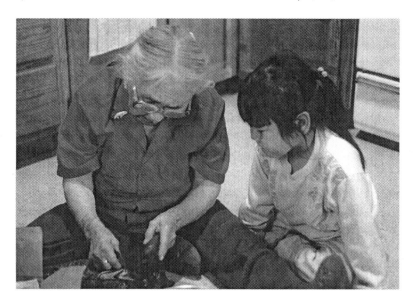

9.1 Rhea cleans a cormorant while her great-granddaughter watches.

surround the time of sunset and sunrise around 2:30 in the morning. When the light days of spring come, it's hard not to think about eating fresh duck or fresh goose or fresh auklets. Some people eat cormorants and a very few still eat sea gulls. It's such a pleasure to change foods with the seasons. Rhea, I know, was very fond of these spring foods and her young hunter relatives used to bring them to us to eat. Even though she was almost blind, she could still clean a bird. The knowledge was in her hands, although her eyes could no longer see. People say that when the auklets arrive, the air smells of oranges. I cannot explain it, but auklets do bring a special fresh smell. And, of course, one can stand along the shore in early morning and late evening to watch long lines of geese, ducks, brants, and dovekies flying low over the open water, with its moving ice floes, on their way to and from their sea-filled feeding grounds. Later, when nests and cliffs are crowded with expectant avian parents, everyone anticipates bird eggs, brought home in huge numbers—especially murre eggs, which are gathered from the cliffs along the coast. Young men usu-ally gather eggs, although some young women do, too. It is a dangerous occupation. In 1996, for example, a young man died after falling from the

Savoonga cliffs while gathering eggs. About the same time, women gather the greens so long awaited, and Labrador tea. The first greens of the warm season are *anguqaq* (dwarf fireweed) and *ququngaq* (willow leaves). Other greens come later. By late midsummer, some time after the Fourth of July, the tundra and undisturbed beach areas are covered with flowers: pinks, purples of all sorts, whites and yellows. For a brief moment, the island is transformed into a softness hardly imagined in midwinter. By late summer, thoughts turn to salmon berries (cloud berries) and the small black berries that ripen just under their leaves in the sandy beaches.

Throughout the spring, summer, and fall, as long as migratory birds nest on the island, young men hunt birds. Auklets, old squaws, and murres are common fare then. In the early years of her marriage, Beda remembered that " . . . all summer we eat birds. Vernon [Beda's husband] used to caught lot of birds and cormorants and murre and auklets. We dried them. We skin them and take out the guts and dried them in the racks. When they dried, we boil it, eat it along with older blubber. Most of them store away for winter" (B. Slwooko 1995, in Jolles 1987ff).

When there is open water, men contemplate the best time to go out in the boats in search of food. Women think about *tepaq* (sea plants and animals) that might wait on the beach for them to collect to add to an evening meal.[4] And, if they can convince their hunter relatives, they might get *uupa* (sea peaches), which are raked up from the sea bottom near to shore with special rakes. Sculpins, what children call "ugly fish," are targeted by older men and women who enjoy a day's quiet fishing. In fact, almost everyone likes to fish, and it is especially rewarding to bring home a bag filled with Arctic char or grayling or Dolly Varden or Tom cod. Occasionally, a hunting boat brings home an infrequent visitor to St. Lawrence Island waters: a shark, perhaps, or halibut or even beluga. For many people, camping and fishing go together. Beda, who grew up with her grandparents at their camp at Tapghaq, remembered all of the food that came in summer, especially the fish:

4. I usually keep my parka pockets full of plastic bags in case I am invited to ride along the beach to find *tepaq*. On my first solo beach trip, I brought home a bright collection of interesting but mysterious plants and animals. I asked Mary to check them, and she carefully removed some bright yellow sea sponges from my bag. Eating these can be fatal! Sea sponges swell up and choke the unwary diner!

They [Beda's grandparents] used to cook lots of different kinds of
fish: Dolly Varden, white fish, grayling, salmon, rainbow trouts.
And another kind of white fish. They dried up some, stored in the
seal pokes. Many years ago that's the way they use to store away
white fish and graylings, in seal pokes, clean ones. And they put
them underneath the ground a bit in the summer time. When
they came here [to Gambell], they usually put them in underground storage.

Many years ago, people in Grandfather's days, they used to clean
up their underground storage every summer, every spring, every
summer. And put clean food in there, some of them maybe clean
down close to the permafrost, . . . They usually call these *Teqaq*
(very bottom), way down bottom, *Teqaq* (the bottomest part).
(B. Slwooko 1992, in Jolles 1987ff)

In fall, as the weather turns cold, people spend less and less time in
camp. Gathering activities gradually subside and families reluctantly return home. School begins in mid-August and by the end of August there
may be snow flurries. Those with school-age children shorten their camping days to the weekends. Everyone waits for the first freeze to solidify the
tundra, making it easier to travel from home to camp on four-wheelers. It
will be November, at least, before it is comfortable to use snow machines.
As the weather turns cold, and before the ice comes down with the polar
ice pack—whose arrival takes longer each year as the world warms and El
Niños complicate weather patterns—women and elders stroll along the
beach edge, hoping for *tepaq* tossed onto the beach by the storms that
come more and more often as the weather turns toward true winter. During all of this time, meat dries on meat racks, a product of the hunts of late
spring and early summer. By August, though, most meat has been stored
for winter in family freezers. When I first came to Gambell, the community operated a village meat locker where everyone could store winter
meat supplies, but it has been out of commission for many years.[5] A few
families still maintain *siqluwat* (pl. form; underground meat storage pits

5. Renovation of the old meat locker storage building began in 1999. When it is
finished, it will be used in conjunction with a bone and ivory resources management
system.

dug down into the permafrost), which are particularly good for aging various meats. Every family used to have one or more of these pits. Now, only a few remain, although many people enjoy aged meat (*aghyughsighaq*), especially *iiqwaq* (aged walrus meat balls). With two village stores, people depend less on the harvests of spring and summer. Both stores usually carry the same popular items: frozen pizzas (which can be popped into a microwave), frozen fried chicken, hot dogs, and hamburger meat. Beda and other elders often speak longingly of the days when all food came from the land and the sea.

> BEDA: In the fall time, around the month of July, part of August, especially the full month of July, that [is] the roseroots and other good eating plants, picking time. Like *nunivak* [roseroot] and *amlluqiiraq, ququngaq* leaves, *alqegkaq*—I don't know what they call in English those, something like spinach, big leaves with a stem in the middle stem. We call it *alqegkaq*. We boiled those when we come home, picking the big leaves, big, big leaves. [The] Stem is partly sweetened. We boil it until it's soft. We put them in another pan when it cool off and stored them in . . . baby seal poke. We stored them—*alqegkaq*. We can make *akuutaq* out of these sometimes with blackberries. Very good eating. Around the month of August, September, that's picking time for roots. Roseroots, [and other] roots I don't know in English those [others]: *qullikaq, qakeqaaq, unataghyaghqaq.* . . . (B. Slwooko 1992, in Jolles 1987ff)

> . . . around October or September, [we had] dried fish and dried seal meat. Dried birds. It's done already. They take down and stored them in a big sack, and stored them in a damp, damp place, so they don't dried. Then all through the winter, we eated those dried seal meat. Dried seal meat, dried bird, dried fish. Grandma always boiled those, every people around here in the winter time boiled those dried birds, something like, cormorants and ducks and other birds . . . . (B. Slwooko 1996, in Jolles 1987ff).

One of the wonderful contradictions of modern island life is that although whaling is superimposed on all things, sacred and secular, walruses and seals feed people every day. I suppose one could say that walruses and seals are like the "hamburger" of the lower forty-eight. Men hunt seals from the shore in late fall, before the ice "comes down," and from the ice in midwinter. Seals and walrus are hunted along the ice edge, which moves south in winter and north in summer. Walruses are found on the ice during winter and spring. As Vernon Slwooko, Beda's husband, remembered it:

> Back then we would try to get as much *maklak*s [bearded seals] as possible. We tried to get many for the skin, but we gathered all the meat, too. We used the hide [*atungaq*] for *kamek* [boot] soles. We always killed seven *maklak*s when we went boating out there in the water. After we killed seven seals, we would head for home. We took everything: the meat, the skin, nothing was wasted. Now the *maklak* hide is just thrown away, just the meat is kept.
>
> . . . We tried to get 100 meatballs stored into meat caches during spring hunt. When we hunted for walruses we would take as much *manguna* [skin] along with its meat, and fill up our boats until we couldn't take any more. . . . we usually [took] 4 walruses. . . . we never killed more than what was needed, and always took all the meat. . . . We needed all that food, because we had a lot of dogs. Howard [Vernon's brother] and I had 40 dogs between us — 20 each — we had a lot of dogs, so we tried to get as much meatballs as we could. We would save them to use as dog food and we would end up eating the good parts [laughing as he said it]. That's the way it was. (V. Slwooko 1992, in Jolles 1987ff)

If the men had too few seals to feed their families and their dogs, they performed a special ceremony, which seemed to help:

> VERNON: . . . when they had a hard time killing a seal, they would inflate a seal's gall bladder and kick it until it popped. [Vernon laughs.]
>
> After they kicked it, they then would go hunting, and they did get seals afterwards!
>
> [Everyone laughs]." (V. Slwooko 1992, in Jolles 1987ff)

Elinor, who was born and raised in Savoonga, was trained to hunt by her father, Albert Kulowiyi, and especially by her father's younger

9.2 *Early in the morning, Vernon Qaqsungiq Slwooko and the late Charles Hughes untangle Vernon's dog team, 1955. Photo courtesy of Leslie Hughes.*

brother, Herbert Kiyukluk. Under her Uncle Herbert's watchful eye, she hunted both seals and walruses. I asked her to tell me about her hunting experiences.

CAROL: Maybe [you could] think a little more about some of your times when you were helping your uncle with hunting?

ELINOR: [My uncle Herbert] wakes me up when they're ready to go out hunting.

I go out real fast, harness the dogs, get things on top of the sled and bring 'em down for him.

Because he's not gonna waste time all the time. He's that kind of a person.

He's gotta go on and on and on. Not wait for other people. So he taught us to be on time all the time. That's one reason I still don't want to be late when I'm working.

I have to be there two or five minutes before. That's why when I'm working I always have my time five minutes back. [Elinor keeps herself punctual by setting her watch five minutes ahead.]

So I won't be late. Because time is important.

He taught me a lot. . . . I think he taught me a lot of things. He showed me how to hunt . . . . [to] Crawl to a seal. and things like that. . . . the first time [I] went out with him . . . It was in April, I think, that they were going out by boat, and me and my brother wanted to go. . . .

My [older] brother had died, and I had [was wearing] his [hunting] clothes.

Skin pants and his parka, and his boots . . . that I wear all the time.

And I went out, and we got walrus with baby out there.

He [Uncle Herbert] let me hold something, or let me cut this part. Showed me this way and that.

Even if it's good weather, we have to, we have to do things quickly. Because the current is always taking us out further away from the village. We have to do it real fast. Bring it home.

And they bring home the catch, and they dump it and go back out again.

I was . . . in the boat with . . . John, my brother, and Hogarth, my cousin. . . . Hogarth and I used to . . . compete a lot in learning things to do, you know. They're my teasing cousins [*ilughaq*]. . . . their mother is my father's sister. That's the way [we] used to do it.

Yes, . . . my uncle's the one who taught me how to crawl to a seal, cut up walrus.

That was exciting. That was also in my blood, because I loved to do it.

And, ah, my father made a smaller net, for bird netting, for me and my brother.

So in summer time and we are at camp, greens picking camp. . . . over the side of that little cliff over in Savoonga. . . . Every spring we used to be over there because my mother needed to pick greens.

So she won't have to go far. Just around there in the creek.

And, me and my brother used to climb up that cliff over there and get enough birds with that net. Enough for one meal till [we] come down. Auklets . . . The cliff birds. Little auklets. . . . me and my brother used to go hunting.

Dean. He was about nine or ten or even younger, probably. I used to take care of him. We used to go fox trapping. With Dad. And one time he got six, six [foxes] in a trap. I had three over me. Of course, Dad, he couldn't put [lift] anything himself because he just had a big surgery. And, we had a baleen toboggan with us. . . . After we got six of them, I put my brother Dean on top of [the load], and surrounded him with foxes. That was easy.

That toboggan's very slick. And coming down the hill, we just sit there and slide.

What else can I talk about? So much for hunting.

CAROL: Well . . . What about the time when you really first began thinking about boys, and thinking about the other boys, other than as hunting friends?

ELINOR: . . . I think I was around sixteen, fifteen years old . . . when I started seeing boys. . . .

And, ah, well, when I became serious with Akulki [Elinor's husband], he knows—I told him everything.

I don't sew. I don't cook. I just go hunting. That's all. Man's work, you know. And, he knows it.

Even my father told Akulki's father, "She's no good for anything except for hunting."

And his family know it, and yet they accepted me. (E. Oozeva 1996, in Jolles 1987ff)

Walrus meat is the mainstay of the diet. It is boiled in large pots on a regular basis. *Manguna*, or walrus with fat and skin attached, is often served with potatoes, which go into the pot with the meat, or with Minute Rice, which is served in a small bowl on the side. When they are available, *tepaq* (beach foods) are cooked in the pot, too. Sometimes, frozen broccoli is the accompanying green—purchased from the store along with ketchup, Thousand Island dressing, and soy sauce. These condiments, into which one can dip one's meat, are often found on a serving tray with the more traditional seal oil. *Qesni*, fat from a female walrus breast, fresh or aged, is another favored part of the walrus.

I myself find fresh *qesni* delicious, but aged *qesni*, unfortunately, is quite beyond me. On one occasion, Elinor invited me to eat with her brother and his family in Savoonga. Her brother's wife spread out a tantalizing array of meats on a tray and we all engaged in serious eating. I suppose I didn't realize how careful my friend, Mary, had always been about the food she served me. Afterward, I remembered that she always told me whether the meat was "old" or not, and I tried each new food at her house based on her recommendations. Anyway, I took a piece of *qesni* from Elinor's sister-in-law's *qayuutaq* (serving tray) and popped it into my mouth. What a shock! The smell of the thoroughly aged meat immediately permeated my senses. My only thought was that as a guest I should not be rude. I must finish this piece of meat. I chewed and chewed and chewed. The meat seemed to have the consistency of a stubborn rubber band. I couldn't chew it up and I couldn't swallow it. Elinor watched me, of course, and slowly she began to smile. Finally, she said quietly, still smiling: "You know, Carol, you are turning green! You don't *have* to eat *everything*."

One special delicacy comes when a walrus is taken after it has eaten clams. The clams are removed from the stomach and then frozen. Later, they are served still frozen and cut into thin slices. Another special food, once included as part of *ramka* whaling ceremonies, is young walrus meat. Young walrus (*qasiqaq*) are hunted in spring and their flesh is aged in the early months of summer. *Qasiqaq* has a flavorful, smoked, piquant taste that rivals any smoked meat served anywhere. Stories are told about people who have just eaten *qasiqaq*. The smell of the meat "sticks" to the hands. After you eat it, you become very sleepy. I'm not sure if the stories are all true, but I do know that the smell of the meat is pungent and seems to cling to one after eating. Once, after eating *qasiqaq*, I attended an evening church service and sat in the back pew of the Presbyterian church with Leonard Nowpakahok, now deceased, and his wife, Beulah. The two of them joked about my smelling of *qasiqaq*, and then, as the service continued, all three of us dozed away. Leonard insisted that I had caused all of us to fall asleep.

Seal meat is served cooked or uncooked, frozen or unfrozen, fresh or aged. Thin sliced frozen seal meat with frozen willow or dwarf fireweed leaves or perhaps a small amount of willow root makes a spectacular noon meal. Seal meat is fried, as is liver of all kinds. (Not polar bear liver, of course; it contains so much vitamin A that it can be harmful if eaten.) Seal intestines are carefully cleaned, braided, and later divided into small sections, which are cooked in a pot along with other meats and served thin-sliced on a tray. Seal meat, and whale meat, too, is often dried into a kind of jerky, called *nefkuuraq*, and cut into bite-size pieces when placed on a tray.

Both women and men regularly set out crab lines and enjoy fishing. In midwinter, usually during the months of January, February, March, and sometimes even later, everyone can be found off the coast of Northwest Cape (which is actually at the northeastern edge of the village), cutting fishing holes into the shorefast ice. This is the king crab season in Alaska, and no one can resist. Going crabbing is like having a winter picnic. Men and women both set lines, one in each hole, hung with bait such as meat or fish scraps. These are wrapped into a piece of old panty hose that keeps krill, which local folks call "worms," from completely devouring the bait before a crab can express an interest in it. (This is the same krill that feeds whales on their northward journey to their spring breeding and rearing grounds in the Beaufort Sea, off the north coast of Barrow.) I am always in awe of the men and women who crab. They stay out on the ice for hours, usually bare-handed, because it is hard to pull up a crab line wearing clumsy gloves.

Crabbing is a good place to relax. Women visit with each other and keep an eye on each other's children and grandchildren. Men and women sit or stand around and smoke while they contemplate the ice, which seems to stretch out for miles. The piles of winter ice create havens that protect the crabbers from too much wind, but it is still quite cold. Crab lines are checked periodically and pulled up carefully hand over hand when a crab is on the line. The unlucky crab is placed upside down in the snow or ice. Sometimes the crab is "stuck" first to kill it. Regardless, it freezes within minutes in the brisk winter temperatures of 10 or 15 degrees below zero. Later, the crabs are stuffed into knapsacks and taken home, where they are put in a quick-frozen pile in *sayuuragaat* (outer entry ways) until they can be boiled and dipped into bowls of melted butter. Occasionally in midwinter someone chances on a pile of small pink crabs (*neghnavregat*), no bigger than the palm of the hand, which have been pushed through a crack or crevice in the shore ice. These are brought home in plastic bags and eaten almost immediately, uncooked. They taste as sweet as new peas fresh from a garden.

One hazard of crabbing is polar bears. They hang around Northwest Cape at the "Point" looking for just such good food. When I went looking for *neghnavregat* with Mary, one of us kept an eye out for bears. We knew we would have to leap onto her four-wheeler in a great hurry if we saw one. Polar bears can move very fast and are not exactly good-humored.[6] Another hazard is shorefast ice. In May of 1996, probably fifteen or twenty people were out on the ice having a great time when a huge section of shorefast ice lost its grip to the shore. Everyone on the ice rushed toward the northern point, where the ice would come to a brief halt before moving out into the current. No one was hurt, but it was a reminder that the sea is never quite safe.

The food most anticipated, the food that truly marks the appearance of spring, is brought by bowhead whales. According to Leonard Apanga-look, "we have been whaling . . . for time immemorial and we claim that we are one of the older whaling communities. . . . we claim that we pushed those whales which were at one time land animals into the Bering Sea when the land washed out. And, that's where we are" (L. Apangalook, in Jolles 1995b:320).

Whale meat (*nguuraq*) and blubber (*mangtak*) are special. Whales that come to the village are celebrated. The taking of a whale generates tremendous excitement, and the infectious and festive atmosphere engulfs the *ramka* that has taken it and extends outward to embrace others, because it tests boat captains to be generous to the whole community at once. St. Lawrence Island identity and values derive from its long history as a hunting community. Nowhere is that sense of identity and purpose so evident as in the experience and tradition of sea mammal hunting, es-

6. Ernest "Tiger" Burch once told me that polar bears are left-handed and that this would help me in an emergency. At the time, I thought Tiger was joking, but later several hunters assured me that it was true.

pecially whaling. All life in the community rests, in a sense, on the organization of community members into whaling cooperatives based on patrilineal and patrilateral ties—the men who hunt together.

As a visitor to St. Lawrence Island, I wished to learn as much about hunting as I could, but I knew that as both a *laluramka* and a woman, I should not ask to witness a hunt. It was and still is uncommon for Sivuqaghhmiit women to hunt, even though women did and do hunt from time to time. Long ago, Anna Okhtokiyuk and her sister Alice Yaavgaghsiq, now in their nineties, accompanied their father, Yaavgaghsiq, when he went out whaling. Anna talked about her experiences in 1992:

> Long ago, when we are going boating, we harness the dogs on the sleds. We went down.
>
> There weren't very many evinrudes [outboard motors] in those days. Ours was only a six [six horse power].
>
> There was long shore ice, so we used to go down to open water by dog team.[7]
>
> When we were all on the boat, our mother would let some of the dogs loose and use two or three dogs to go up [to the house].
>
> We pulled our sails up and went down further, down there [to sail the open water in search of whales],
>
> When someone sees some whales, . . . [we say] "that boat has their flag up."
>
> We tried to see some whales.
>
> When there is not much action going on, we got sleepy, we got sleepy.
>
> Then, "Ahh! that boat has the flag up, Oh, oh, they got a whale!" Someone caught a whale. Oozevaseuk's got a whale. We dropped our evinrude [outboard motor], we put our evinrude down.
>
> We were already reaching them when the whale went under the long shore ice.

7. People in Gambell use the west beach as a directional point. One either "goes down," as in going westward *down* to the beach or *down* to town (to the Gambell Native Store) or one "goes up," as in going eastward, away from the beach and to Sivuqaq Mountain or to the school at its foot.

On the edge of the shore ice, there were boats gathering.

We got there [and] then it [the whale] got up—under the ice it went.

It was too bad. We felt sorry for it there. The floats went with it and we couldn't see it anymore.

They didn't know where it was, somewhere down there . . .

Over there, we're coming up, we come up, we all come up and felt sorry about it, very much.

Tomorrow [the next day], during day time, using those same dogs, we go down.

From there [from that time], there were no more whales. [It was the end of the whaling season.]

We moved to walrus hunting.

When we could see a herd of walrus on top of an ice floe, when we're almost to them, we stayed really still.

When they [the men] shoot them, they [the walrus] wake up and suddenly are alert. . . .

Myself, Alice, Tapiisak, Koozaata and Yaavgaghsiq, that's how many we were in a boat.

So, we caught walrus. We loaded meat especially.

We desired to get blubber to use for Eskimo clay lamps in winter. So we always get blubber.

When we get bearded seals, Tapiisak divides them up. He gives them to each person.

When we came home, we back packed the meat balls to underground caches.

I loved to go dog teaming, so I always bring them up by dog team.

We do not stay out late in evening. Only we play ball, *kalleghta*, which was very fun to play.

Sometimes we used to forget to go home while playing ball that way [see description of *kalleghta* below].

Next day, when we wake up, when the weather is good for hunting, we get up even if we are sleepy and go down. So we go hunting by boat. . . .

When I was a young girl, I was an errand person. I did not sew.

Also many other things I did not do, but I did men's work like guns. (Okhtokiyuk 1992, in Jolles 1987ff)

Still, hunting[8] belongs to men.[9] It is no longer possible to know which came first, the boat crew—with its complement of brothers, uncles, father, sons, and grandfathers—or the *ramka*, based on the assembled patrilineal and patrilateral men and their wives, sons, and unmarried daughters. The same men who hunted together called themselves by distinguishing names, felt a special allegiance to certain settlements and camp grounds, and considered themselves and their children to be of one flesh. The names of place, boat, and person were bound together by the desire and the duty to hunt. Through hunting, the Sivuqaghhmiit world was ordered—both in general and in its specifics. The major ceremonial calendar was articulated and highlighted through the obligations of the hunt, and the ordering of all life cycle activities passed through its lens. Thus, St. Lawrence Island identity and values, past and present, have been derived from its long history as a hunting community. Nowhere is that sense of identity, purpose, and distinctive order so evident as in the experience and tradition of sea mammal hunting, especially the hunt for *aghveq*, the great bowhead whale.

In the early 1900s, even after the devastation of 1878, whaling remained central to community identity and economy. If the cycling of the moon marked the hunting and gathering cycles, whaling was a metaphor and an underlying structure for island residents. In 1982, Willis and Nancy Walunga identified at least eleven *ramket* in Gambell.[10] Within each *ramka* were numerous extended family groups. These groups, today, often possess boats that hunt under the general jurisdiction of the over-arching

---

8. Men's special knowledge, which consists partly of hunting strategies and technologies and partly of a deep familiarity with weather and ice conditions, has been described both by local historians and outside researchers.

9. As a female guest in the community, I have limited my discussion to the religious and the social, since these fall generally within both male and female domains. I have also focused on topics subject to local approval and tried to abide by local rules regarding which stories should be told and by whom.

10. Mrs. and Mrs. Walunga worked with Dr. Lynn Robbins of Western Washington University, Bellingham, Washington, in conjunction with a project directed by Joseph Jorgensen (see Jorgensen 1990).

ramka. In the early 1920s and 1930s, when the population of Gambell was small, consisting of the gathered remains of the once-populous island, each *ramka* was both extended family or lineage and incipient clan. Most *ramka* had only one boat for the hunting men of its group. Each group of men and their extended families performed their own distinctive hunting ceremonies. Henry Collins noted that these ceremonies seemed to differ only slightly, but these differences set apart each group and gave each set of related families within a *ramka* a sense of unique identity. In 1983, Ruby Rookok of Savoonga described how those differences could affect a young person growing up. When she was young, the Siberian relatives used to come to visit in Gambell during the summer. It was a time for athletic competitions, celebrations, and dancing:

> After the competitive events was Eskimo singing and dancing at Suluk's. You know that the Suluks were great singers. Mkklaghhaq, my grandfather, was married to Iknakeneq, Suluk's sister.
>
> Our aunt, Singlenga, wouldn't let us go to (Suluk's) Eskimo singing and dancing. She didn't go herself. But her daughter went with her aunt, Anasuk, because she was considered to be part of the Pugughileq (clan)[fn: Ruby belonged to her aunt's clan and followed their customs, while her aunt's daughter was considered a member of her father's clan which had different social relationships.]. . . . Singlenga used to say to us, "We of the Pagaliq (clan) do not sing and dance." Yes, we are Pagaliq. (Apassingok et al. 1987:139)

In 1985, Lincoln Blassi described how boat crews grew in number. More boats and more hunters meant that as the overall number of hunters within a *ramka* changed, the ordering and inclusion within the established religious ceremonial cycle that each *ramka* followed also changed. By the time I arrived in Gambell in 1987, there were 22 boat crews in Gambell, with an additional fourteen in Savoonga. By 1997, there were at least three more boat crews in Gambell, and additional boats in Savoonga. Until the early 1970s, men from Savoonga whaled with their Gambell relatives. Savoonga, which faces due north, is ice-bound until June, making it impossible to launch boats during the spring whaling season. In 1970, Savoonga men began to travel to Southwest Cape to whale on their own. Since that time the number of crews has steadily grown, as it has in Gambell, with men traveling south to live in whaling camps in order to take advantage of the spring whale migration. By contrast, at the turn of the century, with as few as 150 persons living in Gambell and only a few isolated families living on the south side and at Boxer Bay and Northeast Cape, the overall number of crews must have been much smaller. In many cases a single boat represented an entire *ramka*.

Letters, notebooks, and diaries written by members of the Gambell community since the turn of the century lay out a system of living, a way of life (*kiyaghneq*), that suggests that whaling, as the most honorable and respected single hunting activity, ordered all life. Thus, whaling was not only a metaphor, but also a calendar for island people. Much has been said about the Gambell whaling ceremonies that were known colloquially as "moon worship." These ceremonies, which preceded each *ramka's* whale hunt, encompassed only a small portion of each year. Beginning at the end of January or the beginning of February, from the first full moon of winter to the next, whaling captains and their crews performed specific rites of sacrifice and prayer to thank Apa or Kiyaghneq for the food of the year past and to request, with utmost respect, success in the whale hunt about to commence.[11] These are the ceremonies to which Clement Ungott refers at the beginning of this chapter. The ceremonial activities continued until the end of April. By then, all of the boat crews had finished their immediate religious obligations and were fully engaged in the hunt. Since open water often did not appear around the island until the end of April or the beginning of May, these ceremonial duties preceded the hunt. The ceremonies themselves were elaborate and detailed. They were part of a greater catalog of ceremonies that anticipated the entrance of *aghveq* into the northern seas, marked the gift of *aghveq's* flesh to the community, thanked Kiyaghneq, the creator spirit and overseer of all things, for bounteous gifts, and, finally, returned the remains of *aghveq* after the hunt to the sea—the proper field and receptor of sea mammal remains, which Jonah describes below.

Other ceremonial aspects of whaling addressed the more specific de-

11. The term "moon worship" was coined by early missionaries, who believed, mistakenly, that families worshiped the moon. The Sivuqaghhmiit were seen as pagan idol worshipers who must be converted. Local people, who draw comfort from their ancestors' respect for Apa, the Creator, find this characterization offensive.

9.3 Jonah's whale, 1987.

tails of the hunt and the successful return of hunters blessed with a catch. These included sacred ways to prepare the boat; small ceremonies carried out with members of the crew and their families to create a respectful continuity with the whale and its fierce reciprocal, the polar bear; and, celebrations at the end of June to signify the end of the whale hunt and to initiate the community into the new year, in July.

Many activities, some already mentioned elsewhere, were carefully monitored through whaling. Children's games, courting activity, menstruation, pregnancy, maintenance of the land, and entry onto the land were regulated either partially or entirely by their relationship to hunting. Family celebrations, healing the sick, exchange of women—all were articulated with the hunt. These in turn were overlaid upon the *ramka* system, which was itself an outgrowth and expression of the hunt. Families continue to speak of "our moon" or "our boat" in the familiar language of everyday practice and custom. Hunting is embedded as a deep-seated value in the community through its ordering of all life through hunting, especially whaling.

Even rank outsiders cannot help but be swept up in the enthusiasm that surrounds the annual appearance of *aghveq*. I described in Chapter 2 what it was like in April 1987, my first spring in Gambell, when Pugughilegmiit took a large whale. And, I have always felt that the event welcomed me into Gambell.

The boat captain, who took that whale with one of his sons as striker, was Jonah. When a man tells the story of his hunting life, he mentions the whales he has taken or the whales he has almost taken. Before the hunt, Jonah's sister-in-law had "seen" a whale in a dream. Jonah himself once said that he had not been expecting the whale, and he was surprised when it suddenly appeared practically under his boat.

Jonah had promised earlier that day, before he went out to sea, that if he received something, he would give it all away and he had been true to his word. It seemed to me that spring that Jonah and the others treated that whale almost as if it were his sister-in-law's whale. I have thought about that a lot. Like *nanuq*, the polar bear, the white one, that comes before *aghveq*, the black one, the whale had shown itself first to Jonah's brother's wife in her dream, and then allowed itself to be taken by Jonah. Polar bears "give" themselves to those who see them first, even if someone else is actually responsible for killing them. Had this whale given itself to Jonah's sister-in-law? I remembered, too, that Jonah himself had been given a polar bear that spring. When I first met Jonah's family, one of his sons asked me to congratulate Jonah, whom I had not yet met, for having received a polar bear whose impressive skin was drying on a rack just outside the house. For Jonah, there had been the white one, and it was followed by the black one. I have wondered whether his sister-in-law, too, saw "the white one." Had *nanuq* come out of turn? Was it unusual to see and receive *aghveq* before *nanuq*? Could her status as a woman instead of a man been a factor? Some villagers believed that she had been threatened out on the ice that spring day in May, when she went through the ice while crabbing. Did *nanuq* appear to her on the ice? Was this what caused her death? We shall never know.

Afterwards the villagers talked about the whale, and some spoke with quiet admiration of Jonah's generosity in giving away all that meat. I felt honored to have been present when Jonah's whale was taken and to have witnessed what the family describes as Pugughileghmiit whale weather. After a whale has been safely harvested, the *ramka* expects the skies to close, the seas to rise, and snow or sleet to keep the boat crew at home. In that way, Apa assures that those who have received *aghveq* will respect that gift by staying home. In the past, it was also a time when *ramka* women sang songs. Ruby Rookok described it like this:

> Those who were part of the *iviq* [fn 16: The group of clan women who would sing at the time of a whale catch] would sit outside the [boat captain's house]. As the *llaaget* [fn 17: *Llaaget* and the whale's "extremities," including the flippers, tail, and nose.] were being hauled to the captain's house, the singers would insert the names of the captain and his crew in the [traditional] ceremonial songs. This was a big event performed only by the women. Women who had married into other clans would join their clansman's household to sing with the captain's wife when a whale was caught. (Rookok, in Apassingok et al. 1987:149)

On May 3, 1996, Jonah's boat took another whale. This time his young nephew was the striker. And, once again, because many Pugughileghmiit people are like second family to me, I was immersed in the excitement that a whale brings. Late in the afternoon of the third, under gray skies, a long line of *angyapiget* approached the north beach. This was another big whale. It would turn out to be 48 feet long. The tired smiles on the faces of the returning hunters told their own story. And, the drama of at least twelve whaling boats joined together with common tow lines to bring in *aghveq* was indeed exciting. As the day grew late, the men were still maneuvering the great animal toward the shore.

Unlike times past, whales today are brought up on shore to be butchered, hauled in by community-owned earth-moving equipment with thick pulley lines attached. It is a difficult business. Lines sometimes snap, and everyone must stand out of the path of the tow line once the vehicle begins to pull. The beach itself is a mix of ice and black lava sand. The land surface shifts, and sometimes a vehicle founders in the sand. The current around the north beach is strong, and by the time everything is almost in order, invariably darkness has begun to set in. For this, the community sets up several generators alongside *aghveq* to operate giant floodlights that bathe its body in light so that the men of the *ramka* can see what to do. That night, once everything was set up, the weary men headed for home to eat warm food and rest before beginning the butchering. The captain, in consultation with the elders in his family, gives directions for butchering and sharing. Jonah took most of the responsibility since he was a senior elder in his own lineage and one of several senior men in the larger Pugughileghmiit *ramka*. On the night of the third, I found myself on the beach watching the butchering, which Jonah directed from midnight until dawn. The first sign of morning light came around 4:30 A.M.. For the first part of the night, a picnic atmosphere prevailed. Children slid down icy slopes almost to the water. Young men paced alongside *aghveq*, learning from their elders the best ways to cut into the whale as they did so. It was cold, probably 10 to 15 degrees below zero. Some clanswomen served hot coffee and cookies to anyone who asked for them. The men gradually pulled the giant pieces of *mangtak* back with huge hooks and ran them up onto the shore from the beach. Whales weigh approximately a ton a foot, and even a small piece of *mangtak* is heavy.

As the night wore on, the coffee ran out and the cookies disappeared. Children finally grew tired of playing on the beach and piled four and five at once onto the back and front ends of four-wheelers to be driven home by their mothers and aunts. Some women remained, while the older men of the family continued to work on the beach, handing out shares; they would stay there for many more hours. The butchering took almost two days. Just as the sky began to grow light, some time after 4:30 A.M., the family's whale weather began—that light drifting of snow which keeps a hunter at home.

The next spring, as I listened to several men discuss why they continue to whale, I realized that most, if not all, considered it a sacred duty. That summer, as families scattered to their fishing and gathering camps, I reflected that these sites were once the semi-permanent settlements that carry the all-important *ramka* and sub-*ramket* names. Each time families go to camp, they are reminded of their own long histories on the island, as well as the rules and behaviors of the hunt, which are supposed to govern a person's behavior. As elder Ralph Apatiki explained to me, the hunting universe itself is divided into implicit separable, and distinct fields. These fields should be visited only in the proper manner and in the proper season. There is a time to be on the land and a time to be on the sea. One should take care not to stain the land or the sea, and one should not carry tools inappropriate or offensive to the animals of the hunt to either of these two separate realms. According to Mr. Apatiki:

> In my own learning, they [the ancestors] do to them [the animals which they hunted],
>
> Whatever they first caught, they show them to this Living Being, to the Great-Grandfather, to God.
>
> They went out to [the] mountain, [for] something that first time sprouts, some plants.
>
> They bring them to home. They used to put them to their mouths.
>
> These things [all animal and plant life], all of them, they take very good care of them,
>
> because This [One] had created them.
>
> When [the] time comes, whatever . . . things [they have], they don't waste them.
>
> They return the bones, whatever they are to the fields.
>
> Those [bones] that belongs to the sea, they went to throw away down to sea, they were like that.
>
> That is the one I now still practice up to this day. Some part of it I practice because it is good.
>
> It is very much pleasing, that way of life I have learned in our clan (*ramkeni*) that way.
>
> Whatever things that happens, when it's time that way, they completed everything.
>
> In our society it is a ceremony (*puvallangulghhii*) that is coming. They told it to This One.
>
> It is almost like this long ago sometimes, in my thinking.
>
> They light small lamps. There they sacrifice. The small ceremonial fires are some sort of altars.
>
> They, they have seen it, they practiced it from way back there, long ago.

So much, that on these Holy Books, the Bible, that is written, they practiced it.

They were like that when I came to my senses. These things they complete them.

In my thinking, probably this Creator, they had Him—lived, pleased. . . . So their way of life was good, always have some things. . . .

This island called St. Lawrence Island. . . .

They [the ancestors] had taken very good care of it, just like they honor it, those people.

They take good care of the hunting grounds, these places—all hunting grounds. Respectfully.

They don't go to places until when it is time to go there.

They don't put some things on hunting grounds. They respectfully use them.

Some things they never put to the hunting grounds, some things they kept away from them.

So it always have somethings. During the time of hunting, they use something very carefully.

They carefully take care of this island, they have used it, probably since long time ago.

We have seen it like that. Now, we are sorry about it that it is changing. (R. Apatiki 1992, in Jolles 1987ff)

Hunters and their families interacted with the fields of land and sea, affecting as they did so the results of hunting. Through their conduct, the hunter and his family could either create an environment through which the animals that a man hunted could recognize that proper and respectful attention had been given or had not been given. The sea received the bones of seals, whales, and walrus, and, in a similar manner, the remains of foxes, birds, and other land animals were returned to the land. The fields carry, then, an absolute quality. They represent another level of order, which intersects with the abstract frame imposed by whaling, and, in a perhaps lesser fashion, walrus hunting and sealing, upon those who hunt. These fields separate, within the overall integrating force of whaling, the major components of a hunting life way. Thus, even if a man was not actually hunting *aghveq*, the carriage, demeanor, and conduct of his entire family would ultimately affect his success as a hunter of whales.

Whales and polar bears were given the most ceremonial attention, but all major animals had their ceremonies, whether they were hunted as food for humans, food for sled dogs, or simply for furs to trade for sugar, tea, flour, and other necessities. When I first met Estelle in February 1989, she impressed on me the importance of caring for all animals:

> ESTELLE: As soon as they get that whale and cut it up, . . . the first thing is that they cut the flukes and put them away. The choicest part for ceremonial use. And they just put them up on top of their outer room post, so nobody can touch them.
>
> The other part had been dried up and starts to drip some before it is summertime.
>
> And then they cut [them] up—the first ones they give is [to] their sisters, big pieces, [to] their sisters.
>
> Big pieces, the biggest, the longest—they distribute first.
>
> And also when they get a polar bear, they used to do that but . . . they never make a noise. . . .
>
> After that whale, they hung up two pokes right outside just above the doorway.
>
> And it stays there for five days.
>
> And when they get polar bear, they just brought the skin with the head bone [the polar bear head],
>
> They brought it in and put it on a wooden trough,
>
> And if it be a man, they put a pipe on his mouth for five days or three days, [and] they told some stories. Their relatives get together. Every night they tell some stories [to their relatives and to honor the bear].
>
> Entertained their guests. And if it be a female, they put some beads on to the polar bear.
>
> CAROL: So it would be well-treated?
>
> ESTELLE: Yes, well-treated. They say that we have a good trust here. We treated them that way. Everything they do has . . . an action. They have something to do with that [animal].
>
> Even the white fox, they killed. Before they brought it in, the man called from outside for his wife.

She goes out with [some] soot from the seal oil lamp and just smear it on the fox's mouth before they brought it in.

And for the seal, they hauled it in and the wife goes out with . . . water. They pour that water in the seal's dry mouth. [For] Everything, they do that.

It's very interesting. If I had learned more about it—it would be more interesting.

When I told my children about it, they keep quiet and listen to me. I tried to have them learn something about our culture. Just to remember. (Oozevaseuk 1989, in Jolles 1987ff)

Whaling, especially, provided a "natural" calendar that regulated much of the activity in Gambell up through the 1930s and 1940s. One can see this in the carefully recorded notebooks and diaries that Estelle's father, Paul Silook, kept between 1928 and 1932. While a member of Aymaramka himself, he noted all ceremonies that came to his attention, with greater detail and knowledge reserved for persons and events within his own group. In 1929, for example, Paul told Henry Collins about several games that young people played, usually on the beach. Each game could be played after a particular hunting event. One ball game was played "when a first seal is killed when the ice came at first." According to Collins' notes, the game, which was somewhat like golf, was played in the snow. Another game described by Paul was *Agh vekh tuk* ("throwing rock"):

This is played by boys and men, when a first walrus is killed in winter. They gathered some stones as large as a boy's fist, four to twelve in number. They would divide in two sides, 2 to 6 on each side and each player has two rocks. They set up two large piece of bones on each side and a piece of small bones were set by these two large ones.

$$BB \quad X \quad BB$$
$$X \qquad X$$

X is position of thrower, BB is the big bone

Then one side would throw at these bones. These bones are set about 30 to 35 ft Apart. The first one would throw at them and if he hits one of the bones, they would go to the middle and throw at them. If they hit both of them, the same one would go to the other side and throw at the opposite way. If the misses both them [sic] the other side would throw. Some times they would wrestle when one side would not miss. This they played for a long time. Some times this game may played from noon till the sunset if the weather is not good for hunting. (Henry Bascom Collins Collection 1982)

Girls also had their games. The most important one was played only after a whale had been killed in the spring. This game was probably *Kalleghta*, which Anna Okhtokiyuk talked about so enthusiastically. Here is Paul's description of it:

> The only games of the girls is a ball (game is) which played just (when) a whale is killed, but each time the boys would join with them. The young men and young women also played it in the evenings of spring. The girls can kick a ball when a calf whale is killed. Ball game can be played anytime after the 1st whale of year is killed. Men throw the (ball to) men; girl to girls. Men take this opportunity to kiss the girls. Each sex tries to take the ball from other. (Henry Bascom Collins Collection 1982)

Only when we consider all of the ceremonies connected with whaling and other hunting and gathering activities as constituting a chronological record can we see to what degree whaling overshadowed all other aspects of Sivuqaq life. A section of Paul Silook's diary from 1929 to 1930 (see Appendix B) illustrates how much of daily life was devoted to formal hunting ceremonies, particularly whaling ceremonies. A variety of intricate ceremonies and celebrations, accompanied by prayers and formal restrictions, drew everyone into the ceremonial circle. Whaling was experienced both abstractly and physically from the moment of birth. Before 1900, most people lived in a *nenglu* in winter. These traditional semi-underground dwellings not only mimicked the body of the whale, but were also constructed of his bones. His ribs provided the curved roof supports (and continued to do so when the community, by more or less common consent, began to live in *mangteghapiks*). The plates of his great head supported one end of the dwelling. Other head plates enclosed parts of the sides. His vertebrae sometimes created the hole near the center of the roof through which the smoky residue of seal oil lamps escaped. Thus, the communities of extended families lived their lives within the reconstructed body of the whale. In spring, as dwellings became moist with snow melting into the sod-covered surfaces of the *nenglu*, families moved to small summer houses (*mangteghasqwaaghet*), or small, neat tents made of hide and driftwood poles. Tents could be carried to summer camp grounds. The sturdy winter *manteghat* which eventually replaced them were made of whale ribs, heavy walrus hide roofs, and driftwood sides anchored with great rocks inside, which hung from a center pole (*aghveghaqetaq*) and protected against the ever-present threat of disease spirits. Within, small carvings of humans, perhaps representing the ancestors of the house, waited to be fed through ceremonial offerings. Also, somewhere within the house were the especially sacred objects of the house—the boat captain's sacred bag, the carved image of *aghveq* used only in sacred ceremonies, and the small baleen bucket that the captain's wife filled with offerings each spring to please Kiyaghneq and enable *aghveq* to return. The beautiful ceremonial clothing of whitened seal gut, bound together with minute stitches and decorated with red and blue crested auklet and puffin feathers were stored here, too. Offerings were kept in special sealskin pokes and in small, carefully stored sealskin bags. Whale parts, specially prepared pieces of dried meats, and greens, along with other foods that indicated specific clan membership, were stored here during the year until the proper ceremonial moment arrived. Finally, in a place where no child should look inside to view its sacred contents, the captain's hunting bag was stored. Within it were the sealskin visors worn only when *aghveq* had been taken; stones with unusual properties of power, shape, smoothness, or beauty; elements taken from the eyes and penises of whales and polar bears; and, occasionally, a small dried bird or other powerful symbol. Estelle, whose incorrigible curiosity always got her into trouble as a small child, peeked into her grandfather's hunting bag one day when he was away from home. She said it seemed to be filled with precious gems. She had been told by her father there would be dire consequences if she ever touched the bag, but she said that nothing happened, and her father and grandfather never discovered what she had done.

In the 1970s, the community struggled with issues of identity and belonging. Whales were endangered and an ancient way of life seemed about to disappear. Darrell Hargraves, who taught school in Gambell

then, told this story of the overwhelming sense of loss felt by elder Lincoln
Blassi. Pelassi (Lincoln Blassi) gave Hargraves his own whaling captain's
gear, including his sacred hunting bag, which had been passed down
through his family for many generations, to sell. The story of that gift says
many things about the changes that have taken place in Gambell. According to Hargraves, Mr. Blassi, then an old man, called him to his house
one day and asked if he would like to see his ceremonial whaling gear.
Hargraves was surprised and quite curious to see these things, which he
had never seen up close before. The next day, a Saturday, Pelassi brought
his belongings to the school and laid them out carefully. He explained
each piece and he told Hargraves that he was worried about his things. No
one seemed interested in them any longer. Perhaps they could be sold and
the money used to purchase some hunting equipment for his family's
hunters. It was hard for Pelassi to make this request of Hargraves. Above
all else, Pelassi believed that these things were a sacred trust from his family's past and should never be separated from one another. He asked Hargraves if he would be willing to accept them under certain conditions.
Hargraves should agree never to let these objects be separated from each
other. Then Pelassi asked Darrell if he would like to look inside of his captain's bag. He told him that no one had ever looked inside before, other
than the owners of the bag to whom it was passed down in each generation. As Darrell said yes, he suddenly became aware that Pelassi was crying. He was so moved by this that he didn't know what to do. He just
looked into the bag quietly, observing the ancient dried pieces from former whales and polar bears, the dried eye bits, and the small agate-like
stones. He didn't touch anything and he didn't say anything.

That afternoon, Pelassi left his traditional gear with Hargraves and
went home. The next day was Sunday, and in the morning Darrell saw
people passing by his window on their way to attend services in the Presbyterian Church. Much to his amazement he saw Pelassi also heading toward the church. Pelassi had never been one to attend church before.
Now, it seemed, he had turned his face toward the new way and left the
old behind.

But that is not the end of the story. Hargraves offered Pelassi's things to
the Otto Geist Museum at the University of Alaska, Fairbanks. The museum agreed to purchase the items with the restriction that Pelassi had

asked for, that the pieces should not be separated. They have been displayed from time to time in a case, presumably with the pieces together. The hunting bag into which Darrell Hargraves had once peered is closed. For many years after it received the Pelassi collection from Hargraves, the museum kept all of the items in storage. During that time, the hunting bag was never opened. Gradually, it dried into a permanently closed position. It can never be opened again and is protected finally from the prying eyes of strangers.

Although Pelassi's story seems to suggest that a way of a life ended in the early 1970s, whaling has continued, and the men who hunt whales do so with conviction and devotion to a tradition both ancient and modern. Whaling is founded on an abiding Yupik local identity and history, which embraces both men and women in its web of responsibility. As a philosophy, it weaves together deep meaning and taken-for-granted acts of living (Jolles 1995b:336). Today, those who hunt whales are most often devout Christians.

Like other hunting activities, the practical methodology and the spiritual or philosophical bases of bowhead whale hunting are often discussed. In 1997, Leonard Apangalook, a past vice-chairman of the Alaska Eskimo Whaling Commission, described his education as a whaler:

> Of course, I come from a traditional whaling family, although my grandfather never did catch a whale. It all began with my father. He was a very successful whaler. I began participating on whale hunts when I was about twelve years old. I guess you might say as a cabin boy when I first started, kind of a handy boy around the boat. That's how I began, but like most other jobs, I progressed onto operating the motor, crew man, striker, and, then, finally, captain. I went through all the progressive steps a whaler goes through as he grew up all the way to captain. Like I said, my father was a successful whaling captain. He has harvested, I don't recall how many whales, but quite a few. I, myself, since I took over, have taken only two—two whales. So, that's the extent of my tenure as a whaler as I progressed from my beginning to present. (Apangalook, in Jolles 1999)

Characteristically, Mr. Apangalook first honors his elders, the men of his father's side—his grandfather, whom he never actually met, and his father, a man with many whales to his credit. He outlines his own instruction, that is, his credentials and experience. Implicit here is that he came to his present position as captain because of his extensive training and his willingness to wait his turn. Finally, although he speaks of his own success, he does so humbly. Mr. Apangalook also touches on a significant element of hunting discourse—kinship. Kinship is a major structural component of the hunting philosophy in Gambell. Tied to it is the responsibility to share—across the community—according to specific sharing blueprints. This is the principle of *awalightuq* mentioned by Samuel Irrigoo (see Chapter 7).The whale's body seems to represent both hunting theory and hunting practice, becoming not only a map or embodiment of the community's whale hunting experience, but also a "carved" or written discourse and expression of food distribution practice. Young men learn these distribution maps and the underlying principles of generosity through instruction by their elders whenever a whale is harvested.

Boat captains generally know who will hunt with them, from the moment of the first ice-free or open water to the beginning of June, when, by common decision, men cease to hunt bowheads and begin the spring walrus hunt. Six to eight men, most of them close relatives—sons, younger brothers, first cousins from the father's side—usually constitute a crew. Men who plan to whale await their captain's word. Once notified, the men hurry—out of respect for the whales—to prepare the *angyapik* for the hunt. When men talk about whaling, they generally talk about their family and about the tradition of whaling within their family. Here, Joshua[12] describes his experience: "We started out with my own dad's crew, in those days. And, we were all young. And then, after he passed away, in my sophomore year in high school . . . we joined up with his cousin. And, we whaled with him for a while, I forgot how long it took us. And then, one day, we finally decided we should revive our own skin boat . . . " ("Joshua," in Anungazuk and Jolles 1998). Whale harvest participation highlights family and emphasizes kinship in the broadest sense. Joshua noted that he was filled with a strong feeling of family belonging as men gathered together around the body of a harvested whale. In his words, "I really enjoy it because we get a chance to be with our brothers, our nephews, and the other boys, close together" (ibid.).

12. Pseudonym.

The interrelatedness of family, religious tradition, identity, and practice are even more apparent when the experience of taking a whale is fresh in a man's mind. Kin associations, extending backward in time at least three generations, may flash before him. These relations are beautifully expressed by Brian,[13] a boat captain who took his first whale in the spring of 1997. Brian begins his story by acknowledging the man to whom he turned all through that eventful day.

> Jonah is my uncle, but I look upon him as my oldest brother, [be]cause he is the oldest man . . . in our family group. . . . We were together the day before and we missed by one breath a small whale. . . . The next day, my brother called and . . . said that Jonah . . . asked him if . . . we would be able to go out that day and my brother . . . told him "Yes" . . . and that traditionally, culturally . . . goes back . . . if we had gotten close to a whale then we have to be prepared. . . . ("Brian," in Anungazuk and Jolles 1998)

Understood here is that if one *can*, one *ought* to comply with one's oldest brother's request.

Brian's crew that day consisted of his family—his nephews and his son. Brian later said: "I never realized how emotional our first whale[s] would be, and, of course, all those people that have passed on from my family came into my mind, wondering what they would have thought"(ibid.). While it was happening, Brian was caught by the power of the occasion: "I haven't even talked to my brothers on the CB yet. . . . I couldn't talk. I couldn't talk for a while. . . . I told the boys . . . "Let's wait for Jonah, . . . our closest relative's boat" (ibid.). Only minutes later, Brian made a decision that epitomizes the depth of feeling and meaning made manifest through the whaling experience:

> I called Jonah, since he was . . . just like our oldest brother. I told him . . . "I'm giving you all—every decision—regarding that whale—to you. . . . And . . . that's when . . . I let it go from there. It was Jonah's decision from there on what had to be done or where it should be taken or whatever, because I told him that decision is his, since he was our oldest family member. And, I could see him smile, making him feel good that I hadn't lost our culture (ibid.).

13. Pseudonym.

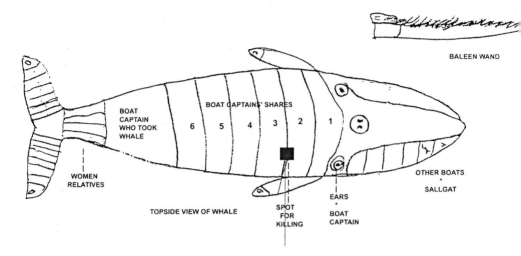

BALEEN WAND

BOAT CAPTAIN WHO TOOK WHALE

BOAT CAPTAINS' SHARES

6 5 4 3 2 1

WOMEN RELATIVES

OTHER BOATS

SALLGAT

EARS

TOPSIDE VIEW OF WHALE

SPOT FOR KILLING

BOAT CAPTAIN

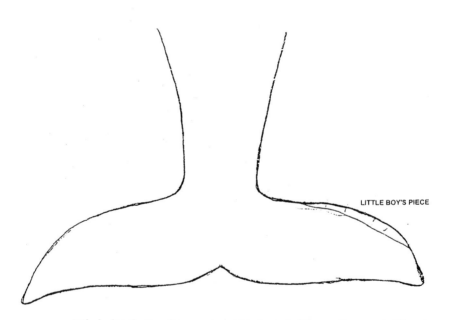

LITTLE BOY'S PIECE

9.4 *Whale distribution diagram (topside) drawn by Vernon Qaqsungiq Slwooko, Sr., Gambell, July 1997.*

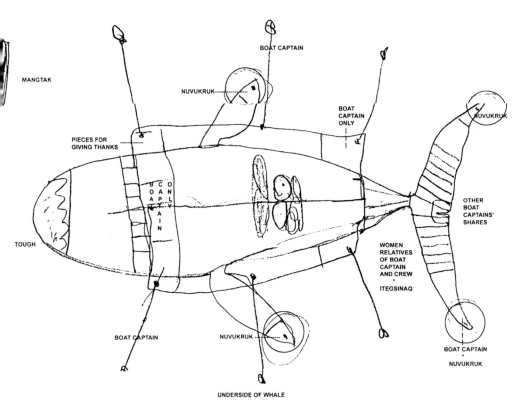

9.5. *Whale distribution diagram (underside) drawn by Vernon Qaqsungiq Slwooko, Sr., Gambell, July 1997.*

The final expression of tradition comes with the distribution of the whale's body. Distribution gives the actual history of the whaling event: it identifies the successful boat captain and crew, the arrival sequence of other participating boats, and the kinship ties of the major participants. Retired boat captain Vernon Slwooko's diagrams (figs. 9.4 and 9.5) give a sense of the orderliness and precision employed by the men who prepare the whale for distribution after a successful harvest.

Brian noted that boat captains must exercise great restraint and humility when the time comes to distribute the tremendous gift of a whale. In the past, members of the successful *ramka* were likely to receive a greater

9.6 *Bowhead whale skulls celebrate heritage and decorate the entrance to a house.*

share of the meat than today. Changes in the distribution system to achieve a more ecumenical sharing across clan boundaries are attributed to Jimmy Otiyohok, who changed his own distribution of a whale as part of his very strong Christian devotion to a more catholic or universal understanding of the sharing concept. Certainly each man and woman who does the work of hunting, processing the harvest of the hunt, and distributing it to members of the community, must wrestle with this issue, because the models for subsistence behavior held up by the community call attention to relationships of blood and marriage and to the generational elements within them. Whaling, the most dramatic harvest of the year, calls upon the community to use traditional models of shared work and distribution, and each participant must acknowledge and contend with the tensions that surround caring for family and caring for community. This is both the challenge and the strength of a hunting life way.

CHAPTER 10

Conclusion:
The Land, the People, the Future

At the end of 1879, St. Lawrence Island was devastated. Its settlements were filled with dead bodies. The strangers whose seductive goods had led islanders to engage in foreign trade had brought diseases whose consequences were awesome. The island, inhabited for centuries, had been reduced to a few remaining families. It is now more than one hundred years since that time, and still there are fewer island residents than before that terrible year. While it might be tempting to dismiss faith, food, and family as obvious functional constructs or as sentimental concepts, these have been the driving forces in the rebuilding of the St. Lawrence Island community. It is not simply that residents who once lived scattered along the shore line in extended family home sites now thrive in two villages made up of those who regrouped in order to survive. It has something to do with the land itself. In spite of the hardship and the tragedy, apparently no one thought to leave. They stayed and they reestablished themselves.

Land holds the stories that exemplify families. On St. Lawrence Island, each settlement is marked by a name that binds that place to families living in Gambell. These are places of the living and of the ancestors. A person's family history can be uncovered by learning the place names, the locations where that person and his ancestors have lived. A few places are no longer used much. For example, at Kukulek, unseen forces—perhaps spiritual, perhaps associated with disease—may still hover among the ruins, but only archaeologists and those interested in ivory or artifacts spend any time here. Northeast Cape, once the camp site of the Kulowiyi family and the Kulukhons, is now polluted, the result of misuse by a U.S.

Army encampment, and unsafe to occupy. Such historical sites have much to tell but are hardly visited.

At each site, the names of rocks, creeks, tent sites long abandoned, underground food caches, and sliding spots for children flavor the land and personalize each settlement, distinguishing its lived history from that of others. The landscape is filled with such names. Many were recorded by community historians in the 1980s (Walunga 1987). That effort revealed more than 348 names along the shore and another 147 in the interior. But the land is more than that. Several family groups draw names from the settlements, which have been used historically by their ancestors. The names of family members create a living link to the land. It is difficult to know how far back this practice of naming people for the land extends. Perhaps it is as recent as the end of the 1878 epidemic. Some names that people carry are referred to as "old" names, names whose literal meaning, but not their cultural or historical significance, is clouded or lost. Other names, while associated with the immediate past and with certain families, do not identify a person with the landscape, even though this kind of name, too, has cycled through the community for many generations. There are also new names, given sometimes to visitors and friends, sometimes to children born to islanders who have moved away. These names often have metaphoric qualities or give enhanced meaning to a person's position in the family. Most people have more than one name, although just one is commonly used in everyday conversation. Commonly used names or the nicknames derived from them are usually recorded as "middle" names, although, as Iyaaka and Kepelgu have pointed out, it would be more accurate to say that islanders have several first names.

My own name, that of an outsider, is one example. In 1987, toward the end of my first visit to Gambell, my hosts, Rhea, Marina, and Isaac, decided to give me a Yupik name. Choosing a name became the topic of conversation for the next several afternoons. These conversations were invariably in Yupik, which I was only just beginning to understand. Selecting a name seemed to involve settling on a single word whose content could be meaningfully associated with the person. The family took into consideration when I had come to visit, why I had come to visit, seasonal events that had coincided with my visit, and my own personality as they perceived it. Other family members joined the debate, too. Names are important.

In the end, I was named Ququngaq, which means "willow leaves." I have speculated that the significance of *ququngaq* is in its seasonal appearance, in the pleasure taken in its reappearance each spring, and perhaps in the slightly bitter aftertaste it leaves in the mouth. I'm not quite sure. Throughout the week in which my name was bandied about, the first branches of pussy willow stalks (low bush arctic willow) leafed out in a vase on the kitchen table. The branches, with their new yellow-green leaves and familiar fuzzy gray buds, had been gathered from the foot of Sivuqaq Mountain by one of Rhea's granddaughters, who had then regaled her grandmother with a lively pantomime in which she pretended to consume the greens eagerly and to strip and chew the roots. Willow leaves are the first greens to make a spring appearance after the long arctic winter. Not only do they herald the coming of summer, but before the introduction of imported vegetables in the Gambell Native Store, they were traditionally the first fresh greens consumed after a winter of meat and, occasionally, soured greens. I understood that the name, given by a respected elder and senior member in her *ramka*, was an honor, although it would be several more years before anyone thought to call me by it. Later that same year, someone from another *ramka* remarked, somewhat unkindly, that Rhea's clan was known for taking its names from the land. Why, he wondered, had they chosen a different kind of name for me? Why, indeed!

This simple act of naming exposes many of the qualities which I have tried to explore here. First is that strangers receive names to draw them into the family circle, to make them more "familiar." Names, even names for strangers, suggest history and are clues to an individual's past and to her place, her belonging in the community. Names both cover the bearer and express the being of the bearer. New names are sometimes drawn from the Bible in creative ways or may denote the protective quality they are meant to carry. For instance, for a teenager whose name translates as "the second coming of Christ," the name shields the bearer against the forces of evil. Earlier I described how Conrad Oozeva, now a senior elder, has given English names to his grandchildren and great-grand-children that derive both from the Bible and from creative combinations of syllables meant to join harmoniously names taken from both parents' families. These English names take on similar kinds of meaning to Yupik names, because they carry with them a substantive history. No one stands alone, and names connote the history that comprises each person. Elders can recite these histories, and young people learn them by listening to the elders' stories about their names.

The changes in naming practices, like so many of the other changes which I have described, demonstrate how community members integrate practices from beyond their own geographic and cultural borders that fit with their own ideas about the place of family traditions and the continuing importance of religious conviction. Naming, to work well in contemporary Gambell, must accommodate both the past and the present.

Since the 1950s, anthropologists working in the North have focused on the importance of subsistence systems in hunting communities. In the arctic, hunting has been central to community survival; the complementary task of gathering is limited to summer and fall expeditions to collect eggs, berries, greens, and fortuitous sea foods and sea plants, which are occasionally thrown up on the beach or appear in open water. Not surprisingly, then, this subsistence cycle continues to be the subject of much research, whether the focus is the economy, of which hunting itself is the centerpiece, or the physical and spiritual activities that comprise hunting systems, or the environment in which hunting takes place. Many studies explore these relationships.

In Gambell, the earliest work was carried out by Riley Moore (1923) in 1912, by Otto Geist and Henry Collins in the 1920s and 1930s, and by Alexander Leighton and Dorothea Leighton, M.D. (1982),[1] in the summer of 1940. Charles Hughes worked in the community during 1954 and 1955.[2] Hughes, whose publications represent the most extensive formal study of St. Lawrence Island culture, worked mainly with men, focusing on formal kinship terminology and the major subsistence practices of men. Recent work by Native researchers and others complements and corrects these earlier ethnographic studies.[3] Most studies focus on subsis-

1. See also Hughes 1953.
2. See, for example, Hughes 1960, as well as 1974, 1958a, 1958b, 1959, 1965, and 1966.
3. See, for example, Apassingok et al. 1985, 1987, 1989; Braund 1988; Burgess 1974; Ellana 1988; Jolles 1989, 1990, 1991, 1995a, 1997; Jorgensen 1990, R. Silook 1976.

tence in one or another of its aspects, although local historians Apassingok and Walunga, were concerned to preserve and record elders' stories (Apassingok et al. 1985, 1987, 1989). Roger Savla Silook, Estelle Oozevaseuk's brother, wished to pass on what he could of community traditions, based on his own knowledge and that of his family. Jorgensen's 1990 study in Gambell was part of a larger comparative study of several Alaskan marine mammal hunting communities and explicitly focused on subsistence. Ellana and Worl both were interested in whaling, whereas Braund was exclusively interested in locally crafted boats used for whaling.

While most studies focus on subsistence, few have considered food itself and the place of food within the overall scheme of a subsistence life. Eating *neqepik* ("our food" or "real food") is so important that to go without it for even a short time is to lose part of one's being, or so it appears to a *laluramka* outsider like me. For this reason I have given special attention to some of the foods that people eat as well as the work required to bring food into the home. People's feelings about food go far beyond a simple pleasure in a particular taste. Food is directly associated with identity and belonging. I have in mind an experience of a few years ago. In 1992, I traveled to the Inuit Studies Conference held at Laval University in Québec City, a French-speaking community just east of Montréal. Two women who are very important to me traveled with me—Elinor, my elder advisor, and Mary, my very dear friend and occasional research partner. We and others attending the conference lived in a motel close to the university. Just down the street was a convenient restaurant. To me fell the task of ordering food.

Years of college French meant that I was the one to translate the menus each day and negotiate somehow with our Québecois servers. That was no problem. That trip was memorable for two reasons. First, I learned that Mary regarded Elinor as her mother-in-law, a relationship that had not occurred to me. Technically, Elinor is the older sister of Mary's husband's deceased mother. Daughters-in-law treat their mothers-in-law respectfully. I knew that Mary honored and admired Elinor, but I had assumed that her respect came simply because of Elinor's elder status. I had not considered that important family ties were a part of those sentiments. The three of us all slept together in the same motel room and were seldom away from each other. We were a somewhat unlikely trio and I worried that by putting us all together in the same room, I had not been very tactful.

It was soon clear, however, that what to eat would be our most pressing problem. Both Elinor and Mary became homesick for "real food." We managed at breakfast and lunch, at a nearby restaurant or on the Laval campus—these are not major Yupik meal times—but by dinner the desire, the need for meat was compelling. We walked the streets of Québec City looking at menus posted in restaurant windows. How much well-done meat could we find listed on the menu, and could we afford it? Night after night we confounded our waiters in the elegant and not so elegant restaurants we selected, by asking for very well done prime rib of beef. That is perhaps the nearest one can approach to a meal of fresh boiled *manguna* (walrus meat with skin) in Québec City. The other items on the plate were unimportant. Each night after we returned to our motel room, Elinor and Mary placed collect calls to their families on St. Lawrence Island. I'm sure their telephone bills were phenomenal when they returned. As the eldest, Elinor Mikaghaq always placed the first call. Practically the first question she asked was "What did you eat for dinner?" Other questions followed: Whose meat was it? Where had the meat been caught? How did they fix it? Who was at dinner that night? After Elinor hung up, my two friends talked about food and what they missed. One night, after we had been there for almost a week, we chanced on a late-night television documentary on seals and other marine mammals. Elinor looked longingly at the animals on the screen and then launched into a discussion about different ways to prepare seal meat.

Food and family are interconnected. In Gambell the most enduring theoretical construct around which daily life is structured is the family. All else develops from that single comprehensive web of living beings. The words *Yupik* and *Yuuk* indicate both a person from St. Lawrence Island and a man known as good and honest. When combined with certain endings (technically, post-bases), the words refer to those whom one thinks would be good boat crew members. Family membership grows out of this conceptual understanding of self. A true human understands what her or his work is. As Elinor Mikaghaq once explained to me, the Yupik word for work holds within its conceptual meaning, a sense of responsibility, of relationship. What you do each day derives from who you are in

relation to all of the other humans within your group. Your group takes
its name from the land, from where families once lived, even if all now
live in one or two communities. Children's names evoke the history of
names, going backward and forward in time. The most important task
which anyone performs is to bring food to the family. Food, in this sense,
can be understood as that which the hunter brings home, the gatherer
brings home, or that which family members process together for future
use, regardless of who first brought it to the household. Food *is* family.
Without food, no one survives. The obligation to feed the hunter is first
and foremost in people's minds. Warm clothing goes to the hunter first.
Or to the one who must walk the beach in search of food. The path
which food travels, once it makes its way into the family, is a way of track-
ing the family. The primacy of food makes it one with family.

This interconnectedness of food and family is accentuated when someone marries into a family from outside the community, something that is
likely to occur more and more often as men and women meet each other
in school, at regional business meetings, and during vacation times on
the mainland. I know of no recent example where a man who married in
from outside the community has been fully incorporated into every aspect of extended family and clan responsibilities. In at least two cases,
laluramket men married local women and settled in Gambell. The men
were employed full-time by a state agency. Both men tried to fulfill their
obligations to their parents-in-law. One hunted from time to time with
men from his wife's family, although not on a regular basis. The other was
not really a hunter. Both men camped with their wives' families. Each
also provided financial assistance when he could to his wife's relatives.
And, both men lived within and at the periphery of their wives' families,
an uncommon practice in Gambell, with its emphasis on patrilineality.
These men did not speak Yupik to their children, and English was the
common language of the home. Even the grandparents spoke English to
their grandchildren, although it was difficult for them and severely limited what the grandparents could teach them of their Yupik culture.

Natives from other communities have also married locally and settled
in Gambell. In one case, a Yupik woman fell in love with someone from
a mainland community, and, since he was already a hunter and appreciated traditional customs from his own community, he came to Gambell

to work for his wife, moving in with her and her family. The difficulty, of course, was that once his groom's work was done, he could not simply bring his wife back to his own family within the community and hunt with his own brothers, uncles and cousins, for his family was from another community. He was often alone and did not speak Yupik; so, in a different way from his *laluramket* counterparts, he, also was both inside and outside of his wife's family. His experience contrasts sharply with that of men who learn the ways of their wives' Yupik families and then return home with their wives to live among their own brothers and their families. It came as no surprise that in the early years of their marriage, the couple thought about moving to the husband's home village. In the beginning, the wife easily found regular employment in Gambell, but her husband had to combine several jobs, including work for other outsiders and a series of home chores. He yearned to hunt on a regular basis, but only after a decade of life within the community was it possible to do so. Change, in this and other communities as well, takes time, time for people to adjust, even if the "change" itself comes swiftly. On St. Lawrence Island a man does not usually live with and depend permanently on his wife's kin. Even in a world of work divided among cash employment, unearned income, and subsistence, a man loses both face and heart when he cannot readily hunt for and with his family and teach his sons to hunt. Sometimes a man hunts only seldom, but his wife feels free to go to his family's meat cache to find food. She could go to her mother and father, too, but she is much more likely to go to her husband's family first.

Choosing a wife or a husband from another community, whether Native or non-Native, is fraught with dangers, just as not having a husband is. Always, the person loses a large support network. Sometimes, as in the case of an in-marrying spouse, that person has much less status in the community than they might have had if they had been married in their home village. The partner loses, too. For women, it means remaining in their birth family, never developing the local friendships and support of their sister-in-law neighbors. Their own sisters, of course, are probably married and much involved in the affairs of their own husbands' families.

Even when young lovers come from strong, traditional families from within the communities, there are obvious signs of change most evident in the somewhat chaotic order that once matter-of-fact ceremonial marrying activities now take. One young couple, for instance, began keeping company several years ago, just after the young woman graduated from high school. For more than a year they "dated," a practice almost unknown thirty years ago. Then, in a reversal of the more traditional practices described by Beda and Estelle, the young lady began to spend the night at the home of her young man's parents. This continued for many months. At some point during this time, the elders in the young man's *ramka* sent a delegation to ask the girl's family for her hand in marriage. As soon as her *ramka* agreed, the young man's family began to prepare for the buying ceremony. But this took place in the 1990s. After the two families had agreed to the marriage, the young couple, like any young couple in dozens of American towns, began to have a series of lovers' quarrels. Whenever there was a quarrel, the young lady came home to stay with her parents. At least twice, the emotions of the young people caused the elders to postpone the buying ceremony. The community today is far more focused on the needs and desires of its young people than it was in the past. Finally, after much discussion among family members, the buying ceremony did take place and all concerned thought it had gone very well indeed. This signaled the commencement of groom's service or groom's work and the young man moved into his newly proclaimed fiancée's home to begin working for her family. This he did, hunting for her family and performing other chores for a year. During this entire time, except when the two had a dispute, they lived together with her parents. When the groom's work was complete, had they adhered strictly to the traditional way of doing things they would have waited for her family to gather up gifts and bring her home to his house. Instead, the young couple wondered how they would ever earn enough money to be able to afford the church wedding which they both wanted. In the meantime, they lived mainly in the young man's parents' home, but still visited, ate, and sometimes slept at the young woman's home. Nothing was said about bringing her home to his house in the old way. And, finally, in the winter of 1998 the two decided to have a legal ceremony while they were in Nome. When they returned home to Gambell, they returned to his parents' house. Soon after, his parents held a celebration dinner to honor the marriage, inviting the young bride's parents to join with them. At some time in the future, it seems likely that the two will eventually have the "bringing home ceremony" to complete their marriage in the traditional sense; and, when they can afford it, they will very likely have a religious ceremony in the church as well.

Whether young people choose their marriage partners from within the community or from the outside, it is still true that almost everyone marries. And, it is not surprising that so few have married outside the village. The cost is high. But times are, indeed, changing. Young people travel—to Nome to go shopping, to Anchorage and Fairbanks to attend school, to other villages for meetings or job training programs or regional athletic events. More inter-village marriages will inevitably take place as opportunities for young people to fall in love with strangers increase. And, it seems likely that more women will remain unmarried as well, raising their children without a spouse. Ideas about family and marriage are reinforced by the school room, by the churches, by television, and by the pervasive images of popular American culture. It seems likely, too, that young people who try to maintain more traditional ways will still have to select from a sometimes-confusing array of choices.

Together the braided structures of family, food, and faith become conceptually one, providing the theoretical construct on which contemporary community life is still based. While the actual structure has changed over time, the philosophical underpinnings of the society are grounded in a theoretical universe which has its origins temporally in an older tradition. Any exploration of the contemporary village relies on these three large categories and on the notion that the past is interwoven into the present. The contemporary community of Gambell is still a profoundly religious one. While not everyone has the same views of the spiritual realm, this acknowledgment of the spiritual basis of things girds round the substance of daily life whether it be foraging in the most traditional sense, hunting with the most modern technology available, carrying out the time-honored tasks of motherhood, or reporting to work at the local post office. My own experience among the marine mammal hunters of Gambell suggests that in the search for the underlying systems of meaning which support what people do conceptually, subsistence is still the focus. I have tried to give some sense of how that system works in Gambell. Those who are responsible for food rely on the powers of faith to bring food to each person. In the past, families relied exclusively on the pow-

erful spirit forces resident in the land itself. As community members gave
up some of the older ways of interpreting and relying upon the spiritual
universe, they turned to a Protestant Christian vision, testing it carefully
in order to assure that this way of acknowledging the powerful spiritual
realm would feed families more successfully than had been the case in
the past. Only then were hunters likely to change—and, as the stories of
Pelassi, Nanghiila, and others so dramatically illustrate, not all changed
at once. Each man, each woman, dealt personally with issues of faith.
People continue to honor the traditions of their ancestors, but where ancient rituals once prevailed, most have been adjusted and reinterpreted
to accommodate a religious system whose strength is equated with the
community's Christian renaissance.

While faith, food, and family are more than simple functional precepts
and indicate a community-endorsed philosophy of considerable depth,
the strains on these three are particularly apparent in the changes in kinship terminology as islanders try to explain themselves to outsider Americans using standard American kinship terms, losing in the process, the
frequent use of Yupik terms, in the persistent effort to be "modern." Modernity itself covers a multitude of categories. At the heart is the need to
make money and to acquire the trappings of American life as advertised
constantly on television screens and in mail order catalogs, both of which
are readily available and in daily use in Gambell and elsewhere in the
north Alaskan arctic.

It is true that in 1998, with a population of 640, Gambell is still a whaling village. No conversation goes on long before someone begins to speak
of the importance of a subsistence life way. And, it is tempting to look
back on life in Gambell over the last decade and to see here a kind of romance, life lived at the edge among a hunter people whose lives "keep
them in tune with nature."

Many of the improvements in "quality" of life which have been introduced into the community in the last ten or fifteen years have created
more creature comforts at the expense of community cohesion and self-
control. Here, as everywhere else, one of the major problems is what will
happen to the children. More than half of the population of Gambell is
under the age of eighteen. The population is growing. There are few legitimate ways to earn cash wages, yet the desire for goods only available

10.1 *Sivuqaq Mountain looms to the east as three little girls carry pieces of their "Barbie doll" house across the open expanse of the village in 1988.*

for cash is increasing. Also, with the availability of television, regular running water, and other conveniences, which are now in almost every home, fewer people regularly meet together to visit, to use each other's tools and utilities, or simply to share a community utility such as the village washeteria. The days when crowds of women and children visited comfortably in the "free" high school showers are gone. Families, *ramka*, and the community itself must now self-consciously generate reasons for coming together on a regular basis so as to instill and promote values that once seemed to develop spontaneously in response to older daily living patterns and traditions.

One of the new sources of values in the community which particularly affects young people is television. As a constant verbal and visual presence in most homes, it has quietly changed children's use of the Yupik language and created a desire for material goods that cannot be supported, given the few consistently high-paying jobs in the community. Children and teenagers here as elsewhere emulate TV stars and the glamorized violence that permeates TV culture. Domestic violence is a problem, too, as is teen pregnancy. Of course, few grow up, train for a life "outside," and leave home, but the old way, the hunting life, has not been taken up universally by the young, for many reasons. Probably first and foremost is that the community has not been directly responsible for the education of its children since the introduction of formal state-mandated education at the turn of the century. In the past, education was not a separate activity, isolated physically and socially from the daily life of the family. Education began early in the home, with a parent, an aunt or uncle, or a grandparent, among one's relatives. The closeness of those family relations and the distress that a person feels when leaving the security of home or camp is illustrated again and again in the stories that women tell about the early days of marriage and that men shyly express in the first weeks of living in the homes of their in-laws to perform groom's work. Education then was aimed at teaching youngsters the skills they would need to participate in a subsistence life way and to prepare them to begin their own families, most often within the household of the husband's parents or grandparents.

Today, however, teaching comes from many quarters. Lessons are learned from the home, from the ever-present television, from school,[4] and from peers. Teaching the underlying philosophy and skills associated with a subsistence life way is often postponed until a young person has reached marriageable age. Young women, especially, are likely to learn skin-sewing and meat-processing tasks only after they are ready to marry and raise a family of their own. Modern marriages, other family relationships, and even living conditions themselves are living examples of the complexities involved when young people try to respect local tradition and accommodate Euro-American family relations and social and economic expectations at the same time. Few families are free of such problems.

One of the most insidious forces of change has been the move to

---

4. The school has only one certified teacher from the community and a handful of teachers' aides, who assist in classrooms.

houses with fewer and fewer family members. In the 1920s and 1930s, a home might hold mother, father, children, grandparents, a man's unmarried brothers and sisters, and perhaps others. Not everyone lived together, but other brothers and "grandfathers" might live next door. Often the interior of the home was symbolically separated into discrete family units, and children learned to respect their elders at an early age. Hannah described this process as she drew a picture of the house in which she grew up for me.

> HANNAH: . . . everyone had to have places . . . the children
> stayed with their families anywhere. But, [and here Hannah indicates a place on her drawing] that was [my father's younger
> brother's] family place, and this was my sister's and the siblings, if
> they want to be, because she was already grown up. And she had to
> have a sort of identification, grown-up identification, and grown-up
> place, and at the same time taking care of all of us younger ones.
> So she needed a regular place.
> CAROL: . . . It's really very formal.
> HANNAH: Yes. I think [they] had a formality of their own, in
> their own way, for things to work. [You] see . . . they're not going to
> roam around all over the place without any place, every one had [a
> place]. And that afforded peace in the family, [for] everyone to
> have a space, everything to have a space. It gave them peaceful
> life. . . . they could feel at home and rest, rather than milling
> around all the time. . . . They sat around themselves here, or over
> here, and the children would play in the middle, too. But, we
> stayed pretty much to our own, you see, our own available . . .
> space, spaces. And in the evenings, when all the men folks were in,
> children usually had to have permission to go over here, go over
> there, and go over here to play with the other children, rather than
> just milling around, because that would disturb the peace, and
> people wouldn't like that. And sometimes our grandparents would
> call us over here to tell us stories. And [our grandparents, too] had
> their space. ("Hannah" 1995, in Jolles 1987ff)

After several generations of "house building," the separations into smaller and smaller family units affect how people relate to each other. It seems likely that homes in which elders might live alone is even a possibility, something that would have been unthinkable fifteen or twenty years ago.

Family life for the last hundred years or more has meant living amongst kin, with journeys away from settlements to trap fox in fall and winter, or to camp in summer while hunting, fishing, and collecting greens, berries, and eggs. Whale hunting brought brothers together and families home for celebrations. Summer sent young men to the cliffs, women to greens and berry fields. Small children were looked after by elderly parents and grandparents. Everyone took care of everyone else and made or traded for necessities. In the old village, along the west beach, one could expect to find at least three generations of family members in a house. After the housing projects of the 1970s and early 1980s expanded the number of available homes, many nuclear families consisting of husband, wife, and children moved out of the homes in the old village to set up housekeeping on their own. In this way, the overall population of the old village "thinned out" as young men took the opportunity to leave their parental homes, which still held their aging grandparents, their unmarried brothers and sisters, plus any men working for their sisters. Population has continued to increase in the community, and, as a result, these newer homes now often hold three generations within them as well.

In the most recent housing addition, young married couples with one or two children and even single parents and their children have moved into large three and four-bedroom modular homes. One young woman friend, for instance, has lived for the last eight years with her parents, her three younger siblings, and her own two children. The parents' home is of 1970s vintage. It is solidly built, and her father has added a large outer entry way, which is used for storing food and gear of all kinds. The house itself originally had a small kitchen and bathroom, a sitting room, and four small bedrooms. Her father added one more room for sleeping and general activity. Like most Yupik homes, the house has very little furniture, but the spaces themselves don't require much. A sofa in the living room doubles as a bed. A television is prominently displayed as well as a stereo unit. The CB sits on its own shelf nearby. The kitchen has space for two people to sit and have tea at a small table. Bedrooms hold mattresses and clothing. Furniture is of little importance in a small room. The people shape the spaces, not the inanimate contents. In the newest homes, the few people within the rooms create an aura of loneliness. My friend seems to me singularly alone in her big home. Sometimes she asks a cousin to "sleep over," and sometimes her parents come so that her children won't wake up in an empty house. In other words, she has asked others to join her to relieve the emptiness by filling the house whenever she can with more family. She has furnished the large living room with two love seats and her television, which sits at one end of the living room. The house has none of the signs which I associate with Yupik daily life: no outer entry way to store the usual boots, hunting gear, and other equipment of a Yupik household, no meat or skins waiting to be processed, none of the interesting confusion of subsistence-related items. So far she hasn't needed these. She still depends on her parents, and her own children are not big enough to begin to fill such spaces yet.

Another family lived until April of 1997 in two and a half rooms—very small by current American standards. Crowded into that space were the husband and wife, their twelve-year-old son, and their grandson, whom they care for. Their teen-age daughter, mother of the baby, lived with them part of the time and sometimes stayed with the child's father. Recently the family moved into one of the new three-bedroom houses. What once was a crowded familial space is now a vast, empty series of rooms with occasional pieces of furniture—the family has a new dining room table with matching chairs, and a sofa, plus new beds in each of the bedrooms. The sense of home once marked by its collection of significant objects has been replaced by modern anonymity. The house has yet to take on the personality of its owners.

The families living in the new homes are genuinely delighted to have them. They have responded to their new circumstances the way any family would who has lived in crowded, sometimes substandard conditions. My reaction to these homes and how people seem to fit into them is certainly mine and not theirs. The effects of these newest living spaces on family and community life won't be known for many years. Perhaps, like the last group of houses, these too will gradually fill with multiple generations, reinforcing rather than deconstructing traditional family life, the subsistence system that supports it, and the religiosity that sustains it.

In the end, the greatest internal challenges facing this community, and other north Alaskan communities like it, are the combined challenges of

10.2 Smiling children embrace the technology of the future.

education, employment, and the maintenance of tradition. The stresses of modernity are starkly revealed each week in the pages of Alaska's oldest newspaper, the *Nome Nugget*. Letters to the editor, obituaries, the paper's weekly police report, and columns addressing subsistence issues together indicate how difficult it is for communities to educate their children for productive futures in their home communities, either in local businesses within the communities in order to provide livelihoods for the next generation of young adults or to promote and maintain a modern version of subsistence to engage and support at least a percentage of young adults. The subsistence life way is an embattled one. Internally, families must continue to interest their children in subsistence skills and knowledge. From the outside, there is the ongoing question of resource exploitation, especially oil and gas. And, there is the long-term problem of environmental degradation and change, in the form of pollution, altering water temperature and raising sea levels. Gambell is not the only village to deal with these issues. It does, however, exemplify many of the same strengths and shortcomings of other rural northwestern Alaskan villages. The community was able to halt exploratory oil drilling in its waters. It successfully took on the responsibility of private ownership of its land. These and other successes in the community have depended finally on the strength of the underlying subsistence ideology, which combines the principles and precepts of faith, food, and family that I have explored. This ideology will be tested and presumably revised again and again as population increases, as available resources change (undoubtedly decreasing as the Bering Sea warms and rises), and as the community continues to modernize and to grow.

Appendix

A. SELECTION FROM PAUL SILOOK'S 1930 DIARY
(BOX 3, HENRY BASCOM COLLINS COLLECTION 1982)

(Winter whaling ceremonies are italicized.)

Jan. 15—Clear in the evening. *During the night I went to Iyaketan which he sings.*

Jan. 31 Friday—N. clear. *Dick Ung. prepare to have a moon worship and he will serve to-morrow by the rising of the sun.* During the day I shot a walrus but wounded it. Frank Iyek caught 1 fox.

Feb. 2 Sun.—N. Part clear and part cloudy. Sleet in the morning *Yoghok held a moon worship which he prepare yesterday. Booshu prepared to have moon worship to-morrow morning.* Wallace killed 1 walrus and several men killed seals. Tatoowi & Nunraela arrived from Camp Collier.

Feb. 3 Mon.—N. high wind sleet. Soonog, Bolowon & Nup each caught 1 fox. Carl killed 1 mukluk. *Booshu held a moon worship. Koonooku prepare to have one.*

Feb. 4 Tues.—N. clear, sleet in the morning, clear up in the evening. Womkon & Chester each caught a fox. Several men killed seals. *We prepare to have moon worship tomorrow morning. Koonooku held one this morning.*

Feb. 17 Monday—N. *clear all day. Womkon prepare to have dancing ceremony which they have every year.* Andrew & Ernest each caught a fox.

Feb. 18 Tues.—N. clear all day the wind is not so high. *Womkon is having a dancing worship.* No body go hunt.

Feb. 25 Tues. 2 P.M. 70, 4 l.b. 8 p., N. Clear.[1]2 Oscar killed 3 seals. *Womkon &*

---

1. In these entries, "1 b" means "number of seal or kerosene oil lamps burning"; "8 p" indicates how many people were in the house; two-digit numbers show the house temperature inside of the *aagra*.

his people came to sing at 2:P.M. 3:P.M. 88, 3 l.b. 26 p. *some dances.* N.
cloudy. They all leave out at 5: P.M., Observe at 6:P.M. 84

Feb. 27 Thurs. 82, 4 l.b. 11 p. S.E. cloudy and snowing all day. *Womkon went
to sing in Koonooku's house & Dicks*

Feb. 28 Fri 78—4 l.b. 11 p. N.E. cloudy & snow. *Yavoghseuk prepare to have a
moon worship*—I killed 1 seal. Lost 1 mukluk & 1 walrus. They day we get
our traps from its places.

March 1 Sat. 6 P.M. 72—4 l./b. 11 p. N. high wind cloudy & snowing all day.
*Yav. held a moon worship.*Yav. held a moon worship.

March 2 Sun. 6 P.M. 74—4 l.b. 10 p. N.E. low wind part clear & part cloudy.
Few men killed seals. some went to get their traps Andrew caught 1 fox.
Lawrence prepare to have moon worship.

March 3 Mon. 6 P.M. 74—4 l.b. 11 p. N.E. high wind cloudy. It was clear in
the morning. *Lawrence held a moon worship.* Lloyd & Henry each caught
1 fox. Arrival of Pungowiyi, Noongwook, Penin, Annogiyok, Rookok & Mr.
Sam Troutman & Marvin from Seevoongu.

March 5 Wed 74—4 l.b. 11 p. N. clear but high wind. The Seevoongu men
did not leave. Several men killed seals on the beach. I killed 1 seal.—*Every
evening the young boys and girls having tag between Jimmie's old house and
James' house.*

B. TRADITIONAL WHALING CEREMONIES FROM HENRY COLLINS' NOTEBOOKS (BOX 4, IBID.)

In 1928, when Henry Collins was excavating Punuk Islands' dwellings and
other sites, he kept both a diary and a notebook filled with stories told him by
Paul Silook, James Aningayou, and others. He was very curious about whaling as were all of the men who came to conduct research on the island. Below
are several pages from his "Ethnology" notebooks which he recorded from
Silook between 1928 and 1931:

> B.1. Jimmie Otiohok, a member of Imaremkeit tribe made a trip to Indian
> Point [Chaplino], Siberia, a week before the Northland arrived to get a
> certain kind of plant needed by his brother Burscha [Booshu [or
> Busaa}—Silook's relative and the man who allowed Geist to participate in
> his ceremonies], for a ceremony, a "whale worship" in commemoration
> of the whale he (B) had killed some weeks before. The Imaremkits claim
> to have come from Indian Point and whenever one of them kills a whale
> he must have for the ceremony that follows this particular plant used by

his forefathers. The Imaremkit people say they are descended from a woman who lived at Kukuliak but who was sold to a man at Indian Point. Her grandchildren then returned to St. L. living at Gambell (Sevuokuk). (Henry Bascom Collins Collection 1982: Unprocessed, Box 3, Notebook: H. B. Collins 1930/Doc.File. Collins 1930.00A: Unnumbered)

B.2. U vuk tuk—A ceremony formerly in use among the Imaremkit and Owahlit as a kind of thanksgiving for recovery from sickness or for having been saved from some disaster. Also after killing a whale. In this latter case: the boat capt, when the whale's struck, calls out the name of ceremonies, asking them (sic) to go ahead of the whale and stop it. After the whale is killed the ceremonies called upon are held. Even if the whale escapes the ceremony is held because calling out the name of ceremony is a promise.

In preparation for the Uvuktuk meat is prepared and the principal (worshiper according to Paul's terminology) or man giving the feast throws into the air a tiny piece of meat or even only touching the meat with a hand—throwing it up and rubs a little on the walrus skin (feeding it). Then all sit down on the skin and eat the meat. Believe that if they eat, the Spirit of ceremony will also, but if not then it will not. When throwing the meat in the air he calls out "Uvuktuk tiwa," (man of the ceremony) then calling out also if he wishes the name of some ailment he or some near relative has and the names of ancestors. All these are offered homage in the same sense; the idea is that if the ceremony is fed it will be strong and so able and willing to help out in time of need. Some meat is divided among the old people. After eating & dividing up the meat (about 1/2 of small walrus or a whale, reindeer or seal or white man's food) the principal steps on the walrus skin and is tossed up into the air by the others. Pcs of rope or thong are tied thru the perforations at the edge and it is by these that the skins is held. Then anyone who wishes is tossed up. Some are tossed as high as 30 ft. Men women or children take part, throwing & jumping—Good jumpers come down straight on the feet, some double over in the air like a high dive.

Additions to notes on whaling—Material for sacrifice pertains to the Imaremkit tribe. Others sacrifice different things. Owalit & Nungpagak sacrifice only fermented plant & walrus blubber. Neskok (Aginaktat) sacrifice only willow leaves, walrus blubber & w- meat, raw-

Ceremony A "moon worship" . . . . : Taking sac.[rifice] material to beach—It is taken to the boat in wooden dishes, placed in the boat which was on the rack. It is dragged to the beach. No women in this.

After men return from beach, then women of the boat capts house (wife), daughters, sisters, (daughters-in-law) go to every house in village and give a small pc of the sacrificial food (fermented plants, codfish, tobacco). In return for this they are given something: cartridges, powder or primers, walrus rope, files, saw blades, sugar, tea, etc.

Anyone can go to one of these sacrifices, regardless of tribe, except that the Imaremkit [Silook's ramket] do not go to those of other tribes altho others may go to theirs. Say that once they went to a sac[rifice] of another tribe & everyone died, so no more. . . . (Henry Bascom Collins Collection 1982: Unprocessed, Box 3, Notebook: H. B. Collins 1930/Doc. File. Collins 1930.00A:4–5)

B.3. The whaling ceremonies "A tagh'hok" are held by each tribe separately, each differing only in minor details from the others. Four ceremonies for a boat captain. The third only if he kills a whale. A. "moon worship" held by certain tribes on certain months, i.e., Feb., March, April; B. if a whale is killed and C. after whaling; D. in November. (Henry Bascom Collins Collection, Unprocessed, Box 3, Notebook: H. B. Collins 1930/Doc. File. Collins 1930.00A:22)

C. SILOOK'S WORK DIARY, JUNE 22, 1928–JULY 5, 1928 (BOX 4, IBID.)

Paul Silook's Note Book—1928 Punuk Island

June 22 (at 2 o'clock): Arrived at Punuk Isl., Mr. Collins, the mate & some of the crew cam ashore to search for a good place for a camp. While we were at the island the fog came and we could not see the ship. We went to the ship leaving the captain on the island. We went by signal of their whistle. Then we load two boat with empty boxes & stuff and cam ashore.

We unload them and after them leave we put up our tents & cook our breakfast & eat and sleep. The same day we stored our stuff between our tents.

June 23: We walk around the island to amuse ourselves.

June 24: Start our excavation. Mr. Collin, Steven & I do the excavating all day. Mr. Collin & I walk around with a shotgun but did not shoot any.

June 25: Dig all day. I cut my finger very deep. Told stories while Mr. Collin writes them.

June 26: While we are digging we saw two walrus. I shot one but it sink. It is about 50

feet from the point. Mr. Collin, Mr. Manca & Steven went out in a canoe to see if the can find it, but it wasn't there. Before, if Steven is good hook thrower he would hook it. He missed it several times. At lunch we saw three more passing by. We did not shoot them. While we are digging we saw another walrus far off from the land.

Steven shot at two seals but missed both of them.

June 27: Dig all day. In the evening I tell story to Mr. Collin.

June 28: Dig again from 11 A.M. Lunch 2 P.M. We see walrus every day. Dig again after lunch came to the tent at suppertime.

June 29: Dig in the morning on the northern part of the island After lunch we all go digging again, but found very few specimens.

June 30: Dig at another place. We see 5 walrus l sleeping. I ran to the tent to get my gun and went to the point. I grunted at them and they would never pay any attention to me. I go dig again then they came near the shore. I ran and shot one but not kill it. Steven shot 4 eider ducks. After lunch we dig at an old ningloo. Steven, Manca & Collin dig, while I dig around where they threw out their dirt. Mr. Collins took my picture by the old ningloo, then after Mr. Collins took Manca's picture while he is trying to take out a skeleton of a man. . . . In the evening I went to Collins tent & tell more stories as he writes them.

July 1: Dig until lunch and find very few speciments. After we had lunch Steven and I went to the N.E. part of the island. Steven brought some wood on his back & when we reach home we saw Mr. Collins was on the other island which he had waded, also Mr. Manka is there.

Afternoon I shot at one seal and at a young mukluk missed both of them. We always on a lookout toward the N.E. Cape to see if a boat is in sight.

July 2:Dig at another place at N.E. of our tent, shot a seal but missed it. Saw a flock of wlrus sleeping near by.

After lunch we go digging again I shot at one seal but missed it 3 times, we done at supper time.

July 3: Dig from 9:30 A.M. to 12 m. I shot at a young mukluk but missed it. After lunch we dig an old ningloo found few specimens. Quit at supper time.

July 4: Dig from 9:A.M. to 12:m go to out tent and eat our lunch while we are digging we find very few things in an old ningloo between the two waters. After lunch Mr. Collins & I measured the old ningloos that we had dugged the other day. While Manca & Steven dig new old ningloo. I shot at a seal three times but not get it. Mr. Collins shot at it once also missed it. We done our digging about supper time. We put all the beach ivory in sacks, because Mr. Collins thinks that the Northland may visit us before he leave to Barrow.

July 5: Dig from morning till noon. I shot at several walruses but did not hit them. Just before lunch Manca shot at the walruses three times, his one just wounded it. We pause to eat our lunch 1/2 hr earlier than usual. After lunch we dig again until supper time. Steven & I go after water. We brought about 3/4 full of barrel.

Glossary

aagra Interior room of traditional homes

aghveq Bowhead whale

akuutaq A mixture, usually of greens or berries and oil

alignalghii Shaman

angyapik (pl. *angyapiget*) Traditional boat with a lumber or driftwood frame and walrus-hide cover. Today's *angyapiget* also use sails and have a well built into the boat for an outboard motor.

angyaq (pl. *angyet*) General purpose hunting boats, such as commercially produced Lund boats

aghveq Bowhead whale

Aymaramka Clan name coming from Chukotka

Kiyalighaq Abandoned settlement site on Southeast Cape

Kukulek Historic settlement located near the present-day community of Savoonga. The settlement was vacated at the end of the nineteenth century after disease swept through it between 1878 and 1879, killing most inhabitants. It was excavated by archaeologists Otto Geist and Henry Collins in the late 1920s and 1930s.

laluramka (pl. *laluramket*) A Caucasian or white person

manguna Walrus meat with fat and skin attached

manteghapik (pl. *manteghapiget*) Traditional home type still in use at the beginning of the twentieth century. These homes were built with driftwood sides, walrus-hide roofs and walrus-hide floors; they were insulated heavily with grasses and mosses stuffed in between interior and exterior walls. They had one interior room, the *aagra*, separated off from the outer area by reindeer hide walls. This was the area of the house that was heated by seal oil lamps.

nanuq Polar bear

nenglu Semi-underground dwellings. These were abandoned at the end of the nineteenth century. Floors were of stone; the walls were of whalebone and driftwood, the sides were covered with sod and, throughout the winter, with snow. The overall shape was dome-like.

neqepik Food taken directly from Bering Sea, or from the island and its many rivers, creeks, lakes and lagoons. One translation is "real" food, in contrast to imported or "white people" food.

Pugughileghmii(t) Person or people from Pugughileq or Southwest Cape

qayuutaq Eating tray, traditionally made of wood. Modern trays are sometimes plastic or heavy aluminum.

qiipaghaak The cloth outer garment that many women wear. It is usually made of decoratively patterned cotton. It falls just above the knees, has a deep ruffle, and generally has additional identifying decoration of red rickrack or narrow red cotton bands around the hem. Sleeves are long, and the garment always has an attached hood.

ramka (sing. and plural) Clan or clans; -ramka is singular if used at the end of a word (e.g., Aymaramka)

ramket That clan, those people; -ramket is plural if used at the end of a word (e.g., *laluramket*)

saayguraaq The outer entries to each home. They are used to store food and equipment. They can be as small as a simple foyer or as large as a separate room.

siqlugaq (pl. *siqluwat*) Underground food storage unit. These units were at least six or seven feet deep. Their deepest parts were at or below the permafrost level. They were entered by wooden ladders. The entrances were covered with whalebone or driftwood and weighted down with large rocks. They were used especially for meat storage such as the walrus meatballs.

Sivuqaghhmiit The people of Sivuqaq

Sivuqaq The Yupik name for Gambell and for St. Lawrence Island

Bibliography

Ackerman, Robert E.

1962 "Culture Contact in the Bering Sea: Birnirk-Punuk Period." In John M. Campbell, ed., *Prehistoric Cultural Relations Between the Arctic and Temperate Zones of North America*. Arctic Institute of North America Technical Papers 11. Montreal.

1984 "Prehistory of the Asian Eskimo Zone." In David Damas, ed., *Arctic* (*Handbook of North American Indians*, vol. 5), 106–35. Washington, D.C.: Smithsonian Institution.

Allen, Paula Gunn, ed.

1988 "Introduction." *Spider Woman's Granddaughters: Traditional Tales and Contemporary Writing by Native American Women*, 1–21. Boston: Beacon Press.

Alowa, Nelson

1985 Tape no. 165. Translated by Deborah Apatiki, May 1988. Materials Development Center, Title VII Bilingual/Bicultural Program, Gambell. Bering Strait School District, Unalakleet.

Anungazuk, Herbert, and Carol Zane Jolles

1998 "Interviews with Whalers: Gambell, AK, 1997." Unpublished manuscript.

Apassingok, Anders

1988 "Family Relationships." Unpublished manuscript. On file, Materials Development Center, Title VII Bilingual/Bicultural Program, Gambell. Bering Strait School District, Unalakleet.

Apassingok, Anders, Willis Walunga, Raymond Oozevaseuk, and Edward Tennant, eds.

1987   *Lore of St. Lawrence Island: Echoes of Our Eskimo Elders, Vol. 2: Savoonga.* Unalakleet: Bering Strait School District.

Apassingok, Anders, Willis Walunga, and Edward Tennant, eds.
1985   *Lore of St. Lawrence Island: Echoes of our Eskimo Elders, Vol. 1: Gambell.* Unalakleet: Bering Strait School District.

Apassingok, Anders, Willis Walunga, Raymond Oozevaseuk, Jessie Uglowook, and Edward Tennant, eds.
1989   *Lore of St. Lawrence Island: Echoes of Our Eskimo Elders, Vol. 3: Southwest Cape.* Bering Strait School District, Unalakleet.

Apatiki, Edna
1989   Untitled. Manuscript in author's possession.

Arutiunov, S. A., and William W. Fitzhugh
1988   "Prehistory of Siberia and the Bering Sea." In William W. Fitzhugh and Aron Crowell, *Crossroads of Continents: Cultures of Siberia and Alaska,* 117–29. Washington, D.C.: Smithsonian Institution Press.

Bandi, Hans-Georg
1969   *Eskimo Prehistory.* Studies of Northern Peoples 2. College: University of Alaska Press.
1995   "Siberian Eskimos as Whalers and Warriors." In Allen P. McCartney, ed., *Hunting the Largest Animals: Native Whaling in the Western Arctic and Subarctic.* Studies in Whaling No. 3, Occasional Publication No. 36:165–83. Edmonton, Alberta: Canadian Circumpolar Institute, University of Alberta.

Bateson, Mary Catherine
1994   *Peripheral Visions: Learning Along the Way.* New York: Harper Collins.

Beechey, Sir Frederick W.
1968   (1831) *Narrative of a Voyage to the Pacific and Beering's Strait to Cooperate with the Polar Expeditions Performed in His Majesty's Ship Blossom . . . in the Years 1825, 26, 27, 28. . . .* (vol. 1: 330–33). London: Colburn and Bentley, original publisher. Reprint.

Berkhofer, R. F., Jr.
1965   *Salvation and the Savage: An Analysis of Protestant Missions and American Indian Response, 1787–1862.* Lexington: University of Kentucky Press.

Blackman, Margaret B.

1989   Sadie Brower Neakok: An Inupiaq Woman. Seattle: University of Wash-
        ington Press.

1991   "The Individual and Beyond: Reflections of the Life History Process."
        Anthropology and Humanism Quarterly 16 (2): 56–62.

Boeri, David

1983   People of the Ice Whale: Eskimos, White Men and the Whale. New
        York: E. P. Dutton, Inc.

Bogoras, Waldemar

1904–09 "The Chukchee." Memoirs of the American Museum of Natural His-
        tory 11. (New York.)

1913   "The Eskimo of Siberia." (The Jesup North Pacific Expedition 8[3],
        Franz Boas, ed., Memoirs of the American Museum of Natural History
        12.) Leyden, Holland: E. J. Brill.

Boolowon, Reena

1998   "Components of a Traditional Siberian Yup'ik Marriage." In Susan B.
        Andres and John Creed, eds., Authentic Alaska: Voices of Its Native
        Writers, 128–30. American Indian Lives Series. Lincoln: University of
        Nebraska Press.

Bourdieu, Pierre

1977   Outline of a Theory of Practice. Cambridge: Cambridge University
        Press.

Bowden, Henry Warner

1981   American Indians and Christian Missions. Chicago: University of
        Chicago Press.

Braund, S. R.

1988   The Skin Boats of Saint Lawrence Island, Alaska. Seattle: University of
        Washington Press.

Braund, Stephen, and Elizabeth Moorehead

1995   "Contemporary Alaska Eskimo Bowhead Whaling Villages." In Allen
        P. McCartney, ed., Hunting the Largest Animals: Native Whaling in
        the Western Arctic and Subarctic. Occasional Publication No. 36,
        Canadian Circumpolar Institute, University of Alberta.

Burch, Ernest S.

1971   "The Nonempirical Environment of the Arctic Alaskan Eskimos."
        Southwestern Journal of Anthropology 27:148–65.

Burch, Ernest S., ed.
1984   "The Central Yupik Eskimos." Supplementary issue. *Etudes/Inuit/ Studies* 8.

Burgess, Stephen
1974   "The St. Lawrence Islanders of Northwest Cape—Patterns of Resource Utilization." Ph.D. diss., University of Alaska, Fairbanks.

Burn, June
1921   Unprocessed papers. Bureau of Indian Affairs record box. Gambell Elementary School (carbon copy: original lost).

Burridge, Kenelm O. L.
1969   *New Heaven, New Earth: A Study of Millenarian Activities.* New York: Schocken Books.
1978   "Introduction: Missionary Occasions," In J. A. Boutilier, D. T. Hughes, and S. W. Tiffany, eds., *Mission, Church and Sect in Oceania.* ASAO Monograph No. 6. New York: University Press of America.

Campbell, Edgar Omar, and Louisa K. Campbell
1904–11 Unpublished journal, volumes 1–5. Presbyterian Historical Society Archives, Philadelphia.

Carius, Helen Slwooko
1979   *Sevukakmet: Ways of Life on St. Lawrence Island.* Anchorage: Alaska Pacific University Press.

Collins, Henry B.
1937   "Archaeology of St. Lawrence Island, Alaska." *Smithsonian Miscellaneous Collections* 96.

Cruikshank, Julie
1990a   "Getting the Words Right: Perspectives on Naming and Places in Athapaskan Oral History." *Arctic Anthropology* 27(1):52–65.
1990b   *Life Lived Like a Story.* Lincoln: University of Nebraska Press.

Damas, David, ed.
1984   *Arctic.* Vol. 5 of *Handbook of North American Indians*, William C. Sturtevant, general editor. Washington, D.C.: Smithsonian Institution.

Dorothea Leighton, M.D., Collection (DLC)
1982   Field notes (1940) of Dorothea Leighton and Alexander Leighton. Archives of the University of Alaska, Fairbanks.
1983   "Eskimo Recollections of Their Life Experiences: Collected by A. H.

and D. Leighton, Gambell, St. Lawrence Island, 1940." *Northwest Anthropological Research Notes* 17:1–2.

Doty, William Furman, Teacher
1900   "The Eskimo of St. Lawrence Island." In Sheldon Jackson, *Ninth Annual Report on Introduction of Domestic Reindeer into Alaska, 1899*, 186–223. U.S. Department of Education. Washington, D.C.: Government Printing Office.
1900–1910 "Log Book, St. Lawrence Island." In *Report on the Introduction of Domestic Reindeer into Alaska*, 224–56 (United States Education Bureau). Washington, D.C.: Government Printing Office.

Dumond, Don
1998   "The Hillside Site, St. Lawrence Island, Alaska." University of Oregon Anthropological Papers No. 55.

Ellana, Linda J.
1988   "Skin Boats and Walrus Hunters of Bering Strait." *Arctic Anthropology* 25(1):107–9.

Elliott, Henry W.
1896   *Our Arctic Province: Alaska and the Seal Islands*, 444. New York: C. Scribner's Sons.

Feld, Steven, and Keith H. Basso, eds.
1996   *Senses of Place*. School of American Research Advanced Seminar Series, Douglas W. Schwartz, editor. Distributed by University of Washington Press, Seattle.

Fienup-Riordan, Ann
1986   "The Real People: The Concept of Personhood Among the Yup'ik Eskimos of Western Alaska." *Etudes/Inuit/Studies* (10):261–70.
1990   *Eskimo Essays*. New Brunswick, NJ: Rutgers University Press.
1994   *Boundaries and Passages: Rule and Ritual in Yup'ik Eskimo Oral Tradition*. Norman: University of Oklahoma Press.

Fitzhugh, William W., and Aron Crowell
1988   *Crossroads of Continents: Cultures of Siberia and Alaska*. Washington, D.C.: Smithsonian Institution Press.

Gambell, Vene
1910   *The Schoolhouse Farthest West: St. Lawrence Island, Alaska*. New York: Woman's Board of Home Missions of the Presbyterian Church.

Geertz, Clifford
1973   *The Interpretation of Cultures.* New York: Basic Books.

Geist, Otto W., and Froelich G. Rainey
1936   "Archaeological Excavations at Kukulik, St. Lawrence Island, Alaska: Preliminary Report." *University of Alaska Miscellaneous Publication* 2. Washington, D.C.:Goverment Printing Office.

Geist Collection. Dr. Otto W. Geist Collection
c. 1916–61 Alaska and Polar Regions Archives, University of Alaska, Fairbanks.

General Conference of Seventh-day Adventists
1959ff Record Group NA 9, Series: Conference Directories, North American Division/Conference Directories, Alaska Missions Section. Washington, D.C.: Office of Archives and Statistics.
        Roll 11 (1959–68, 1971–75)
        Roll 23 (1976–82)
        Roll 34 (1983–85)

Giddings, J. Louis
1967   *Ancient Men of the Arctic.* Seattle: University of Washington Press.

Guemple, D. Lee, ed.
1972   *Alliance in Eskimo Society.* Proceedings of the American Ethnological Society for 1971. Supplement. Seattle: University of Washington Press.

Henry Bascom Collins Collection, National Anthropological Archives, National Museum of Natural History, Smithsonian Institution
1982   Box Unnumbered—Unprocessed [Collins Notebooks, Field Notes—Resolute, etc., Alaska]:
        H. B. Collins—Archaeology Notebook—1930—Gambell, St. Lawrence Island (especially notes following entry Cut 16); H. B. Collins—1930—Ethnographic notes—Memo Notes—Book B (written on front of notebook); H. B. Collins—Archaeology notebook—1930 (J. A. Ford's notes); Loose pages from Henry Collins notebook—approximate date 1920– 1930.
        Box 3—Unprocessed—[Collins Field Notes etc.] Notes on Games taken down from Paul Silook, 1929; Notebook H. B. Collins 1930; 1928 Silook diary; 1929–1930 Silook diary; H. B. Collins 1930—Ethnographic notes—Book A (written on front of notebook).
        Box 4—Unprocessed—[Collins field notes, etc.]: Memorandum Book—Ethn—1928; Notebook: "Collins 30.00A" ed.; Notebook:

"Collins 30"; "Notebook of James Ford—Henry B. Collins"—1930; Paul Silook—archaeological Notebook 1930–1931 (for the Smithsonian 1931 Expedition); Loose-leaf notes from a memo book; Paul Silook (H. B. Collins) Folk Lore.

Hooper, Calvin L.
1881   "Report of the Cruise of the U.S. Revenue Steamer Corwin in the Arctic Ocean, November 1, 1880," 10–11. Washington: Government Printing Office.

Horton, Robin
1971   "African Conversion." *Africa: Journal of the International African Institute* 16(2):85–108.
1975   "On the Rationality of Conversion, Parts I and II." *Journal of the International African Institute* 45(3):219–35, 373–99.

Hughes, Charles Campbell
1953   "A Preliminary Ethnography of the Eskimo of St. Lawrence Island, Alaska." Master's thesis, Department of Anthropology, Cornell University.
1954–1955 Field Notes. In possession of Mrs. Charles Hughes.
1958a   "An Eskimo Deviant from the 'Eskimo' Type of Social Organization." *American Anthropologist* 60(6):1140–47.
1958b   "The Patterning of Recent Cultural Change in a Siberian Eskimo Village." *Journal of Social Issues* 14(4):25–35.
1959   "Translation of I. K. Voblov's 'Eskimo Ceremonies.'" *Anthropological Papers of the University of Alaska* 7(2):71–90.
1960   *An Eskimo Village in the Modern World.* Ithaca, NY: Cornell University Press.
1965   "Under Four Flags: Recent Culture Change among the Eskimos." *Current Anthropology* 6(1):3–69.
1966   "From Contest to Council: Social Change Among the St. Lawrence Island Eskimos." In Marc J. Swartz, Victor W. Turner, and Arthur Tuden, eds., *Political Anthropology*, 265–63. Chicago: Aldine.
1974   *Eskimo Boyhood: An Autobiography in Psychosocial Perspective.* Lexington: The University Press of Kentucky.
1984   St. Lawrence Island Eskimos. In David Damas, ed., *Arctic* (William Sturtevant, general editor, *Handbook of North American Indians*), vol. 5, 262–77. Washington, D.C.: Smithsonian Institution Press.

Hughes, Jane Murphy

1960   "An Epidemiological Study of Psychopathology in an Eskimo Village." Ph.D. diss., Department of Anthropology, Cornell University.

Irrigoo, Clarence

n.d.   Manuscript in the author's possession.

Irrigoo, Samuel

1979   Tape 25. Translated by Deborah Apatiki, May 1988. Materials Development Center, Title VII Bilingual/Bicultural Program, Gambell. Bering Strait School District, Unalakleet.

Isaacs, Harold R.

1975   "Basic Group Identity: Idols of the Tribe." In Nathan Glazer and Daniel P. Moynihan, eds., *Ethnicity, Theory and Experience*, 29–52. Cambridge: Harvard University Press.

Iutzi-Mitchell, Roy D.

1989   "Strong Man, Spearman, Bowman, Chief: An Introduction to the Classical Martial Arts of the Asiatic Eskimos." Paper delivered at the Alaska Anthropological Association meetings, Anchorage.

Jackson, Rev. Sheldon, D.D.

1880   *Alaska and Missions on the North Pacific Coast.* New York: Dodd Mead and Company.

Jackson, Sheldon, comp.

1895   *Report on Introduction of Domestic Reindeer into Alaska, 1894.* Washington, D.C.: Government Printing Office.

1898   *Report on Introduction of Domestic Reindeer into Alaska, 1897.* Washington, D.C.: Government Printing Office.

1900   *Ninth Annual Report on Introduction of Domestic Reindeer into Alaska, 1899.* U.S. Bureau of Education. Washington, D.C.: Government Printing Office.

Jacobson, Steven A., ed.

1987   *A Dictionary of the St. Lawrence Island/Siberian Yupik Eskimo Language.* Compiled by Linda Womkon Badten, Vera Oovi Kaneshiro, and Marie Oovi. Fairbanks: University of Alaska.

1900   *Report on Introduction of Domestic Reindeer into Alaska, 1899.* Washington, D.C.: Government Printing Office.

Jolles, Carol Zane

1987ff   Field notes and tapes in the author's possession.

1989   "Salvation on St. Lawrence Island: Protestant Conversion Among the Sivuqaghhmiit." *Arctic Anthropology* 26(2):12–27.

1990   "Being Yup'ik, Being Christian: Ethnicity and Christianity in Sivuqaq (Gambell, St. Lawrence Island, Alaska)." Ph.D. diss., Anthropology Department, University of Washington.

1994   "Cutting Meat, Sewing Skins, Telling Tales: Women's Narratives in Gambell, Alaska." *Arctic Anthropology* 31(1):86–102.

1995a   "Paul Silook and the Ethnohistory of Whaling on St. Lawrence Island, Alaska." In Allen P. McCartney, ed., *Hunting the Largest Animals: Native Whaling in the Western Arctic and Subarctic*. Studies in Whaling No. 3, Occasional Publication No. 36:221–52. Edmonton, Alberta: Canadian Circumpolar Institute, University of Alberta.

1995b   "Speaking of Whaling: A Transcript of the Alaska Eskimo Whaling Commission Panel Presentation on Native Whaling." In Allen P. McCartney, ed., *Hunting the Largest Animals: Native Whaling in the Western Arctic and Subarctic*. Studies in Whaling No. 3, Occasional Publication No. 36:315–37. Edmonton: Canadian Circumpolar Institute, University of Alberta.

1997   "Changing Roles of St. Lawrence Island Women: Clanswomen in the Public Sphere." In *Arctic Anthropology* [Power, Resistance, and Security: Papers in Honor of Richard G. Condon, Steven L. McNabb, Alexsandr I. Pika, William W. Richards, Nikolai Galgauge, Nina Ankalina, Vera Rakhtilkon, Boris Mymykhtikak, and Nikolai Avanun, edited by Pamela R. Stern, George W. Wenzel, and Sergei Kan] 34(1)86–101.

1999   "When Men Speak of Whales." Paper presented at the Oral History Association meeting. Anchorage.

Jolles, Carol Zane, and Kaningok

1991   "*Qayuutat* and *Angyapiget*: Gender Relations and Subsistence Activities in Sivuqaq (Gambell, St. Lawrence Island, Alaska)." *Etudes/Inuit/Studies* 15(2)23–53.

Jorgensen, Joseph

1990   *Oil-Age Eskimos*. Berkeley: University of California Press.

Kotzebue, Otto von

1821   *A voyage of discovery, into the South Sea and Beering's straits, for the purpose of exploring a north-east passage, undertaken in the years*

1815–1818, at the expense of His Highness . . . Count Romanzoff, in the ship Rurick, under the command of the lieutenant in the Russian imperial navy, Otto von Kotzebue. Vol. 1. London, Longman, Hurst, Rees, Orme, and Brown.

1967   A *Voyage of Discovery into the South Sea and Beering's Straits,* vol. 2. Bibliotheca Australiana. New York: Da Capo.

Krauss, Michael

1988   "Many Tongues—Ancient Tales." In William W. Fitzhugh and Aron Crowell, eds., *Crossroads of Continents: Cultures of Siberia and Alaska,* 144–150. Washington, D.C.: Smithsonian Institution Press.

Krupat, Arnold

1994   "Introduction." In Arnold Krupat, ed., *Native American Autobiography: An Anthology,* 3–17. Madison: University of Wisconsin Press.

Krupnik, I. I.

1983   "Early Settlements and Demographic History of Asian Eskimos of Southeastern Chukotka (Including St. Lawrence Island)." In H. Michael and J. VanStone, eds., *Culture and History of the Bering Sea Region: Papers from an International Symposium,* 84–111. New York: International Research and Exchanges Board.

1993   *Arctic Adaptations: Native Whalers and Reindeer Herders of Northern Eurasia.* Hanover, NH: University Press of New England.

Kulukhon, Lawrence Qilleghqun

1965   "Rules for Living." Manuscript.

1966   "How Christianity Began on St. Lawrence Island." Manuscript on file, Wycliffe Bible Translation Office, Gambell, AK.

n.d.   Untitled tape in the possession of Willis Walunga.

Langdon, Steve J.

1986   "Contradictions in Alaskan Native Economy and Society." In Steve J. Langdon, ed., *Contemporary Alaskan Native Economies,* 29–46. New York: University Press of America.

Langness, L. L., and Gelya Frank

1981   *Lives: An Anthropological Approach to Biography.* Novato, CA: Chandler and Sharp Publishers, Inc.

Lantis, Margaret

1947   *Alaskan Eskimo Ceremonialism.* Monographs of the American Ethnological Society, edited by Marian W. Smith. New York: J. J. Augustin, Publisher.

Leighton, Alexander H., and Charles C. Hughes
1955   "Notes on Eskimo Patterns of Suicide." *Southwestern Journal of Anthropology* 2(4):327–38.

Little, Ronald L., and Lynn A. Robbins
1982   "Ethnographic Baseline: St. Lawrence Island." Final Technical Report, SLI-4. Minerals Management Service, Anchorage.
1984   "Summary: Ethnographic Baseline: St. Lawrence Island." Technical Report, United States Department of the Interior, Minerals Management Service, Reston, VA.

Little, Ronald L., and Lynn A. Robbins, with Joseph C. Jorgensen
1986   "The Yupik Eskimos of St. Lawrence Island, Alaska: Social Impact Assessment of Proposed Energy Development." Napa, CA: John Muir Institute.

Marsh, Gordon H.
1954   "A Comparative Survey of Eskimo-Aleut Religion." *Anthropological Papers of the University of Alaska* 3(1):21–36.

Mauss, Marcel
1967   *The Gift: Forms and Functions of Exchange in Archaic Societies.* New York: W. W. Norton and Company.

Moore, Riley D.
1923   "Social Life of the Eskimo of St. Lawrence Island." *American Anthropologist* 25(30):339–75.

Morningstar Gallery
1999   *Masterpieces of Antique American Indian Art,* 58, No. 07228.

Morrow, Phyllis
1990   "Symbolic Interactions, Indirect Expressions: Limits to Interpretations of Yupik Society." *Etudes/Inuit/Studies* 14 (1–2):141–58.

Murphy, Jane M.
1964   "Psychotherapeutic Aspects of Shamanism on St. Lawrence Island, Alaska." In Ari Kiev, ed., *Magic, Faith and Healing,* 53–83. London: The Free Press of Glencoe/Collier Macmillan Limited.

Nelson, Edward
1983 (1899) *The Eskimos about Bering Strait.* New York: Johnson Reprint Corporation.
North Pacific Union Gleaner 68(1):12–13.

Nuttall, Mark
1992 *Arctic Homeland: Kinship, Community, and Development in Northwest Greenland.* Toronto: University of Toronto Press.

Oswalt, Wendell H.
1963 *Mission of Change in Alaska: Eskimos and Moravians on the Kuskokwim.* San Marino, CA: The Huntington Library.

Pratt, Mary Louise
1986 "Fieldwork in Common Places." In Clifford, James and George Marcus, eds., *Writing Culture: The Poetics and Politics of Ethnography*, 27–50. Berkeley: University of California Press.

Presbyterian Historical Society
n.d.   Confidential history files: Bannan, Ann; Campbell, E. O.; Campbell, L. M.; French, Arthur E. (Folder 1); Gall, Alwin; Green, Alice S. (Folders 1, 2); Hickox, Dean; Irrigoo, C. M.; Kristiansen, S.; Ng, William DeShue; Parker, Elmer E.
n.d.   Yukon Presbytery, Section: St. Lawrence Island—1894.
1877–1908 Jackson, Sheldon, Photograph Collection, Roll 238, 1–2.
1878–1984 Reports on Alaska. Minutes of the General Assembly of the Presbyterian Church in the United States of America. Board of National Missions.
1894–1960 Record Group 98 (Alaska Missions): Box 1, Files 10, 11, 33; Box 2, Files 18, 19, 28, 37, 43, 48; Box 3, File 29; Box 4, Files 11, 12, 21; Box 6, Files 4, 5, 6, 10, 11, 12, 13, 19, 32, 33, 35, 36, 50, 51, 54, 55; Box 7, Files 32, 46.

Rainey, Froelich G.
1941 "Eskimo Prehistory: The Okvik Site on Punuk Islands." *Anthropological Papers of the American Museum of Natural History* 37(4):453–569.

Ray, Dorothy Jean
1975 *The Eskimo of Bering Strait, 1650–1898.* Seattle: University of Washington Press.

Ridington, Robin

1988   *Trail to Heaven: Knowledge and Narrative in a Northern Native Com-
        munity.* Iowa City: University of Iowa Press.

Robbins, Lynn

1986   "Upper Skagit and Gambell Eskimo Indian Reorganization Act Gov-
        ernments: Struggles with Restraints and Power." Paper given at the
        Annual Meeting of the Society for Applied Anthropology, Reno.

Schneider, Jane and Shirley Lindenbaum, eds.

1987   "Frontiers of Christian Evangelism." Special issue. *American Ethnol-
        ogist* 14(1).

Schweitzer, Peter

1989   "Spouse-exchange in North-eastern Siberia: On Kinship and Sexual
        Relations and Their Transformations." In Andre Gingrich, Siegfried
        Haas, Sylvia Haas, and Gabriele Paleczek, eds., *Vienna Contributions
        to Ethnology and Anthropology.* Vol. 5, *Kinship, Social Change and
        Evolution: Proceedings of a Symposium Held in Honor of Walter
        Dostal,* 17–38. Frankfurt, Germany.

1992   "Reconsidering Bering Strait Kinship and Social Organization." Paper
        given at the 91st Annual Meeting of the American Anthropological As-
        sociation, San Francisco.

Sheldon Jackson Correspondence

1899–1903 Letter to Sheldon Jackson from Edgar O. Campbell, October 9,
        1903, *Pioneer Presbyterian Missions* 15:346–49. Archives of the Presby-
        terian Historical Society, Philadelphia, PA.

1904–1908 Letter to Sheldon Jackson from Vene Gambell, July 17, 1995, *Pio-
        neer Presbyterian Missions* 17:154–56. Archives of the Presbyterian His-
        torical Society, Philadelphia, PA.

Shinen, Marilene

1963   "Notes on Marriage Customs of the St. Lawrence Island Eskimos."
        Anthropologica n.s. 5(2):199–208.

Silook, Roger S.

1976   *Seevookuk: Stories the Old People Told on St. Lawrence Island.* An-
        chorage: Alaska Publishing Company.

Turner, Victor W.

1982   *From Ritual to Theatre: The Human Seriousness of Play.* New York:
        PAJ Publications.

U.S. Bureau of Indian Affairs

1977a   "Savoonga: Its History, Population and Economy." BIA Planning Support Group Report 242. Billings, MT.

1977b   "Gambell: Its History, Population and Economy." BIA Planning Support Group Report 243. Billings, MT.

U.S. Congress

1896   *Report of the Commission of Education for the Year 1894–95.* 298(2):1425–26. Washington: Government Printing Office.

1897   *Report of the Commission of Education for the Year 1895–96.* 234(2):1435, 1446–47. Washington: GPO.

1898   *Report of the Commission of Education for the Year 1896–97.* (2):1604. Washington: GPO.

1899   *Report of the Commission of Education for the Year 1897–98.* 258(2): 1753. Washington: GPO.

1901   *Report of the Commission of Education for the Year 1899–1900.* 276(2):1741–42. Washington: GPO.

1902   *Report of the Commission of Education for the Year 1900–01.* 288(2): 1466–67, 1478. Washington: GPO.

1903   *Report of the Commission of Education for the Year 1902.* 330(2):1230. Washington: GPO.

1905   *Report of the Commission of Education for the Year 1903.* 342(2):2343, 2355–56. Washington: GPO.

U.S. Education Bureau

1900–1910 *Report on the Introduction of Domestic Reindeer into Alaska.* Washington: GPO.

VanStone, James W.

1964   "Some Aspects of Religious Change among Native Inhabitants in West Alaska and the Northwest Territories." *Arctic Anthropology* 2(2): 21–25.

1980   "Alaska Natives and the White Man's Religion: A Cultural Interface in Historical Perspective." In Antoinette Shalkop, ed., *Exploration in Alaska.* Anchorage: Cook Inlet Historical Society.

Walunga, Willis, comp.

1987   *St. Lawrence Island Curriculum Resource Manual, Revised and Expanded Edition.* Gambell: St. Lawrence Island Bilingual Education Center, with the assistance of the U.S. Department of Education.

Watson, Lawrence C., and Maria-Barbara Watson-Franke

1985　　*Interpreting Life Histories: An Anthropological Inquiry.* New Brunswick, NJ: Rutgers University Press.

Williams, D.

1977　　"Gambell: Its History, Population and Economy." BIA Planning Support Group Report 243. Billings, MT.

Index

Printed in the United States
200530BV00003B/1-78/A

9 780295 981888